D1112204

SLAYERS & VAMPIRES

ALSO BY **MARK A. ALTMAN** AND **EDWARD GROSS**

The Fifty-Year Mission:
The Complete, Uncensored, Unauthorized Oral History of Star Trek:
The First 25 Years

The Fifty-Year Mission: The Next 25 Years: From The Next Generation to J. J. Abrams: The Complete, Uncensored, Unauthorized Oral History of Star Trek

SLAYERS & VAMPIRES

THE COMPLETE UNCENSORED, UNAUTHORIZED ORAL HISTORY OF **BUFFY & ANGEL**

EDWARD GROSS

AND

MARK A. ALTMAN

A TOM DOHERTY ASSOCIATES BOOK

NEW YORK

SLAYERS & VAMPIRES: THE COMPLETE UNCENSORED,
UNAUTHORIZED ORAL HISTORY OF BUFFY & ANGEL

A Tor Book
Published by Tom Doherty Associates
175 Fifth Avenue
New York, NY 10010

www.tor-forge.com

The Library of Congress Cataloging-in-Publication Data is available
upon request.

ISBN 978-1-250-12892-8 (hardcover)
ISBN 978-1-250-12893-5 (ebook)

First Edition: September 2017

Printed in the United States of America

0 9 8 7 6 5 4 3 2 1

FROM MARK A. ALTMAN

Dedicated to the **West Coast Altman Family** cats **Giles and Willow** (and, of course, our not-so-sweet **Ripley,** who recently left us, presumably to fight aliens on LV-426. We miss you!).

And especially my wife and Sunnydale High graduate, **Naomi Altman**. She saves my world . . . a lot.

Also, my future Slayer, **Ella Altman,** and Watcher in training, **Isaac Altman.** (Although he does his fair share of watching right now with *Star Wars* and *Star Trek*. Ah, the classics.)

Thank you to my wonderful grandfather and inspiration, the late **Seymour Isserson,** for being the first published author in the family. Still on that "road to self-improvement."

Special thanks to the original Gentleman, our editor **Brendan Deneen**, who never tells us to Hush (though no doubt he's sorely tempted).

And the word-count slayer, my partner in crime, coauthor, and jocular journalist **Edward Gross**. Nobody does it better . . . makes me feel sad for the rest.

And finally, **Ken Wahl** and **Jonathan Banks,** because *Wiseguy* still rules! (Right, Dad!?!)

FROM EDWARD GROSS

Dedicated first and foremost to my wife and best friend, **Eileen,** who's been slaying me for over thirty years (in the best possible way).

To my little "Angels," **Teddy, Dennis,** and **Kevin.**

To my daughter-in-law, **Lindsay,** who went from Potential to the real deal.

To **Mark A. Altman,** for being such a great collaborator and friend.

CONTENTS

PART TWO: ANGEL

"Fangs, don't fail me now."

PART THREE: ACROSS THE BUFFYVERSE

"If there is no great glorious end to all this,
if nothing we do matters,
then all that matters is what we do."

ONCE MORE, WITH KNEELING

"She's cool. She's hot. She's tepid. She's all-temperature Buffy."

BY **Mark A. Altman**

Make no mistake, Joss Whedon is a god.

Not a Zeus-like god who hurls thunderbolts from the sky and demands sacrifices of goats, chickens, geese, and the occasional vestal virgin, but an honest-to-goodness writing deity, a wizard of words, a maestro of the macabre and liege of letters. Not to mention he's far more partial to plaid button-downs than togas. But, not unlike Vargas on the receiving end of a spear gun from 007, you get the point (or Mr. Pointy, in his case). If that fact got lost on us during his less-than-halcyon days, when Whedon wrote for the mouthy Roseanne and Dan, resurrected *Alien,* or even when he debuted the first *Buffy,* who failed to slay audiences on movie screens in 1992, by now it should be abundantly clear to those of us fortunate enough to have been hip to the oeuvre of Joss Whedon, this is a man of boundless creativity, thoughtfulness, passion, intelligence, and wit.

Are you not entertained?

In a medium and a genre in which sexy blond girls were cannon fodder for the creepy-crawlies that go bump . . . and slash . . . in the night, Whedon flipped the script. Instead of being the prey, the lithe little blond girl with the silly name was the predator, keeping the troubled town of Sunnydale safe from all manner of nefarious and apocalyptic threats to her friends and family, from points north, west, south, and east. It's been said before but it's worth reiterating that *Buffy* didn't take place in the high school world of a John Hughes comedy; it used its supernatural trappings as a metaphor for the challenges and pain of adolescence. Not many of us could relate to growing up in a small town terrorized by soulless vampires, goblins, and ghouls, but most can relate to stories of unrequited love (or lust), sexy and soulful mysterious strangers, insular high school cliques, and cheerleaders whose bodies are possessed by their obsessed mothers. OK, not so much that last one.

High school drama had come a long way since Glenn Ford in *The Blackboard Jungle*. And what makes *Buffy* so unique is that it stands as perhaps one of the last vestiges of a more innocent age of adolescence, before social media and iPhones. When *Buffy* was created, it was still the era of creaking plot mechanics that could hinge on a missed ring on the landline phone, and in which the only social network in a town like Sunnydale was hanging out at a place like the Bronze while listening to music from a procession of great to middling '90s bands. *Buffy* was delivering its swan song to the more innocent days of high school just as the first glimmers of social networking were arriving on the scene with Friendster (remember that short-lived precursor to Myspace and Facebook?). *Buffy* would be a very different show today: the denizens of Sunnydale would be snapchatting and tweeting about Mayors transforming into giant lizard gods and hellish Halloween celebrations. "For god's sakes, stay away from Ethan's and lay off the Band Candy." Is that more than 140 characters?

Meanwhile, Whedon's spin-off of *Buffy, Angel,* is a miraculous story of survival against all odds. The series debuted with David Boreanaz's titular vampire as Philip Marlowe lite attempting to redeem himself on the mean streets of the City of Angels in a ham-fisted, noir-tinged detective drama. Sputtering for nearly half a season, the show began to find its own distinct identity, miraculously and brilliantly reinventing itself several times, first when Cordelia was bequeathed the visions of the late Glenn Quinn's Doyle, and then when Angel Investigations took up residence in an abandoned art deco hotel, and, finally, when Angel and company would find themselves in charge of the evil law firm Wolfram & Hart. What was stunning was that despite the seemingly inane, high-concept *TV Guide* description—"Angel, the vampire with a soul, is forced to run an evil law firm in Los Angeles" (redundant, to be sure)—the show's dramatic reinvention for its fifth season was a home run, and, much like *Next Generation*'s darker, more brooding spin-off *Deep Space Nine, Angel* often outshone its progenitor, despite having a smaller audience and receiving far less critical acclaim.

Embracing a more serialized structure than its progenitor, *Angel* required a more serious commitment from viewers of the pre-DVR age, who would be amply awarded for their loyalty (although I vaguely recall purchasing my first TiVo around that time, and I still have my plush Mr. TiVo to prove it). As *Buffy* began sputtering to its inevitable conclusion, *Angel* continued to evolve, culminating in one of the great series finales of all time, a supernatural *Godfather* denouement, a cliffhanger that is, regrettably, unlikely ever to be resolved. Not since Mike Torello and Ray Luca grappled violently in the cockpit of a rapidly descending Cessna in the second-season capper of *Crime Story* had a series left you hungering for more as the axe swung.

And since the respective conclusions of *Buffy* and *Angel,* Whedon has continued to amass quite the filmography (a subject for another book, surely). He rarely repeats himself and, no matter how disparate the material, marks his work with a singular style and wit. Even without Joss Whedon's name in the opening credits, it'd be hard to miss his unique imprimatur on such a diverse array of film and television as 2002's *Firefly,* the addictive, short-lived cult sci-fi Western about a ragtag group of underdogs and misfits long before *Guardians of the Galaxy* made such things *en vogue,* and 2012's *The Avengers,* featuring a distinctly different band of underdogs and misfits who save the world and transformed Whedon from a revered cult figure to a bankable blockbuster film director, all while he knocked out the microbudget adaptation of Shakespeare's *Much Ado About Nothing,* a charming and delightful retelling of the Bard's whimsical comedy, which gets a very Whedonesque makeover and was shot in his backyard. He made the film on a shoestring between Hammer time and Hulk busting. Doesn't this man sleep? Apparently not.

Meanwhile, there was the far less successful Eliza Dushku vehicle for Fox, *Dollhouse*; the genre-subverting *The Cabin in the Woods,* directed by *Buffy* veteran and future *Martian* Oscar nominee Drew Goddard, which Whedon and Goddard cooked up in a matter of days and that harkens back to horror classics like Sam Raimi's *Evil Dead* but has a distinctly Whedonesque spin; and the beloved *Dr. Horrible's Sing-Along Blog,* with the always delightful Nathan Fillion as the preening, narcissistic superhero Captain Hammer, a dastardly and lovestruck Neil Patrick Harris as Dr. Horrible, and an adorable Felicia Day. (And I would know since I've been lucky enough to work with both of them, the awesome and avuncular Nathan on *Castle* and Felicia on *The Librarians,* where we played hours of *Lord of the Rings* pinball with Sean Astin, but that's a story for another time.)

As a television writer myself, it's hard not to appreciate Whedon's sheer talent and prodigious output, which I've always enjoyed, respected, and admired. My personal connection to Whedon predates this book by over two decades. When I first moved to Los Angeles and was working as a journalist for *Sci-Fi Universe*, the self-proclaimed magazine for science fiction fans with a life that I had started for Larry Flynt, of all people, I attended a Writers Guild mixer, where I first encountered Joss, in his ubiquitous and unmistakable uniform of T-shirt, jeans, and button-down plaid shirt. We talked for a while about his new film, *Toy Story*. He was excited and equally trepidatious about the film's imminent release, Pixar's first. He'd already become one of Hollywood's most accomplished go-to guys for script fixes, doing substantial uncredited rewrites from films ranging from 1994's *Speed* to 1995's infamous *Waterworld* which contributed a new twist to the seemingly immutable Hollywood axiom: Never work with kids or animals and definitely never, ever shoot on water. We all know now, of course, that the first *Toy Story* is a triumph, one of the great animated films of all time, and became a perennial favorite for a generation of children (and adults). But I'll never forget walking out of the Crest Theatre in Westwood during the opening weekend to find Joss ensconced in the shadows of the back row quietly watching the film—and the audience. Surprised, I approached him and asked what he was doing watching his own film, which he had assuredly seen many times already. Chagrined and embarrassed, a nervous Whedon smiled, answering he didn't want anyone to recognize him, hoping to anonymously see if the film played with a real, paying audience. Indeed, it did—it was nothing short of a masterpiece. That was the last time I ever saw that side of Joss. Success didn't make him an egotist or an asshole, as it does for many in our business, but it did make him deservedly self-confident . . . and a better dresser.

After that, I would regularly run into him on Tuesdays at the late Pico Boulevard haunt, Laser Blazer, where we both used to pick up the latest laserdiscs and, later, DVDs and Blu-rays. We would have brief and amiable conversations, but I can't say I ever got to really know him very well, although we were bonded into that community of pre-Amazon obsessives who would march out to the store every Tuesday to pick up the latest new releases on the day they came out—often leaving them in the original shrink-wrap for years. (As anyone who is still part of the dying breed of connoisseurs of physical media will adamantly and lovingly tell you, sometimes it's just enough to know they're there.)

Perhaps my most embarrassing run-in with Joss was years later at the Saturn Awards, the awesomely kitsch, sweet, nostalgic, and charming awards show devoted to genre entertainment held annually by the Academy of Science Fiction, Fantasy and Horror Films. For years, my wife had been consumed by a question that she desperately wanted answered. Now, you have to understand that my wonderful spouse, Naomi, is a die-hard fan of the Whedonverse and a devoted fan of *Buffy* and *Angel*. Not only did we have a string quartet play the beautiful "Sacrifice" theme from "The Gift" at our wedding and name two of our rescue cats Giles and Willow, but for her first Mother's Day I took her to Torrance to see Sunnydale High School (aka Torrance High School) and the original Summers residence nearby. In fact, when she first moved to Los Angeles, Buffy was a great solace to her since she had left behind so many of her close friends in Chicago, and it was the gang at Sunnydale High that helped her acclimate to her new life in a new city with new friends, not unlike the Slayer herself. So you see, even though I ducked having to ask her question for several years, unfortunately, when she heard that Joss was going to be at the Saturns, there was no way I was extricating myself from this unwelcome task. Naomi insisted that I talk to Joss and get a definitive answer to her vexing query.

What did she want to know? you may ask. Not far from where we live in Beverly Hills, there was a three-way intersection; at it stood the Willow School, Wesley Street, and, nestled between them and now long gone, the imposing Angelus Shoe Factory. Naomi thought perhaps this had been an inspiration to Joss when he was creating Buffy. I, of course, thought I'd never eat lunch (dinner or brunch) in this town again if I posed her question, but when your wife asks you do something—other than take out the garbage—you do it and so I did. Mortified, I approached Joss at the afterparty, and, after exchanging familiar pleasantries and downing a few vodka-enhanced beverages, I finally, reluctantly, asked him if indeed this had been an inspiration for *Buffy*. Smiling amusedly but taking pity on me by not outright laughing, he answered quietly and thoughtfully, "You can tell your wife, definitely not." And so ended one of the all-time great, longheld mysteries of *Buffy* for our family.

Hopefully, however, in this volume you now hold in your hand, Ed Gross and I will be able to clarify many other mysteries, dispel some apocryphal myths, hip you to the best craft services, and reintroduce you to the wonderful worlds of *Buffy* and *Angel* in a new, candid, and exciting way. The joy of writing these oral histories of such beloved pop culture staples is not only to revisit worlds we love (like *Star Trek* in *The Fifty-Year Mission* and Sunnydale and Angel's City of Angels in this volume) and share insider stories with passionate fans about the creation and making of these iconic series, but also to showcase the behind-the-scenes tales and many of the unheralded talents of so many of these wonderful shows with those who may have never encountered them before.

At twenty years old, there's an entire generation of TV viewers who didn't grow up with Buffy, Willow, Xander, Cordelia, Faith, Angel, Spike, Giles, Willow, Dawn, Flutie, Snyder, Anya, Kendra, Gentlemen, Masters, and Mayors. Once they read this volume, it's our hope they will feel as if they did. *Buffy* and *Angel* are distinctly products of their time. They were created early in the second golden age of television, after the emergence of series like *Hill Street Blues* and *St. Elsewhere* changed the medium indelibly forever but before the renaissance of *The Sopranos, The Wire, Mad Men*, and *Breaking Bad*. But for as long as girls love boys, kids endure the endless tortures of high school, and we question the myriad sounds that go bump in the night, *Buffy* and *Angel* will remain timeless. The visual effects of Mayor Wilkins turning into a giant snake notwithstanding, of course. *That* does look pretty lame now.

October 29, 2016

VAMPIRES AND SLAYERS, OH MY!

"I may be love's bitch, but at least I'm man enough to admit it."

BY **Edward Gross**

Growing up in the 1960s, I had a number of pop culture obsessions, most of which are still with me, including Superman, James Bond, *Star Trek*, *Planet of the Apes*, *The Odd Couple* (I saw the movie when I was eight and have loved the concept ever since), and vampires.

As to the latter, I was fascinated with the classic Universal and Hammer horror movies, most notably Bela Lugosi and Christopher Lee's takes on *Dracula*. But that was nothing compared with my genuine obsession with Barnabas Collins, the vampire star of television's only gothic-horror daily soap opera, *Dark Shadows*. From the moment I encountered that character one afternoon after school, he'd never fully gone away (a memory solidified by the fact that there was a period in the 1980s when I was hanging out with the man who played him, the late Jonathan Frid).

Strangely, the idea of Slayers—those whose chosen path was to take down my beloved vampires, among other supernatural threats—was appealing to me as well. (I don't even want to get into the psychology of wanting to see the thing I love destroyed.) The first person I recall doing that slaying was the reporter Carl Kolchak, played by Darren McGavin, in the 1972 TV movie *The Night Stalker*, in which he discovered and took down a vamp haunting Las Vegas. A year later Kolchak returned in *The Night Strangler* and, a year after that, in the weekly series *Kolchak: The Night Stalker*. There was also Roy Thinnes in 1973's *The Norliss Tapes* TV movie, Gene Roddenberry's 1977 TV movie *Spectre*, 1984's *Ghostbusters*, the following year's *Fright Night* (which introduced audiences to Roddy McDowall's Peter Vincent), and 1993's *The X-Files* (of course).

But then there was *Buffy the Vampire Slayer*, debuting in 1997, which was an entity all its own, capturing the imagination with horror, humor, and (shockingly) three-dimensional characters as it introduced the world (and me) to Sarah Michelle Gellar's Buffy Summers and the rest of her particular Scooby Gang. And in *that* mix came the vampire with a soul, Angel, as played by David Boreanaz.

One TV show with a vampire *and* a Slayer? My mind was boggled, and since I had been a journalist for a great metropolitan newspaper . . . sorry, that was Clark Kent . . . that is, for a number of magazines, I was given an inside look at the making of the series and also of the spin-off, *Angel*.

But even before there was a *Buffy* TV show, there was Joss Whedon. Back in 1995, I was an editor at *Cinescape* magazine, and it was announced that a fourth movie in the *Alien* franchise, ultimately called *Alien: Resurrection*, was going to be made (*really* big news at the time) and that someone named Joss Whedon would be writing it. Well, back then, before every bit of information about a film fell under the full and complete control of studio publicists or the talent involved was terrified of speaking out of turn, I figured there couldn't be too many people named Joss Whedon out there, so I called 411, information. A moment later, I had a phone number and decided to give it a call. Joss answered, I introduced myself, and we stayed on the phone for about an hour or so, engaging in what would be the first of many hours of conversation over the years. Eventually, when *Buffy* did become a TV series, Joss continued to make himself available to me, and he even made it possible for me to speak to many of the other writer/producers of both series. As a result, next to *Star Trek*, I don't think there were any other TV shows that I covered as much as I did *Buffy* and *Angel*.

This book, then, is the culmination of my lifelong obsession with both vampires and Slayers. In telling the story of *Buffy the Vampire Slayer* and *Angel*, particularly in the oral history format, it was our hope that this would be the most in-depth and intimate look at two shows that, whether people realized it or not, evolved the medium. A lot.

December 31, 2016

PART ONE

BUFFY

THE VAMPIRE SLAYER

"She saved the world . . . a lot."

BLONDE ON BLONDE

"If I had the Slayer's power . . . I'd be punning right about now."

The year was 1997 and a new series debuted on the WB network with the unlikely and unpromising title *Buffy the Vampire Slayer.* Based on the critically reviled 1992 film of the same name, few would have anticipated that the series would soon become one of the most beloved television series of all time and pave the way for a succession of empowered female protagonists on television, including Sydney Bristow on *Alias,* the titular *Veronica Mars, Battlestar Galactica*'s cigar-chomping Kara Thrace, and later Gwendoline Christie's noble Brienne of Tarth on *Game of Thrones*—not to mention *The Walking Dead*'s badass katana-wielding Michonne, among others.

In the wake of the jingoistic, testosterone-fueled action fantasies of the '80s with Sylvester Stallone refighting and winning the Vietnam War in *Rambo* and Arnold Schwarzenegger mowing down hundreds if not thousands of adversaries, female heroes were few and far between. It's ironic given the dominance of such smart-mouthed and capable women like Carole Lombard, Jean Harlow, Myrna Loy, Katharine Hepburn, and Greta Garbo in the screwball comedies of the 1930s like *It Happened One Night, The Thin Man, Bringing Up Baby,* and *Ninotchka*, which paved the way for the powerful Barbara Stanwyck and Lana Turner in noirs of the '40s like *Double Indemnity* and *The Postman Always Rings Twice*. But women had rarely been considered action heroines; more often, they were the damsel in distress or, more likely, the scantily clad love interest for Schwarzenegger, Stallone, and Norris, who seemed more interested in stroking their weapons than their women. But that was all about to change. Ridley Scott introduced a new kind of female protagonist in 1979's *Alien* with Sigourney Weaver's smart, savvy, and sexy Ripley, and James Cameron took her matriarchal (and Xenomorph-slaying) power to a whole new level in *Aliens* a few years later.

By 1993 there was Johnnie To's *The Heroic Trio,* a kick-ass Hong Kong chopsocky in which a trio of female superheroes defeats an evil master who is raising kidnapped children into a superarmy. Sound vaguely familiar?

But it was in the year 1997 that a new and thoroughly unexpected female superhero debuted on television, Buffy the Vampire Slayer. As in the great Stan Lee comics of the '60s, this was a superhero who knew that with great power comes great responsibility (even if Buffy was more X-Men's Kitty Pryde than Spider-Man's Peter Parker) and who also found that her everyday problems as a student at Sunnydale High School often far exceeded the challenges created by her birthright as a vampire slayer.

It is a show that changed the small screen forever, and, while it'd be hard to consider television an auteurist medium, *Buffy* is one of the few shows whose success and tone can be almost entirely credited to one man, Joss Whedon, the visionary writer/director/producer who brought the Slayer to life . . . death . . . and life again.

JOSS WHEDON
(creator/executive producer, *Buffy the Vampire Slayer*)

Buffy came from watching a horror movie and seeing the typical ditzy blonde walk into a dark alley and getting killed. I just thought that I would love to see a scene where the ditzy blonde walks into a dark alley, a monster attacks her, and she kicks its ass. So the concept was real simple. After all those times of seeing the poor girl who had sex and got killed, I just wanted to give her the power back.

SARAH MICHELLE GELLAR
(actress, Buffy Summers)

For a long time I think there was a lack of strong female characters on television, especially for young people, and it's so hard because that's the age you really want to identify with someone. You want to have a hero and the thing I liked about Buffy, and Willow as well as Cordelia, is that they are OK with who they are. They're not the most popular or the most beautiful at school. Willow is the smartest, but they're OK with who they are and there's a comfort in their individuality.

SARAH LEMELMAN

(author, *"It's About Power":* Buffy the Vampire Slayer*'s Stab at Establishing the Strength of Girls on American Television*)

Buffy the Vampire Slayer was revolutionary for its time as it created fresh images of females, and demonstrated this to an important demographic—young teenage girls—who are fed all sorts of conflicting and dispiriting representations of women. The show established that girls no longer had to adhere to the standards for females in society. *Buffy* showed that it was not acceptable for girls and women alike to degrade themselves in order to fit into society, as society should accept all versions of females—ladylike or virile, timid or outgoing, polite or crass, and even heterosexual or homosexual, among many other conflicting personalities and characteristics for women and girls.

ANTHONY C. FERRANTE

(director, *Sharknado*)

Whereas in most horror movies, the female lead became a "survivor," *Buffy*'s female lead became a "hero." She didn't need to become ripped like Linda Hamilton in *Terminator 2* or Sigourney Weaver in *Aliens*. She was able to be feminine and tough at the same time. The magic of *Buffy* is that you could relate to her. She still had insecurities, needs, and desires, but at her core she also had to be a hero and a fighter to save herself and the ones she loved.

SARAH LEMELMAN

The world of *Buffy the Vampire Slayer* was a refreshing escape for the female sex. Women were seen enacting change on their own accord, and were equalized to—if not stronger than—men. *Buffy* asserted that women could, in fact, be valued in society. Unlike its predecessors in *Wonder Woman* and *The Bionic Woman*, *Buffy the Vampire Slayer* showed that young teenage girls could be powerful, too. The members of its cast became role models for girls to escape demeaning female stereotypes that had been laid down for so long and instead showed girls that it was perfectly acceptable to define themselves.

ANTHONY C. FERRANTE

Ripley [in *Alien*] started out a lot like *Buffy*. She was the everyperson on that ship. The unlikely survivor and hero. She learned to become a badass and a hero, while not sacrificing being herself in the process. Could Buffy have existed without Ripley in *Alien*? Probably, but Whedon has great taste and, again, understood what he appreciated about great horror movies of the 1970s and 1980s and did his spin on it, taking the best qualities from the best movies and making it into its own.

SARAH LEMELMAN

Before *Alien,* movies that showed female empowerment focused on sex appeal—*Charlie's Angels, Wonder Woman*—which is not the case in *Alien*. Obviously, *Buffy* focuses on the title character's sex appeal, but the point of that is to undermine stereotypes. You can be beautiful *and* not in need of saving. Sigourney Weaver is this tireless fighter, which is something that is seen in *Buffy*.

ANTHONY C. FERRANTE

Buffy really paved the way for more empowered female characters in the genre. Slasher films always had the strong female lead who was the "final girl," but in some ways it was the process of elimination that made them the final survivor. In *Buffy,* it was less about a survivor and more about becoming a hero. In many vampire movies, women were under the thrall of a vampire and the victim in many instances, who needed to be saved by a Van Helsing–like character. *Buffy,* on the other hand, looked like the victim but was Van Helsing instead—but with a healthy sense of fashion and pop culture smarts.

CHARISMA CARPENTER
(actress, Cordelia Chase)

She was just a normal kid and she just wants to be a girl. My worldview at that age is not the same as it is now. I was twenty-four at the time. We weren't going through what we're going through right now. There wasn't an Internet, there wasn't empowerment, there wasn't a female presidential candidate. I don't think woman power came into my consciousness until *Buffy*. I guess when you feel empowered in general you aren't really propagating it because you don't really need to. I never felt held down or held back or anything like that, but I learned discrimination did exist for a lot of women. I didn't go to college, so I didn't have the experience with civil rights. I was a little bit naive.

SARAH LEMELMAN

It may seem like a laughable idea that a show made up of vampires and young high school girls could possibly help pave the way for the future of women in television, but it in fact did just that, and became a popular culture phenomenon in the process. The program's heroines are presented as feminist role models to its largely teenage-girl-based audience, showing that women should fight for what they want and not be discouraged by the limits that a patriarchal society places on women. *Buffy the Vampire Slayer* constantly pushed the boundaries of how the female form was represented on television and showed its audience that feminism can be a normal part of everyday lives.

JOSS WHEDON

I was watching a lot of horror movies and seeing blondes going into dark alleys to get killed and I thought it would be interesting to see the blonde go into the dark alley and be the one who kills instead. So that became *Buffy the Vampire Slayer*, which I wrote and was promptly rejected by everyone in Hollywood till Fran [Rubel Kuzui] came along and found it and produced and directed the movie. Then a couple of years later, Fran and Gail Berman, who was working with Sandy Gallin who had the rights, came and asked if I'd be interested in doing a TV series of it. I thought about it a while and said, "Gee, that would be cool." High school as a horror movie pretty much sums up my life. I thought there was a whole series there.

ANTHONY C. FERRANTE

I really enjoyed the original *Buffy* movie, but the TV show lived up to the potential of the concept. Joss Whedon decided to use all the tropes of high school and growing up and then mask it with a vampire-show template.

GAIL BERMAN

(executive producer, *Buffy the Vampire Slayer*)

One of the things we did when we went to see Joss, Fran [Kuzui] and I, was to talk about this character and see that we were simpatico about her being a young empowered woman. Probably the most important thing we went to talk about originally. There weren't any young empowered women on television and it struck us that this was a real vacuum that could be filled. Not only creatively, but it was important for women to see someone empowered on television.

JOSS WHEDON

Everything I write is about power and helplessness. And somebody being helpless and their journey to power is the narrative that sustains me. A lot of it has to do with being very helpless and tiny and I had two terrifying older brothers and a terrifying father and a withholding mother and, generally speaking, I knew I was on my own and I had no fucking skills. I was like, I don't know how to survive. I got mugged every time I left the house. Just like people were waiting in line. I'm pretty sure one in six New Yorkers has in their lifetime mugged me. I would just be walking around in my head creating these narratives where these little tiny people that nobody paid attention to kicked everybody's ass in one way or another. Why they are always female I'm still not sure, but I'm not uncomfortable with it.

SARAH LEMELMAN

It may seem odd that a man, rather than a woman, had a passion to write and produce a show with a strong female lead, but Whedon—who was clearly ahead of his time—wanted to show that powerful and captivating young women can be a part of everyday life. As a graduate at Wesleyan University, he studied both film and feminist theory, and is a self-proclaimed feminist, stating that he has always found strong women interesting because they are not overly represented in the cinema [and] that there are a lot of ways to break new ground without having original thoughts. Perhaps one of the most important projects he worked on prior to the *Buffy the Vampire Slayer* movie was *Roseanne,* which starred a housewife who showed the world a new type of independence, while still relying on, and embracing, her femininity. This seems to have inspired and influenced Whedon, and with the success of *Roseanne,* he continued to hold on to *Buffy.*

JOSS WHEDON

It took a while, actually, to figure it out. I wanted to do this girl who was different and had powers. Plus I love vampires; they're so cool. But it started with Buffy. Before the vampires became part of it, I knew that I wanted to make her this special person. Someone who wanted desperately to fit in, but had a higher calling. That's how the idea of her being a vampire slayer first came to me.

STEVE BIODROWSKI

(editor in chief, *Cinefantastique*)

The evolution of vampires on page, stage, and screen paved the way for *Buffy the Vampire Slayer* in the sense that, as the depiction of the undead changed, something was lost. To coin a phrase, the bat had been thrown out with the bloody bathwater. Old-fashioned, frightening vampires became passé if not outright cornball while literature and cinema focused on sexy, romantic immortals suffering existential angst.

A serious depiction of a life-and-death battle between good and evil risked being laughed off the screen. Joss Whedon found a way to give us evil vampires again and undercut the risk of unintentional laughter by affecting a droll tone, somewhat akin to the 1960s spy series *The Avengers*: treat the important stuff in an offhand way; treat the trivial stuff as if it were really important. So *Buffy* may have been averting a vampire apocalypse, but she really would have preferred to focus on fitting in at school and making friends.

JOSS WHEDON

The title is one of the things I fought for. The only disagreement I ever really had with the network was I would not let go of the title. A lot of people said, "But it's stupid, and it's the title of a comedy movie, and people won't take it seriously." I'm sure there are some people who still don't.

DAN VEBBER

(co-executive producer, *The Simpsons*)

I was a huge fan of the show. You hear the stories all the time about how hard it was for him to keep the name *Buffy the Vampire Slayer* instead of just calling it "Slayer" because people wouldn't watch a show called *Buffy the Vampire Slayer.* As a fan I found that to be the case, too; it was hard to convince people how good it was, because it just had a silly name.

I agree with Joss, though, that he absolutely should've kept the name, because it's essential to the mood and the tone of the show; that's what the show is called and it says everything you need to know.

STEVE BIODROWSKI

One interesting thing about *Buffy* is the appellation "vampire hunter." The notion of a vampire hunter is pretty much a cinematic invention. Stoker's Van Helsing was a professor called in to consult on an unusual medical case, who recognized the signs and then read up everything he could find; in other words, he was not a professional vampire hunter. The same could be said of Kolchak, at least in *The Night Stalker* telefilm. The main difference between Buffy and these examples is that Buffy has a normal life—or tries to, anyway. None of us really knows what Van Helsing or Kolchak would like to do in their spare time; in fact, the very notion of them relaxing and hanging out is almost comical.

But Buffy would love to go to a club and just enjoy a night out with friends. Which brings us to probably the main reason for the success of *Buffy the Vampire Slayer*: it gave high school girls a protagonist they could relate to, who lives in a world that, at least on the surface, resembled theirs. For high-school-age people, everything seems to be of life-or-death importance; every failure is the end of the world. The series' little joke is that, for Buffy, this is not a metaphor but literal reality: her life is in continual danger, and she is trying to prevent the end of the world.

SARAH LEMELMAN

Women have historically been subjugated to men in both the home and workplace and I think that has permeated into literature and the media. In terms of the "girl in peril" trope, essentially, women are not capable of saving themselves. They are typically young and beautiful and need the big, strong, brave man to offer help and protection against some foe, or to get the girl out of a distressing situation.

Whenever I think of the modern girl-in-peril trope for television, I think of Marissa Cooper from *The O.C.*, who is this beautiful girl, who always seems to get herself in the worst situations, and has another character, Ryan Atwood, who saves her. In recent times we've connected the damsel to blond girls, because of the stereotype that blond girls are dumb/ditzy/incapable of making decisions for themselves, so therefore they're the most likely in need of saving.

The beauty of *Buffy* is that Joss purposely plays to these stereotypes—Buffy is blond, beautiful, petite, and a cheerleader. Also, let's be honest, the name "Buffy" doesn't sound very threatening. Instead, Joss shows that Buffy can do the saving, despite looking the part of the typical "girl in peril" trope. Moreover, he plays on this with inserting Xander as someone who needs constant protection. In earlier seasons, Xander is seen bullied in school and becomes the "damsel" in distress, who is saved by Buffy, the new hero.

HOWARD GORDON

(executive producer, *Homeland*)

Adults can love it and kids can see themselves in it. It just had that voice that makes you sit up and pay attention. I would say that its cult status was burnished because it really was the crucible of adolescence; particularly, being a strong, powerful young woman really resonated with a certain portion of the population that elevated it to cult status.

ANTHONY C. FERRANTE

Buffy is surprisingly responsible for how a majority of television has been reinvented. It took some of its cues from *The X-Files* in the sense of having an overall mythology mixed throughout, but it also deviated from what *X-Files* did to evolve the television genre itself. The first season of *Buffy* featured a "Big Bad," a concept most TV series use as a buzz word during development, even though it came from *Buffy,* while doing stand-alone episodes as well.

SARAH LEMELMAN

The use of long story arcs was not the only tactic that was used which influenced modern television. As the title *Buffy the Vampire Slayer* suggests, vampires were a crucial component to the success of the show. While vampires have always captured the minds of readers and viewers alike, *Buffy* has revitalized the vampire genre. Angel is depicted as a romantic hero—with the catch-22 that he can never truly be happy or fulfilled, otherwise he will revert back to his soulless self, Angelus.

In the first three seasons of *Buffy,* he is essential to the story line in helping Buffy fight the forces of evil. Angel is despised by other vampires and demons, as he is expected to be torturing defenseless victims, not helping them. His heroic acts and inner sufferings create the image of the "sympathetic" vampire, which the viewer loves and approves of.

ARMIN SHIMERMAN

(actor, Principal Snyder)

Buffy fell in love with a vampire. If she let herself get too close to him she could get hurt. And yet with the growing love for that vampire, she wanted to be closer to that person. You don't have to go very far to see that as a metaphor for young people's sexuality. That a young girl is in love with a young man whom she's frightened of. I assume she hasn't had a sexual experience yet and that's what he's going to want and that she could get hurt by that. And yet, because of her growing love for that person, she wants to but she's terrified because of how she might get hurt. She might say yes and then the guy may leave her. All kinds of decisions and fears that I, as a man, have no understanding of. But the writers on *Buffy* did.

ANTHONY C. FERRANTE

The characters grew up on *Buffy,* they graduated, they fell in love with different people. The downfall of many shows is doing the same thing all the time. *Buffy* took a lead heroic character, Angel, and in season two turned him into the "Big Bad" halfway through. It was a ballsy move, and paid dividends. *Buffy* explored same-sex relationships in a way that didn't feel jaded or a ploy for shock value. And *Buffy* had shocking deaths of major characters throughout its run—something most shows do almost too ritualistically today.

SARAH LEMELMAN

Typically vampire films—and shows—are meant to represent the marginalized groups in society. The most obvious and blatant in-your-face example is the use of vampires in *True Blood* to represent the LGBTQ community and civil rights in general. It's set in an unaccepting southern community where people know that vampires exist, but [the vampires] are largely frowned upon.

In its title sequence, there's a sign to a store that says "God Hates Fangs," and the phrase "coming out of the coffin" is used in multiple episodes. In its concluding seasons, the government creates "Hep-V" which is fatal to vampires, and it is clearly meant to be an allegory for HIV/AIDS. We also see this idea of movies representing marginalized groups, in *X-Men,* where mutants are seen as freaks, and not deserving of equal rights. On a broader level, vampire films are used to represent more straightforward, abstract things, like fear, or the "other."

ARMIN SHIMERMAN

Buffy spoke to the fears, neuroses, of young people. Primarily to young women who were just learning about their own sexuality, about their own emergence as adults. A great deal of the episodes were metaphors for that emergence. I remember one episode, in particular, where there was a girl who had been neglected, overlooked by all of her classmates and she became invisible and took out her revenge by using that invisibility. Well, I can imagine there were hundreds of thousands of young girls who felt that they were neglected in school and would like to be invisible.

SARAH MICHELLE GELLAR

I remember Joss saying the basic principle of the show is you take all that is horrible about youth and all that is scary, and we literally made them into monsters. But I think anyone can relate to what high school is like and how that is the worst monster for you and the worst nightmare, and it was something that was so relatable.

MARTI NOXON
(executive producer, *UnReal)*

These people—Buffy, Oz, Xander, Willow, Cordelia—they are teenagers. They make mistakes—and they should, for emotional reasons. They do stuff that isn't very smart just as most of us do when we are that age. When I was trying to decide if I wanted to take the job, which wasn't a very hard decision, but I hadn't seen the show, so I was watching the episode "Angel," when Buffy is fighting Angel at the very end and then she bares her neck to him, and says "Go ahead, take me, if you can, go ahead and kill me, if you can." I thought, this is the coolest thing I've ever seen, because she's the hero, but she's an adolescent, and she's going to make decisions sometimes out of total emotion, out of passion, as opposed to her head, which makes it that much more interesting. That's one of the things I loved about these characters: they're fighting evil, but they were still teenagers.

STEVEN S. DEKNIGHT
(director, *Pacific Rim 2: Uprising*)

All the writers were giant fans of this genre and if I have one big complaint about other genre shows I see on TV, it's hearing about people who work on them and getting the sense that the creators, the people who run these other shows, don't have the love of the genre. If you don't really have the love of it, you don't understand it. That's where you get things that seem creaky and a little too earnest and clumsy. It's because that's what they think the genre is. And it's not. You go back to the original *Star Trek*. It's the beautiful metaphor that you can tell a story about gay marriage, you can tell a story about terrorism, you can tell a story about racism, under the guise of flights of fancy. By God, we need another Rod Serling!

THOMAS P. VITALE
(executive vice president, Programming and Original Movies, Syfy and Chiller)

Unfortunately, aside from the notably great sci-fi and supernatural shows we all know and love, most genre television series before the 1990s weren't made with the fan in mind . . . and probably most of them weren't made *by* fans. In fact, there are too many mediocre genre shows in television history in which the sci-fi or supernatural elements are just used as a "setting," but not much more. In other words, if you removed the genre elements from the show, the story would still work.

Conversely, in the best science fiction and supernatural literature, the genre elements are critical to the stories and those elements work as metaphor in addition to being used as part of the plot. But *Buffy* was important in the history of genre shows, because the genre elements are crucial to the story. Most important, Buffy was made by fans for fans. *Buffy* succeeded on every level—great characters, great stories, great metaphor and symbols, great homages, and great buzz among its target audience.

ARMIN SHIMERMAN

So, why is it endearing? Because it speaks to universal problems that young people have. And then of course it spoke to other things as well. It was a very powerful cast, with very good directors, and of course incredibly good writers.

TIM MINEAR
(executive producer, *American Horror Story*)

It also had a sense of humor, but because it was called *Buffy,* I don't think that the network or some of the executives ever really understood what it was. I think they all thought that it was John Waters on some level, that it was camp. In fact, this was as far from camp as can be. It was serious hero drama . . . with some funny.

DAN VEBBER

For me, it was always about the characters. They were the smartest and funniest written characters that I'd seen at that point on a television show. That's just Joss's character voice that he writes in. It's very quick banter and very pop culture savvy driven by goals which are heightened compared to real world characters. At first, it was the dialogue that appealed to me. Plus, being a genre fan I did enjoy the horror stories. I immediately latched onto the metaphor of the show: that high school is hell. I saw it as a place I could really pitch some stories that I thought would be really funny.

DAVID FURY
(executive producer, *24*)

When I met Joss, he was specifically looking for comedy writers. He kind of knew what the tone of the show was and he was also aware that a lot of drama writers can't do comedy and so when the show was initially in development, he had a lot to figure out, but he knew he wanted comedy writers.

DAN VEBBER

At that point I was exclusively a comedy writer, so I only thought in terms of, "Will this be funny or not?" That was always my first thing. And that was a detriment to me working on a show like *Buffy,* because emotion on *Buffy* is such a huge part of it. That's something I did not have a lot of experience in and I was learning from Joss about the basic things involved in constructing a dramatic story for a one-hour TV show, because I had never done it before.

ANTHONY C. FERRANTE

Like any genre, the vampire genre itself had been run into the ground right before *Buffy* arrived. There had been clever deviations on the formula. There were horror comedies like *Love at First Bite, Vampire's Kiss, Fright Night,* and *Vamp* that had fun with the vampire concept and you had groundbreaking reinventions like *The Hunger* and *Martin*. But what was brilliant about Joss Whedon is that he has a unique voice that looks at the world and genre in a different way. That allowed him to approach *Buffy* from a different vantage point, first with the original movie and then later with the TV series. He appreciated the conventions that came with the genre, but he wanted to find a way to subvert it by grounding it in metaphor as well.

STEVE BIODROWSKI

I'm not sure any vampire films in particular had a big effect on Joss Whedon. The impression I get is that he caught bits and pieces on the late show and mashed them together for an audience that wouldn't know the difference. I suppose the Hammer vampire films were influential, at least indirectly, in that they tended to feature action. Count Dracula was never staked in his coffin—at least not successfully—there was usually some kind of struggle or fight scene, the most memorable being the one in *Horror of Dracula,* with Christopher Lee's Dracula and Peter Cushing's Van Helsing fighting to the death. And, of course, Hammer gave us *Legend of the Seven Golden Vampires* (aka *The Seven Brothers Meet Dracula*), which combined vampires with martial arts.

ANTHONY C. FERRANTE

I also think *Buffy* owes a huge debt to [the] *Kolchak: The Night Stalker* series as well. The *Buffy* movie felt a bit broader than the TV show, which is more in line with Whedon's quirky sensibilities. And as he gained more of a footing as a show runner, and later director, the show's identity really came to the fore. Whedon is a great storyteller who understands why great genre movies work—they were about something more than just the monsters. Strip away the vampires and monsters from *Buffy* and it's about a high school girl coming of age. Look at George A. Romero's Dead movies, and those films are allegories for other things.

HARRY GROENER
(actor, Mayor Richard Wilkins)

Part of its success is not just the vampire myth. It's the sense of humor of it. It's funny. It doesn't take itself too seriously and it has a moral. It teaches something. It can be about abuse or it can be about bullying or it can be about whatever it is. And the monsters are actually monsters.

JOSE MOLINA
(co-executive producer, *Agent Carter*)

What resonated with me and what probably resonated with a lot of people was that it was a high school story, first and foremost. The monsters she was battling were all metaphors for the travails that a high school student goes through while they're in school. The other thing that I found really unique about Buffy is that here she is, this beautiful former cheerleader, all the boys think she's cute and want to date her. But the people that she chooses to hang out with are these couple of misfits. And she's a bit of a dork herself. I had never seen that before. I'd never seen a girl who looked like Sarah Michelle Gellar being one of us. One of the nerdy, geeky, high school losers. She was a relatable action hero who you kind of identified with. You either wanted to hang out with her or be part of her gang.

SARAH LEMELMAN

One of the major reasons that *Buffy* was able to garner such interest from fans and scholars alike is the fact that the program's main characters are marginalized and considered outsiders, which . . . was not a typical formula for television in the 1990s, and even today. Rather than most teenage television series that showcase "popular" high schoolers, such as jocks and cheerleaders, Catherine Siemann calls *Buffy*'s protagonist the "ex-cheerleader who fell from grace," who is paired with two other outsiders, the shy Willow considered a "brainiac," and the awkward Xander, who uses humor to deflect derision from his classmates. Joss Whedon stood firmly behind the idea that "the show is about disenfranchisement, about the people nobody takes seriously" and [consulting producer] David Greenwalt stated that "if Joss Whedon had one good day in high school we wouldn't be here."

STEVE BIODROWSKI

Xander, to me, seems to be in the tradition of sidekicks like Harry Sullivan, from the Tom Baker era of *Doctor Who*: Harry looked like he should be the archetypal male hero, but since that role was already taken, Harry was a bit of a third wheel, who had to settle for providing comic relief, though his assistance did come in handy from time to time. The only difference is that Xander was playing second fiddle to a woman.

SARAH LEMELMAN

Obviously, Whedon himself faced struggles that the average, day-to-day teenager faces in high school, and not many television shows have been keen on portraying this. The Scoobies, ignoring their involvement with the supernatural, do not fit into the mainstream, and Whedon wanted to embrace this, hoping that it would provide a connection for viewers who were not always accepted by their high school peers.

HARRY GROENER

Everything has been pretty much said about how talented Joss is. He was just incredibly perceptive, and in tune and in touch with those kids. He knew how to write for them. He knew how to characterize the angst that was going on in these kids and he's fast on his feet.

JOSE MOLINA

There was a sense of inclusiveness, which is a word we use a lot nowadays. But even back then I felt like the Scooby Gang was open to anybody who wasn't an asshole. And even if someone was an asshole like Cordelia, if her heart was in the right place, she was still welcome.

SARAH LEMELMAN

Whedon's portrayal of high school "rejects," aside from the Scooby Gang, is especially shown in the earlier seasons, most notably in the episodes "Out of Mind, Out of Sight" and "Earshot," which depict a girl who feels ignored by the rest of the world—and turns invisible—and a bullied boy who attempts to commit suicide, respectively. *Buffy* addresses these struggles to any ostracized students and sends the message to viewers that "belonging" does not mean a person has to be "cool" or popular but that having a supportive network of friends and family is more important than fitting into mainstream society.

JOSS WHEDON

It was about four years after the end of the run of *Buffy* that I really just went "Oh, I was Buffy! The whole time." I always thought I was Xander before he started getting laid. I'm the wacky sidekick. Then I had this shocking moment of idiotic revelation that I'd been writing about myself that whole time.

HELLMOUTH OR HIGH WATER

"A Slayer with family and friends. That sure as hell wasn't in the brochure."

In the beginning, there was the movie. And the movie kinda sucked. It certainly wasn't what its writer, Joss Whedon, had intended. Not entirely surprising considering that he was "only" the film's writer, attempting to move from working on such television shows as *Roseanne* and NBC's first attempt at bringing the movie *Parenthood* to TV into features—which was long before he ever contemplated putting *Iron Man, Captain America,* and the rest of the Avengers through their cinematic paces.

Whedon, who would go on to become one of the most successful and highly paid script doctors in the go-go '90s, when it wasn't uncommon for a scribe to get a million dollars for a week's worth of rewriting on a big-budget action film, grew up on the tony West Side of Manhattan, in a family for whom the performing arts were nothing new, seemingly right out of a Noah Baumbach movie like *The Squid and the Whale*.

JOSS WHEDON

(creator/executive producer, *Buffy the Vampire Slayer*)

My parents were theater geeks in a big way and also just film lovers. They would just take us to things that were wildly inappropriate or strange. I saw *The Exorcist* in the theater when I was like nine. It didn't damage me. And my mom was head of the history department and every year she would abuse her power to rent a bunch of 16 mm movies and throw them up on our living room wall before she showed them to her students. Every year for like ten years we watched *The General, Steamboat Bill, Nosferatu, Grand Illusion, The Seventh Seal,* and a couple of others. Not only did I get to see movies a lot with my parents, but I got to see the same ones over and over and over and over, which is really the key. That's the thing that makes you go, oh, wait a minute, now I want to know how that's done. I'm not saying *Star Wars* didn't help. That also.

The big moment, it feels so stupid because I was so old, I was like sixteen, the moment of like "Oh, somebody directed this" was the Big Wheel shot in *The Shining*. That's when I went, "Hold on a second, somebody decided to do this." And that set everything sort of in motion. Right after that I got *Truffaut/Hitchcock* which was just the bible and the best comic book I'd ever read at the same time.

I went to Winchester in Southern England. The year I graduated we celebrated our six hundredth anniversary. The queen came, and I got to sing for her, which was pretty exciting. Then we had a big opening for our new theater and I had a little solo in the number. We watched the news that night and there was my little solo on the news. I was just like, can anybody imagine how drunk I'm about to get?

There's no way that Stan Lee and those guys weren't influenced by Shakespeare. He invented a lot of the structures and rhythms that we understand and that we've built off of. I feel like Shakespeare was absolutely about let's take this grand spectacle of theatre about kings and queens and gods and fairies and absolutely bring it down to earth. That was his genius. Let's humanize this. Let's tell stories about ourselves and pretend that they're kings and queens. I'm always doing something large and dire in my scripts and in my ideas. There's always genre, there's always some big sort of concept I can build off of. The world is often threatened or the lives of the people, it's not very Sundance-y, I don't have a Sundance-y vibe. Nobody is going to go on a road trip and reconcile with their family. Unless they take an evil road trip.

It wasn't long after graduating that Whedon decided he wanted to pursue a career in writing. He quickly discovered how much he liked it and that he had an aptitude for the craft.

JOSS WHEDON

I knew I wanted to be an artist and by that I mean not really work. Not do actual human work. I didn't actually study writing, it was just something I did for fun. When I got out of college, I was like, I want to make movies and I just sort of assumed I'd write them, but I didn't really think it through.

I didn't have a plan. I was like, "I'm going to make movies! Writing is perfect joy." The moment I started writing a script I was like, "This is my true love, this is why I'm on the planet if there's any reason at all." And that's *still* the case. Even after things sometimes don't go the way you wish they would.

I've always been working since I started writing, and that's good. It's required a lot of work and there were many times when it was heartbreaking and awful, but just in terms of day-to-day life, as long as I've been able to write, I've been able to make money at it. Hopefully I'll move up and forward every time I try to do something and get to that next level. But that's all about the writing; that's all about doing the best job that you can.

I really needed money. My dad wrote for television and my grandfather also wrote, so my father suggested I try my hand at an episode of a TV show so that I could make enough money to move out of his house. So I did, but it was strange. I was a film major; I was supposed to make movies and I never thought about writing, but I just assumed I would without ever thinking about writing. I did a bunch of TV-episode spec scripts. First I tried to get an agent and then I tried to get a job. I ended up on *Roseanne*.

Roseanne was a groundbreaking sitcom and a huge hit for ABC. Starring comedian Roseanne Barr and John Goodman, *Roseanne* was the story of a working-class family of five in which its outspoken matriarch struggles with the never-ending problems of marriage, children, and work.

SARAH LEMELMAN

(author, *"It's About Power":* Buffy the Vampire Slayer*'s Stab at Establishing the Strength of Girls on American Television*)

Roseanne is another situational comedy that starred its namesake, Roseanne Barr. *Roseanne* is different than its predecessors, in that it not only features a strong and independent woman but also shows that she is far from the ideal image of what a woman is supposed to be. Although she is a married woman who deeply loves her husband and children, she still desires time to herself and to be free of traditional wifely duties. *Roseanne* changed the tide for women, showing to its audience that every body type is beautiful and feminine and that a woman who enjoys her independence and strength could still embrace the family around her.

Roseanne seemed to be a huge victory for feminists. It was an instant smash hit and had one of the most successful runs of programming during its time, as it reached the top of Nielsen ratings for most of its stretch while it aired on television.

JOSS WHEDON

Roseanne was quite a carousel ride. It was an extraordinary year. I liked the speed at which you had to turn the stuff out. It teaches you a good discipline. I would never have written anything if I hadn't spent a couple of years on TV. We actually got so behind at one point that the plot of the next episode was listed in *TV Guide* before we'd written it. It all depends on the show. In TV, it's all about the process. If you're turning out a quality show where it's consistently good, then you do have to go through hell, but there are certain times when it becomes only about the process. Then it's about this guy's power and this guy's vanity and all of a sudden *all* you're turning out is work. Toward the end of the year I was on *Roseanne,* that started to happen, which is why I quit. There were a lot of different factors, but basically the show started to suffer and it was all about, "Who's angry at whom?" and none of it was about, "What's happening this week on *Roseanne*?" I can't help but learn a lot every time I do something. Just once I would like *not* to learn something.

Shortly after leaving *Roseanne,* Joss began writing what would become the 1992 *Buffy the Vampire Slayer* feature film, a tongue-in-cheek affair that cast Kristy Swanson as high school cheerleader Buffy Summers, who is recruited to battle the undead. Although he was satisfied with his original script, the final result was disappointing, creatively and financially. In addition, Whedon butted heads frequently with Swanson's costar Donald Sutherland, a long-time genre fan himself and notorious pain in the ass.

JOSS WHEDON

I started writing the *Buffy* movie right after, but I spent a year on *Parenthood* [the 1990 series], that ill-fated show. Then I was working on a pilot for a while and that didn't go anywhere. At that point I had had enough of that and pretty much wanted to do movies. [The script for] *Buffy* had gone out and had been pretty much ignored and then the woman who eventually directed it got a hold of it—Fran Kuzui.

STEVE BIODROWSKI
(editor in chief, *Cinefantastique*)

Outside of Paul Reubens's death scene, I have a hard time remembering the feature film. I do think that the movie took a bit more of a silly comedic approach to the material, assuming that the very notion of a blonde high school Vampire Slayer would be automatically entertaining. The series wanted us to laugh at the character's jokes, not at the premise of the show itself.

JOSS WHEDON

What I started with was a horror action comedy. It had fright, it had camera movement, it had acting—all kinds of interesting things that weren't in the final film. Apart from the jokes, and there were a lot more of them—and all of my favorite ones got cut—it was supposed to have a little more edge to it. It was supposed to have a little more fun and be a visceral entertainment rather than a glorified sitcom where everyone pretty much stands in front of the camera, says their joke, and exits.

I wasn't happy about anything—although there are some people who are faithful to it. I had one advantage from it: the direction was so bland that the jokes kind of stood out, because they were the only things to latch on to. In a way, that kind of worked for me, because it got people to notice it. But, no, that was a big disappointment to me. It could have been a lot more than it was.

FRAN RUBEL KUZUI
(director, *Buffy the Vampire Slayer* [1992])

Joss Whedon had written the original script, which, in all honesty, had been rejected by almost every studio in the United States. When somebody showed me the script, I saw an enormous potential in it. I optioned it, and then paid Joss to rewrite it accordingly to my concept and idea. Joss's screenplay had Buffy just romancing around, sticking stakes through vampires' hearts. There was no humor, and absolutely none of the martial arts that you saw in the final film. I think Joss envisioned his story as being a De Palma–type movie, something like *Carrie*. Also, he had written the character of Buffy as being so stupid and empty; she was totally unbelievable.

JOSS WHEDON

The movie is pretty different from what I originally intended. I like horror, but the movie ended up being more of a straight-on comedy. While it is an absurd story, I wanted to go for the thrills, the chills, and the action. The movie wasn't as focused on that as I was. They lightened up the tone, and I always like things as dark as possible. In my original draft there were severed heads and horrible stuff going on. Camp was never my interest. I can't really write camp, because it takes you away from the characters. I don't like laughing *at* people. I like laughing *with* them.

ANTHONY C. FERRANTE

(journalist, *Fangoria* magazine)

There's a lot of 1980s influence in Whedon's *Buffy* work. Less so with vampire films, but horror movies that successfully mixed horror and humor—where the humor was organic and not forced. *An American Werewolf in London, The Howling,* and *Return of the Living Dead* come to mind.

SARAH MICHELLE GELLAR

(actress, Buffy Summers)

In my opinion, eighties horror films became almost comical in a sense. It was almost funny. It was the "babe" running in the woods; it was decapitation and gore and guts and blood. Truthfully, after a while it's not scary; it's funny.

FRAN RUBEL KUZUI

I was a very big fan of John Woo and his original Hong Kong marital arts movies. I especially admired Woo's use of humor; he could have you watching a bloody fight yet have you chuckling at the same time. I showed the films to Joss and suggested that we use the elements of martial artist and humor in *Buffy*. That's how all the tongue-in-cheek fighting got in the movie. I saw the whole concept of *Buffy* as very much about girls in high school who don't want to acknowledge that they're different. They're encouraged to marry the brightest, smartest, best-looking guy who is going to take care of them, but then they find out that they're not destined to just be somebody's wife. I emphasized that detail in the story, because I wanted girls to know that it was OK to be different, it was OK to kick serious butt. I also wanted them to know that even with acknowledging their power, they might be able to get a hold of that bright, smart hunk anyway.

KRISTY SWANSON

(actress, *Buffy the Vampire Slayer* [1992])

So many people have gotten confused. They say to me, "You're Buffy, the Vampire Slayer, aren't you? You're the girl on the TV show?" I tell them, "No, I was the original Buffy—the one in the movie." Then they ask, "Did they ever ask you to play the part in the show?" When I tell them no, they ask, "Doesn't that bother you?" And I go, "No, not at all. Why would it?" I was too old to play a high school girl. Secondly, I've already played Buffy, already made my mark in a film that's something of a classic. People get the wrong idea. They think I'm sensitive about talking about the TV show, whereas I'm actually proud to discuss it. The series is very different than the movie. Other than the fact that some of the characters are basically the same, it had nothing to do with the film whatsoever. First of all, the show was shot differently; it's darker, more Nancy Drew-ish. And also the TV show is much more serious. The film was a lot lighter, fluffier, with more satire.

It wouldn't be long after the original *Buffy* movie came and promptly left theaters that Whedon began work as a highly paid script doctor on a succession of major Hollywood films following his critically acclaimed work rewriting 1994's *Speed*, which became a huge hit for Keanu Reeves and Sandra Bullock.

JOSS WHEDON

Once you start making the big money or working on the big projects, then all of a sudden there are movie stars, a giant budget, and there are suddenly a bazillion people who are trying very hard to make this work their way and there's really no place for the writer. No one's ever really going to listen to the writer. As a writer you may get to play in the big leagues, but we never get the ball because they've got this big guy, the big director.

Basically, when they are making a movie already and they should not be, they called me in. That can be, "Gosh, this one scene doesn't work," or "Wow, this script sucks." What it is, for me, is connecting whatever dots they already have. It's taking whatever they're wed to and then trying to work something good in between the cracks of it. In the case of something like *Speed,* there were a lot of opportunities to do that. They had the entire premise and I couldn't change a single stunt, but I could change every word.

Apart from rewriting about 90 percent of the dialogue, the best work was stuff that nobody would ever notice: just trying to make the whole thing track logically and emotionally so that all of those insane over-the-top stunts, one after the other, would just make sense. That's the biggest part of script doctoring that's actually interesting to me. When somebody says, "We've got a guy and he's falling off a cliff, and later he's hanging from a helicopter and we need you to tell us why. We need you to make the audience believe that he's doing it"—*that's* what *Speed* was about, apart from writing the jokes.

What I like about that is taking a scene and saying, "OK, she's married to him, but he's shooting at her, so wouldn't he feel *this*? What if we do it like *this* instead?"—all without changing who gets shot. I think that's really fascinating, because a lot of scripts, even when they're well-wrought, people will throw something in and they won't track it emotionally. They'll say, "This would be cool, this would be cool, this would be cool," but then you have to go in and say, "How on earth did that happen?" Even if it's just throw in some jokes, throw in some action, it's all about making my contribution fit with what they already have.

The success of *Speed,* which is the best of the *Die Hard* knockoffs ("*Die Hard* on a bus"), which included movies like *Under Siege* ("*Die Hard* on a boat") and *Cliffhanger* ("*Die Hard* on a cliff") led to work on a succession of other films including *Titan A.E., Atlantis: The Lost Empire,* and 1996's *Twister,* also directed by *Speed*'s Jan de Bont, about a team of storm chasers who pursue a deadly tornado. But no film had a bigger cinematic impact than *Toy Story,* the Oscar-nominated film in which Whedon collaborated with seven other writers, including the film's director, John Lasseter.

GLEN C. OLIVER
(journalist/pop culture commentator)

Despite some stumbles during its production, *Toy Story* is, as far as I'm concerned, the most well-balanced, artfully conceived, and skillfully executed project Whedon has been involved with to date. I believe every creator/artist has one shining moment that stands far above the rest of his or her work. In regards to his writing involvement, I strongly suspect history will show that *Toy Story* is such a title for Whedon.

On a side note: since seeing *Toy Story,* it has been a great deal harder for me to throw away, or donate, toys or potentially precious items. Someone should conduct a broad psychological study to determine if there was an uptick in hoarding proclivities throughout the world after the release of this movie. Fuck you, Joss.

DAVID GREENWALT
(co-executive producer, *Buffy the Vampire Slayer*)

Toy Story comes out and I know I'm going to take my kid to the Crest Theatre in Westwood and I know I can have a nice nap in the theater and take him to a kids' movie, right? We go, we sit down, this movie comes on. I had the same feeling when I read the *Buffy the Vampire Slayer* script. It's one of the finest movies I've ever seen. It's like when I saw *Pulp Fiction* not knowing anything about it, or *Silence of the Lambs* at the premier and you're like, "Somebody got it right, somebody cared." It really worked and it makes it worthwhile. I had that experience watching *Toy Story.*

GLEN C. OLIVER

Twister made quite of bit of money—nearly half a billion dollars in theaters alone—so it can't really be called a failure in that sense. But as a piece of filmmaking, it's a bit of a tepid mess. Whedon has himself indicated that a number of elements in *Twister* were not realized in the way he'd intended, so it's not entirely clear whom to blame for this wreck.

Early teasers for the film, featuring a terrified family—presented largely in complete blackness, lit only by the briefest flashes of lightning—cowering in a storm cellar as a tornado hammers the crap out of their home above. A hugely impactful promo. Yet not one single moment in the actual film lived up to the power of that short teaser.

A few years earlier, Whedon had previously worked with *Twister* director Jan de Bont on *Speed*—a film that very much nailed the energy it was going for with investment-worthy characters and a great atmosphere in a hugely entertaining and smooth way. Clearly, the de Bont/Whedon reteaming may not be entirely to blame for what happened with poor *Twister*—but it does further beg the question, Where and how did such a seemingly sure thing go so very wrong?

One of the highest profile films Whedon would become involved with was the assignment of writing *Alien: Resurrection* for 20th Century Fox. He would be charged with the challenging task of resurrecting the Alien franchise after the box-office implosion of 1992's *Alien 3,* a responsibility that came on the heels of his own enormous success as a highly sought-after script doctor along with the high-priced sale of his original spec script, *Suspension,* which was lauded at the time as "*Die Hard* on a Bridge."

JOSS WHEDON

Quite frankly, I don't know what makes a big spec sale. I think certain things will sell, but it's hard to pinpoint exactly what they want and why they think they should pay a lot of money. I *know* they don't revere writers. Although I've been treated well by good people a lot of the time, I have the usual bitter, "They're jealous of us, they need us and they hate us because they need us" writer thing, which is probably true. I think that on the totem pole, writers are still pretty much the part of the totem pole that's stuck in the ground so that it will stay up.

I think the compensation and the high profile has to do with the whole media being more insider than it used to be, with people knowing more about directors and the industry. Everything is becoming sort of more high profile. But I think that, ultimately, the industry's attitude toward writers is pretty much the same: "How can you facilitate our blockbuster and how can we push you around?" The fact that they're paying them a lot of money doesn't really have anything to do with that. In a way, I found that the more successful I got as a writer, the less power I had.

Alien: Resurrection, released in 1997, would eventually be helmed by French auteur Jean-Pierre Jeunet, the brilliant director who was part of the critically acclaimed duo behind the masterful *The City of Lost Children* and *Delicatessen.* It was an odd pairing with Whedon's distinctly American sensibilities and colloquialism, and the film would please few, including Whedon himself.

JOSS WHEDON

I got the gig for *Alien: Resurrection* by writing a treatment that did not involve Sigourney [Weaver]. Then they said they wanted to get her in it. At first my response was, "Bullshit, she's dead." I had to figure out how to bring her back. We didn't just say, "We've brought her back, let's make the movie." It's the central issue of the movie, the fact that we bring her back. We knew that once you do that, everything must be different. Somebody comes back from the dead, especially in a movie where death is the ultimate threat, you can't just say, "It's OK, anybody can die and come back because we can do this now." It was very important to me that it's a very torturous, grotesque process so that people will viscerally feel what it's like to be horribly reborn in a lab.

I enjoyed the bleakness of the third film, but it played that and it played it to its logical conclusion. Originally my whole pitch was that she wakes up and she's got to be pretty angry, and she's got a lot of shit to work through. What's interesting about this was she could be all kinds of different people at this point rather than just play that same note again.

GLEN C. OLIVER

I'd argue that much of what Whedon chiefly intended throughout his screenplay drafts made it to screen—more or less at times, in other instances exactingly. I can see Whedon trademarks stamped throughout the film—both on paper, and on screen. One example: characters project a vibe, a 'tude, which can be spotted fairly easily and can be correlated to Whedon's approach to characters in his other works. There are some innate Whedonesque thematics present as well.

JOSS WHEDON

I saw *Alien* when I was fourteen and there's not another movie that had as big an impact viscerally and aesthetically on me. *Alien* changed the face of science fiction, even more than *Star Wars*, into a working man's universe. It was a submarine movie. It's like that thing in *Star Wars* where Luke looks at the Millennium Falcon, which is the coolest thing I'd ever seen, and says, "What a piece of junk." All of a sudden you're not in robes proclaiming, "Mars will explode!" You're in a science fiction universe inhabited by *us*. I think that's a huge part of it.

Also they created a monster that was not only genuinely new, but sort of horribly resonant. For the first one, that was the huge thing. *Aliens* just made brilliant changes on it. That's what was disappointing about the third one for me. I thought the attitude and the feel of it was great, but people want to see those changes. They say, "We know the Alien and we know it intimately, what's new? What's different?" Cameron did it big just with the title, and *Alien 3* said, "Yeah, well this one is small and kind of slow."

They weren't rushing to make another one afterward. I think they were disappointed, because it wasn't the film they were hoping to make. And, again, how does that happen? How does a bunch of guys with a ton of money and a great franchise set out to make a certain kind of movie and then say, "Oh, I don't get it"? They all felt that the matter was kind of closed, and Sigourney had dissolved into a pit of lava, so it wasn't like they thought they had a star. *Alien 3* was beautiful, but it was neither exciting nor scary, which is a travesty. It needs those things.

My friend Tommy had an interesting theory about what was wrong with the third one. He said that all of the Alien movies were very specific. The first one was a bunch of pros on a submarine, the second one was an army movie, and the third one was a prison movie, only it wasn't a prison movie and *that's* where it failed. As he said, it was just a bunch of bald British guys and you couldn't tell one from the other. That's *not* prison genre. In prison genre, they're Americans very specifically. That was a big mistake in terms of trying to evoke a prison movie, because they carry their own level of terror and it was hard to be scared of these guys. Making them all British totally undermines the prison movie idea. I think the fans were robbed in the third one. You know what they did in the third one that just upset me beyond imagining?

They actually had a scene where people we didn't know were killed by the alien. That's bullshit, because nothing is more boring than people you don't know being killed. I just want every scene to contain something amazing. I want to do *Evil Dead,* where it's really menacing and then about twenty minutes into it the action starts and never stops.

GLEN C. OLIVER

One of the brilliant conceits of the Alien franchise is that each of the film installments has represented radical stylistic departures from the previous entries. Thus, I don't think it would be fair to say that what director Jean-Pierre Jeunet and Whedon were attempting was categorically less relevant or worthy than previous films in the cycle. Each movie has its own approach, its own aesthetic, its own thematics, and its own voice. Which, for my money, is exactly the kind of diversity that should be reflected in an ongoing big screen franchise. So, *Resurrection* got that part right, at least.

JOSS WHEDON

I fucking hated it! I thought it was as badly directed as a movie could be and I thought it was bad in ways that I didn't know movies could be bad. I learned more from that movie than anything I've ever been involved in. I thought it was badly cast, badly shot, I didn't like the production design. Everything that was wrong in the script was incredibly highlighted by it, and everything that was right about the script was squashed with one or two very minor exceptions. I just couldn't believe how much I hated it.

GLEN C. OLIVER

Jeunet's overall execution of Whedon's "vision" is highly suspect. When viewing the movie, I've always perceived a sense of conflict and struggle within the filmmaker. At some level, he was clearly aware of the enormous dramatic potential of the project. Ripley's discovery of her prototype clones in the Auriga lab somehow manages to be both horrific and touching and thrilling simultaneously—not an easy feat to accomplish for a director. Our heroes taking on the alien beasties underwater is both quite striking and very smartly executed. In moments like these, Jeunet shined as the amazing and provocative filmmaker he can often be. The filmmaker this particular project needed more of.

JOSS WHEDON

I wasn't really involved in production. I went to the set once, because I was busy doing *Buffy*. I went to dailies once and thought, "This doesn't seem right, but I'm sure it's fine." I saw the director's cut with the studio brass and I actually began to cry. *Then* I started to put on a brave face and tried to be a team player, but I can say with impunity that I was just shattered by how crappy it was.

I worked really hard on it for a really long time. But you know what? It was an epiphany, a wake-up call. After that I said, "The next person who ruins one of my scripts is going to be me." I have always wanted to direct. I'm not just a bitter writer trying to protect his shit. I think they're two very different talents, but there is an element of, "Enough already." I was making an argument in the past that I had yet to really live, as far as I was concerned. It was the final capping humiliation of my crappy film career.

GLEN C. OLIVER

Where the film suffers most greatly—and deviates most significantly from Whedon's intent—there are frequent instances where Jeunet is clearly viewing the source material as little more than a glorified B movie. Certain action and suspense movements feel not that far removed from the less disciplined days of Troma or New World. Some moments here feel like they've been carved from a less thoughtful, respectful version of the franchise. Not quite parody, but not fully reverential, either. There were times when I wondered if Jeunet was making an Alien movie, or . . . in some weird way . . . if he was lampooning the "scruffy crew in a compromised setting" genre on the whole. It's a strange, and unclear, tone at best—one which I think resulted in no small portion of pushback from audiences.

JOSS WHEDON

A lot of writers become directors because they want to protect their material, and after *Alien: Resurrection* anybody would feel that way. Directing is the other half of storytelling, and that's what I wanted to do. What I only ever wanted to do is tell stories, and sometimes it was very frustrating to me that I'm not this incredible lens man. I'm not the most adept. I see people who can shoot so much better than I can and it's a little frustrating. But I also have a little bit of that glint thing of, Was the gun in the frame? I know what's important and it's what they're feeling and what I'm feeling about what they're feeling and for the rest, I'll do my best. I'll work very hard, but it will also take care of itself. But writing was always just the first half. And back then when I started, you wrote a script and then maybe a studio would buy it. But I had ten scripts I wrote, one hundred pages plus each that nobody ever made. So the act is somewhat masturbatory. If you don't get the partner, if you don't get the other person involved, if you don't see it to fruition, then you're just telling stories to yourself like when you masturbate.

GLEN C. OLIVER

I can't fathom that, given the body of his work on the whole, Whedon ever once conceived that the characters in *Alien: Resurrection* shouldn't connect with viewers more fully. If an audience doesn't care for the characters on screen, the audience doesn't care what happens to them either—and the fabric of the film quickly begins to unravel. Which I very much feel happened here. And the fact that the film's principal iconic contribution to the franchise—the alien "Newborn"—looked like a rubber chicken which had been left in the sun too long didn't help much, either.

Whedon also was involved with an even more notoriously troubled feature film, Kevin Reynolds's 1995 would-be sci-fi epic, *Waterworld,* in which most of the Earth is underwater after the polar ice caps have melted. Kevin Costner's Mariner befriends Helen (Jeanne Tripplehorn) and her young companion, Enola (Tina Majorino), as they escape from an artificial island pursued by Dennis Hopper and his malevolent Smokers in the hopes of finding the mythical Dryland.

JOSS WHEDON

I lost the patient! That experience was pretty interesting and a pretty good example that, by the time I got there, there was too much going on for me to make a real difference. They were too far into it. With *Speed,* I had leeway to kind of really work on it. With *Waterworld,* there were only tiny cracks I could get in between. I will tell you that that film is one of the projects that proved to me that the higher you climb, the worse the view.

BEN EDLUND
(creator/executive producer, *The Tick*)

I ended up working on *Titan A.E,* which was a late '90s sci-fi, which actually had eighteen writers that worked on it, but the credits ended up landing on myself, Joss Whedon, and John August. We were the ones who got screen credit. But I had actually not worked ever a moment with either of those dudes. We all did our own individual drafts, but I had actually been cocredited with Joss on a movie and had never met him.

After a succession of these unsatisfying but financially lucrative writing gigs, Whedon got the phone call that would change his life from the WB (forerunner to the CW), a fledgling network that was attempting to stake out the young audience that had all but been abandoned by ABC, NBC, and, especially, CBS. The idea was to come up with programming that would never be greenlit by the mainstream networks, and *Buffy the Vampire Slayer,* despite its failure as a feature, somehow seemed ideally suited to their needs at the time.

GEORGE SNYDER
(former assistant to Joss Whedon)

I'd worked for the producers of the *Buffy* film and was introduced to Joss by Gail Berman. Then Joss mentioned that the Warner Bros network was talking about doing a pilot of *Buffy* for television and wanted to know whether or not I had ever done a pilot. I told him, "No," and he said, "Neither have I. Let's do it."

JOSS WHEDON

I thought a series would be very different from the movie, but there is an idea in the "high school horror show" that would sustain . . . an entire television show [and] keep it going for years. The movie, the idea, the premise is really just for one piece. Where the show would be different is we could broaden it out a little with different monsters, different problems, new characters, and things like that. It was appealing to me as an idea for a show, but I hadn't thought of it until they brought it to me.

DAVID GREENWALT

Gail Berman worked at Sandollar at the time and she was the one that said, "The vampire story should be a TV series." They said to her that you got to get Joss Whedon, knowing that he'd already sold a million-dollar script and done all this stuff in movies. Gail went and got Joss, whom we thought would never do TV, because he's a big movie guy. But he doesn't care if it's TV, movies, that *Dr. Horrible Sing-a-Long* thing, or a play in his backyard. He only cares about quality, and he was disheartened with the movie version of *Buffy,* which was very camp. It was a great script that I don't think was that well executed, and he wanted to do it right. They made a deal with him that they only owned him for the first twelve episodes. That's unheard of, not to own a guy for at least two or three years who's going to be the igniting element in the show. He just stayed and did it because he loved it, and because he was getting it right. Gail turned out to be pretty smart.

FRAN RUBEL KUZUI

I wanted to make the sequel in Hong Kong, and make it even more of a martial arts movie than *Buffy.* I lost interest in it, though, and it wasn't until a few years later that Gail Berman approached me about possibly turning *Buffy* into a TV series. Gail's timing must have been right, because I agreed to go ahead and do it. I loved doing the movie, loved so much of it that I was ecstatic when I was given the opportunity for it to have another life as a TV show.

IAN WOOLF

(first assistant director, *Angel*)

What happened was that the Kuzuis produced the feature film and had the ancillary rights in perpetuity. We never saw them. I used to do a funny thing early on in the first and second seasons. On the first day of principal photography on the first episode of that season, I would call the Kuzuis' office and call in for a shot. They were like, "Who is this?" "It's Ian Woolf, first AD on *Angel*. Just calling in the first shot for the Kuzuis." They're like, "What?" because they don't know. It's kind of a joke, because, typically, when you get the first shot, it's always called into the production office or called into Fox, because they like to know when the first shot rolls and when the break for lunch is and all that stuff. I just used to fuck with the Kuzuis and call in the middle of the show.

But they had nothing to do with it; they just got a check and that was it, basically. When they would do crew jackets for everybody, they'd always ask the Kuzuis for money, because we felt it was a waste of money. The crew jackets just end up in somebody's closet. We prefer to give the money to a charity. But the Kuzuis never gave money to the crew. They were real assholes.

CHARISMA CARPENTER

(actress, Cordelia Chase)

Joss had no desire to have another awful experience where his idea was there to get basically trampled on, and where he has no voice because he sold it and they're going to do it their way. In the end, he wanted control over his vision, and he had no desire to have another bad experience where he didn't get to do his vision. So when Gail [Berman] was able to go, "No, no, no, you will have total creative license," she was able to kind of talk Joss into it.

He has always been sort of a pioneer—I remember after *Buffy* and *Angel*, after I wasn't on the show anymore, he called me and asked if I would participate in this round robin with some of the writers and actors from the show and talk about stuff. I always thought he hated me and one of the things he said is how we have to own our own content and how important it is to do it ourselves and not let big budget or studios control it. He's a rebel. If you want something done right, it has to be your voice. You can't have any interference from the financier.

STEVE BIODROWSKI

I see parallels with *Dark Shadows* in the sense that *Dark Shadows* started with the vampires and branched out to include just about everything: witches, ghosts, werewolves, even "Diabolos." I think that's how the devil was billed, though never so named out loud. It was an attempt to recycle familiar, well-loved horror clichés in a television format. The "rules" of these creatures might be bent a little bit, but there was generally no overt revisionism. In the same way, *Buffy* might have played around with the nature of vampires, but they didn't sparkle in the sun.

SARAH LEMELMAN

Dark Shadows started off as not even having any supernatural elements, and then much later into it, we're introduced to Barnabas Collins. My mom has said that's who she remembers from the show and I think that just speaks to the popularity of vampires. She said it had werewolves and time traveling, but she, and everyone who watched it, remembers Barnabas. He was this charismatic character that drew in the audience, especially with the love story between him and Angelique. It's likely that Joss was aware of *Dark Shadows,* and may have partially based the relationship of Angel and Buffy off Barnabus and Angelique. I think it's safe to say, people love forbidden love. That's why Romeo and Juliet or Tristan and Isolde have stayed popular for centuries. Vampires shouldn't be with people, and when a vampire falls in love with a Vampire *Slayer,* now *that's* a captivating story.

STEVE BIODROWSKI

The other parallel between *Dark Shadows* and *Buffy* would be that both retained the basic notion [that] vampirism was a bad condition even while allowing that individual vampires might have a conscience. Barnabas Collins didn't want to be a vampire, but occasionally he was able to use his unwanted powers for good (several of his victims were villains we were glad to see him kill). On *Buffy,* Angel was a sympathetic if conflicted vampire, and of course he got to put his undead powers to good use on his spin-off series.

GEORGE SNYDER

Gail Berman went around to the major networks and was literally laughed out of the room. People said to us, "Why did you go to this little network?" and Joss would say, "Well, they were the only network that would take us." Fox, who were producing it, said they already had their own vampire show, which was *Kindred: The Embraced,* but they would produce. It was Gail Berman who said, "This has got legs," and *she's* the one who asked Joss if he would be interested in pursuing it as a TV series. He thought it could be intriguing as long as he could do what he wanted to do with it. Then it was a matter of trying to sell it.

DAVID GREENWALT

She's great and we had a lot of fun, and then she ran Fox Network. My wife always liked Gail, because Gail never treated her like she was a piece of shit because she wasn't in our business.

GEORGE SNYDER

The reason I think the WB took on the show is that they were very smart people; it was a little network that had nothing to lose at that point. I think they just got the idea and a lot of people didn't. Hybrid shows, shows that play with genre . . . there was just something very different, but they got it. As Joss has said more than once, they were very nurturing. They were willing to take the risk, they could afford to take a risk, but it was a risk nonetheless.

JOSS WHEDON

The idea of the movie was that Buffy is someone who is completely ignorant to the world, who was never expected to do anything except be pretty. And someone who's nice but self-centered and kind of vacuous who learns about the world, basically because she has to learn about vampires and stuff and becomes a more mature person in the process. This Buffy is dealing with the same stuff, but she's already a Slayer and has been a Slayer for a while. She is instinctively a hero, but at the same time there are some things she will always be dealing with: the pain of adolescence and growing up, but her journey is not quite the same. In the series she's already empowered; she's just trying to deal with how that empowerment affects her. She tries to put the events of the film behind her a little bit, but basically she accepts what she is. It's just a question of balancing her life as a Slayer and her life as a teenage girl who would rather go out on a date than spend the night killing vampires.

THOMAS P. VITALE
(executive vice president, Programming and Original Movies, Syfy and Chiller)

The original *Buffy* movie was fun and entertaining, but if considered in a vacuum, I don't think that movie would ever be considered an "important" film. Beyond that, I don't think anyone in the *Buffy* movie audience could have imagined that little film turning into an iconic and long-running television series. The fact is that very few film-to-television projects ever become hits. The "prebranding" of a theatrical movie definitely helps with the original launch of the show, as familiarity can attract viewers to sample the series version. But if the television series doesn't stand on its own and have something new to say, it won't last. Out of the countless television dramas ever made, I'd estimate there are only a couple of dozen film-to-television series that have become hits, and maybe none as special as *Buffy*.

STEVEN S. DEKNIGHT
(executive producer, *Spartacus: Gods of the Arena*)

I remember when I heard they were doing a *Buffy the Vampire Slayer* TV show, I thought, "Well, that's not going to work." Like everybody else, I wasn't a huge fan of the movie. Then I watched the first episode and I'm like, "Oh, wait a minute . . ." I think by episode three I was like, "This is the best thing ever. This is brilliant." I really, really loved it. I started watching it before I had broken into the business.

JOSS WHEDON

Truthfully, I can spot the similarities between *Buffy* and my other scripts. It's not that different. Our approach on *Buffy* was to make little movies. The good thing is that I had no idea what I was doing, so a lot of that works to my advantage. We shot a little higher than we should and it's easy to break rules when you're not sure of them. At the same time, I'm very traditional. I like to tell a good story, I care about my characters and all that stuff.

It's not like *Twin Peaks* where it's completely out there. I'm actually a very conservative storyteller. We're always so dedicated to "What is the emotional reality of being locked in a cage by the substitute teacher who then turns into a giant praying mantis?" And we're very serious about it. Otherwise it becomes jokey. If you can't connect your story to some emotional reality to your characters, then there's no reason to tell that story.

GEORGE SNYDER

The WB got the metaphor. When you go in to pitch a show, you pitch some ideas for possible episodes. The two Joss went in with were what eventually became "The Pack" and "Out of Mind, Out of Sight." The pitch for "Out of Mind, Out of Sight" was that this is a girl who is so shy and so unpopular that she doesn't get noticed to the point where she becomes invisible. Well, everybody got that. It was one of the hardest episodes in the end to write, but that pitch was something they got. The high school metaphor, the idea of being lonely in high school, Buffy's problem of, "I can't be a part of this, because I'm a Slayer," translates to, "I'm too tall," "I'm too short," "I'm too funny looking," "I'm not athletic." Whatever teen issue I'm burdened with keeps me separate, and this is a story about that alienation. We were off and running.

JOSS WHEDON

It made sense to me, but it definitely surprised most people. Why are the best writers in TV? Because they can control their product, they're given something resembling respect, and they see what they create come up on the screen not only the way they want it, but also within a few months as opposed to, like, four years. Plus it's steady work. That's my theory, because most movies are so bad that you have to wonder who in their right mind would want to write those. I love movies and want to make more movies, but if the idea is to tell the story, then TV is the best way to do that.

SUSANNE DANIELS
(president of programming, WB Network)

Every once in a while you meet a writer whose passion and vision just blow you away, and that's what happened when we met with Joss Whedon for the first time. As soon as we saw Joss's pilot script, we knew we had something unique.

SARAH LEMELMAN

Susanne Daniels was sold on the idea as she was looking to reach the profitable teenage audience. For Daniels, the targeted teenage, and moreover young girl, demographic was critical, as in the late 1990s they were seen as an ideal target market that spent an estimated eighty-five billion dollars per year. It certainly helped that during that time frame, third-wave feminism was taking its hold on America, and media depictions of "girl power" were everywhere. Its reach ranged from magazine cover stories and spreads to newly formed female music groups, like the Spice Girls, who headlined festivals and tours across the world and disseminated the girl power mantra. The time was ripe for a show to be broadcasted about female empowerment, and Daniels wanted to take full advantage of this.

JOSS WHEDON

Buffy starts in a new school, hoping to leave her vampire-slaying days behind her. Unfortunately, the school is built on a Hellmouth, which is kind of a mystical portal between our dimension and the demonic dimension. So in this high school, *anything* goes. Right from the start, we had witches and werewolves, giant insects, and, of course, vampires. She and her friends—who find out her secret—become the core group to fight them. What's fun about the concept is that our characters go through all of that and then have to worry about school. The humor comes from, "I have a test, I have a giant insect attacking me, and I have to deal with both of those realities." And they deal with both of those realities, because they have to. They can't get kicked out of school and become bums. They're hoping that if they can stop the monsters, normal life will continue.

SUSANNE DANIELS

In fact, it's a show that we thought appealed to the Goosebumps audience at the same time it captured *X-Files* viewers. *Buffy* was much more than a Vampire Slayer. She's the chosen one, chosen to fight all of the forces of evil she comes upon, and in this series evil ranged from powerful modern-day witches to a seven-foot praying mantis disguised as a teacher.

JOSS WHEDON

Early on there were *so* many ways that people described the show as everything from "*Clueless* meets *The Night Stalker*" to "*90210* meets *The X-Files*." Those things were a great way of selling the show. *Clueless* was a bit of a mislead, because that's really a camp show where everyone is laughing *at* the characters, and *Buffy* is an actual hour drama where, although it's got a huge amount of humor, it takes itself seriously. It's not one of those post-modern things where everything is referential and everything is a big joke. Visually, I don't think the show was quite as dark as *The X-Files*; it had a lighter side and all of the actors weren't Canadian. But that was definitely the closest forebear at the time, because we weren't just vampires. We were dealing with all kinds of monsters and demons. We weren't interested in doing variations of the same thing every week.

SARAH MICHELLE GELLAR

What we did was take the concept of the movie of this sixteen-year-old aching that everyone felt in their adolescence: Am I an adult? Am I a child? And, suddenly, she has to save the world. Now she's an outcast. She doesn't fit in. She doesn't know if she wants to be a cheerleader or fight vampires, and that is what makes her interesting and believable. Buffy is a person who is lost, who doesn't know where she belongs, and you can feel for her. Junior high was my time to feel that I didn't know where I fit. I tried to be a jock.

I tried to be cool. And I couldn't find my place. I think that is what Willow, Xander, and Buffy were all going through. That's what made them such wonderful friends—they helped each other to get through this time.

JOSS WHEDON

The people of Sunnydale sort of had a notion that things aren't right. Terrible things happen all the time at this school; kids are dropping like flies, but everyone else is pretty oblivious. The group and Buffy's Watcher are the only ones who *really* know what's going on. Believe me, they *want* to have normal lives. Hopefully the high school situation we presented was not totally unrealistic. It's not, "Oh, there's a nerd; there's a jock." We tried to show people the way they act in high school. We tried to create a little more of the reality of high school, because, of course, that's where the horror is really coming from. A lot of these stories were supposed to work as fun-house-mirror reflections of normal life, so that the werewolf story would be a puberty nightmare, basically.

Then we do a story about a girl who is so unpopular that she becomes invisible; there's a story about a witch who tries to get on the cheerleading squad, and it's basically a story about girls and their mothers, which also happens to have a witch, magic, horror, and all that stuff. Everything was supposed to come from high school. We were facing a sort of almost absurdly huge and horrific extension of our own normal everyday high school experience.

SARAH MICHELLE GELLAR

High school *is* horrific! Let's be honest—it's the most horrific time in life. Kids are vicious for no reason. You're labeled with your reputation as a freshman, and it's virtually impossible to change that throughout high school, and you live like that.

JOSS WHEDON

It's also why I wanted to do the show. I wanted to do the movie because I liked the character and I liked the premise, but that won't carry a show.

What carries the show is that it's about high school. It's not just *in* high school, it's about the human relations that are going on in there. Those things are just blown so out of proportion that instead of having a sensitive heart to heart, we had to deal with a terrible, horrible beast. But it's the same issue. I've said it before and I'll say it to my grave: high school was a horror movie. And a soap opera. And a ridiculous comedy. So we go from the sad scene at school where Buffy finds out that the guy she likes is interested in somebody else, to the slaughter of innocent people.

DAVID GREENWALT

At that time Joss had longish hair that kind of came across his forehead. As years went by and the hair began to disappear, I used to tease him mercilessly. Sometimes I'd come in and I'd go, "God, I have all this hair." I thought he was sweet, very smart, and my first impression was you know this is a really smart guy who has his own style, his own language, and he's come up with this great concept. In the horror movie where the blonde goes into the dark alley and kicks the shit out of this person who attacks her, the reverse of what all of the horror movies have been based on.

CHARISMA CARPENTER

Oh, gosh, it was like, who's this guy in charge? We shopped at Abercrombie & Fitch, he wears layers, he picks his buttons, he's kind of sheepish, funny, awkward. It was like, *he's* in charge? Never had such a young boss! But wicked smart, and very educated, and he studied in England, and was a Shakespeare authority. He's changed so much even now; now when I see him he's a man.

We were all just kids. I had all this respect for him, and definitely aimed to please and do my best, and wanted his approval, of course. And then Gail [Berman], I wanted to be next to her; if she was on set, I wanted to be anywhere she was. I wanted to hear what she had to say, because I was able to identify with the woman in power in her. She is the embodiment of female power; I felt that she made it happen—if it wasn't for her, there would be no *Buffy the Vampire Slayer.* It wouldn't have gone to TV.

JOSS WHEDON

People always say comedy and horror are different, but they're actually quite similar to me. Because a lot of great comedy comes from a character's lack of control; the unexpected, not knowing what's coming from out of the frame. Not just slapstick. Look at *Groundhog Day,* which is a movie that I adore. The guy is not in control of his environment and is just completely confused by what's going on. And a horror movie is sort of the same thing. It's also, "What the hell is going on?" Only in that case you've got a guy with a really big axe or it's a slimy monster. A horror movie is very much about, "I don't understand the space I'm in and I don't have control of the situation." An action movie is, "I have control of the situation and I understand the space that I'm in." Cameron is a great action director. The thing about his action is that he tells you exactly what the space is, what the problem is, where the people are, what you need to do, what's going to happen, and then he uses that space. So you know exactly where everybody is. What's exciting is seeing a person in control of the space that they're in. That, for me, is textbook great action filmmaking. Horror is the opposite.

The hardest thing about the *Buffy* series is you had to put a heroic character and her friends into peril, and at some point she has to take control and become an action hero, so we played both things in the show. One of the things we were always saying is, "We need a space that's small and dark so it will be scary, and big and bright enough for her to kick ass in and us to get that epic sense that she's a hero."

HARRY GROENER
(actor, Mayor Richard Wilkins)

I like all the Anne Rice books. I thought her interpretation of what a vampire is supposed to be was much more interesting than Bela Lugosi. As soon as you have a vampire that can have sex and all that, and the idea of everything is human. It's just transitioned out of you. It's all about love and power and you get stronger and stronger and just live all these years gathering information and understanding for almost a thousand years. That's fascinating to me. The idea that they've been around and have seen how the world has changed is why I loved the Anne Rice books. Joss took that and mixed it with all the high school stuff. Am I pretty? Does everyone like me? Do they hate me? Do I have a boyfriend?

JOSS WHEDON

Buffy was the most manic-depressive show on television. It ping-ponged from, "Oh, it's light 'n' fluffy" to "It's Medea." The show's appeal early on was that it spoke so plainly to the high school experience, which is something you just don't really ever get over. Everything's bigger than life. In high school, my internal life was so huge and so dark and strange and overblown and dramatic that this show seemed kind of realistic in comparison. What's funny about the show is that we never knew from scene to scene which way it was going to go. A scene that started out very dramatic could end up quite funny, or something truly horrible could happen.

KELLY A. MANNERS

(producer, *Buffy the Vampire Slayer*)

Many years ago I was offered *Buffy* as a first assistant director and I turned it down. An executive friend of mine, Jamie Kleinman, said, "Kelly, I've got two shows you can be the AD on. One's called *Buffy the Vampire Slayer,* which is a mess of people running around in rubber masks, and one's called *L.A. Firefighters.*" She goes, "*Buffy*'s going to be twelve episodes and out, *L.A. Firefighters* is going to go five years." I picked *L.A. Firefighters* and that was twelve and out and *Buffy* went seven years.

HIGH SCHOOL CONFIDENTIAL

"It's my first day. I was afraid that I'd be behind on all my classes, that I wouldn't make any friends, that I'd have last month's hair. I didn't think there would be vampires on campus."

After a pilot was given the green light by the WB, Whedon shot a presentation reel rather than a full one-hour pilot. Shot on 16 mm, which was grainier and cheaper than the 35 mm film most television was shot on at the time, the presentation reel was a relatively bare-bones affair with primitive visual effects and action. Stepping behind the camera to shoot it would be Whedon himself, but while the presentation itself was unimpressive, the writing and the casting were, which helped get the series on the air.

Among those considered for the titular role early on were Katie Holmes, who would later go on to star on the network's *Dawson's Creek*. But the first person cast by Whedon along with casting director Marcia Schulman was Anthony Stewart Head, who loomed large in the cultural zeitgeist at the time in a series of serialized Folgers coffee commercials (yes, you read that right, Folgers—coffee—commercials), in which Head flirts with his female neighbor over coffee. Such were the nineties for those of you who weren't there.

JOSS WHEDON

(creator/executive producer, *Buffy the Vampire Slayer*)

I was very careful to make sure that my leads were really specifically drawn out so that they're not so generic: "I'll be pretty this week; I'll be snotty this week." I hate that shit! You've got Buffy, you've got Giles, you've got Xander, and Willow, and what's great about her is that she is also someone you just respond to emotionally whether she's in jeopardy or being hurt, you're just completely open to her in the same way that you're open to Sarah.

GEORGE SNYDER
(former assistant to Joss Whedon)

With Giles, Joss knew exactly what he wanted. Tony just *so* nailed the part.

ANTHONY STEWART HEAD
(actor, Rupert Giles)

Early on, Giles didn't have the faintest idea what he was doing. He just knew it was his duty and his life's mission to find this girl and to teach her how to deal with vampires. She is *the* One. The One who possesses all of the talents. Giles is the Watcher, so the fact that she had no desire early on to get on board was infinitely annoying to me. And the fact that she was this young American high school girl and I'm very English, so there was a lot of fun to be had.

GEORGE SNYDER

What's amazing to me is that the English got *Ally McBeal* before they got *Buffy* and they said, "You can see that *Buffy* comes out of the *Ally McBeal* mold." Whoa, whoa, whoa, quite the reverse, and that's no reflection on David Kelley.

In addition to his relative fame in the Folgers commercials, Head had also had guest-starring roles in such shows as *Highlander: The Series* and *NYPD Blue* and had roles in films like *A Prayer for the Dying, Devil's Hill,* and *Lady Chatterly's Lover.* On the London stage he appeared in *The Rocky Horror Picture Show, Julius Caesar, The Heiress, Chess,* and *Rope.* To genre fans, he was probably best known for his costarring role in the short-lived *VR.5,* in which he more or less "watched" over that show's star, Lori Singer.

ANTHONY STEWART HEAD

I read the *Buffy* script and it was really exceptional. You never know what will happen, of course, but I had never seen anything like it on TV before.

I chose to take the script with me when I popped out for something to eat. I sat there eating with my script and found myself laughing out loud, which is a bit embarrassing when you're sitting on your own. But it is something that is strangely accepted in L.A.—people sitting at tables reading scripts and trying desperately not to look obvious that they're reading a script. I couldn't stop turning the pages to find out what happened, but at the same time I couldn't help but crack up.

This was amazingly new stuff, so I couldn't wait to meet them. I met Gail Berman, Joss, and a few others. Had no idea who Joss was. He was so young anyway that I probably thought he was an intern or something. I didn't pay him much attention the first time around, but then again when you're greeted by a bunch of faces in a room, you don't really know who's who. Joss has apparently said that I picked up the part and walked away with it under my arm at that moment.

JOSS WHEDON

The poor man had a ton of exposition on the show, because we wanted everyone to understand what's going on. He's got such extraordinary range, yet at the same time he's extremely funny and plays the person who is so hapless and confused by this young American so perfectly. People used to ask why he was cast. We heard him read. Then that was over. Soon as he did, we knew we had our guy.

ANTHONY STEWART HEAD

The first test I did was for Fox, and just before I went, my agent said, "Have you seen the movie?" I said, "A long time ago." He suggested I see it and I was saddened, because it wasn't at all what I had read. I thought, "This is bizarre. This is not what I envisioned at all." Later I saw Joss in the hallway, and, by that point, I had worked out that it was him and said, "I saw the movie," and his face fell. He said, "Well, we're not doing that." I'm a great believer in instincts and intuition, and I knew then when I talked to him, I just felt it would come together.

So I had to audition in front of a bunch of Fox executives, which is bizarre, because it's a room of about twenty people. Very crammed, like a small Equity Waiver Theater. You go in and do it. Some of them laugh excessively, because they're working very hard to make you feel at home, and some people are completely blank and you have absolutely no idea how you're going down. It's rather like being a bad stand-up comic. Added to that, you sit in the corridor before you go in and they give you a contract to sign, so flashing through your mind is, "OK, I'm going to be away from my family for five to seven years. Do I know what I'm doing? What's going to happen?" At the same time, they're bringing pages of the contract that have been faxed from the agent with points that have been renegotiated or changed. You're flipping through this contract trying to figure out what you're saying that you'll do instead of being able to concentrate on acting. It's bizarre.

RAYMOND STELLA

(director of photography, *Buffy the Vampire Slayer*)

He's always got his glasses. That was his big thing. That is a distraction that keeps you busy. He loved his props.

MARK HANSSON

(second assistant director, *Buffy the Vampire Slayer*)

Anthony was the brother of Murray Head from *Chess* and *Sunday Bloody Sunday*. He was a very nice man, but he has some birth-defect hand deformity. I remember he was always careful to never show that on camera.

CHARISMA CARPENTER

(actress, Cordelia Chase)

One day, Tony and I walked up and everyone was surrounding Tony's trailer. Joss had a CD cover from the show in his hand. I remember I looked at it and said something that was pretty funny, like, "Is this a joke?" His face was made up like KISS, but with colors. And Tony says, "Actually, no, it's not a joke." He's very hip, very cool. The first time I ever saw him, it was funny. We were in the casting office and he had earrings in and he was dressed in baggy pants and Converse high tops and he's *nothing* like his character.

JAMES MARSTERS
(actor, Spike)

I had said the word "bollocks" and I had pronounced it "bull-locks," and that was the final straw. He came to me and said, "We don't say it like that, you prat. You're embarrassing me back home." He tutored me by force for about six months until I got my accent right. Without Tony Head, we would not be having a conversation about what a great British accent I had.

The role of one of Buffy's best friends, Xander Harris, went to Nicholas Brendon, who began his career as a production assistant on the sitcom *Dave's World* before securing a recurring role on the soap opera *Another World* and on stage in *The Further Adventures of Tom Sawyer, My Own Private Hollywood,* and *Out of Gas on Lover's Lane. Buffy* represented his first genuine big break.

GEORGE SNYDER

A couple of guys came in to audition for Xander, but Nicky just hit it out of the park. He, like many of the characters, begged the question, "Which is more Joss, Willow or Xander?" In a way, probably Xander, in another way Willow. There is some part of Joss in all of the characters.

NICHOLAS BRENDON
(actor, Xander Harris)

I *was* Joss Whedon in high school. I think what Joss wanted is a situation where he could completely manipulate and write the situation the way he saw fit. He played God. If he wanted that girl, by golly, by going through me he was going to get that girl. He could say all the funny lines and have all the retorts quickly, very witty and wry. I liked that. I think he went to high school in Europe at an all-boys school, so it wasn't a typical high school situation. I think it made him even more insecure when he went out into the real world. We had that conversation where he told me that Xander was him in high school.

JOSS WHEDON

Nick Brendon is extraordinarily likable. He's real good-looking and brought a humbling quality to the character, which is extremely charming. He can also play a range of emotions.

NICHOLAS BRENDON

I was horribly insecure in high school. I wanted to be funny, but I had a stutter. One of the reasons I got into acting was because I have a stutter, and that's why I'm hard on myself when I act. I lived my whole childhood life and high school with a stutter that I couldn't control. It took a lot of hard work. When I want to do something a certain way, it has to be that way; otherwise, I'll beat myself up for it.

Brendon had hoped to be a professional baseball player, but an arm injury cut that dream short, and he pursued an acting career instead. After some commercial work and a recurring role on *The Young and The Restless,* he appeared in *Children of the Corn III: Urban Harvest.*

NICHOLAS BRENDON

I went into acting. I was a great player, but there are so many politics in baseball and you have to be really lucky and in the right place at the right time. It sounds similar to acting, but with acting I was really naive.

Charisma Carpenter, whose first name was inspired by an Avon perfume, was born on July 23, 1970, in Las Vegas, Nevada. Her early credits include a succession of local lounge shows and beauty pageants. By the time she had finished high school, though, she was seriously leaning toward a career in teaching English. College would lead her to a position as an aerobics instructor and then a one-year stint as a cheerleader for the San Diego Chargers.

CHARISMA CARPENTER

Since I was five I was in a dance studio, and I was always involved in the arts. I went to the School of the Creative and Performing Arts, so we learned stage technique and opera and acting, and all sorts of things under that umbrella. One summer I took a three-day seminar and there was scene study, so I was given a scene and you learn your lines and you act it out. There was this one woman who it was impossible for her to give a compliment, and she was kind of wowed by me, and it really caught my attention; something about us heartbroken artists need to have the attention of those who don't approve of anything.

I grew up in Las Vegas and I was very involved in the community and I was involved in the Young Entertainers, which is basically a talent group for young children. We used to tour the local Travelodges at every entrance and exit of the Las Vegas freeway, of which there are two, and we would do little bars, and we would do the March of Dimes, and we would do old folks' homes, and I was in talent contests. I was always performing at a very, very young age. On top of that were the recitals, so I feel like, with that kind of background, to be in front of people performing, it came second nature to me, so acting, when that came about, made sense. It was like the next level.

In 1992 she went to L.A. to visit her boyfriend and never moved back. At first she took a job as a waitress at California Pizza Kitchen, and then, after the inevitable questions from her customers whether she was an actress, she decided to actually give it a try. Acting school followed, which in turn led to over twenty television commercials, including two years as the Secret antiperspirant spokeswoman.

CHARISMA CARPENTER

I was in my early twenties and had moved to Los Angeles from Las Vegas to be with a boy. I didn't know what I wanted to do, so I got a job at a restaurant on Sunset Boulevard called Mirabelle, and one day an agent asked me if I did commercials and I said no. He said, "What are you doing with your life?" And I said, "I'm here and I'm waiting six months to pay college tuition to go back to school, because it's an exorbitant fee," and he said I should really consider acting, because it's a lot less time-consuming than waitressing. I'm like, "Oh, tell me more." He introduced me to his son, who was a commercial agent, and I started doing commercials, and then I started studying acting with Robert Carnegie and Jeff Goldblum at Playhouse West and fell in love with that.

It was a really tough school and we had to do book reports. Our teacher was constantly reminding us how impossible it was to make it and this work ethic was kind of pounded into our heads; how often were you working on your craft, if you're trying to earn a wage, how many hours a week are you really putting forth? We had to do book reports, we had a reading list, and we had to read 1,500 pages a week, because it was imperative we understood what good writing was. So he provided a reading list, and, in a matter of a few short pages, [we had to] be able to discern what is good writing and what is the essence of a story and what is character development. It was quite the curriculum.

Stage roles in *No, No Nanette* and *Welcome Home Soldier* were followed by a guest-starring turn on *Baywatch,* which caught the attention of Aaron Spelling. Ultimately, Carpenter was cast as the bitchy Ashley Green on Spelling's short-lived *Malibu Shores*.

CHARISMA CARPENTER

I was auditioning for *Buffy* while I was doing *Malibu Shores*. I guess they knew it was going to get canceled soon. So I auditioned wearing overalls, a leather jacket, and flip-flops. It was really a bizarre day. I was actually reading for the character of Buffy. Then they wanted me to read for Cordelia five minutes later. I did and I guess they really liked it. Joss Whedon was there and I didn't know that it was for producers only. Cordelia was always looking for attention and never got it. The fan mail was disheartening too, saying things like, "Are you ever going to be nice?" My response is, "I *am* nice. They're meaner to me than I am to them."

When I was on *Malibu Shores* and went on to *Buffy,* I suffered from extreme anxiety. I didn't really know how debilitating it was. I remember when I was dancing in these talent shows and I would compete in pageants, and I would blank on what the next step was in my routine. You have to remember, I would have four-hour private rehearsals on a Saturday and a Sunday and I had been doing the same dance for a year. It's not that I didn't know the steps. For whatever reason, and I could never predict it, which created even more anxiety, I would forget. So in *Buffy*, I really wanted to do a good job and I believed in what I was doing, but I just never felt safe; I never felt I could trust myself or remember, and it created a really bad confidence problem which was just getting bigger and bigger.

When you find your passion and you know what you want, and you're living that dream, you want desperately to never lose it—there's just this pressure that I put on myself, and then there's the absolute pressure in making TV, which is expensive. At the time we were using film and so it was two takes and you're done. By the time you've shot seven people for about fourteen hours and it's your close-up and it's time for you, and you don't get it in two takes, it's a problem. It's an economic problem, it's a morale problem, and it's a confidence problem.

GEORGE SNYDER

Originally, Joss was looking for a black actress for the role of Cordelia. But one of the stumbling blocks there was the way we knew Joss anticipated the relationships shifting and changing. There was some concern at the network at the time that interracial relationships would be problematic. At that point the WB was a different kind of network. I know that came up and Joss said, "I can't have restraints on how I mix and match the dynamics. That's part of the fun of the show, that Willow is in love with Xander, Xander is in love with Buffy, Cordelia can't stand any of them yet finds herself drawn to Xander." Joss decided it wasn't worth fighting that fight at that particular time, but he didn't want to be hindered in the dynamic of the shifting triangles.

CHARISMA CARPENTER

I had gotten a call on *Malibu Shores* from my agent for this audition. She said the word on the street is that *Malibu Shores* was not going to continue, so she got me an audition to keep me employed. I went in, I got the monologue, the Buffy monologue that was the audition with Giles in the library, just talking about why she doesn't want to be the Slayer and she doesn't want that responsibility—she wants to be a kid—that was the speech. I read for Joss Whedon and [casting director] Marcia Schulman and it was a rainy day and I was in these overalls and bright orange JCrew flip-flops that were plastic, and it was a really bad choice. I don't know how they saw Cordelia in any of that, but I read for it, and they loved me; they just said, "Can you do me a favor, how do you feel about reading for this other part, Cordelia?" I'm like, sure. And they were like, "Can you just go prepare it, go in the corner and come back in fifteen minutes?" I was more fearless then, so I did, and they loved it.

I went back to work on *Malibu Shores,* and I got a call that they wanted me to go to the network and meet with Garth Ancier, who was running the WB at the time, which no one had heard about. It was a crazy story, because I was at work at *Malibu Shores* and I knew I had to be in Burbank at 7 P.M., and my job was cooperating, to get me out, which was nice, and it's rush hour and I'm in Long Beach and I had to get to Burbank. I'm driving this Nissan Sentra, my very first car, with no air-conditioning, no radio, and the next thing I know I'm in gridlock traffic in the middle of downtown L.A. and I'm freaking out, because I'm late. And I get this 911 beeper message from my agent. I get off the highway and stop at a liquor store with a phone booth to call her back, and she's like, "Where are you, they want to leave, they're hungry." Literally, I said to them, which is *so* Cordelia, "Wendy, you tell them I have been in gridlocked traffic for the last hour and a half and I will be there in the next ten minutes and they should wait and order pizza! They're going to see me today. I'm coming, I'm almost there, and they can't bail now, not after everything I've been through to get there. They don't know my pain." So that was it and the rest is history. I got the part. I was in a 7-Eleven parking lot when I got the offer. It was thirteen days after the final audition. I was going crazy. I just went into the 7-Eleven and started telling people.

DAVID GREENWALT

(co-executive producer, *Buffy the Vampire Slayer*)

They were all so funny, particularly Aly, Charisma, and Nicky Brendon. I wrote a line for Nicky in "Teacher's Pet," I can't remember it now, and he was just so good. He could use these words that he didn't necessarily know what they meant and Willow could give him grief. They were funny and they could play all this. Willow's got a thing for Xander, Xander's got a thing for Buffy, Xander gets a thing for Charisma that blows everybody's mind. They were eighteen, Nicky was maybe a hair older, but they were all really young and suddenly making a lot of money. It changed everybody's lives. It was a big deal.

CHARISMA CARPENTER

I really liked that I was the truth woman. There's also another word for that. One of my favorite lines was something that takes place, where Giles says to Cordelia, after she says something rude to Buffy, "Do you actually have any tact?" And my response is tact is just not saying true stuff. So forget it. I enjoyed that very much, that I could be vulnerable and at the same time express myself.

It was a great part. I wish I was as witty as her. One of my favorite lines is, "That's just propaganda spouted out by the ugly and less-deserving." She said hilarious stuff. I had Joss speaking in my ear 24-7, so thankfully some of the wittier things in her way of speaking sunk in. There's got to be some of that in me, or I wouldn't be able to do it.

JOSE MOLINA
(former assistant to Howard Gordon)

Charisma was never supposed to be part of the regular cast, but she was so great in that character that everybody just started writing toward her, and so this girl who had been created to be a thorn in Buffy's side and nothing else became a regular. She and Harmony were basically the same character and there was no depth, because they were just the bullies. So when they'd decided that she was going to be a part of the show, then they had to figure out, well, how do we show different parts of this without taking up too much broadband from the other characters that everybody's already in love with?

CHARISMA CARPENTER

I was a series regular that wasn't going to be in all shows produced, which is a fact my agent kind of left out of the equation and it wasn't good news. I think they were really happy with me and decided to keep me, which is why they tried to make me a part of the Scooby Gang, if you will. They probably never initially had any plans to do that, which is why I never fully fitted in, because the role was never meant to be like that. I think they finally started to develop the character a little more when she and Xander got together.

One of the many unlikely recurring stars of the series was Mercedes McNab, who played Harmony Kendall in the unaired presentation reel, returned for "The Harvest," and then appeared in a recurring role throughout much of the series and into *Angel,* where she became a series regular in its last season. A member of the "Cordettes" who is later turned into a vampire, McNab's other clique was even more exclusive: she was one of the many actresses on the series who had auditioned for the titular role of Buffy.

MERCEDES MCNAB
(actress, Harmony Kendall)

I auditioned for *Buffy* like pretty much every other girl in L.A. at the time. I went back in a couple times and then I never heard anything. After all, it's just not that unusual. Then they just called out of the blue and said they had a role, and they wanted to offer it to me, and it was the role of Harmony. It was just a guest star, not a huge part, nothing to write home about, really. But I was excited, because I wanted to be a part of the project. Of course, I would have much preferred to be Buffy.

At the time I didn't think that my character would ever return to the show. As far as I knew, it was just a one-time-only kind of a gig. I was in high school at the time and I remember I was allowed to drive on the freeway. I had just gotten my license and it was the only time my mom and dad would let me drive on the freeway since I was going to work, so that was kind of a bonus.

I just thought I was Cordelia's sidekick and I didn't think anything would come of it. I had no expectations. I really didn't think it would get picked up, let alone that it would be on the air. Then to last eight years was even slimmer. I don't think anyone thought anything of it.

CHARISMA CARPENTER

I barely worked first season, but at the beginning of the second season, I was hung upside down on a meat hook by my feet. The pace was much swifter than first season. I don't know if I was sick from nerves, but in my episode "Out of Mind, Out of Sight," toward the end I was throwing up. There was a scene with the invisible girl in the bathroom and it was a really convenient location because right after that scene was over, I threw up three times. It must have been nerves or something.

MERCEDES MCNAB

There wasn't really a difference between me and Cordelia originally in the first season. From the point of an audience, I wanted it to be a little bit more interesting. And then also have the opportunity to stand out, because you don't necessarily need two of the same characters in one show. There was an opportunity for that when we were in that computer science class. I remember this pretty vividly. We were doing some project on our computer and I just remember taking a moment playing that I'm not just the bitchy girl, but I'm also just *so* dim. I thought maybe that could differentiate me from Cordelia's character.

Before landing the role of Willow Rosenberg on *Buffy,* Alyson Hannigan began her career in Atlanta, where she started shooting local commercials, moving on to national spots such as those for McDonalds, Six Flags Amusement Parks, and Oreo cookies. At age eleven, she moved to L.A. with the hopes of breaking into film and television.

ALYSON HANNIGAN
(actress, Willow Rosenberg)

I moved out [to L.A.] to be near acting, because that's what I always wanted to do since I was a kid. I started commercials when I was four, and I've been doing it all my life. It was an after-school sort of thing. Some people would go off to ballet; I would go to a commercial shoot. Commercials are just a day here or a day there and I didn't miss much school. And I loved it. I also had regular activities. I was on the soccer team. I was a kid; I just had a job that I loved.

My first picture was *My Stepmother Is an Alien.* An interesting thing is that Seth Green also played my boyfriend in that film. After *Stepmother,* I did a short-lived sitcom called *Free Spirit.* It was sort of a *Bewitched* kind of show. It went for thirteen episodes, then got canceled. I did some guest spots here and there, nothing really too wonderful—movies of the week and all that stuff. But nothing great until *Buffy.* By far *Buffy* was the best thing I'd done. I did some movies of the week that were horrible, but they weren't the same thing as a horror series.

GEORGE SNYDER

The casting of Willow was a problem, because the network said, "Why don't we just get an Aaron Spelling girl and put glasses on her?" The notion of casting a not classically beautiful girl—"beautiful" in the television sense or Spelling sense of the word—was something Joss was absolutely committed to. He had somebody in mind that didn't work out and then there was somebody else who didn't work out. There was a lot of shuffling actresses to the network and the studio and finally, in the midst of it all, came Alyson. And that's when he said, "You know, this is the one!" Fox got it, I think. The WB was a little reluctant at first, and her look—as you watch through the first season—changed a bit. Finally they began to realize that she had a look that was equally important. Joss basically said, "Trust me." The WB did, and she got all the prisoner mail in the first season. Actually, in the first season her mail was second only to Sarah's.

ALYSON HANNIGAN

I almost didn't get the part of Willow. My agent had submitted me, but for some reason they wouldn't see me. They had cast someone else for the presentation, but then she got fired when the show was picked up. I finally was able to get an audition for the recast . . . and I auditioned for what seemed like forever. Then I waited and waited, but didn't hear anything. I'm not the most patient person. After a while, I was at the point of, "Oh, please, just tell me yes or no, because I will kill myself if I don't find out!" I figured, even if it was bad news, at least I would know. Well, I was at a 7-Eleven store one day when I got a page to call the producers. After all that auditioning and waiting, they told me I had gotten the part! I was like, "All right, cool!"

On the first day of shooting I was a little bit nervous. Nick [Brendon], Charisma [Carpenter], and Sarah [Michelle Gellar] had all known each other from the pilot episode, and I was pretty much a stranger. But it didn't take very long for all of them to become very good friends of mine. Everyone involved with the show was so great and nice. During the first season hiatus, I had my tonsils taken out, and Sarah visited me in the hospital and brought me a little Beanie Baby.

JOSS WHEDON

Alyson Hannigan played the shy, bookish one and what's great about her is that she is also someone you just respond to emotionally. Whether she's in jeopardy or being hurt, you're just completely open to her in the same way that you're open to Sarah. She is also sort of a temptress. She brought a real life to the character and made her very much a part of the group. If these four didn't have different perspectives on stuff, they were going to be boring.

ALYSON HANNIGAN

I'm a fan of the genre, but such a wimp when I watch the movies, because I will basically jump into the lap of the person next to me. There was an episode, "Prophecy Girl," where there's this huge, enormous slimy monster attacking my leg. It's wrapped in a tentacle around my leg and is pulling me. They gooped it up with the slime stuff. It's really disgusting and really scary, and then they turn on these air things so they would flop around and they would make this hissing sound, so I was genuinely screaming to myself at that point. I watched the footage and my hands were up in my face and it looked so fake. It was my natural reaction, but it looked really fake. Of course, only I noticed it, because I'm so critical, but I thought, "What a dork."

JOSE MOLINA

I was probably a cross between Xander and Willow. I kind of wanted to be as funny as Xander, but I was more dorky and studious like Willow and you know, like Xander, Buffy was a dream girl. Who doesn't want to date her? But there is a moment in the season one finale where Xander does ask Buffy out and Buffy is like, "I don't know, we should just be friends." And then I think Willow asks him, "What are you going to do tonight?" And he just says, "I'm going to go home and listen to country music. The music of pain." As a guy who sat with a lot of sappy music and licked my own wounds in my time, I could definitely relate to that.

Aspiring actor David Boreanaz—who was making a living parking cars, painting houses, and handing out towels at a sports club—was famously discovered by an agent while he was walking his dog. This led to guest appearances on *Married with Children*, the TV movie *Men Don't Lie*, the stage shows *Hatful of Rain*, *Fool for Love*, and *Cowboy Mouth*, as well as the feature films *Aspen Extreme*, *Best of the Best 2*, and *Eyes of the World*. Whedon cast him as Angel, an early protector of Buffy who quickly became her love interest, and revealed himself to be a very soulful vampire.

DAVID BOREANAZ
(actor, Angel)

I wanted to be everything. I wanted to be the fire guy, I wanted to be the police guy, I wanted to be the cowboy, the Indian. I guess I didn't say I wanted to grow up and study the Shakespearean art of acting. I'm not good at that kind of stuff. I love people. I love experiences. I love going out. I love traveling. I love adventure, I love learning, and I love involving myself in things where I'm going to learn more about people and seeing people. I'm extremely voyeuristic; I like to look at things. I can go to parks and watch people and their personalities. I didn't study at the Royal Shakespearean Academy or whatever. I have a high respect for those people, but my method is trying to get down and dirty with it. I understand the level it takes in order to achieve the impossible dream, and for me, the dream is, "Be very simple." And that's very hard to do. It's very difficult. It takes a lot of work, a lot of effort. I just want to work hard and do what I'm doing.

DAVID GREENWALT

That's a hard part to cast, a young really good-looking guy who maybe isn't a star yet, but probably could be one. I remember David came in and in the scene he's supposed to be riding a motorcycle. He turned a chair upside down and kind of sat on it as if he was on a motorcycle. Gail Berman and Joss and I, particularly the women, really responded to David. Then, you know, I think it was about episode seven, somewhere around Christmas, where this first kiss between Buffy and Angel happened. I just said, "I'll just write the episode." I didn't know it was going to be that big a deal. It went on the air and, you know, the rest is history.

Recalled casting director Marcia Schulman at the time, "The breakdown said 'the most gorgeous, mysterious, fantastic, the most incredible man on the face of the earth.' I think I saw every guy in town. It was the day before shooting, and a friend of mine called me and said, 'You know, there's this guy that lives on my street who walks his dog every day and I don't know what he does, but he has all the things you're describing.' And the minute he walked in the room, I wrote down in my notes: 'This is the guy.'"

DAVID BOREANAZ

I've always liked horror films. When I was a kid, *Frankenstein*, the original movie, scared the hell out of me. I've always been fascinated with the film *Nosferatu*, and when I saw the film the first time it was eerie. You had no choice but to get into the genre when you were on the show, because you're surrounded by all these vampires and it's amazing when you have all these extras in vampire makeup, or you're in the graveyard shooting and you look around to see vampires hanging out. The show itself was really well written and it just goes to show you that if you have the writing and the right chemistry between the cast, things really do work out for the best.

JAMES MARSTERS

I like [David] so much. The man does not whine. He refuses to whine. One time I saw him break a two-by-four with his head. He was trying to get into Buffy's mom's house, because he saw me in there. He was supposed to try and get in, forgetting that he wasn't invited, so there was a force field that kept him out. The way that we did that was to rig him with a steel cable out of his back so that when he got to a certain point, he'd be pulled back by a cable. Well it was one of those things—dusty floors, maybe. God knows what it was, but the cord was shorter than he expected and he got yanked off of his feet, back through the porch, and splintered a two-by-four in half. Not just a crack, he splintered it! The whole set hushes. They think David is going to the hospital and we're shutting down for a week. But David pops up and says, "I'm fine, I'm fine."

The other story is that when I went over to *Angel*, he had just gotten rear-ended on the highway at high speed. They just took him to the hospital because they suspected whiplash, but the doctor says it wasn't and he should just be careful. He went back to set and he was strung up on chains and hung off the floor for sixteen hours while we tortured him. The man would not complain. The one time I realized he was in pain was when he thought no one was looking at him. I saw his face go ashen. But he's like a stunt guy; he won't admit it.

SARAH LEMELMAN

(author, *"It's About Power"*: Buffy the Vampire Slayer*'s Stab at Establishing the Strength of Girls on American Television)*

The first real iteration of the sympathetic vampire came about with the publication of Anne Rice's *Interview with the Vampire,* in 1976. In it, Rice introduces Louis, a vampire who is repulsed by the joy his maker, Lestat, takes in killing and feeding on his victims. While Angel is not the first sympathetic vampire, his character certainly helped popularize this new conception of the vampire, as following the end of *Buffy* and *Angel,* both television and the movies saw a rise in this depiction of a vampire, which seems to have become a staple of the vampire genre.

In 2008, much to tween girls' delight, the vampire Edward Cullen was brought to life on the big screen, in *Twilight*. The same year also saw *True Blood,* a television program which showed the southern gentleman—and vampire—Bill Compton. The following year, in 2009, television viewers were introduced to Stefan Salvatore of *The Vampire Diaries*. All three characters are essentially the same type of vampire, refusing to feed on humans and wanting to help, rather than hurt, humanity. Since then, there have been dozens of other less popular sympathetic vampire roles on television and the movies, as the fascination around this now prototypical vampire has grown immeasurably.

GEORGE SNYDER

Angel was not designed as an ongoing character. What would you do with Buffy and Angel? If we froze them in time, if we had stayed in high school forever, maybe we could have kept it going. Anybody else would have been tempted to stay in high school and stay with that unrequited love. What is more boring than that? It's Sam and Diane from *Cheers*. No, you don't let them go to bed, and we all know that when Sam finally did get into bed with Diane, it was the end of an era. So your gut reaction is, "Let's just keep him a dark, mysterious, brooding guy who helps out Buffy." Joss said, "No, at some point you've got to go to the next step. Up the tension and go for the dark." What's the last thing you have happen? A Slayer in love with a vampire! So you do it. But having done it, oh my God, now he's bad.

Of course the mail came in: "Turn him back, turn him back." Even the network came in with, "He gets cured next week, right?" Joss is like, "Oh no, not next week. First of all, he's never going to be cured. Second of all, he's not going to turn back and he has to go to Hell." They said, "He's a very popular character and we're a little concerned." But, again, it was the narrative driving the show. Then, of course, we did turn him back and he was redeemed. Then the question was, "Now what?" Of course that led to him being spun off into his own show.

KELLY A. MANNERS
(producer, *Buffy the Vampire Slayer*)

David's a good friend of mine but an odd duck. As a matter of fact, I'll tell you a story about his show, *Bones*. My daughter went to work on it on season two, and she said the assistant directors don't even look at David Boreanaz when you go to set. I said, "Well good, when you get called to set, I want you to run up to David and jump in his arms and when the ADs freak out, then you better whisper real quick you're my daughter." She said the assistant directors went crazy, but David loved it. He's a good guy. As with most actors as they got more and more famous, some of them change drastically. David's a good guy. He has a big heart. David *did* get his nose up in the air toward the end, but he was still a great guy. Let me put it this way: I got fired by Don Johnson. There were no Don Johnsons on set.

RAYMOND STELLA
(director of photography, *Buffy the Vampire Slayer*)

I remember he was always kind of an asshole. I worked with him on *Angel*, too. He was kind of stuck-up a little. Married a *Playboy* model and he liked to play golf.

DAVID GREENWALT

I thought the way David handled his position on *Buffy* and his relationship with Sarah was really great and terrific and also very smart. He always treated her like she was the star of the show and then he got his own show and, of course, did a lot of crossover stuff. I never saw him misbehave in any way on any of my shows with him.

The producers couldn't have hoped for better casting when Sarah Michelle Gellar entered the process as Buffy. Already an acting veteran, having appeared in many television commercials, in 1980 Gellar moved over to the daytime soap opera *Guiding Light,* and guest-starred on *William Tell; Love, Sidney;* and *Spenser: For Hire.* In 1989 she cohosted the syndicated teen show *Girl Talk* before costarring in the teen soap opera *Swan's Crossing.* A fairly big break came in the form of the TV movie *A Woman Named Jackie,* in which she played the young Jackie Bouvier. Small roles in several films were next, followed by Neil Simon's Broadway play *Jake's Women.* This was followed by a two-year stint on the soap opera *All My Children,* for which she was awarded an Emmy. As her tenure on the soap was coming to an end, Gellar went to the *Buffy* office to audition for the part of Cordelia and walked out with the lead.

JOSS WHEDON

Sarah Michelle Gellar embodies Buffy extraordinarily, and she brings an intelligence and depth to the character that I certainly couldn't write. She is so incredibly sympathetic—she's somebody that you just love to watch—but she's also this extremely intelligent actress who thinks her way through everything. So she makes Buffy an emotionally very-connected character, which is huge. It's never, "Oh, look at her, she's a dork," even though she's kind of an eccentric. It's never, "Oh, laugh at her and her silly ways." You're completely sucked into her story, because Sarah is so gifted.

GEORGE SNYDER

We had seen a lot of actresses for the role of Buffy. She read for Cordelia, but then they had her read for Buffy and knew she was right. The other actresses couldn't get the balance. Somebody said to me, "It's very interesting that for a girl as beautiful as Sarah is, she nevertheless has been able to sell the idea of being an outcast." That's no small feat. There's a vulnerability there. Your initial reaction is, "Yeah, right, *she's* not the most popular girl in school?" Yet when you watched, you got it. She sold it.

SARAH MICHELLE GELLAR
(actress, Buffy Summers)

My manager spoke to the WB and they mentioned they had this *Buffy* show. He thought it would be a great opportunity to use my tae kwon do and do comedy and drama. I probably had eleven auditions and four tests. It was the most awful experience of my life, but I was so driven. I had read the script and heard about Joss Whedon and how wonderful he was. I went to the audition the week he was nominated for his *Toy Story* screenplay. I thought, "I'm going to have this role." He tells me I nailed it, but I still went through eleven auditions.

JOSS WHEDON

There was no second place. We read tons of people and several were staggeringly untalented. Buffy is a tough part. It is a character actress in the part of a leading lady. This girl had to look the part of the blond bimbo who dies in reel two, and yet she's not that. Buffy is a very loopy, very funny, very strange person—kind of eccentric. Sarah has all those qualities and you don't find them in a beautiful girl very often.

She gave us a reading that was letter perfect and then said, "By the way, it doesn't say this on my resume, but I did take tae kwon do for four years and I'm a brown belt. Is that good?"

Finding Buffy was the biggest challenge, and I think if we hadn't found Sarah, the series might not have happened or lasted. What Sarah brought to the part was her intelligence. At the same time, she had the hormonal idiosyncratic goofiness that made Buffy not just the Terminator. She approached the vampires with total irreverence, which drove them crazy. I called her Jimmy Stewart, because she suffered so well.

SARAH MICHELLE GELLAR

I picked up tae kwon do when I was about nine or ten. It just seemed like something interesting to do at the time. I thought it would be fun, kick around a few people, get a couple of aggressions out. I studied for about four years and had my brown belt when I stopped training. So when *Buffy* came up, it was a wonderful opportunity to be able to use that. We shot the fight scenes very carefully. We usually tagged the other actor, which is sort of just a light kick. We used stunt doubles when necessary if it was really dangerous. Martial arts is a form of meditation—it's an art form—and what I studied was a defensive form, not an offensive form.

JOSS WHEDON

My attitude is the show wasn't so good that it's worth anybody getting hurt for it. Sarah was always covered with bruises and I was saying, "Sarah, don't do this stuff. We'll get the close-up of you saying the funny thing after." "No, no, I can do it," she said, and then she gets this giant black-and-blue mark on her arm. "Sarah, stop, please!"

SARAH MICHELLE GELLAR

When I was growing up I watched Mallory worry about her dates and her boyfriends on *Family Ties*. I watched Blair on *The Facts of Life*. There were no strong female characters. I'm sorry, Tootie was not a role model. But with *Buffy*, we were showing real situations. Buffy was not the prettiest girl in her school; she was not the smartest. She made mistakes; she made good decisions and bad decisions. She was dealing with real situations that we can put on a fantasy level.

As an actor, you can always bring parts of yourself to the characters, but hopefully it's only a small portion of it, and the rest is a new character that you developed. My junior high school was like Buffy's. I was kind of a nerd. I didn't have many friends and I was an outcast. But I think Buffy was an amazing role model, because the one thing that I was able to do at my high school was to be an individual. The problem with most high schools is they don't stress individuality. Buffy showed girls it's OK to be different.

GEORGE SNYDER

I think *Buffy* was different from other high school–based shows in that it allowed its characters to move through their grades naturally. They all got to grow up. A decision Joss made early on was he didn't want forty-year-olds in high school. So the decision was made that they would be sophomores, juniors, seniors, go to college, etc. Actually we weren't sure what she was going to do, but we knew that she was going to graduate from high school in three years. This attitude allowed us to change the looks and to let them evolve as actors and in their characters.

SARAH MICHELLE GELLAR

It's always interesting when you go from being a child actor to an adult actor. *All My Children* was really that transition for me. *Buffy* was a really wonderful opportunity for me to play someone a little closer to myself and the situations I'd been in. Minus the vampires.

JOSS WHEDON

We had scenes where we've shot her reaction and she makes the entire scene even if she doesn't have a line. I was the luckiest man in show business.

SARAH MICHELLE GELLAR

Usually, you're doing one thing on television, you're funny, it's action, and there were few shows on television where all of us get to do all of it. We got to be funny, sad, we got to fight. As an actor that's your dream, to get to do all these amazing things.

HOWARD GORDON
(consulting producer, *Buffy the Vampire Slayer*)

One of the genius things that Joss did was to *not* take the Buffy character and go with someone in terms of looks like Charisma Carpenter or Kristy

Swanson, who played her in the movie. To *not* make her an airhead, but someone who's beautiful and accepted by those girls, but at the same time is essentially a nerd herself. So I think Sarah Michelle Gellar was a great bit of casting, and she made her a more substantial character who fit in among the nerds *and* would have been welcomed by the popular kids had she chosen to do that. I think that was a genius reinvention of Joss's original premise.

DAVID GREENWALT

I love Sarah. I directed a bunch of these and directing her was like driving some really high-class Lamborghini automobile. Sarah was very young, but she was very old for her age. I think she was eighteen when that thing started, but she'd been working since she was a kid. Sarah loved to have a director pay attention and give her notes. I swear to God, you could go up to her, it could be a big scene, maybe four or five pages, and give her eight or nine notes, and she would do every one of them in the next take. She was just born to do that job.

RAYMOND STELLA

Sarah was brilliant. She hardly needed more than one take. She really knew what she was doing and she was a joy. She would do more than one if the director asked. She started in soaps and commercials where she was the second person and the lead didn't show up who had all the lines, and they were wondering what to do. *Sarah* knew all the lines. They weren't even her lines, but she knew them and read them and they gave her a chance apparently and from there on she got a reputation that she knows what she is doing.

DAVID GREENWALT

She liked to have somebody important like Joss or me watching her performance, and I was sort of like, "I'm not going to spend all my life on the set doing this." I do remember one time she said, "Well, are you going to be here?" I said, "No, I'm not." Then Joss ended up having to soothe her a little bit, but she always delivered.

ARMIN SHIMERMAN
(actor, Principal Snyder)

When they cast me and I got the offer for Snyder, I'd already been watching the show, because my friend Kenny was on it playing Principal Flutie. I really liked the show a great deal and I wasn't watching it for Kenny anymore, I was watching it because I really enjoyed it. But when they called and said, "You're going to be doing this show," I wanted to know who I'd be working with and what Sarah Michelle Gellar's background was. They told me she's a nineteen-year-old soap opera actress and I, being a theater actor and an older guy, went, "Ooooh, a soap opera actress." I had a bad attitude about that. When I got to the set on the first day, they had me walking down an aisle in an auditorium and I thought, "Oh my God, I'm going to have to deal with these kids. And I've got a regular job, why am I doing this?" My attitude was not very good. And that's Snyder. Snyder grew out of that attitude. They just built on it.

JAMES MARSTERS

If you know your lines and you show up on time, she was like your best friend. The beautiful thing is that no one screwed around, because Sarah doesn't. Sarah doesn't pull shit or diva stuff. She didn't come in late, she's always prepared, she always has little jokes to keep the set light without messing around. She's pretty amazing.

ARMIN SHIMERMAN

After about the fourth or fifth episode of *Buffy* that I had done, I marched myself up to Sarah's trailer and knocked on the door. She was surprised to see me, because after all she only knew me really as Snyder. We hadn't really talked much and there was some antagonism between the two characters. I said to Sarah, "I need to apologize to you." I told her the story about my initial reaction and then I said, "But I've come to realize you're one of the finest actresses I've ever worked with." And it's true. I've rarely worked with actors as gifted, as talented, as amazing as Sarah Michelle Gellar. After that, we became great friends and we were very close off camera.

MARK HANSSON

All the makeup and hair people would do a synchronized hand movement from above their heads to their waists, saying in unison, "She, who must be obeyed," whenever Sarah's name would be mentioned. It's from an old sci-fi movie.

RAYMOND STELLA

I remember before *Buffy* I was up to take over *Gilmore Girls* and the leading lady was, like, forty and that's much harder to light. On *Buffy,* I had to make Sarah look better than everyone else and keep her on your good side. I remember she got so pissed off at me one time and I didn't even think about it. The director never came back. He's got Sarah somewhere and he goes, "I need a real wide lens right up here when she comes up out of this trash bin at the Doublemeat Palace," or something, and she's going, "This camera is too close and it's too wide." She got me in a corner and laid it out. And I'm going, "I'm sorry I wasn't thinking. I won't let him do it." She was *pissed,* and so he never came back. I didn't think about it. But, she'd get so tired. You just go with it.

JOSS WHEDON

I've worked with my share of divas. But I also have enormous respect for divas. They're usually people who do something extraordinary and know it and show up and do it. And you have to deal with a lot of other stuff but they usually come in and say, "You're going to have to deal with a lot of other stuff. I'm a diva. So here we go." And then you get this beautiful work and you're like "OK, good, and thanks for the heads-up." Really toxic people I avoid. I cast for sanity. That's a very important thing to me. But toxic people are different than divas. Divas are complicated but they know that there's a simplicity to what they're going to give you that you need and want. Truly toxic people are just about trying to tear something down. Whether it's somebody else in the thing, whether it's the story—they're about power. Those people have no business in my life as far as I'm concerned in the industry.

HARRY GROENER
(actor, Mayor Richard Wilkins)

Sarah's been doing it since she was an embryo. She is such a pro. There was never any crap on the set. They all seemed to like each other and enjoyed working together. That's a wonderful environment to be part of and you want that.

Gellar's first efforts as Buffy were showcased in the original half-hour presentation reel for the series—directed and written by Whedon—that sold the series.

ANTHONY STEWART HEAD

That presentation was pretty ropey. I don't think anyone would disagree with the notion that it left a lot to be desired. There were elements in that script that were strong, though. There was one really cool moment with me and Buffy in the library. We had a library set that was two tiers. There was a mezzanine balcony with a spiral staircase coming down from it. In the middle of a conversation Buffy is on top and I'm down below. While she's talking, she does a handstand on the banister rail and flips twice and lands on her feet. At that time we had two stunt doubles, one to do acrobatics and one to do fight scenes. The acrobat was just astonishing; she did this great flip.

SARAH MICHELLE GELLAR

That was Joss's first directing experience and he didn't have a very good support team behind him. We didn't know what we were doing with the show. It was like all these ideas in your head and they're not working out right on paper. We had a whole summer to fix it by the time we did the real pilot, and I think we did a pretty good job. What made everything work is we needed to find Alyson Hannigan. She was the best and what allowed Nicholas Brendon and myself to become a threesome. Once she came aboard, everything clicked.

ANTHONY STEWART HEAD

Joss did *not* have a very sympathetic crew for the presentation. Generally you hope when you pull a crew together and it's your directorial debut, there will be some give and take and some leeway. But they were very odd. I'm being very general here, because some people were great and some people were off, but they weren't very generous, which was all rather surprising, really. By the time we got the unit together for the series, it was a very different matter.

This presentation reel featured a different actress in the role of Willow, Riff Regan, who didn't make it to series. Cherubic and acerbic, she was completely different from Alyson Hannigan but would later nab a starring role in the popular NBC series *Sisters*.

The pilot presentation begins with Julie Benz's seemingly innocent Darla sneaking into school with a boy who appears to have malevolent intentions, when she turns into a vampire and chows down on him. The next morning Buffy arrives at Sunnydale High and is greeted warmly by Principal Flutie (played for the first and the last time by perennial character actor Stephen Tobolowsky [*Groundhog Day*]), after which she meets Xander and the mysterious librarian, Giles, who throws a *VAMPYR* tome in front of her—at which point she flees the library. She is befriended by Willow when the Cordettes, comprised of Cordelia and Harmony, attempt to co-opt Buffy for their own clique.

Only after finding out there's a dead body on campus and learning it is the work of vampires does she return to the library, where Giles tells her she can't escape her destiny. But Buffy insists she's given up vampire slaying for good. Meeting Xander at the Bronze, she learns Willow has gone off with a mysterious stranger, prompting Buffy to take up her old ways, defeating several vampires in the process. The reel ends with Xander and Willow now hip to Buffy's secret and her throwing a stake through the heart of a handbill for an upcoming screening of *Nosferatu* on campus.

Watching the twenty-minute presentation, it's easy to see why the WB saw something in the show. Most of the performances are terrific (particularly the troika of Sarah Michelle Gellar, Nicholas Brendon, and Charisma Carpenter), Joss's trademark puns and wit are all in evidence, and the sales reel, despite its clear lack of budget, is original and charming. Whatever it lacks in polish, it makes up for in heart. Also, it is certainly abundantly clear that Regan was the wrong choice for the role of Willow, not just physically—it required a more wispy (not to mention willowy) actress and the playfulness and neuroses of Alyson Hannigan's effortless portrayal.

DAVID GREENWALT

They had shot a pilot, but they replaced the character of Willow with Alyson Hannigan, who is now my good friend, as is her husband, Alexis Denisof, who appeared in *Grimm* for me.

ANTHONY STEWART HEAD

[Regan] was the opposite end of the scale. Basically, she was a very different concept of Willow. I must admit that when I first saw her, she wasn't how I envisioned Willow. Alyson is *exactly* the way I envisioned the character. The girl who played her was lovely, really gorgeous, we had great fun, but she didn't feel comfortable in the part. She just didn't feel comfortable in the gawkiness of it, which was hard to play. It just didn't fit right, and I think she would be the first to admit that.

The first thing we had to film was the last scene when we say, "Well done," and pat ourselves on the back and go on to the next thing. I was playing it as I thought they wanted me to. When you've tested three times and each time you're thinking, "Christ, what was it I did last time that they really liked? What was it that got me this job?" It does make you self-conscious and you are desperately searching for whatever it was that got you the gig. But in that last scene, I was appalling. Seriously appalling. And luckily, as fate would have it, my dressing room was next to the room they were using to show dailies. I heard my voice coming from next door, so I puttered in and had a look, and was appalled at what I saw myself doing. I was then able to pull back from that.

I was play-acting the man instead of *being* the man. So then the scene that Sarah Michelle Gellar and I had in the library was the one that made all the sense and the one that felt completely right. It was night and day. Very different. Thankfully, there were a couple of good scenes like that, and that offset this dreadful scene.

MERCEDES MCNAB

I'd seen the original movie and liked it because it was very clever and relatable. So I liked Joss's work, but didn't translate completely to this show. Obviously, the show was a lot different. I was a fan of that. But him personally, I just thought Joss was very creative and smart and kind of goofy and quirky, and there was just so much going on. We really didn't have a ton of time to connect in that first pilot presentation.

Based on the presentation, the WB greenlit the series for a mid-season debut in 1997. That meant Whedon and his cast and crew would be producing the first twelve episodes without any feedback from either the critics or the audience as production on the entire season would be wrapped before it even aired.

SARAH MICHELLE GELLAR

We finished the entire first season before we went on the air, so we were able to do it in a bubble without having anybody on the outside interfering. When I was in North Carolina shooting *I Know What You Did Last Summer,* we didn't get to see it, because it was on a cable channel we couldn't get in the town we were in. I was able to avoid the craziness, although Alyson called me every week going, "You don't understand, every time you go past a grocery store there's a *Buffy* billboard."

We sort of felt it was time for the show, because the network bought it. And they wanted to do the exact kind of show we wanted to make. And they were interested in making it with us, which is good. I sort of figured they would say, make it stupid. But they didn't. It pretty much went the way we planned except it dug down a lot deeper. And we just didn't know we could put so much pain up on the screen and how good it would make us feel.

JOSS WHEDON

I don't think we would have existed anywhere else. No one else would let us do it, they wouldn't have been there with us, they'd try to micromanage it into something they understood.

SARAH MICHELLE GELLAR

The network wasn't exactly sure what we were doing in the beginning. After the praying mantis episode, they said, "We're just not sure if we're sending the right message." We're like, "What message? You have sex with her and she bites your head off." These are situations that children can relate to. The themes throughout the show are common: loving a friend, being at an age when you're having problems with Mom, and wanting to be an adult and wanting to be a child at the same time.

DAVID GREENWALT

We wrote episode one and two and took a lot from the pilot presentation. Everything was shot from scratch.

SARAH MICHELLE GELLAR

All of my friends felt sorry for me, because I was on a mid-season replacement show, on a network no one had heard of. People would look at me and go, "At least you got a pilot your first time out! That's great! Next year you'll get one that'll go."

BEWITCHED, BOTHERED, AND BUFFY

"I'm reading about death all the time, and I've never seen a dead body before. Do they usually move?"

With the series greenlit by the WB, Joss Whedon, who had never run a show before, would have to assemble a team of writers for the first twelve episodes, which would debut mid-season on the network. One of the first writer/producers to join the series was co-executive producer David Greenwalt, who became an important consigliore for Whedon over the years, eventually leaving *Buffy* after the third season to cocreate and run the spin-off, *Angel*.

Greenwalt had recently worked on *Profit*, the acclaimed series starring Adrian Pasdar, which was beloved by critics but failed to find an audience despite anticipating the milestones of peak-TV shows such as *The Sopranos* and *Breaking Bad*.

HOWARD GORDON
(consulting producer, *Buffy the Vampire Slayer*)

It's an almost impossible tone to strike, and so many people have tried to do it. It's like Supreme Court Justice Potter Stewart's definition of pornography: you know it when you see it or hear it. Joss created a show and a voice and found other writers to help him execute that vision that was kind of unlike anything we'd seen before.

JOSE MOLINA
(former assistant to Howard Gordon)

I was so intimidated by Joss. He was so busy, he'd never run a TV show before, so one of the reasons that 20th partnered him up with David Greenwalt was because they wanted an experienced TV guy to hold his hand while he figured out how it worked. Joss had been a feature guy for a long time and did some TV as a staff writer or story editor. But he was never a producer on TV.

DAVID GREENWALT

(co-executive producer, *Buffy the Vampire Slayer*)

I had my choice of almost any show I would want to be on, because everybody in the industry loved *Profit*. It was the first show with a sociopath villain as the hero. It was before *The Sopranos* and all. I got a huge sack of scripts and I met with Steven Bochco [*Hill Street Blues, L.A. Law*] and I met with a lot of other people, and here was this *Buffy the Vampire Slayer* script in the pile. And I was like, this is not only the best pilot of the year, clearly it's one of the best scripts I've ever read. Somebody has to introduce me to Joss Whedon.

JOSS WHEDON

(creator/executive producer, *Buffy the Vampire Slayer*)

David and I worked on all the stories together. We came in and tried this and that. We knew generally where we were headed. But, beyond that, we filled in the blanks and once we figured out a story, "OK, Xander's going to be a hyena," we spent anywhere between a couple of days and a week, just breaking down the story and figuring out each scene and what everybody is doing. That was the hard part. The writing was a little easier, because it's all set up for you, but it's figuring out how to move the story, how to keep in character, not make every episode Mulder's dead sister. We repeated ourselves, although we tried not to. David Greenwalt was incredible.

DAVID GREENWALT

I started as a movie writer with Jim Carroll in the late '70s and early '80s, and we had a pretty good time getting some movies made then. Then I got really bored with movies—they're a pain in the ass to make and they take too long. I could've made a fine living as a script doctor, but I hated it, so I got into TV and started with *The Wonder Years*. By the way, my style had always been either adventure/comedy or romantic/comedy. It wasn't really a genre. I don't think I'd ever written anything in the genre. Then John McNamara and I did *Profit* for Fox and it just died a terrible quick death, but it made a big splash within the industry.

KELLY A. MANNERS

(producer, *Buffy the Vampire Slayer*)

They were a great team. Between Whedon and Greenwalt, you could always get a straight answer. If Joss was having one of his days, David was there to back him up and take over business for the day if he was in deep thought about the next script or whatever was on his mind. He was probably plotting out *The Avengers* back then. I can't say enough about all the people on the show who were really great. It was a great experience.

DAVID GREENWALT

I met with Joss and we got on. He had loved *Profit* and supposedly he needed a show runner. He had been on *Roseanne,* but hadn't done that much TV. He needed a show runner like I need another arm. He's kind of a genius, but we worked together great. It was a love affair from the first. What I learned about genre very early on was it had so much more power than regular drama. You can take a metaphor like, "Oh, I feel invisible in high school" and literally have a girl turn invisible. So that the emotional connection is strong, but the fact that it's fantasy or genre separates the audience enough from it that they can really get into it without having to suffer too much. We got a letter on *Buffy* early on from a woman who was a lawyer, and who was agoraphobic and had not left her house in a long time. She said, "That episode last night gave me enough courage to walk out the door and walk around the block once." You never get letters like that on regular stuff, you just don't.

SARAH LEMELMAN

(author, *"It's About Power":* Buffy the Vampire Slayer*'s Stab at Establishing the Strength of Girls on American Television*)

Buffy is no blond damsel in need of saving. She saves the world and those she loves. She is her own savior, and when she cannot save herself, she is willing to die for the cause, like Joan of Arc. Buffy is no meek girl, but a strong female character, and shatters the perception of masculine qualities and gender binaries, instead choosing to transcend traditional sex roles.

DAVID GREENWALT

Julie Benz, who played Darla, had this little thing in the teaser of the first episode and it made a statement about don't trust these pretty blondes in the horror movies, because they can be badass, too, which is perfect. Then, boy we used her a lot, and she came back and back and back and, of course, had this whole thing with Angel.

Season one debuted on March 10, 1997, with the two-part "Welcome to the Hellmouth" and "The Harvest," which set up the series premise and introduced Mark Metcalf, neither worthless or weak, as the malevolent Master, best known for his work in *Animal House* as the loathsome Niedermeyer. But early episodes quickly established that Buffy wasn't just a Vampire Slayer: episode three, "The Witch," was a standout, about a domineering, embittered mother who uses witchcraft to switch bodies with her daughter so she can relive her glory days as a cheerleader in high school. *Freaky Friday,* it's not.

ANTHONY C. FERRANTE
(writer, *Fangoria* magazine)

Even though *Buffy* is about "vampires," it also explored other types of villains, creatures, and monsters to keep the show fresh. Joss Whedon was a restless creator that shook things up all the time on the show, so the show itself could evolve. Some detours worked, others didn't, but looking back at the series as a whole, it really was groundbreaking.

JOSS WHEDON

David [Greenwalt] had come up with the idea that a mother was jealous of her daughter's youth and had stolen it from her. It was absolutely the essence of the show. It took the idea of "oh, there's good guys and there's bad guys and there's monsters and we love these people" one level further into what people are capable of and, in particular, what David Greenwalt is capable of. That was a seminal moment for me, because it made me realize there was more to this. And he figured out the very real, very ugly twist that set the tone for the whole series.

DAVID GREENWALT

With "The Witch," I came up with the twist that it's really the mother has traded places with the daughter. Joss always recounts that to me as when he realized he made the right choice in hiring me and knowing this guy needed to be in my camp. Frankly, I am not the world's greatest story breaker, but I did have that idea as we were breaking the story and said, "What if the mom traded places?" Joss always says that's the point where he knew he could trust me, and he fell for me as a writer. That was, like, a historic moment forever.

Subsequent episodes included "Teacher's Pet," about a substitute teacher who is apparently infatuated with Xander, but is revealed to be a giant praying mantis who subsists on the men she seduces; while "Never Kill a Boy on the First Date" focused on Buffy finding work-life balance between slaying vampires and trying to be a student at Sunnydale High. In "The Pack," hyenas from Africa possess the minds of students–including Xander–which was an effective parable about the insidiousness of high school cliques, while "Angel" reveals that Buffy's mysterious and enigmatic admirer is not only a vampire, but one with a soul.

CHARISMA CARPENTER
(actress, Cordelia Chase)

I remember Gail Berman coming to set early on in *Buffy* when we were shooting "Reptile Boy" and it was me and Sarah chained to a wall and screaming. I was so wiped out and my mom was visiting that day and Gail asked, "Hey, is there anyone you'd want to work with, is there anywhere you'd want to be?" I just remember saying to Gail, "I'm exactly where I need to be, right here and right now."

On the surface, you're looking at damsels in distress and big bad boogeymen and a girl who fights vampires in a graveyard. If you look at it superficially, it can seem like a very silly show. But the themes and metaphors were really deep and it had really talented people saying things in a really interesting way using verbiage and cadences and sentence structure that had never been heard before. Right then, I knew where I needed to be and it was the people I was working with like Joss Whedon. She just looked at me quizzically and said, "Interesting."

In the first year, a Buffy tradition was born, the slaying of the high school principal. Played by Kenny Lerner (who replaced Stephen Tobolowsky from the original presentation reel), Principal Flutie met a quick and ignominious end shortly into the season in the episode "The Pack," surprising audiences who never anticipated his early demise.

DAVID GREENWALT

We worked and worked to break that episode and we knew we were going to eat the principal. He's a great actor, that guy. He was in my movie *Secret Admirer*, but we wanted to get a new principal, so we knew we were going to eat him. We were working and working and working and we suddenly said, "What if Xander becomes infected with this thing and starts really coming onto Buffy?"

That unlocked that particular episode and it was like a template for us—it's better when it's happening to your main characters. In his mind he might have felt like pushing her up against the soft drink machine and scaring her, but he would never do something like that except if he was infected with this thing. There were a lot of stand-alones that first year.

Lerner was quickly replaced by a moonlighting Armin Shimerman, who was already a lead actor as part of the interstellar ensemble of Paramount's *Star Trek: Deep Space Nine,* playing Quark, a devious Ferengi, here essaying the memorable role of Principal Snyder on *Buffy.*

ARMIN SHIMERMAN
(actor, Principal Snyder)

While I was doing *Star Trek: Deep Space Nine,* I had an audition for Flutie, which was the principal before Snyder, and that didn't work out. My friend Kenny Lerner got the part. As I was leaving the room, I was walking down a hallway of various offices and I passed one room. I glanced inside and I saw that there were two cardboard cutouts. One of Major Kira/Nana Visitor, and one of Worf/Michael Dorn. As I walked past the door, I stopped and said, "Why don't you have a standee of me in here?" And then we started to chat for about two minutes and then I walked back to my car, finding out I didn't get the role. Fine.

HARRY GROENER
(actor, Mayor Richard Wilkins)

I auditioned for the role of the first principal [Robert Flutie] and there's a memorial bust of him right outside the cafeteria door on set, so every time in rehearsal when we passed the bust I said, "That could have been me."

ARMIN SHIMERMAN

Many months later, my agent called and said there is a straight offer for you for this new principal, Principal Snyder. I said to the agent, "Well, is this a recurring character?" And they said yes. I said, "Listen, you know that I have a day job. I do *Star Trek* on a regular basis." And they said to me that they're going to rotate principals on a regular basis. They're going to kill them off and I said OK. Maybe it'll be two or three episodes and that's it. To this day, I'm not sure whether it was the audition that got me Snyder or it was that two-minute talk in what I later learned was the writers' room.

My life is about that. About just turning left when I should have turned right and vice versa. It's possible that that conversation in that room was more influential than the reading I gave. I was sorry that Kenny lost the job but I was very grateful for the role. Because they had told me that principals were going to be killed off on a regular basis, I was enormously surprised for the next three years that I was still there. When they'd come to the end of a season, I would always go to the back page first of the script and say,

"Well, how do they kill me off?" And had been surprised for years that I was still there.

DAVID GREENWALT

The deal they made for me to go to *Buffy* was only for twelve episodes ordered and it was like, "Go help this guy Joss get his little show off the ground, and then your reward will be to go to *The X-Files*." By the way, I admired the shit out of *X-Files*, but I could not write it to save my life. At the end of these twelve episodes, it was a big love fest with Joss and most of the actors, and there's a picture where Joss went around with all the actors and one of the producers basically looking very pleadingly into the camera and saying, "David, please don't go."

I went to *The X-Files* while we were waiting to see if *Buffy* would be picked up, and I spent about a month or two there. Howard Gordon was kind of my savior there. I watched eighty-four of them in a row. I was so amazed. What a piece of work. *X-Files* set the bar for TV production and excellence. They reshot whatever they didn't like before they were a big hit. They had this high level of production and Chris Carter is very good at writing this kind of stuff. That's *not* me. I couldn't get the emotional connection. It was always about, "Oh, it's an alien, no it's bees, it's small pox, it's this thing, that thing. It's nothing." I went running back to *Buffy* after about two months on *The X-Files*. My real reward was working with Joss all those years.

In the second season Howard Gordon briefly became a part of the *Buffy* staff as consulting producer, joined by his assistant, Jose Molina, who himself would eventually become a story editor on *Firefly* for Whedon, and went on to much success on a series of popular shows, among them *The Vampire Diaries*, *Castle*, *Agent Carter*, and the Amazon iteration of *The Tick*, and who would cohost the screenwriting podcast *Children of Tendu*.

That second season also saw the arrival of husband and wife writing team of David Fury and Elin Hampton (though of the two only Fury—who had previously worked on *The Jackie Thomas Show*, *Dream On*, and *Life's Work*—would ultimately stay with the show, eventually rising to the rank of co-executive producer over subsequent years). Marti Noxon joined as a writer and became story editor mid-season, also rising over the years to become an executive producer and show runner for seasons six and seven. And, in season three, *The Onion*'s Dan Vebber joined as a staff writer, later rising to a co-executive producer on such popular series as *Futurama, American Dad,* and *The Simpsons.*

JOSE MOLINA

I was a huge *X-Files* fan, which is how I came to work as Howard Gordon's assistant in the summer of 1997. I was working as a PA at Warner Brothers feature animation, which is the division that produced *Space Jam* and *Quest for Camelot*. Right as it became defunct, they produced *The Iron Giant*. So I worked on *Iron Giant* technically for a heartbeat. But when *Quest* came out and it didn't do anything, they essentially curtailed the division down to the very bare essentials. So, of course, what's the first salary that has to go? That fat PA salary has to go and they saved four hundred bucks a week by *not* paying me. Coincidentally, though, the head of the department, whom I really liked, was Howard Gordon's sister. I sent out two résumés cold and got an interview with Howard. He interviewed me in his *X-Files* office, which was packed up at the time because he was leaving *X-Files* at the end of season four. I told him my story of *X-Files,* which included a pitch and meeting my wife, whom I've now been with twenty years, in an *X-Files* chat room. I think that endeared me to him, knowing that his show had changed someone's life completely. One interview, one cold résumé, and I got the gig. That's how that happened.

DAVID FURY

(co-executive producer, *Buffy the Vampire Slayer*)

My wife had seen *Buffy* on opening day. We skipped out of work and said let's go to a matinee of *Buffy the Vampire Slayer,* because I just thought this is a great premise. I love a great horror-comedy mash-up, and I thought this was going to be a lot of fun. I didn't love the movie. Just tonally it was wrong, it wasn't funny enough, it wasn't scary enough. Although I loved the premise.

When Joss talked to us about writing for the series, I told him off the bat, "I was so excited about this, but I was disappointed in the movie." He recognized all the problems in the way his script was produced and started to explain how that was going to be fixed in the TV series. The more he talked about it, the more he talked about how the stories were allegorical and he gave the example of the invisible girl, the girl you go to school with whom nobody pays attention to and is kind of invisible to everyone else—and then she becomes literally invisible. I went, "Oh my God, that's exactly the kind of thing I love to do."

When we were done with the meeting, I said, "I want to work on the show." I loved everything Joss had to say. He was funny in the meeting and so I really wanted to work for this guy. I told my agents and they said, "Are you crazy? This is six episodes on the WB which no one knows exists, and it's a mid-season show." The other meeting we had at the same time was a sitcom on ABC to premiere in the fall, sandwiched between *Roseanne* and *Home Improvement,* which were like the number one and number two shows on television at that time. "This is a surefire hit; you have to do this show," and we listened to our agent and turned down *Buffy* and went to the sitcom.

The sitcom was eighteen episodes and out. Meanwhile, *Buffy* premiered mid-season and was almost off the bat a phenomenon. It was getting magazine covers. We watched it, because I really wanted to see how he pulled stuff off, and we loved it. We were kicking ourselves. We fired our agent and moved to another agency, which was the same agency that Joss was at. When they asked us what other things we were looking to do, I said I wanted to get back in at *Buffy* and pitch to Joss.

We got to get back in and pitch to Joss at the beginning of the second season, he bought our story, and we got to write "Go Fish." That resulted in a job offer, but Elin, my partner, wanted to stay in sitcoms. She loved doing sitcoms, so she went to *Mad About You*. I wanted to go to *Buffy* and Joss was going to give me a script to try me out as a solo writer. That's what kind of propelled me into hours. And then the progression of how does a comedy writer wind up there? Every successive show got more and more serious. *Buffy* then *Angel,* which was a little more serious, and then *Lost,* which was more serious but still [has] room for comedy. And then *24,* which has no room for comedy. Once you're in that kind of mode, that becomes how people see you, "Oh, you're a *24* writer." "No, I'm a comedy writer, believe it or not."

DAN VEBBER

(staff writer, season 3, *Buffy the Vampire Slayer*)

I was a huge fan of *Buffy*. It was my first staff writing job. I had been at *The Onion* previous to that. Moved out to Los Angeles so my background was really in comedy, but I had written a spec script for *The Larry Sanders Show,* which was my miracle script. It got me in pretty much any meeting I wanted, and then I wrote a spec script for *Buffy,* because it was the one show that really had the voice that I was trying to write with. My agent warned me up and down—everybody said, up and down—"Don't ever write a spec script for the show that you want to write for." But I'm one of the rare instances where it actually worked. My spec script got to Joss, because we were at the same agency, UTA. I went in for a meeting with Joss and we had a good meeting and he hired me this day.

Pretty much as soon as I exited the meeting I had a job offer from them—he said at the time that I was just very good at capturing these characters' voices, which speaks more to my ability to write comedy than my ability to write drama. Mimicking character voices is easy, because that's just an element of satire and parody which I had honed working at *The Onion,* and that's how I ended up there season three.

DAVID GREENWALT

Joss has been very generous and many times he's said that *Buffy* wouldn't be if it wasn't for me. I have no idea what I brought to it. I worked my ass off, I'd get up at five in the morning with a thesaurus, because of what he did. He invented a language for these kids in *Buffy,* because he felt if he went to a junior high [or] high school and just overheard stuff, it would be old in two years, right? So he invented an entire language and I did what I beg other writers to do when they work for me, which is that your job here is to not so much express yourself and your feelings and your childhood as it is to replicate what the creator of the show has done and is doing. Like I said, I'm a pretty good mimic.

I don't suffer like him, but I would get up very early every morning with a thesaurus and write my ass off and try every different word I could think of for every piece of dialogue. You could use words like "skedaddle" and all these wonderful words that you couldn't use in a regular show. I just stalked him every day and sometimes I would stand outside the bathroom and would push to get things done and we broke stories together and it was amazing. I have no idea what I brought.

JOSE MOLINA

I went to work for Howard Gordon in June of 1997. He was in an overall at Fox and he was developing and they asked him to consult on this show. There were a couple of shows that needed people and he chose *Buffy*. That was my first exposure to the show. I'd never seen the movie and I'd heard that they were making a show out of the movie. My reaction was the reaction of most of us cynics, which was, "Oh my God, they're making a shitty show out of that shitty movie that nobody saw." But Howard had a couple of tapes in his office and I watched them and I was like, "Holy shit, this is good!" And I went back and I watched the movie—clearly the movie is not as good as the show. Howard was consulting, which meant he got all the scripts, which also meant I got all the scripts season one. He started working at the beginning of season two, which was also Marti Noxon's first year on the show. I was instantly addicted to the show. More so than Howard, who was working on it.

HOWARD GORDON

I don't know if it was my experience or my temperament, but I'm also very self-critical, so I sort of recognized that I'm not singing exactly in this key, but I was experienced enough and a hard enough worker to get some serviceable material. I guess I felt lucky to have a front row seat to something that I hadn't done.

JOSE MOLINA

I remember specifically he was writing a script, he was supposed to do the teleplay for "What's My Line?, Part One." He was having a really hard time with it. His voice isn't naturally that funny, quirky, dialogue-heavy, Whedon voice, which I absolutely loved and like to think I still sort of write in a similar voice to. I asked him, "Hey, do you want me to write a couple of scenes? Maybe I can help you out and you don't have to tell anybody, just let me show you what I can do." I went home one weekend and wrote a few scenes in "What's My Line?" and I brought them in and he wound up not using them, but he paid me a great compliment which was he had other scripts and other pages from people on his desk that he was trying to read and emulate the style as he was trying to figure out how he was going to write his script, and he said that he couldn't tell the difference between my pages and their pages, which made me go, "Well use my fucking pages!" But he didn't. He had enough pride that he wanted to do it himself.

Eventually, when it came down to how long it was taking him and how hard a time he was having, he actually wound up cowriting that script with Marti [Noxon] because Marti was writing "What's My Line?, Part 2" and she had finished her script already in the time that Howard had done about half of his. So that was the beginning of me with *Buffy*.

In addition to the standing sets for the series that were built adjacent to the production offices in Santa Monica, Sunnydale High exteriors were shot at Torrance High School in Torrance, California, as were the exteriors of the Summers house a few blocks away at 1313 Cota Avenue. Angel's residence as well as the mansion occupied by Drusilla and Spike was shot at the legendary Ennis House, designed by Frank Lloyd Wright. Offered Joss Whedon previously, "We were very much on a tight budget. It's really kind of sad, actually. The outside of the warehouse also doubled as the entrance to The Bronze."

Although the initial cemetery scenes were filmed at a real graveyard in Los Angeles, a smaller, makeshift series of tombstones was constructed by production designer Carey Meyer for the second season in the parking lot of the production studios, where most of the cemetery scenes were shot. Said Whedon at the time, "It made our lives a whole lot easier, but it doesn't give you the scope you get from a real graveyard."

DAVID FURY

A lot of the times what happens when your show shoots in Vancouver or cross-country or wherever is that camps start to form. There's the production camp. Then there's the producer-writer camp. There's kind of a lack of trust, because they're bitching over in production about something that you don't know they're upset about. Whereas you can fix it immediately if you were there, but it's difficult to do when you're in different time zones. That's something I sorely miss from doing *Buffy*, the fact that we had our own stages and a little back lot of downtown Sunnydale right outside our offices. It was three warehouses; then behind the warehouses they created a downtown outside exterior where the Bronze was, and the magic shop was there for exteriors. They would lay sod across the parking lot and put up tombstones and that would be our cemetery. It worked! On as tiny a budget as we had, it worked great.

RAYMOND STELLA

(director of photography, *Buffy the Vampire Slayer*)

We were shooting in a warehouse that was a converted lumber warehouse right on 28th and Olympic. I think the metro is going through it now. It had small ceilings. We didn't have any [lighting] grids to work off of. We had ladders—we'd be either putting stands above the sets or tacking it with C-clamp lights to the tops of the sets. But we didn't have any gridwork to work off of. People were falling off ladders. So it was slow in that respect. You didn't have anyone up there on the catwalks and stuff. It made it challenging. We made it work, but we had our limitations, so it kind of tended to make it look a little low-budgety if you weren't careful, because you are shooting in the house on the stage and the windows have to look fairly decent.

MARK HANSSON

(second assistant director, *Buffy the Vampire Slayer*)

One funny story was when shooting in at Torrance High School, where a lot of the first season took place, we were getting ready to do a basketball scene in the gym. Alyson wanted to pull a prank on Nicholas Brendon, so in front of the whole company and a hundred plus extras, when he was jumping up for a shot, she ran up and pulled his shorts down. Well, it took everything with the shorts, so he was totally naked in front of everyone, which was funny but embarrassing. It was a rehearsal and cameras weren't rolling at the time. Alyson was mortified, but Nick took it in good humor.

RAYMOND STELLA

I had a good gaffer and a lot of good people around me working hard and it was fun. That was a challenge. I had come off features where you shoot two or three pages a day and here we're shooting ten a day. Seven to ten pages, which is a lot of work. So, that's a challenge. You don't know whether to look at your meter or your watch half the time. We waited a lot on actors, too, because after you get into four, five, six, or seven seasons, they're, like, not going to be rushing around too much. So we're lit and it takes them about ten seconds to get off the stage and about twenty minutes to get back once you're ready.

The first people that the producers come to when you're behind is the camera crew. I told them, "I can light circles around these actors, the problem is that they don't come back. If you can keep them on the stage we could push this thing." I wasn't going to take the brunt of it. It took time to light here and there, but we had a good crew; we knew what we were doing.

DAN VEBBER

I remember it being pretty tense on set, but because I had so little experience working on live-action shows, I don't know how much of that is normal and how much was unique to that show. I didn't get the sense that a lot of rewriting was being done on set.

MARK HANSSON

Buffy was not a very happy experience for many people, even though it was a good show. They asked me to continue, but after so many people in my department got fired that first year in 1996, I elected to just do the first season. Never regretted not going back, even when the show became a hit.

JOSE MOLINA

I had no idea what I was doing, so my priority was to stay the hell out of the way on set. But I remember a conversation I had with Sarah Michelle Gellar while they were shooting one of the big fight scenes with her and Kendra. Fights take a lot of time, so there was a lot of downtime. She was very nice and was willing to talk to the consulting producer's assistant, who was just the visitor. As I managed to do more often than not, I planted my foot firmly in my mouth.

Sarah had a movie opening that weekend; little thing called *I Know What You Did Last Summer*. That weekend was also the opening weekend of a much lesser known David Duchovny movie called *Playing God*. So I'm talking to her and she's wondering aloud how well her movie is going to do. My response was that I thought she was going to get stiff competition from that David Duchovny movie. Thankfully she did not punch me in the face.

DAVID FURY

We all knew the *Buffy* actors really well, because we're in the same space. If you have a break, you go down, you watch them shooting, you talk, you have lunch with the actors. On *Angel* we never saw anybody, because they were across town. Unless we had a reason to go to the set. It was a pleasure to be able to be on the set of a show I had been working on for years but only occasionally visited. Did not know the crew as well, because, again, we just didn't have the opportunity to drive across town to go to the stages where they're shooting *Angel.*

JAMES MARSTERS
(actor, Spike)

Acting, for me, is much simpler and less important than I thought. It feels like every time I learn something new about acting, it's just about simplifying and not acting and letting the words work for you. An actor needs to know enough about structure and quality writing to be able to choose good words. But once you've chosen those words and signed the contract, get out of the way. Don't bring attention to yourself, bring attention to the words and let them make the money for you. At which point it becomes brutally simple and easy to look cool. I always say that a character is defined much more by what they say than how they say it, which means that how the actor says it is important, but it's not nearly as important as what the writer is saying. Acting then becomes the breath and life under the words.

DAVID FURY

It was helpful to talk to the cast. To know how they would feel about things. That's something that's very rare now in Los Angeles, because very few shows now are shot there. I was in Budapest for *Tyrant* and Berlin for *Homeland.* Nobody is shooting in L.A. What was great about doing *Buffy* and

Angel was you're there with each other all the time. You're there with your collaborators. You're part of a repertory company. You get this great experience to trust each other, because you see each other all the time.

RAYMOND STELLA

On any set, there's so much food around and if you're on a film that takes time lighting, you tend to wander over and graze a lot. At the end of *Buffy*, between all the work we'd start out at seven or eight in the morning on Monday and work our way into four or five on Friday. With twelve hours' turnaround, because you'd work until four or five in the morning on Saturday. You're a zombie that day and Sunday. Forget it, you're so tired you just have to recoup. It takes its toll, so it's a young man's business, an episodic twenty-four-show season.

CHARISMA CARPENTER

We were literally sheltered. On *Buffy* we had our own soundstage, we were in Santa Monica, we worked so many hours. We barely had a life; our life was each other.

KELLY A. MANNERS

We had a crew that liked to have a good time, though the hours were torturous. Being vampires can't go out in the daylight, that was torturous, because we were working many, many all-nighters. Through it all we kept a good sense of humor and we had fun. I'll never forget, I was sitting in a room with the executive producers . . . and we're talking about demons. I said, "I can't believe there's six grown men in here talking about demons." It was wacky and it was fun. It was good storytelling.

RAYMOND STELLA

I would have probably liked it more if it was not such so much of a night shoot. Those are hard on you. [Line producer] Gareth Davies was interesting. He'd come on the set looking for me when we were behind, and I'd be hiding. I'd see him come on and I knew he was looking for me to kick my ass about something. But it was OK. It wasn't that serious. He'd look around and he'd storm off and I'd come out of hiding.

MARK HANSSON

Unfortunately, Gareth Davies, a not very nice British producer, also known as Dr. Death, fired people left and right, so it was kind of a dreadful set.

HARRY GROENER

The worst thing about working at a real high school was all the night shoots and everyone had to be out of there before the students came to school in the morning. So to see everyone scrambling, all the technicians, to get off campus before the sun came up was very funny considering it *was* a vampire story.

JOSS WHEDON

I honestly believe that we had a good vibe on the set and I honestly think it made the show better. Is art worth pain? Yes it is. Is it worth me feeling pain? Yes. Is it worth me *causing* pain? No. It doesn't mean that I'm nice to everybody. I try not to be a dick, but I have to get stuff done. But if everybody feels like they're actually part of making something that they like, they give everything they have. At one point I was just so exhausted. Somebody comes over and says, "What prop should we use?" "I hate this show. God, why do we have to have props? What happened to mime? Mime is a great art." And everybody is like, "Whoa, PMS on the Joss man." It truly takes your life to do TV, because you always have a deadline.

David Greenwalt and the staff we had were the best writing staff. They came up with great stories. It's never cheap, it's never bullshit, it's never how do we vamp until the end? It's always, "How can we make this story better?" So when it comes down to the prop guy, we know there's a reason, that he cares about it. It applies to us as well as everybody else. If we don't love the stuff that we're putting out on the screen, it ain't worth the pace.

DAVID GREENWALT

The network was afraid of Joss. They almost never gave notes. Occasionally they'd call me and say, "Does Willow really have to be gay? Can't you talk him out of that?" I always ran to Joss like Robert Duvall as Tom Hagen in *The Godfather* and would always say, "My employer is someone who likes to hear bad news fast." I would tell Joss whatever was going on. He was right. Willow was gay before every show had a gay character.

JOSS WHEDON

They really let me get away with murder. They got what the show is, how strange it is, how it's all over the place, how edgy it sometimes is, and so there was never really a problem. We never had a story thrown out or a real disaster. We've had standards and practices issues, which you have on every show, but they got what we were doing and they didn't interfere. I've seen networks that do it the other way and this is the ideal.

CHARISMA CARPENTER

We were a bunch of young kids, we'd get together every week and watch the show, most of us, and we were already together all the time. It was very informal on set, to be honest. I get a little mushy thinking about it; it was a really sweet time. We worked and played together and we were going through this crazy life together and no one understood it better than us because we were doing it together. So it was special.

After work we would sometimes go to the pub or if we'd have a great guest star, we'd all go out with them. David Solomon directed a lot of episodes and we'd loved him, so we'd watch the show with him. It was a really special experience. We always celebrated together. I remember having my first New Year's Eve party at my house and Joss came and it was so fun. We were very supportive of each other.

The first season culminates with "Prophecy Girl," in which Buffy finally confronts the Master and is briefly killed. Filmed and completed before a single episode aired, the fate of *Buffy the Vampire Slayer* was uncertain as the crew went to the first-season wrap party, but one thing was clear: creatively, *Buffy* had lived up to the potential of what Joss Whedon had articulated for the series, and then some.

SARAH LEMELMAN

The first season shows Buffy struggling to find her identity as a Slayer, and the heroine is truly at a crossroads when Giles discovers a prophecy that describes what is to become of her fate in the final episode of the first season: "Prophecies are a bit dodgy. They're mutable. Buffy herself has thwarted them time and time again, but this is the *Codex*. There is nothing in it that does not come to pass. Tomorrow night, Buffy will face the Master and she will die." In Buffy's moment of shock, she no longer is the plainly confident hero that the viewers have come to love. In a conversation with her mother, Joyce surprises Buffy with an expensive prom dress that Buffy has been eyeing at a store. When Buffy tells her mother that she cannot go to the dance, Joyce authoritatively states, "Says who? Is it written somewhere? You should do what you want." In this moment, Joyce is oblivious to the fact that Buffy's fate is indeed written, but the message is still clear. Joyce begins to plant the seed that the role Buffy is supposed to play in the prophecy, and society, does not have to be the way it ends.

Despite this message, Buffy faces the Master, and indeed dies at his hands. She is bitten and thrown into a shallow pool as he leaves his lair, free to ravage Sunnydale. Luckily, Xander and Angel show up in time and resuscitate Buffy. Buffy may have died, but she is now reborn, and a prophecy means nothing to her. She can write her own story, and this renews her strength and confidence to kill the Master.

Whedon once again stepped behind the camera for the finale, which, as far as the cast and crew knew, could be the series finale. Although he had directed the pilot presentation, this was really his first time directing a real hour of television that would actually be aired.

JOSS WHEDON

Basically, there is usually something I desperately want to say, a moment I want to capture, an idea I want to try out. I like to create. To me, the writing is the most important thing. If I'm going to take the time to direct something, to take the time out of my schedule, I usually want it to be something of my own. It would certainly be an interesting exercise to direct other people's material.

RAYMOND STELLA

Joss's episodes always went, like, twice as long. I loved working with him. He put a lot into it and I enjoyed every minute of it. He's so proud of that musical, "Once More, with Feeling." He'd take it to his alma mater and show it, which was really fun. That one went fifteen or sixteen days.

JOSS WHEDON

I was afraid at first. I didn't study directing. And so, you know, that feeling you have that I'm a fraud and they're going to find out. I was! I was an actual fraud. I was bullshitting. I thought there was some secret language they all knew that I didn't and they were going to find out. But the only thing I had in my arsenal was the truth. "This will work better if it's like this." That's all. And that's all anybody wanted to hear was the truth. A *nice* version of the truth. And so it became very easy, very quickly—and then very exciting.

J. AUGUST RICHARDS

(actor, *Agents of S.H.I.E.L.D.*)

Joss was unlike anyone that I had ever auditioned for and still is. It's so hard to describe, but I would later just come to understand that he is really a genius, but his level of creativity and his ability to communicate with actors is unparalleled. My last scene in *Agents of S.H.I.E.L.D.*, he was able to direct me in a way that in some ways he reintroduced me as an actor to people, because he just knows how to calibrate you in a way that is so effortless. It's so hard to describe. For me, I say a director can either inspire me to greatness or just de-inspire me by the things that they say. Joss has a way of saying something to you that just completely turns you so on that you forget about the cameras, you forget about the fact that millions of people are going to be seeing it, and you're so invested in your character that it just translates in a new way.

CAMDEN TOY
(actor, a Gentleman)

Joss was incredibly even-keeled. He never showed any tension, but you got to know there was tension. When I did [fourth season's] "Hush," he had just launched *Angel* and was in the middle of a season of *Buffy*. And yet he was always the first on the set; he was always the last one to leave. He never looked tired, there was never any drama, even though I'm sure he had sleep deprivation. There was one point with this little gag we did shoot with the scalpel touching the skin and blood coming out. We ended up not using that, which I think was really wise, because, instead, everything was left to your imagination, but we did shoot it, and unfortunately that gag wasn't working. Joss was like, "We have to move on." Instead of him getting angry—"We can't stop working!"—he's like, "OK, we just have to move on." And, because of Joss being like that, he really inspired us to work even harder. Sure enough, within minutes somebody had it working.

J. AUGUST RICHARDS

I'll never forget the one note he gave me for my final scene on *Agents of S.H.I.E.L.D.* I was doing the scene very emotionally and I was crying and just feeling sorry for myself as a character. Joss just came over to me and said, "You know what, I think your character has more pride than that." That little bit just took the scene from being average and something you would expect to just something that I'm so proud of to this day.

IAN WOOLF
(first assistant director, *Angel*)

I AD'd [assistant directed] on a bunch of episodes for Joss. I love working with him. He's a character who's got his own kind of style. I kind of equate Joss with David Lynch. I did two movies with David Lynch, *Dune* and *Blue Velvet*. The two are very similar in the way they direct and their mind-set.

RAYMOND STELLA

Joss is just one of these guys that knows what he is talking about. He's very intelligent. I always look at writers as very intelligent people. It's hard to write. To make something good. He knew how to direct, too, and get what he needed. He was easygoing, but when he needed to be forceful, he was, to get his point across.

CAMDEN TOY

He was incredibly even-tempered. He didn't give us a lot of instruction, you know, 95 percent of directing is really in the casting. If you're micromanaging the actor's performance, you've probably cast the wrong actor. So he would give us little adjustments occasionally, but really let us do our thing. He was incredibly generous.

RAYMOND STELLA

I saw him gain a lot more confidence. At first, he hadn't done a whole lot and this was big and it started steamrolling big-time for him. As you get bigger and better, you become more confident and you can see that with him. He made decisions easier. He had more clout, too, because he was on a roll. That helps.

JOSS WHEDON

When I finally directed the season finale and the first episode of the second season, every fucking grip in there was busting his ass because, I think, they were enjoying making the show.

By the end of the season, the show was already a hit, if not in the ratings, with fans. At the time of its debut, *The New York Times* dismissed the show, claiming, "Nobody is likely to take this oddball camp exercise seriously." In retrospect, TV critic John O'Connor's criticism of Sarah Michelle Gellar is particularly laughable: "Given to hot pants and boots that should guarantee the close attention of Humbert Humberts all over America, Buffy is just your average teenager, poutily obsessed with clothes and boys." But the show rapidly earned a small but fervent (and demographically desirable) cult following and was championed in such popular magazines as *Entertainment Weekly* as well as *USA Today* and *TV Guide* back when that actually meant something.

JOSE MOLINA

I had a feeling it was going to do pretty well, because this is an era where WB and UPN were just starting out. And it didn't take a whole lot to stay on the air on one of those networks. Even from the get-go, probably because of Joss's background as a script doctor, having worked on stuff like *Speed* and *Waterworld,* he was pretty well known. The term "script doctor" sort of became well known at around that time. So because of that I remember seeing right from the get-go articles in *Entertainment Weekly* about Joss himself and about *Buffy.*

Given the fact that a little WB show was registering with a major publication that didn't often cover a lot of sci-fi or a lot of genre stuff at the time, I wasn't particularly worried that it was going to go away. I didn't realize, of course, that it was going to become the touchstone for so much genre, especially female-led genre, that came after it.

JOSS WHEDON

I can almost never experience total, naked surprise. I can never see it with perspective. I've said before, I always intended for this to be a cultural phenomenon. That's how I wrote it. In the back of your mind you're picking up your Oscar and your Saturn and everyone is playing with their Buffy dolls. You go through so much rejection and so much negativity—and believe me, I did—you sort of have to develop this shell of incredible hubris, this arrogance, where you say, "This is going to be huge." Because if you don't believe that, you have so many people you're going to fail or it doesn't work, and you sort of just crumble.

So you sort of take it for granted and when it happens, when it goes the way you hoped that it would, then you're sort of striding along, and every now and then you'll take a moment of total perspective where you forget about all your arrogance, you forget about everything you've been through, and you just see it in perspective for the first time and it's boggling. It's *so* intense. But it doesn't happen very often. You just have to believe that it's going to so strongly that when it does, you don't get the fun of going, "I can't believe it."

BEN EDLUND

(creator/executive producer, *The Tick*)

I was working on something like *Santa Claus Conquers the Martians.* I was out in California and I remember watching the pilot in a hotel room and going, "That is amazing." It was amazing to me for someone to reclaim *Buffy the Vampire Slayer,* since I remembered the movie and felt like, even in the movie, there was something going on, it wasn't tracking right, but there was something going on that was intriguing in the writing. Joss was able to re-mount that as a TV show.

The pilot, the way it functioned so well. It was a very arresting moment, and I went, "All right, that's a guy . . ." I didn't really know about his history as such a prolific script doctor. I started to hear that he had done really well on *Roseanne.* That he was, to use a cultural term, *big-brained.* So I became aware of him.

THOMAS P. VITALE

(executive vice president, Programming and Original Movies, Syfy and Chiller)

The morning after *Buffy* premiered, everyone at workplaces across America was talking about it. I was working at Syfy at the time, and the show was truly "water cooler" programming and what's best is that the show got better. Some shows start out great and then fade. *Buffy* strengthened beyond its pilot.

DAVID GREENWALT

We knew we were onto something when three weeks of *Buffy* being out there was a *Buffy* question on *Jeopardy.* We knew we'd cut through the noise pretty good.

SOUL MAN

"From now on we're gonna have a little less ritual and a little more fun around here!"

If season one had proved there was quite a bit of life in the undead, season two is when the series truly came into its own. The show introduced the dynamic vampire duo of Spike (James Marsters) and Drusilla (Juliet Landau), Xander began dating Cordelia; Willow started a relationship with Oz (Seth Green), who is revealed to be a werewolf; and, in the most exciting, compelling, and shocking twist, Angel, after Buffy and he consummate their relationship, loses his soul and becomes evil. *Truly* evil, betraying Buffy repeatedly; torturing Giles and murdering his girlfriend, Jenny Calendar; and threatening to suck Earth into hell, forcing Buffy to turn Mr. Pointy on the former object of her affections.

HOWARD GORDON

(consulting producer, *Buffy the Vampire Slayer*)

I came on after the first season for season two. *Buffy* was just starting to get some notice; people had begun to sit up and notice that there was something special there. It certainly hadn't reached its cult status. I think the newness connected with people. The emotion. Joss always minded the store in terms of emotion. These characters were real. It's the same thing that draws anyone to a hit show is that these characters become incredibly real, incredibly vivid and have emotional lives—and it's wildly entertaining and moving all at the same time. And funny.

DAVID FURY

(co-executive producer, *Buffy the Vampire Slayer*)

When my wife and writing partner, Elin [Hampton], came in to pitch to Joss and to David Greenwalt at the beginning of season two, they both let us in on little things that were coming in the show. The whole idea of the Cordelia-Xander relationship was like, "Oh my God, that's great." But we never really got a sense of the staff, because it was really just Joss and David we were talking to. I noticed Howard Gordon's name on the door and I knew Howard's work from *The X-Files* and I was a big fan. But I never saw him there. I never actually saw a lot of the writers. We only just saw David and Joss and they were still very clearly figuring out the show. As much as they had and were able to accomplish in that brief first season, they were still trying to find something that was going to stick.

HOWARD GORDON

I was incredibly welcomed by Joss and David Greenwalt. I had a deal at Fox and I went on to *Buffy* as a consultant. I was actually blown away by Joss. I don't know if Joss's reputation as a genius had gotten around, but I was just blown away by the show. Just how clever it all was. I was a young writer then, and Joss was younger still. He mostly had a background of working in sitcoms and script doctoring on features. Just the way he was able to mash up a rich crazy filmography and bibliography and summon them at will . . . What I admired and saw him do again and again is that some writers just write the first thing in their heads and sort of paint themselves into a corner, and Joss I noticed right away just had this architecture in his head where you could really see the wheels turning. It was always a total pleasure to see.

JOSS WHEDON

(creator/executive producer, *Buffy the Vampire Slayer*)

Season one we found out that we had a show. That people liked it. I thought people were going to laugh at the Buffy-Angel thing and say, "Well clearly he's a vampire. This is so hokey." But they couldn't get enough of it. It definitely made me realize—and by "Prophecy Girl" we had incorporated it—the soap opera aspect of it; a continuing story of the romance and the people and their emotions was really what was fascinating. The monsters were all very well and good, but in the first season we were like, "Let's take our favorite horror movies and turn them into high school stories." By the second season, the horror movies were gone and the horror came from the story, the high school, the emotion.

DAVID FURY

A lot of the first season was silly fun, it was *Kolchak: The Night Stalker.* But season two is where the show really found itself.

SARAH LEMELMAN

(author, *"It's About Power":* Buffy the Vampire Slayer*'s Stab at Establishing the Strength of Girls on American Television*)

The relationship of Angel and Buffy is frequently thought of as the greatest romance for Buffy, as it is her first foray into love, and clearly her most passionate. Despite the fact that Angel provides tender love for Buffy, and the two are madly and deeply under the other's spell, the series still uses this relationship to present to viewers the anxieties of teenage girls, especially in losing one's virginity and what it means when the partner may disappear or ignore the girl, as in the case of Buffy and Angel.

DAVID FURY

It was still early in the writing stage of the second season and we sold the story which was later "Go Fish," which was about the swim team turning into monsters. I had just read an H. P. Lovecraft short story, "Shadow over Innsmouth," which is a story about these townspeople who were gradually turning into these fish monsters, and it really affected me. I was also a big fan of *The Creature from the Black Lagoon*. They had already done a Frankenstein story and the Mummy ["Incan Mummy Girl"] and clearly they'd done Dracula, although not literally yet, but vampires, so I was trying to think of what other classic monsters they hadn't done. That's how that story got pitched.

They weren't quite sure where the episode would fit in, because it was very much a stand-alone episode, and after Angel's turn when he sleeps with Buffy is when the show became so rich and emotional. The metaphor of the first guy you sleep with becoming an asshole. As soon as you let him into your pants, he becomes a complete dick. That was a fantastic metaphor. They reached the depth they hadn't reached before in terms of the characters. Suddenly our little fish story felt frivolous and so out of place.

DAVID GREENWALT

(co-executive producer, *Buffy the Vampire Slayer*)

I used to have soccer moms come up to me and say, "What's going on with Buffy and Angel? Are they going to get back together?" People really got addicted to Buffy. The age of the people that watched *Buffy* was like seven to seventy. Grown forty-five- to fifty-year-old women were really concerned about the romance, and I knew we were onto something really good.

JOSS WHEDON

In the second season we had "Innocence" and the Angelus arc that really let the audience know that we were interested in change; we were interested in shaking things up as much as possible and interested in just making things as grown-up and complex as we could get away with. The triangle with Spike, Dru, and Angelus. Originally, we thought Spike and Dru would be fun, more hip, and they won't be trapped in a cave like the Master, so they can actually interact. As it grew and the more we thought about it, the bigger it got until it became a really complex, adult kind of show.

JAMES MARSTERS

(actor, Spike)

It was really satisfying, because it was so obvious that Spike did not fit into the pegs of this story at all. But in a way, that's what made it great. He was able to take the theme and put it on its head, because the theme is, How does one grow up? How does one become one's best self? It was frustrating a lot, because I really would get just two to three pages of dialogue a script. I often felt that I was at this enormous banquet with the best food I'd ever seen in my life, but my portion wasn't always that big and I was salivating after everyone else's plate. But that is a glorious place to be as an actor, because what it is not is having to mumble a bunch of crap—which is death. So, both frustrating and rewarding. Actors are so greedy—we want everything.

I had been doing regional theater for ten or fifteen years. I was very happy and very poor. And then I had a son. I remember looking at his beautiful, bloody face on the bathing table and he's being wiped off, just seconds old, and I had an epiphany. Whereas *I* chose to be poor—a poor artist—my son *didn't* make that choice, and I was going to have to do my best to try to make some money. So I called a childhood friend, who was a casting director in town named Robert Ulrich, and asked him if he could help me get an agent. He was very gracious; he said he would. He's been a supporter of mine since high school and we'd known each other when we were both in New York when I was at Juilliard. I told my agent that I was not coming to Hollywood for awards or to prove myself as an actor; I had done that on stage. I was here for money. I was here for diaper money. I needed health care. I needed diapers. I need formula. I needed clothes for my son. And my agent was very happy with that and started booking guest spots on cop shows, and before long I got a call that I had an audition for *Buffy the Vampire Slayer.*

I said, "Well, no, not that. Not *Buffy the Vampire Slayer.* I saw the movie, man. No thank you." My agent said, "It's Tuesday night. Why don't you watch it and call us back to see if you might change your mind. It's a different animal than the movie. The writer's actually producing it and it's got a lot of buzz around it." I watched about fifteen minutes of it and fell in love and called my agent back in desperation saying, "Jesus Christ, yes. Holy God, it's amazing."

I went in and auditioned for the casting director's assistant. They were three days away from filming at this point. They had their backs up against the wall. They'd been looking for a Spike for a while but hadn't found someone they liked. I guess Joss had put the word out to scrape the bottom of the barrel in Hollywood . . . calling all the people that normally wouldn't be seen. That's how I got the audition. I remember wanting the role very badly. I didn't realize the size of the role. I was only given sides to one scene, but it was a very good scene, the introduction of the character and Drusilla. I had no concept that it was going to be any bigger than one scene. It was a great scene, and I remember trying to psych out the other actors in the audition room by reciting Shakespeare, because I'd just come off of a successful production of *Macbeth* in Seattle. I thought that if I did some of those soliloquies, I could prove that I was the best actor in the room. I was new to Hollywood and I didn't realize that Shakespeare's meaningless down here. All I was proving was probably psychosis.

I'm someone that respects film acting deeply. But Shakespeare's not in the toolbox. I'm sure all the stares that I was getting were just wondering who let the psychotic in the room. I was lording it over the other actors, so I went into the audition very full of myself, which worked for Spike. I think the reason I got cast was I got along with Juliet Landau. I was her boy toy for that story arc, and she was the character that was going to continue in the story arc and I was going to be killed off after about five episodes. But both

Juliet and I were from theater, so we kind of connected on that level very quickly. That's how I got the role.

DAVID GREENWALT

James Marsters was one of my favorite people, too, and a really interesting actor. Something about his acting let you know everything he's thinking all the time. It's very simple and direct in a way and in other ways it just bamboozles me, and, of course, Drusilla was great, too. Juliet Landau and James were so interesting.

JULIET LANDAU
(actress, Drusilla)

Joss has described Spike and Drusilla as the Sid and Nancy of the vampire set. I really like that analogy. Even their look was a cross between period, Victorian-looking, and Kate Moss cheap. But there was also a sweet, sentimental side to their relationship. That's one of the things that made them interesting villains. It sort of balances out the evil, horrible deeds they do.

JAMES MARSTERS

Part of what I like about acting is being able to safely explore places in myself that normal life would not allow me to explore. I had just come off of a successful production of *Macbeth* in Seattle. To play Macbeth I had to get comfortable with the idea that I was a man who slashed people in half as a day job and had no problem with that. That a normal day for me was to take my sword out and just disembowel large groups of people. I had always grown up thinking of myself as a nice guy. That was a challenge for me, because a lot of actors when they approach Macbeth, they always play him like, "I know this guy's evil, too" and I think that's a mistake. I really did not want to go down that road.

So I did some research into being a soldier and I found someone saying that one of the things that soldiers can't talk with civilians about is the fact that murder is fun. There's a rush that happens when you take a life. There's a sense of power to that. And one of the things that soldiers have to deal with for the rest of their lives is the guilt that they feel having felt this animal reaction. Civilians really don't understand when you talk about it. Luckily, I had already played a role where I became comfortable and didn't feel guilty about this rush of excitement, imagining doing that act.

DAVID FURY

The most helpful thing is you can articulate your thoughts to the actors to get the cast excited. "Here's what I'm thinking, here's what I'd like to see you do, what do you think about this?" It was wonderful to be able to have that relationship, I loved working with James Marsters. It was great, because he relished it. Some actors don't really want to talk about it, but James loved talking about it. I would tell him something for Spike and he would just get so excited.

JAMES MARSTERS

When I took Spike, there's a saying in theater: it's called a play for a reason; no one pays to watch you work. They'll pay to watch you play really well. And so, it's always about fun. You have to have fun in what you're doing. It seemed . . . the way to make the [Spike] character work was just have this guy having the best time doing the most vile act and that's just sick . . . just horrible. But if you can give yourself over to it, it can be a wild, weird ride for the audience. I was able to give myself over to that. And then once you do that, you're just through the looking glass. You're just in new territory. Macbeth was bloody but not sadistic, and Spike asked me to enjoy the sadism. And, you know, it's all safe. No one got hurt. I got bruised as much as anyone else, but it was a weird ride. That was probably the most enjoyable part of it initially. The character grew way beyond that. But the first rush was that.

DAVID GREENWALT

Then Spike, who was this ballsy, dangerous, scary guy, you find out was this very fey poet to begin with and then to have the idea that Spike and Buffy would someday get together. You would never think you could pull that off.

JOSS WHEDON

I do think that the balance is necessary, that you need to go from something like Xander becomes uberpopular to Ms. Calendar gets killed. I don't think you can have one without the other. That, to me, was our most manic-depressive moment with doing those shows back to back. I love them equally for totally different reasons. It was kind of a relief to get back to the high school from the unbelievable, world-shattering angst that is the real sort of mythology episodes.

DAN VEBBER

(staff writer, season 3, *Buffy the Vampire Slayer*)

Joss would come in and say, "Here's the arc for the next season." Now, for all I know, he might have worked with Marti Noxon or Dave Greenwalt before I even came into the room, so I don't know to what degree other writers might have had a say in it. But in terms of the point when I was brought into the room to break the stories or to see the arcs of the season, it was already figured out by Joss. He knew what was going on. There was some leeway in coming up with episode ideas, but then it became about, "How does this fit into the overarching arc"?

DAVID FURY

That was the brilliance of Joss. He had these things that you just wouldn't have expected. Especially coming off of sitcom writing. A lot of it is always the status quo remains the same. People don't change. They'll go through funny situations and they'll have little moments together, but ultimately every episode you're starting from scratch. So when he would have these dramatic turns like this Angelus thing, it was incredibly daring. He and David would run through this stuff with us. He would try to keep us abreast of what they were doing as the season went on, because of the whole process of us writing this freelance script. It went over several months so we just kept seeing a prize of new developments. I would just kind of be flabbergasted by, "Oh my God, that's great."

DAVID GREENWALT

This was the most brilliant twist ever in the show and this is what got all the soccer moms so involved, because the curse of Angel was that if he ever knew a moment of pure happiness, he'd turn evil, right? Of course Buffy is a virgin. He finally sleeps with her . . . they'd been waiting. We really built up to it beautifully and then he turns into an asshole. If that is not a metaphor, I don't know what is. Every woman at some time in their lives loves a guy, they give it up for him, and he turns into an asshole.

DAVID BOREANAZ
(actor, Angel)

The transformation of Angel from good guy to bad guy was hard for me, both personally and professionally. I was in tune with Good Angel, but I wasn't coming home for Evil Guy. I think if you've played a character long enough, you subconsciously carry that character with you into your private life. You can shut it off to an extent, but there's a part of you that still consciously lives with it. On the set, it was particularly hard doing scenes with Sarah, because she didn't see Angel as an evil type and all of a sudden there he was.

DAVID GREENWALT

Sarah was so good at this stuff. The scenes where she's saying, she can't believe how he's behaving. And he's saying, "Yeah it was all right. You were OK, you know a little inexperienced." My favorite thing was where Buffy's father comes and needs to talk to her and really the whole reason the marriage broke up was because of her. That and Angel turning into an asshole were really two of my favorite things in the series, because it was so emotional and your worst fear coming true in the case of Buffy and her father, and then with Angel that great sexual metaphor. It drove season two. I remember when I first watched it and how shocked I was at how much power it brought, because he was so good at being the evil Angelus. Your heart just broke for Buffy. It was unbelievable.

JOSS WHEDON

"Innocence" was the show where everything really fell into place with Buffy going through a hero's mythic journey, being couched in the terms of losing your virginity and your boyfriend doesn't call. It really felt like we hit both levels at once; it speaks to people about their experience and elevates it to something bigger.

DAVID BOREANAZ

For the most part, the relationship between Buffy and Angel had been almost a Beauty-and-the-Beast type of thing. Buffy knew what Angel was, but she still loved him. Then the transition came, and it was hard for her, and also for me, to adjust. To help Sarah with the transition, after each scene I made it a point to confirm to her that, "I'm here for you. I'm not here against you. This is not who I am." I believe there has to be a coming-down period where you hug the other actor or help the other person, and even help yourself get out of the turmoil that's been created, instead of being submerged in it. As harrowing as that can be sometimes, it's part of the acting process, and one that I would never even think of giving up.

DAVID GREENWALT

David [Boreanaz] was cool with it. When I did *Profit,* in which the leading man [Adrian Pasdar] kills his own father in the pilot with a syringe, he said, "You're sure you want to do this on screen, because a lot of people are going to freak out." No, it absolutely had to be done. I never heard anything from David about it. I think he loved it. It was fun and most actors love it if they can play some opposite version of their character if they can justify it. You knew it had to swing back. You couldn't do it forever, though. Once you got all the emotion out of it, it was time for him to suffer like a son of a bitch.

JOSS WHEDON

The first time when I wrote Angel turns evil because he and Buffy made the beast, I wrote the scene where he basically pretends that he just doesn't care about her and just acts like a dick. I didn't drop my pen, but I actually looked at it and was like, "Oh my God, I had no idea I was such a dick." Like, I accessed this terrible person and I was just so happy that I had this darkness in me that was just appalling, and this has been happening with this script just over and over and over. Probably too much.

DAVID GREENWALT

The great thing I like about Joss is that he would really go there. He wouldn't protect the audience. He used to say, "You have to give an audience not so much what it wants, but what it needs." He would really go to these places where you can't believe what you're seeing. It really would change up the game. Doing that takes enormous balls and it's what made the show really good. People responded. People loved it. His stuff feels like real life, a little bit heightened, but it feels so real to people.

MARTI NOXON

(executive producer, *Buffy the Vampire Slayer*)

For me, personally, the emotional substance of *Buffy* is very real. I don't think I'm alone in that assessment, either. The killing off of [Giles's girlfriend and Sunnydale High teacher] Jenny Calendar was one of those surprises that we keep coming up with to keep our viewers on their toes. In one of the episodes I wrote, coincidentally titled "Surprise," Jenny turns out to be a gypsy with a vendetta against Angel.

That was an idea that just grew on its own; it wasn't something that Joss, David, and I were purposely planning on. I don't think we even thought, at the outset, that Jenny was going to be connected to Angel in any way, but it soon became obvious that she was. That's the wonderful thing about learning from Joss. His mind is completely open to do things that are unexpected. When Joss told us Angel was going to murder Jenny, I stood up and said, "No! You can't do that to us!"

Joss was so pleased, because that was just the reaction he was looking for—you know, something strong and emotional. So our characters are always turning out to be involved in stuff that I didn't think they were going to be involved in. But it's not always by design. A lot of times, as with "Gypsy Jenny," we went, "Oooh, wouldn't that be cool? Let's do it."

JAMES MARSTERS

Initially, it was that Angel and Buffy were going to at some point have sex, at which point Angel goes evil as many boyfriends do in real life. And Angel would kill Spike, thus becoming the Big Bad and take up with Drusilla so that Buffy would get her heart broken. That was the original plan. And they kept most of that but then didn't kill me off.

It let Joss kind of explore Spike as the sidekick—as the jealous little brother, rather than the Big Bad that originally came to Sunnydale. Once you decide not to kill Spike off, the problem is how do you get him up off that ladder of cool and back down to earth so he can actually be explored as a three-dimensional, interesting character? That was one of the big ways to do it. I think ultimately what Joss came to with Spike was that Spike was the most successful poser in the history of the world. Like most people who want to seem tougher than they are, they just buy some leather pants and the right car or whatever. But Spike actually was made into a vampire so that he could get away with posing. Because he was super strong now and he could heal quickly and all of that stuff, he actually could pose and get away with it. That's really interesting. The beginning of that was just to show him as the jealous little sidekick of the much cooler Angel. And luckily art imitated life enough that I was thoroughly jealous of David Boreanaz. I *hated* David Boreanaz for a while . . . to my shame, because he was nice to me from day one.

My girlfriend at the time became jealous of Drusilla and me, who struck up a close friendship. We never became romantic in real life, but we became quite close as collaborators and as friends. My then girlfriend just couldn't stand that. So she told me that she had a crush on David. And so that's all she wrote. I was like, "F— you, David."

And so, as jealous as Spike was of Angel on the show, I was jealous of David in real life. I kept it to myself. And, truly, David was supportive of me from day one and kept telling me to keep doing what I'm doing, because he started out on the show exactly where I was. He kept telling me how positive people's reactions to the character were and that I should not lose hope and that I would probably become a large part of the show. He was just my biggest supporter from day one, and I was just blinded by jealousy for a long time.

DAVID FURY

When they finally said we're going to put "Go Fish" at the end of the second season when the whole season was coming to a climax with Spike and Drusilla and Angel killed Jenny, it was tough to have emotional grounding to an episode that was meant to be a funny lark, and it felt out of place. The fact was that Joss and David were thrilled with it and that's all we cared about at that time.

When they called, they called gleefully from the trailer. They were jumping up and down with happiness. That was the greatest feeling to know we nailed the first hour of television we had ever written, having only done sitcoms and animated series prior to that. It was a big deal for us and it was really exciting, and so we had that to hang on to. Even as a lot of fans trashed it.

On its own merits, it's a fun episode. But I'm with the fans when I say that's the last thing you want to see when all this great stuff is happening on the show and you really want to bring it to the climax and you get this little side trip where Angel has one tiny scene in the episode and it's inconsequential. People are just going, "What is this episode we're watching? We want to see Angel and Buffy." And we weren't seeing it.

Another surprise for viewers as well as the staff was Whedon's decision to have Xander and Cordelia become a couple only to have Xander cheat on her with Willow, who had long endured an unrequited crush on him, breaking Cordelia's heart.

DAVID FURY

It was the couple that you would never have thought would happen and it happens so quickly. And it's smart, because it brought Cordelia into the mix as opposed to always standing outside the gang making snarky comments at Buffy. It was a way of bringing her in. Every move they made was so smart. I kind of held my breath.

Joss lives in the pain. He taught all of us that that's where the best stories live. He really did. Coming from genres that don't convey that kind of depth of human emotion and pain and anguish and suddenly you're writing it, I thought, Why haven't I been writing this all along? Why haven't I been trying to strive for this in everything I do?

CHARISMA CARPENTER
(actress, Cordelia Chase)

As the show got more popular, they had to rely on servicing the ancillary characters more, and that served the show in a great way. I wasn't in the writers' room, but that might have been the cause of exploring those characters, bringing in Oz, being forced to build story lines for Willow. And I think that created a lot. I felt like there was a big difference between season one and two.

We learned that Cordelia's heart is broken when she sees Xander cheat on her, and that was the first time we see Cordy vulnerable and heartbroken. That changed a lot about the way audiences saw Cordelia; seeing her in a new light they could identify with her, because it's a universal theme. You see this woman who is so acerbic and vain get sad, and that made it even more powerful.

MARTI NOXON

I can venture to say that I used my experience to punch up the relationship between Xander and Cordelia. It's kind of pathetic in a way because their constant feuding, then making up, is very close to how my own romantic life was. Joss often said to me, "Marti, if you had had a happier teenager-hood, you wouldn't be here."

The justly lauded teenage metaphors of the series were never more ubiquitous and potent than in the second season of the show, all thanks to the wisdom of Whedon, who was learning to become a show runner while producing some of the most meaningful television the medium had ever seen for a generation of adolescents.

JOSS WHEDON

I didn't read Robert McKee. I didn't do any of the things you were supposed to do. I was raised by an angry pack of comedy writers. Structure is always hard and it's the most important thing. Structure is work, it's math, it's graphs.

JOSE MOLINA

(former assistant to Howard Gordon)

Joss is pretty easily the best writer I've ever encountered. He is so fast and he thinks so differently. It's something that I learned from him as a writer that there's a way of telling a story that is the traditional way. You go from point A to point B. Well, you know, once you've been writing for more than a minute, you learn, well, what if I do that backward? What if I just flip it? And what if I do B to A? And what I learned from Joss is, don't turn it around, turn it sideways. Flip it in some unexpected way. Can you go from A to Q or from R to C? What is the thing that you didn't see coming? And do that not just in episodes, but in scenes and in line to line to line; where you might expect a person to ask a question and get an answer, what if a person asks a question and gets another question? OK, that's simple: What if a person asks a question and gets a recipe for french fries? OK, I didn't see that coming, now what does that mean? That's what he has an incredible facility with. He can see that strange, off-kilter, unexpected way of approaching a moment or a scene or a story. I still aspire to that level of it. When I have to work on it. When I have time to think about it, I need to twist this scene and then I can put myself in that kind of head. But to him, it's just natural.

JOSS WHEDON

I will do color charts for everything that looks like I'm doing a PowerPoint presentation. This is where it's scary, this is where it's funny, and everything has got to find its flow and intersect. That can be appallingly hard, but the act of writing, the macro and the micro, which is having ideas and then actually writing scenes once you figure out what they need to be, is perfect bliss. It is the greatest thing anybody got paid to do. I'll never capture that feeling in any other way and I don't need to. Characters are the reason I'm there and they're the most fun to think up. It's very easy to go, "You know what would be really cool . . ." Even a premise is not a movie—although that's something in American cinema that people have forgotten sometimes. So, structure is an absolute.

DAVID GREENWALT

He's a really good fucking writer. Joss's scripts generally start a little slow and you just think you're in real life. Sometimes even just the first ten or eleven pages of one of the TV scripts we wrote or he wrote or we wrote together would almost start to get a little boring, and then some incredible twist happens and you're off and running. It's emotional, it's funny, it has a point.

JOSS WHEDON

Two times in my life I have had an idea that had a third act in the idea. And one of them was the biggest spec sale I ever made, and I knew it would be the moment I thought of it. The other one was *Cabin in the Woods,* which we wrote in a weekend. You have to know where you're going. Now, some people can write a different way and I wrote a couple of episodes where I didn't, but there was enough structure around them like the dream episode of *Buffy* ["Restless"], where I was like, I know enough that I can just sort of let this flow like poetry. But almost without exception, if you don't know where you're going, you're never getting anywhere. And it doesn't matter how cool the idea is and how cool the characters are. You've got to figure out that *reason* why there's a whole movie about it. So structure, structure, structure.

DAVID GREENWALT

The trick with Joss Whedon is not just that he is a genius, the trick is he works harder than anybody else. Maybe he's a genius with that Jeff Katzenberg work ethic. At least in those days, but as you get older and the family becomes more important it's harder. Writing a story with him was like watching Mozart play, because you would work and work and work and then wait and wait and wait. Then eventually he'd just go to the board and start writing these beats and you'd go, "Oh, they're perfect." They're inevitable, but they're surprising, they're emotionally connected. He always says, "I'd rather have a moment than a move. I'll sacrifice a move if I can have a moment." Our stuff was very emotional. We were crappy detectives and, you know, our detective work probably left a little to be desired, but that wasn't what we were interested in. We were interested in the emotional journeys of the people.

JAMES MARSTERS

The writing, especially as far as dialogue is concerned, is something that you'd have to go back to the films of Billy Wilder or Preston Sturges to match. Really, something kind of interesting or pleasing happens every five seconds. It'll be a turn of phrase or an event that happens, some joke that happens with such frequency that it starts to froth. Usually a movie will give you something interesting happening every three minutes or so. I feel a little weird comparing him to Billy Wilder, because that's like comparing him to Shakespeare, but Wilder never had to crank this stuff out every week.

JOSS WHEDON

What ends up connecting with people is that if you're not writing about yourself, why are you writing? For me if you're not telling a story, spinning a yarn is fine and there are some people who are great at it. And they are great at things that I'm not great at. You know, like intricate heist plots and things that I admire and envy, but if you're sitting down to write something or make something that's going to take three years out of your life, why would you not want to tell people something that is important to you to say? I don't mean a moral, I mean an examination of the human condition.

You want to be able to talk about the politics of personality. That's something it took me a while to find. I started to find it on *Alien: Resurrection*, which is the last thing I wrote before *Buffy*, before the show. That was the first time I went, "Oooohh, this is a metaphor" and the only way this works is if I feel the way she feels, and that was sort of like the beginning of becoming a storyteller instead of a yarn spinner. To me, if I can't do that, if I can't make that connection, then I'm wasting people's time. As much as I may look back at anything I've made and go, "flawed, flawed, flawed, flawed, flawed, embarrassing, embarrassing," I never feel like I wasted somebody's time.

HOWARD GORDON

I learned the importance, and it may be self-evident, of the architecture of each season. Joss sort of knew the story he wanted to tell, didn't quite know how he wanted to tell it. As a show runner, it's become increasingly important—you have to know how to ask the right questions. You may not always have the answers, but you have to know how to ask the right questions and that's what Joss is particularly good at. Joss was truly a great show runner. It wasn't always easy. I don't think I learned it from Joss, but certainly along my path I saw how important it is, when you see something and your staff doesn't always see it, so it's about having the patience and wherewithal to communicate something that you're not always entirely capable of understanding yet in its entirety, but keeping the conversation going. Keeping them invested in it. Giving them ownership of it. And everyone *did* feel ownership in that show. It's not an accident that so many people stayed with that show through the whole run or moved over to *Angel*.

DAN VEBBER

(staff writer, *Buffy the Vampire Slayer*)

Joss is a terrific guy. At the beginning of the year, he was a lot less harried than he was at the end of the year. So by the end of the year, the chummy guy who'd be your buddy and was willing to talk about pop culture or whatever got replaced by the guy stalking through the hallways and completely in his own world, because he just got so freakin' busy. But he's definitely very confident about his voice and his vision and deservedly so. I don't have anything negative to say about him. When he didn't renew my contract, your ego is hurt, but the next time I saw him in public, he was very gracious and said, "Look, you're a great writer, you're a great comedy writer, and you're going to land on your feet."

DAVID GREENWALT

There's certain of us that really fit in that Joss mold, in that Joss world, and certain others did not, and never the twain shall meet. Edgar Allan Poe would've done really well there. Thomas Smart Hughes, who was actually a happy, well-adjusted guy—he would've done terrible there. You had to be really vulnerable and willing to dredge up all the horrible things that have happened to you.

DAN VEBBER

Leaving *Buffy* at that time, you know, like I said, my ego was bruised and I was stressed out about it, but that ended up being right when they needed people to work on *Futurama,* which ended up being a show that I had a far, far better fit with. And since then it's been those animated comedies that I've been working on. It doesn't wound my ego to say that I have deficiencies in writing drama scripts, because I'm so confident in my ability to write adult primetime animated-type comedies with just jokes to make people laugh. To a certain degree, that sensibility helped me on a show like *Buffy,* but I think it also kind of hindered me, because I wasn't thinking in terms of what's going to be best for the emotional drama of the story.

DAVID GREENWALT

Joss was always kind and generous and one of my favorite things about him is whatever his troubles or demons may be, he didn't take them out on other people like so many people in our business. He would be in his own world, with his blinders on, and you'd have to remind him this shoots Tuesday and we better have some words. I used to plant myself outside the bathroom. He'd come out and I'd be face-to-face with him telling what we had to do next. He would always forget his jacket or his teacup in your office. He was just so focused on what he was doing. One day we were in a big art department meeting and, for some reason, he just laid down on this table in the middle of this big serious meeting.

JOSE MOLINA

He's one of those people that you hear about that needs to create. That needs to write. That's not me. I would be perfectly happy taking long vacations and traveling the world and fucking around and spending time with my friends and my family and playing board games and video games. If I was never able to write again, I would miss it but it wouldn't kill me. I think it would kill Joss. It's kind of like air to him. He needs it to be able to function properly.

ARMIN SHIMERMAN
(actor, Principal Snyder)

I had been working on *Star Trek* for a long time. I'd worked a lot of shows before, but I wasn't educated to the ins and outs of set behavior and politics until I was involved in the Star Trek franchise. So when I went to work at *Buffy,* every day of every episode that I ever worked on, Joss Whedon was there. This was not the policy that Rick Berman had at *Star Trek*. Rick Berman was a very busy man, and we rarely saw him on the set of *Star Trek,* so I was not used to seeing the executive producer on the set. So a thought occurred to me, is he here checking on me? Is that why the executive producer is here? Because I'm not used to having an executive producer around.

After I had done five or six episodes, I actually posed the question to him. He said one of the places he liked to write was on set. And then with my asking, "When do you get time to write here?" he said, "Between takes." He was an amazing man on *Buffy*. He was the executive producer, he was the head writer, he was the person that sold the show. And because the cast was relatively young, at least younger than the cast in *Star Trek,* I can say he was the chief babysitter as well. He was there, I came to understand, probably for lots of reasons, but one of the reasons was to make sure that if there were problems on set, he could take care of them before they grew into larger problems. That was a remarkable ability that probably nobody ever talks about. He is, of course, a phenomenal writer and a phenomenal producer and a great creative mind. But he's an incredible babysitter, too.

HARRY GROENER

The very last two shows of the third season ["Graduation Day"] they sent an email, because we didn't have a script yet and we had to go to work the next day and they said, "Well, there's a synopsis, but there aren't any words yet. Just come to the set." So we go to set, we get ready, we get our costumes on while we're waiting for some words. Finally, some words come. So we say, "OK." We get the scene, we go in and rehearse it, they light it, and while that's happening, Joss is back over in a corner writing the next scene.

JAMES MARSTERS

I remember being terrified of Joss Whedon. I knew that he was the creator and head writer, so I went in with a lot of respect for him based on what I had seen on the show. I remember he came in and selected my costumes, thank goodness. The costumer had pulled a lot of glam rock, kind of clear plastic shirts and stuff. And Joss knows punk rock and he just axed all of that stuff, thank God, and got me into something that worked.

JOSE MOLINA

I didn't have a lot of exposure to Joss. I'd never been on a working set. I'd visited sets, but it was one of those things where I saw an opportunity to learn something. So I spent some time on set with Marti Noxon first season and she was amazing. I'd already read a couple of her scripts and it's the worst kept secret in town that she did an uncredited polish on the episode "Halloween." And her voice was quickly becoming the strongest voice on the show that was closest to Joss, which ultimately led to her running the show seasons six and seven.

MARTI NOXON

One of the reasons that Joss and I work so well together, and why this partnership was so fruitful, is that much of the time what he wants is naturally—and not in ass-kissy way—what I want.

DAVID GREENWALT

Marti's great. She started as a staff writer, as low as you can be, and she went to executive producer in not that many years. Joss, Marti, and I used to talk about ourselves as the evil triumvirate.

MARTI NOXON

I was nervous, because Buffy was actually my first staff job. My father, Nicholas Noxon, is the head of National Geographic Documentary Division and I used to hang around him all the time when I was a kid, because I always knew that I wanted to do something in the film business. But I found out that I really didn't want to be a documentary person—I found it very frustrating watching and waiting for animals to do things. I wanted to give them direction. I went to film school at UC Santa Cruz, and when I graduated I just worked in a bunch of different jobs in the industry, mostly as an assistant to a writer and then to a writer/producer, and I just wrote a lot. I did spec scripts, both feature and television. I actually did have one produced, and that was for the show *Life Goes On*. After that, I got signed by one of the biggest agencies for television and talent and they passed my material to Joss at *Buffy*. I met with Joss and David, and I thought it had gone miserably, and I was never going to get the job. I couldn't tell if they liked me, but much to my delight, they did.

I think one of the reasons they liked me was because I had a real taste for the macabre. When I was writing spec scripts, most of them were ghost stories, or had some sort of supernatural element to them. One of the specs I wrote was for *The X-Files*. I loved that show. I have always been obsessed with ghost stories, and it seemed that David and Joss were able to pick that up. That is why *Buffy* was such a great fit for me.

JOSE MOLINA

Even as a staff writer she was a force to be reckoned with and very cool and down to earth and approachable and accessible. You know, enough that she hung out on set with another writer's assistant who was just there loitering.

MARTI NOXON

My agent at the time, there were definitely people telling me not to take *Buffy*. When I first got the job, my mother was like, "Oh, that's too bad. Something better will come next year." She was excited for me, but thought there would be something better. The attitude, even two and a half years after the first season, is that I was slumming a little bit. It wasn't like I was having offers coming out of the trees; it was my first season on a staff. I was just going on a gut instinct and the fact that, considering all of the stuff that I could have possibly worked on, this really resonated with me. And to see that kind of paid off—it's so gratifying to see that people who love it really love it and really get it. I felt that way about the show. I feel that way about Joss and his work, and . . . knowing that you would be watching the show if you weren't working on it was pretty gratifying.

When I came in to meet with them, they sent me a bunch of tapes. My agents scrounged up as many tapes as they could find. I went and watched pretty much one through twelve, trying to get ready for my meeting. By about episode four, I was hooked. I was watching one after the other, ordering take out. And then when the whole Angel thing started happening in the first twelve, I was completely addicted.

DAVID GREENWALT

I learned a lot from Joss. So many things like what we call "first thought theater." Many television writers want to do it too quickly and they won't wait until the idea is correct. One thing I learned from Joss is wait a long time before you go to the whiteboard and start writing down possible beats of a possible story. Like one time, [writer/producer] Jane Espenson came in with a story idea about a student who could read minds. We said, "Oh, that has to be Buffy," and then the story broke in twenty minutes and we never had that experience again. Most of them were laborious. They took five to ten days to break. The breaking was the hardest part and the part where the most attention had to be paid. Joss hates to rewrite, so he will wait. Once we have the story, he will wait and pace and pace and pace—he loves to walk and drink tea. Then he'll sit down and eventually write a script that needs, you know, three line changes.

DAN VEBBER

Buffy was not a very collaborative show. At least not for me. It was very much Joss's show. So that was my first experience with the idea of a show runner who pretty much will do a page one rewrite of your draft. I'm always reticent to talk about my experience on the show, because people will compliment me about the episodes that I wrote. For the most part, the things that they were so impressed with are purely, one hundred percent Joss and not me. And I don't want to take credit for it.

It was Joss's show for better or for worse, and for the most part it was definitely for better. I still think it's the best thing that Joss has done. That and more recently when *The Avengers* came out, which is my favorite superhero movie ever. The Joss Whedon voice works so well in certain things and *Buffy* was the absolute pinnacle of that. It just happened to be his first big breakthrough thing that he did.

NICHOLAS BRENDON

(actor, Xander Harris)

After a while we started thinking, "When are the great scripts going to stop coming?" But they didn't. I felt so fortunate to be doing such good material.

KELLY A. MANNERS

(producer, *Buffy the Vampire Slayer*)

Joss is a genius. Some days Joss would walk around with a dark cloud over his head, and you can just tell he's either really deeply thinking of something and you know to stay the hell away from him, but most of the time Joss was a fun-loving guy. He called me Meat Pie. Meat Pie was a nickname he gave a friend of his in school.

I'll never forget Sarah wanted to take a week off and she announced this after we were already prepping a script, and after the weekend Joss wrote a script for her where she turned into a frog. I couldn't believe it. It was just remarkable how that man could adapt.

DAN VEBBER

It was very much a case of him standing at the whiteboard saying, "Here's what our story is, here's what the outline is, go write it." Then you would go write it and he would rewrite it. He would take snippets of my dialogue, which was always nice because, you know, in theory, that's why he hired me, because I got these characters. I could talk in their voices. But when you look at an episode like [third season's] "Lovers Walk," everyone always points to that great speech that Spike gives about the nature of love and stuff and I can't take credit for any of that. I wrote a version of that, but the version that's in the show is one hundred percent Joss's doing, which he did . . . in his rewrite.

KELLY A. MANNERS

You didn't get scripts early with Mr. Whedon, so I got to a point on *Buffy* where I'd break down his outlines and guess the page counts to just get an idea if we should build a set, do this or that. I'll never forget about the second time I did that. I put out a one-liner based on guessing page counts and everything else.

Joss went and pondered it and talked to his writers and said, "Does this scene bother you as much as it bothers me?" They all said, "No, but we weren't going to say that." Joss came back to me the next day and said, "You're right. I was going to reshoot it for selfish reasons. I had something else in mind." He was an approachable guy. If you had something to say, you better know what you were talking about instead of wasting his time. He's a genius, and, like all geniuses, he has a quirky side as well.

JOSS WHEDON

In the sense of dialogue, it comes down very specifically to just the musicality of a phrase and because I'm a wannabe actor, obviously I say everything as I'm writing. Also because I type very slowly. You can hear when something feels really awkward or abrupt or wrong. And sometimes it's nice to throw something off, but when I'm being specific about it, I'm very, very attuned to how that's going to fit in the mouth, how is this going to roll off and into the next line. In terms of meaning, and in terms of rhythm. And for a long time when I started, I would be in constant conflict with people about saying things exactly as I wrote them, because I was doing something a little different than anybody was used to.

And then over the years two things happened. One: I chilled the fuck out. I started remembering it was a collaborative process. And two: I realized that people no longer had as much of an issue with the way I wrote; that it had sort of entered the mainstream enough that it was now something that people understood and they would come in and they'd go, "Oh, yeah, I don't need to replace this with the generic version of it. I get it." Which was gratifying.

DAN VEBBER

What surprised me is that, as a staff writer, there were days when I just had nothing to do. I would come in and sit there, but Joss was just so busy doing every aspect of the show that he wouldn't be around. I did learn a lot about story structuring and just a lot of the basics that people who go to school for this type of thing learn in classes. Like how you construct a drama script. I had never done it before. It was like a master course from Joss Whedon, which was really cool.

STEVEN S. DEKNIGHT

(executive producer, *Spartacus: Gods of the Arena*)

What I loved about what Joss did, and I saw other show runners on other shows kind of just fumble their way through a season, was he came in and knew the beginning, middle, and end, which are the important parts as long as you have that structure. At the beginning of each season, often at the end of one season, he'd start talking about the next one. He would have an idea of, "OK, this is how it starts. This is what happens in the middle. This is what we're building towards." With twenty-two episodes, there's a lot to figure out. He would always have that big-picture idea. A lot of times, he would have the idea for what the episode was about or the main thing he wanted to have in the episode.

I remember episodes were usually assigned on a rotational basis. It's like from the top of the pecking order to the bottom; the top would usually get the first episode and then it would just go in order. Then it would rotate back around. You were never quite sure which one was coming up for you. I remember I got an episode called "Seeing Red," where Tara gets murdered. I thought, "Oh, this is a tough one."

JOSS WHEDON

We'd spend a few days breaking a story, figuring out what to write. Then someone goes off and writes it and that took a couple of weeks—or a few hours, if that's what we have. We shot in eight days; then we had two days to edit. We tried to figure out the story lines far in advance, but we also tried to be flexible. Like something'll pop up and we'd go, "Jenny could be a gypsy."

DAVID FURY

As Joss has the big ideas, he doesn't always know exactly how they're going to be executed and what they're going to be. He gave us a lot of free rein, which was really wonderful and important in that he gave us the big ideas, but where we found some of the story was in things that we, being the staff, were able to create and make work. In other words, his ideas weren't always entirely worked out. He knew where he wanted to end up, but he didn't always know how we were going to get there. He knew some of the devices we were going to use. He knew the events he wanted to explore. But beyond that, it was up to all of us to work out and work through. He was not this guy who was dictating everything to us. He was somebody who just gave us the building blocks of what the season will be and then we got to be the ones to figure out how to get there with him. The really enjoyable part of working with him was that he was not so locked into an absolute. He was basically looking for help. "This is what I want to do, help me get there."

JOSE MOLINA

Howard's involvement on *Buffy* was cut short because he got a pilot picked up which was called *Strange World*, which is a show that nobody ever saw, which explains why it lasted all of eight days on the air. We produced thirteen episodes and my first ever writing credit was actually on *Strange World*. But, because we did the thirteen episodes, that took him out of the Whedonverse for a while. But the minute the show got canceled, it was a similar situation again, where he was still on a deal and they were launching *Angel* and they wanted Howard to come and join *Angel.*

HOWARD GORDON

I left the show because I had a pilot that was shooting that got picked up. In a way, I came on as a consultant. I had an overall deal and in some ways Fox was servicing my deal, but it wasn't a perfect match.

JOSE MOLINA

Let me give you the roster of the fucking heavy hitters that were there. Upstairs on *Buffy* you had Joss, of course; Marti Noxon; David Fury; Jane Espenson; Doug Petrie; Drew Z. Greenberg; Drew Goddard; Rebecca Kirshner; and Tracy Forbes. On *Angel,* by the time *Firefly* was up and running, you had Sarah Fain and Liz Craft, you had David Greenwalt, you had Tim Minear, Steve DeKnight, Jeff Bell, Mere Smith, and then on *Firefly* it was Joss and Tim, Ben Edlund and me and Brett Mathews, and Cheryl Cain was a story editor. So, you had kind of three murderers' rows of writing staffs. People who would go on to have huge careers.

HOWARD GORDON

The writing room really was a bunch of really smart people: David Greenwalt, Marti Noxon, Jane Espenson, David Fury—really good people. Joss would come in and gingerly look at the work that had been done. He was very good at not dismissing it outright, but kind of rearranging it or revising it. I have to tell you, it was a pleasure to watch him work. You would see it in his face when he sort of got it and everyone knew the process was moving the furniture around until Joss gets it, and when he did, it changed fast. It was the perennial marching back and forth, until the light went off and you could almost see the light go off. You'd wait for it. He created a great culture, and a great group of people who really respected him and got him and got *it* and were happy to be there.

STEVEN S. DEKNIGHT

Joss was so great to be around. Look, running a show is a pressure-filled job. Nobody can be nice all the time. He had his good days. He had his bad days. He always loved his writers. He always said that, with his writers, you could be the best writer in the world and if you don't get along with the family, he doesn't want you there. He really considered it a family. At that time, obviously, he had *Buffy*. He had *Angel*. When I was on *Angel*, he had *Buffy*, *Angel*, and *Firefly*. I don't know how you run one show that goes twenty-two episodes a year, but he was taking a stab at three. He must have never slept.

JOSE MOLINA

We all parked in the same parking lot and a lot of the times we would walk in at the same time. You get into the lobby and then the different people went in their different directions. The *Buffy* guys went upstairs, the *Angel* guys went to the left, the *Firefly* guys went up the stairs to the right. Then we would all sort of meet at various hours of the day out in the smoking patio, where even the nonsmokers would come out, because that's where people were hanging out. So the three staffs got to know each other. Jeff Bell was there on *Angel*. And he actually became the show runner that year. But Jeff was not a smoker and he would come out. The Drews would come out every once in a while. Fury would come out to bum cigarettes, because he never had a pack on him because he was trying not to smoke.

ELIZABETH CRAFT

(executive story editor, *Angel*)

The group of people we got to work with was extraordinary. We were just starting out and we were working with Joss, Tim [Minear], Steve DeKnight, and David Fury. Jane Espenson was upstairs and Marti Noxon. Drew Goddard was just starting on *Buffy* when we were starting on *Angel*, and Ben Edlund. It was just a great group.

JOSE MOLINA

It really became one big group of like-minded writers who were all desperately craving Daddy's attention. Because by the time Joss was running three shows, he didn't have enough time for any of us. Running one show is enough of an enterprise, running two is crazy, running three is certifiable.

ELIZABETH CRAFT

There was a façade over our office window, a *Buffy* [set] façade over it. We would constantly be having pigeons getting trapped there and beating against our window. Another thing that added to the atmosphere of working on *Angel*.

STEVEN S. DEKNIGHT

In the *Angel* episode where Fred dies, there was that argument that Angel and Spike were having about who would win: astronauts or cavemen? And the story behind that is Doug Petrie, who was working on *Tru Calling* at the same time, which was in the same building, came down one day and wrote on the [dry-erase] board, "Who would win, astronauts or cavemen?" We knew it was Doug, because he tends to throw up stuff like that. Would you rather be invisible or able to fly? So we were all in the room and Joss was there and we kind of looked at it and laughed and it ended up turning into a two-hour argument about who would win.

It was a really heated argument, because *that's* the kind of stuff we love. And, of course, when you're in the room breaking the story, you'll talk about anything except the story for as long as you can. It was such a fun time working with them. Sometimes I wanted to kill them, but most of the time, it's just like family. It is just the best place ever to have grown up, just amazing.

JOSE MOLINA

We would always meet out in the smoking patio and the first question everybody asked was "Did you get him today?" "No, we got him yesterday; we're supposed to get him later today." "Oh no, he's directing now, we won't see him for a week." So we would always be comparing notes. "How are you doing? Are you ahead or are you behind? What's the story you're breaking?" Because we all knew everybody else's shows and we all got each other's scripts so that we would be up to date on what the other shows were doing. We would kind of collaborate and give notes and pitch in ideas. I don't know how many ideas ever made it across staffs, but I had a ton of conversations with Craft and Fain and with Mere Smith, who were on *Angel* at the time. And with David Fury and you know, whoever came knocking. Sometimes creative, sometimes personal.

The Mutant Enemy writers really became one team, which is interesting because when I was an assistant on *Angel,* I found out about this softball league called the Prime-Time Softball League. The Prime-Time Softball League is a league where all the TV shows play against each other. If you're not on a TV show, you are not welcome to play in this league. So when I was an assistant on *Angel,* I had two shows to cull from in order to cobble together a team. And I brought it up to Joss and I was like, "Hey Joss, how would you feel if we put the Mutant Enemy shows together and play in this?" And he was like, "Great!" He was so into it for a non-sports guy. He paid for the jerseys and the hats out of his pocket. We were Team Mutant Enemy, and that was the beginning of the cross-pollination between *Buffy* and *Angel.*

Funny story, though: I was in charge of getting the shirts and the hats and Joss was so upset when he saw the shirts and the hats, because they were so fucking ugly that when I came back for *Firefly,* he wouldn't let me have anything to do with it.

KELLY A. MANNERS

I remember Joss on all fours, giving pony rides in the production office to Alyson and Sarah. It was hysterical to see this genius millionaire giving pony rides in the production office.

DAVID FURY

It was extraordinarily unique. There was no social media at that time, but Joss was one of the very first. He told me about "The Bronze," the fan-site posting-board group. They took the name from the club in the show. Joss loved to engage the fans on the posting board with every episode. He said you've got to go on and try this. He was excited about this feedback he could get immediately, and the fact that they treated the writers like rock stars.

When we would go onto the message boards, I can only describe it as being like throwing bread into a pond. Suddenly, all the ducks came in. You'd go on and I'm talking to dozens and dozens of people who were so excited to talk to me, to talk about the writing process, and the show. It was remarkable. It was great and an exhilarating time. I know Joss told the story of when they first went to Comic-Con after the first season and it wasn't even what it is now. They went there and they were mobbed. It blew everyone's mind at the time. They didn't know anybody was watching. They didn't know anybody cared.

YOU GOTTA HAVE FAITH

"Congratulations to the class of 1999. You've all proved more or less adequate. This is a time for celebration, so sit still and be quiet."

The third season finds Buffy lost and confused after season two's heartbreaking finale in which she sends Angel—his soul restored at the last possible moment—to hell to save the world. But with the help of her friends, Buffy begins to slowly rebound from the tragedy until she learns Angel has returned to Sunnydale, a revelation that she hides from everyone else. One of the most exciting additions for the new season was that of actress Eliza Dushku's Faith, a charismatic but highly unstable Vampire Slayer who was created in the aftermath of the death of Kendra the previous year. Initially appearing to be an ally, Faith becomes a formidable agent of the quirky Mayor Richard Wilkins, the season's Big Bad, who is intent on completing a ritual that will allow him to ascend and transform him into a giant demonic snake. And by season's end, the groundwork was laid for David Boreanaz's Angel to be spun off into his own series.

In addition to marking the final year of high school before graduation, the show continued to become even more serialized, eschewing many of the stand-alone stories that had typified the previous seasons.

JOSS WHEDON

(creator/executive producer, *Buffy the Vampire Slayer*)

Third season proved that there was life after *Romeo and Juliet*. How do we keep this fresh? Getting to explore Faith and the dark side of being a Slayer and calling that whole thing into question was really exciting. Also, knowing that we had a countdown on high school stories when we'd only been in high school for two and a half years. There was discussion of whether we should be *Saved by the Bell* and they're in high school forever, and the decision to have them graduate meant that for the first time we were going to get into some serious changes just in terms of the look and the feel and lineup.

DAVID FURY

(writer, season 3, *Buffy the Vampire Slayer*)

There was a change between season two and three. It was kind of that fractured quality. In season two, it didn't seem to be quite coming together yet, and suddenly—and a lot of it was because of the Angelus story—by season three the show was so clearly defined. The staff seemed much more relaxed; there was a little bit more confidence there. The people who were there were just lovely, funny, great people. They were very nice and they were very cordial to me. I'd stop in and introduce myself and tell them I'd just read an episode they wrote or an outline. The thing in the third season that was different from the second was Joss now was more than just filling me in on what they were doing: he wanted me to read their scripts, he wanted me to read outlines, he wanted me to be completely up to date on what they were doing.

JOSS WHEDON

We knew that Angel was going to be leaving. Knowing we had limited time to play up both high school and the Angel-Buffy romance sort of galvanized us and made us pull out all of our stops with what we could do. We also dealt with the last great metaphor, sex. The bite in "Graduation Day, Part II" was a big deal.

JOSE MOLINA

(executive story editor, *Firefly*)

Buffy started out very much monster of the week. There were definitely instances in season one and two of *Buffy* where you could watch an episode not having any idea of what the serialized story was and walk away having enjoyed it. The way you would a Star Trek, for instance, or *The X-Files*. Starting in season three, the season of Faith and the Mayor, it became the first season where if you missed an episode you were missing something because of the Mayor's plot and Mr. Trick and Faith and what they were doing to help the Mayor's plan. The show evolved kind of naturally into 80-20 monster of the week to being more 50-50, and by the time they launched *Angel*, the network wanted monster of the week and something that people could pick up without having seen anything else, and that, honestly, didn't work.

SARAH LEMELMAN

(author, *"It's About Power":* Buffy the Vampire Slayer's *Stab at Establishing the Strength of Girls on American Television*)

Another relatively unused television tactic that the show helped promulgate was the use of long-story arcs. When the program aired in 1997, the most common form of storytelling was episodic storytelling, where the stories of each episode started and ended and never carried over into succeeding episodes. While *Buffy* was not the first show to break this stand-alone episode format, it was one of the few shows in the late 1990s that consistently used long arcs successfully with its "Big Bad" evil plans of the season. In this way, viewers became "addicted" to the show and had a reason to return since the completion of an episode did not mean the completion of a story line. This type of storytelling is now commonplace and a standard in television.

DAVID GREENWALT

(executive producer, *Buffy the Vampire Slayer*)

The networks were terrified of too much serialization at that time.

THOMAS P. VITALE

(executive vice president, Programming and Original Movies, Syfy and Chiller)

Buffy was a binge-worthy show at a time when the only primetime shows with truly serialized story lines had been the nighttime soaps—earlier shows like *Peyton Place, Dallas, Dynasty, Knots Landing,* and *Soap,* and shows contemporary with *Buffy* like *Melrose Place* and *Beverly Hills 90210. The X-Files* waded carefully into serialized storytelling, reserving only a portion of episodes each season for mythology, but the majority of *X-Files* episodes were purely monster of the week; *X-Files* never fully embraced serialized storytelling.

STEVE BIODROWSKI

(editor in chief, *Cinefantastique*)

Buffy the Vampire Slayer was definitely part of a trend toward what I would call tribalism, in which popularity was dependent less on churning out great episodes than on using continuing story lines to hook viewers, who began to see themselves as "insiders" who "got it" while everyone on the outside was hopelessly out of it.

The X-Files fell into this trap a few years before *Buffy*. And a year after *Buffy* ceased production, *Lost* picked up this approach and ran with it big-time. David Greenwalt started *Grimm*'s first season with mostly stand-alone episodes, but now it's totally into series continuity. *The Walking Dead* almost ritualistically pads its season with do-nothing episodes, knowing the audience will stick around because they've invested five years in watching the characters.

STEVEN S. DEKNIGHT

(writer, season five, *Buffy the Vampire Slayer*)

Joss admits it himself that he works best in the serialized format. We had to try to strike some kind of balance, because the network really liked stand-alone episodes because they can re-air them. And when it's serialized, the numbers for re-airing them are very low. So it's that kind of balance. It was the same thing with *Alias* and *24*—although *24* was designed that way. If it's serialized to the point that we were, somebody just dropping in won't understand what the hell is going on.

JOSS WHEDON

Something else that our audience seemed to eat up was our switching from stand-alone episodes to the episodic ones, the ones that prolong our running plot. We got that idea, actually from *The X-Files,* but it wasn't like, "Oh, let's try it because it worked for them." It was more like, we know what we want to do, we have continuing relationships and have things change, and have arcs for people. We wanted to do stand-alone monsters. The thing with *The X-Files* for us was that it just showed, yes, this can be done, and very efficiently.

DAVID GREENWALT

Even on *The X-Files* they said that even a regular fan is seeing every second or third show. Only the rabid people were seeing every episode. There was so much natural serialization of *Buffy* because we were so into the emotions of all the characters. We could do stand-alone episodes but that still had all the great Buffy-Cordelia conflicts. We serviced a lot of that kind of stuff. But you can't all be just about feelings and stuff. You still need a villain and a crime.

THOMAS P. VITALE

Buffy broke ground in serialized television, especially for television aimed at a young adult demographic, which previously hadn't been offered many quality continuing stories. After all, most primetime soaps were aimed squarely at an adult audience, not a teen–young adult audience. It can even be said that Buffy paved the way for all of the serialized superhero shows currently finding a teen and young adult audience on the CW. And like those CW superhero shows, Buffy appealed to both fanboys/fangirls as well as the general audience, and from a demo perspective, *Buffy* appealed to teens and young adults but also to a more mainstream older audience.

DAVID FURY

They offered [my wife] Elin and me a job for season three, but Elin decided to do sitcoms so he couldn't offer me the job until he saw what I could do on my own. He allowed me to pitch stories for season three and that was a story that became "Helpless." It was about Buffy turning eighteen years old and had to do with these tests that the Watcher's Council puts Slayers through on their eighteenth birthday.

My original pitch was that Buffy was going to be drugged by Giles, but she was going to hallucinate and think that her friends had become vampires and she comes home and her mother's a vampire. Basically, it was a way of taking away her support group—the family unit she has that's the basis of her support—and how does she respond? Is she able to? How is she able to function along those lines? I pitched that and they liked it, but I think they had just come up with the episode "The Wish," where Willow is a vampire and different people from her life are vampires, so they couldn't do that. Joss came up with the idea of taking Buffy's powers away.

Here is the pitch, and this is my sitcom thinking, by the way. I said that after Buffy fails, Giles would be fired. This would be like the midpoint of the episode, and by the end Buffy does something to somehow make amends and Giles gets rehired again. But the thing that Joss really responded to was, "Oh my God, Giles gets fired." He just wanted that. It's an episode where Giles is no longer a Watcher. I was going, "I don't want to lose Giles's job. I pitched this, but I wanted him to get his job back." Somehow the idea became a permanent part of the mythology of the show. A significant event that Joss would hang on to is Giles will never be her Watcher again. He most responded to that.

The pitch was bought, the changes made about Buffy losing her powers, and instead of Giles getting his job back, he *never* gets his job back. That's what they bought and that's what I got to go write. I didn't know what was going to happen with Giles, but Joss said Giles getting fired will give us an opportunity for Buffy to have a new Watcher. It opened the door for Wesley, who showed up a couple of episodes later in an episode Doug [Petrie] wrote.

As important as Alexis Denisof would become to the show as Wesley Wyndam-Pryce (as well as to costar Alyson Hannigan, whom he met on the series and would marry a few years later at the tony Palm Springs spa and resort, Two Bunch Palms), looming equally large in the series mythology was the arrival of Faith, played by Eliza Dushku, all grown up from her turn as Arnold Schwarzenegger's pouty and profane daughter in James Cameron's *True Lies*.

JAMES MARSTERS
(actor, Spike)

I remember getting off the show after the second season and the character was done with at that point; there were no plans to have him back. I remember thinking over the summer break, "Try to do the show without me now. Never, never succeed without me now that you've tasted it—now that you've bit into the mountaintop; you won't be able to help yourself." And, of course, Joss made up the character Faith. I remember watching a couple of episodes with Faith and then being like, "God! He can do it without me. No problem. He doesn't need me at all."

ELIZA DUSHKU
(actress, Faith)

Buffy really came out of the blue for me. It had been two years since I had worked. Sarah Michelle Gellar and me had an agent and manager in common, and so I had met her probably years before. I originally went in for five shows in season three and then they kind of came up and said, "Would you be the villain this season?" and I'm going, "Yeah, that would be amazing."

I knew that it would be a fun job to take on, and by that point I knew I loved working with those people. So I stayed on and just through the writers and I, we just kind of created this character that the fans really responded to. For me, it was almost like a little bit of therapy. When I first started playing Faith, I had just graduated high school. I was seventeen years old. All of a sudden I'm out of the house and I'm moving out to L.A. I was actually enrolled in a university before I got *Buffy* and I had to withdraw.

SARAH LEMELMAN

Faith is a true Madonna figure, in that she not only embraces her sexuality but also enjoys the male body as well. She takes full advantage of what Camille Paglia calls "woman's cosmic dominance" and uses her magnetic nature to allure men. Men flock to her, as is seen in "Bad Girls," when her provocative dancing at the Bronze attracts a crowd of male dancers around her. Faith is frequently seen in control of men, drawing power over them through her sexuality. She is the type of woman that Paglia describes as "a prowler and predator, self-directed and no one's victim." With her nonchalant attitude of sex and her ability to dominate men with her body, Faith thoroughly transgresses sex roles. Faith shows that women should not be afraid of their sexuality, and instead wield it as a weapon—a temptation no man can resist.

CHARISMA CARPENTER
(actress, Cordelia Chase)

Eliza is Mother Nature on wheels; that's how much of a force she is. Adore her—she's still very much a live wire. She's changed a lot over the years and I forget how young she was. She's just a weird combination—she has this really strong energy and she's very powerful and forceful. It's so interesting to watch her process.

ELIZA DUSHKU

High school was hell in a way. It was *so* hard. I went to public school in Boston after having been an actress since I was ten years old, so I had that element of just being different in an environment where any kind of difference you have makes you kind of an outcast and an automatic target. I really built up this tough shell, and it was all no-bullshit. It was a bit of a façade, but at the same time it was my reality, because just to survive you kind of have to have the attitude, "Nothing hurts me; you can't get through to me." I was kind of this really hard Boston chick. That worked well for Faith and for the creation of that character Joss really zoned into that and we worked with it.

DAVID GREENWALT

She has a really natural talent, you know? She just had this kind of power and it was a good mixing of part and actor. She was a little green, I believe.

ELIZA DUSHKU

Sometimes they seem to be different manifestations of my different personalities. I think we all do have interesting people in us. I try to mix it up, keep it fun, keep it real, keep it interesting. But it's always a circumstance where the grass is greener. When you're on a comedy, you're like, "I need to do something serious." I was doing *The New Guy* and *City by the Sea* pretty much simultaneously. It was night and day. The characters were so different. It makes it fun and kind of interesting. For me, I think I have to see a streetwise element to the character. I like to see intelligent young women in roles and as characters. I gravitate toward that streetwise element.

I grew up with three older brothers, so I thought I was a boy until I was like ten! I was all about having a crew cut and wearing hand-me-downs, and cheerleading was a girly sport in a way, unless you're a guy being a cheerleader. So I was just never into that.

KELLY A. MANNERS
(producer, *Buffy the Vampire Slayer*)

We had to emancipate her. She was only seventeen that first season, and she knew that this was her big break. She brought high energy and the character was fantastic.

ELIZA DUSHKU

It was really not as black and white as "I divorced my parents," which I know happens a lot in this business. My mother has never been a stage mom. I lived in Boston my whole life, even like the seven or eight years that I was doing films, and she always wanted me to be in high school. When my grades weren't doing so well from on-set tutoring, she said, "Forget the movies, girl." She is a government professor at a university and she said, "I want you to come back to town, go into public school and get good grades in your junior and senior years, and just live the life of a junior and senior in high school." It really was always her just wanting the best for me, and so I graduated high school with my class, went to the prom, and enrolled at university in my mom's school. I was all set up, I went to orientation, I had my dorm all sorted out. Meanwhile, my mom was already planning to go to Romania to write a book for the year, so she was going to be out of the country.

I was seventeen when I graduated, so when *Buffy* came up, it was really a hard choice because, originally, they only wanted me for five shows, which turned into more. But at the same time I was really, really excited about going to school. So we did the emancipation knowing that my mother was going to be out of the country and because I was ready to go out and be independent. In fact, the sole reason for the emancipation was so that I could be a legal adult for work, and especially the night shoots on *Buffy*, because otherwise, if you're classed as a child, you can't work past a certain hour.

DAVID GREENWALT

When I was on *The Wonder Years,* of which I wrote three and directed four, I had the time of my life. Fred Savage was just born to do that part and he had really good parents. They gave him $10 a week allowance. He comes up to me one day and says, "I got this date and I can take her to a café or a movie, but I don't have enough money to do both." I said, "You got the greatest parents in the world."

KELLY A. MANNERS

I did *Dollhouse* with Eliza as well. She could bring a conflict that we didn't have before; she came between Buffy and Angel and just the whole group of them. She was a great addition. It brought a darkness to it, too, which was nice and welcome. It always had its dark elements, but Faith was such a dark character. It made the show that much better.

ELIZA DUSHKU

Truthfully, though, I get misunderstood sometimes, because everyone says, "Oh, you just love to play the bad girl because she's so bad and because it's just so fun to be evil." It's not just about that. It's about I have a connection to a bad-girl character that makes it more than just so black and white, and more than just so evil. People that were watching Faith were really surprised when, at times, they felt sympathy for her or they felt compassion and it wasn't just, "Oh, here is this black-and-white monster bad girl." I think that it's more about just playing interesting women and having contrast so that there is more to the girl next door.

DAVID FURY

It's another example of bringing up Sarah's game and having another layer on the show, one who plays up her sexuality. Playing bad girls is better than playing good girls for an actor; there's always going to be more ripeness to it. There never seemed to be any tension between them that I ever witnessed. But certainly the characters themselves—you kind of have to raise your game. Her character was just the sexier version of what Buffy was, because Buffy is the good girl and more grounded. Buffy is beautiful and can play a great romantic scene, but to have someone with Eliza's sexuality out there, dancing, there's always that homoerotic quality that's going on between them, too. They were two sides of the same coin.

SARAH LEMELMAN

Mayor Richard Wilkins is the Big Bad of season three and serves as both an ally and loving father figure to Faith. After Faith accidentally kills a man, she becomes out of control and is rejected by Buffy and the rest of the Scooby Gang. It is then that the Mayor takes her under his wing and treats her as if she is his own daughter.

HARRY GROENER
(actor, Mayor Richard Wilkins)

That was a very interesting and special relationship, because it was unconditional. His seeming love for her I felt was unconditional, and I don't think she ever had that before. It doesn't matter what you think; I'm going to love you no matter what. Faith got that kind of relationship, and he got a daughter that he could never really have, because he's immortal.

DAVID FURY

The Mayor character becoming a daddy figure to the bad girl was great. Giles is always the father figure to Buffy. The Mayor became the father figure to Faith. It just created this great dichotomy. It's always fun to write villains; it's fun to write bad girls, which is why we played around with Buffy in later years where she becomes a little bit of a bad girl with Spike. That's always much more of a fun place to be.

SARAH LEMELMAN

At first, Faith very clearly does not understand the Mayor's impetus to spoil her—he is the first character on the show to treat her as a human being, rather than a monster or outsider. Slowly, she warms up to the Mayor and the two share an eerily disturbing bond, where Faith is depicted as an equal as well as a young daughter to him. In one scene where the two are discussing a plan, the Mayor breaks off and says, "You know what I wish? I wish you'd pull your hair back. I know, fashion isn't exactly my thing, but gosh darn, you have such a nice face, I can't understand why you hide it!"

HARRY GROENER

A lot of the fans say over and over again that one of the things that was so scary about the Mayor was that he's like your neighbor. He's like your uncle. He's just your guy next door. A lot of it was on the page, so it was just how you interpreted it. Joss and I were on the same page about that particular thing. He would always be the person to check me if I ever got to a point where it was too mustache-twirly. He would always say, "No, just throw it away, throw it away." That was a great note. Because he's so sure of himself. Mayor Wilkins is so sure of the course of his trajectory and where he's going. He seems to be very clear about it. The only time that confidence is in jeopardy is when Faith is in jeopardy. When she is in trouble, that was a weakness for him and that was eventually something that took him down.

SARAH LEMELMAN

The Mayor effortlessly changes conversation topics with Faith: at one moment talking about an assassination, to the next moment, where he wants her to "load up on calcium." He is the ultimate patriarch; Richard Wilkins leads the town of Sunnydale, is the ruthless head of a dark organization, and is a kind and caring father to Faith. Like the Master, the Mayor represents a failure of familial patriarchy, because he cannot protect that which he holds most dearly. Once a stranger, Faith becomes an inspiration to him, but in one of their missions to distract Buffy from the Mayor's actual agenda, Buffy puts Faith in a coma. As the doctor in the hospital describes to the

Mayor the injuries that Faith sustained, his face changes to pure horror. At that moment, he overhears a nurse speaking about another case that has just come in the hospital, and by the description, it is clearly Buffy.

With no remorse, he moves to suffocate Buffy, until Angel pulls the Mayor off of Buffy. The Mayor's response to this is his shriek of "Murderous little fiend! Do you see what she did to my Faith?" This act of trying to kill Buffy solidifies his bond with Faith, as he is painted as a father having lost his daughter. Faith's growing dependence on the Mayor and her demise at the hands of Buffy show the failures of familial patriarchy. The Mayor is unable to protect Faith, despite his great power and affection for her.

ARMIN SHIMERMAN
(actor, Principal Snyder)

I had cast Gregory Itzin, who's an old friend of mine, as the Mayor in my head. But lo and behold, one of my dearest friends is Harry Groener. So I was tickled when Harry got cast, and Harry did a brilliant job as the Mayor.

HARRY GROENER

Mr. Trick was a wonderful Steppenwolf [Theatre Company] actor named K. Todd Freeman. In fact, I had seen him in a fabulous show on Broadway, and Ladysmith Black Mambazo was the chorus. It was one of the most brilliant pieces of theater I'd ever seen. And he was the lead.

Less well known was the fact that, unbeknownst to most, Charisma Carpenter was still grappling with severe anxiety that had complicated her work on the show from the beginning of the series.

CHARISMA CARPENTER

It's amazing what people will and won't put up with. I feel people will put up with bad behavior before they'll put up with something that's costing them money. That's just the facts. If you're late or you're mean to people or you're challenging ideas and you're creating angst among people, it's not appreciated and people will talk about it. But I was having meetings in which my producers were calling me in, my agents were being called, and it was just an awful situation. I could cry just saying this: obstacles are so important; they give perspective, so when they come, you can go, "I earned this, I deserve this," and you're not lost in that, because you worked for it—it wasn't just given to you. I had to overcome a lot and it keeps me grounded.

I've had huge things to overcome, and I tried really hard to learn as much as I could and absorb as much as I could and, fortunately, I worked with a lot of professional people who've been doing it for a long time and they were great examples. But I remember a cameraman being so mad at me that I wouldn't hit my mark, and it was literally my first job. When I first did *Buffy*, I was still doing *Malibu Shores* with not a lot of experience under my belt. We were shooting both shows at the same time and I didn't have a lot of on-set experience, and this cameraman was like, "What's wrong with you?" He was so annoyed, saying, "It's really important you hit your mark." I made a joke about putting a sandbag down. I just learned on the job and am thankful for the people that surrounded me at the time who had been doing this for a long time and am grateful to have learned from them.

I didn't know it was anxiety at the time. I just thought I was stupid. I beat myself up about it, and I would obsess about my dialogue, and I would study for hours. I'd bought my first house in 1999 and I'm living with someone and I was never present. I couldn't enjoy my house, because I was constantly trying to figure out what was happening. Do I just need to study harder, memorize longer? There was no space left in my head to just be. It just got really nasty—it was a really big thing to overcome for a few years, but I think my bosses knew that it wasn't about me not trying or putting in the work, because they would see me with my script and my coaching lessons and I would break down the script and write it out a hundred times.

I would apply what I learned in school and I knew that writing it out for me would help. Then I would have an acting coach help me memorize stuff at home where you toss a pillow back and forth and I would try to recite the stuff when you're doing an action and you try to recall things; it makes you work both sides of your brain. I did everything. I went to a psychiatrist, I took antianxiety medications, whatever would assist me to put my best foot forward.

HARRY GROENER

In television you have to make your choices very quickly and you develop a kind of short-term memory. You can keep it in your head for twenty minutes. And then after that it's gone until you put it back in. Just enough to get the take. We did that. You had the short-term memory where you kept it all for the rehearsal and for shooting, but the next day it's gone.

CHARISMA CARPENTER

I think my bosses knew my heart and knew how much I cared, so they wouldn't fire me just because of my work ethic and because of my passion and my extreme effort to overcome what I was going through. Then there came a time, I think it was the third season of *Buffy,* when they were like, "What can we do to help you?" And I said, "I need an acting teacher on set to run lines with me." Really, what I probably needed to do was to stop running lines. I needed to stop and relax, which is easier said than done. That's so cliché: how do you let go when you're driven like me?

So that was my big thing, and my costars were probably annoyed and it didn't bode well with my relationships with them. *Not* that they were mean; there was no drama like that. But you know, poor Sarah, spending thousands and thousands of hours on a set, I just can't imagine that this girl, six years younger than me, who was working her ass off, consummate professional, and then, it's Charisma's turn! There was shame around it and the anxiety and fear and really empathizing with everyone I was working with.

With all of that, Carpenter was also dealing with insecurities over the fact that the show's growing fandom had not yet embraced the character of Cordelia, the actress believing it having to do with Cordy's perceived bitchiness.

CHARISMA CARPENTER

I remember in the first season how when fans would come to set or come to our location they were there to see Willow and, of course, Buffy. No one was looking for Cordelia. I say it because she was so mean. I remember the difference when I made the jump between *Buffy* and *Angel* and she became more fleshed out.

First of all, they loved to hate her, and at some point—I think it was in season three of *Buffy*; it was during the homecoming episode, and I have to do this spatula thing, where I'm swatting the air with my spatula and Buffy is looking at me like, God help me—and I remember just going to Joss and David and saying, "I'm so tired of being the damsel in distress, the stupid one, the idiot." Like that's such a good idea! I had all these ideas about Cordelia, like why does she have to be such a slut and making out all the time and I don't like that; I don't like this image. I probably said only those two things in the entirety of the series, and I remember being shut down so succinctly. Joss said to me, "But that's why America loves you." I was like, "OK, I'll just keep doing that then."

Honestly, I never felt that fan love for the first three seasons of *Buffy*. I would go everywhere and people knew I was on the show, but people would never come up to me. I guess I was a very convincing bitch. People even to this day on Twitter never call me by my name, they called me Cordy or Cordelia. It's silly. I laugh at it, but then it's hard from tweets to discern whether they're doing it to be sarcastic—it's a beloved character, and I'm so grateful that she's finally beloved. It took a while for people to warm up to her.

In the penultimate episode of the third season, Angel is poisoned by Faith, and the only way to save his life is for him to drink the blood of a Slayer. A reluctant Buffy attempts to procure the lifesaving antidote by killing the only other Slayer in Sunnydale, which leads to a violent fight between the two in which a defeated Faith falls off her apartment building and onto a truck, putting her in a coma. In a desperate effort to save Angel's life, Buffy decides to let him feed off of her as Mayor Wilkins prepares for his ascension, culminating with his commencement address to the students of Sunnydale High before he transforms, destroying the school in the process.

ARMIN SHIMERMAN

When they finally did kill me off, they did exactly what I asked Joss to do, which was to have me eaten. When I knew that they were going to graduate from school, I didn't know how they were going to graduate, but I knew that they were seniors and were graduating and I knew that I was no longer needed. I said, "Listen, I know you're going to have to get rid of me one way or another, but I want to be eaten." Because Flutie was eaten. And they agreed to my wishes.

HARRY GROENER

During the transformation, they rigged the suit to sort of fall apart. There were two people on either side, holding twelve fishing lines each that they were to pull at the appropriate time and it would fall apart. So the transition starts and I feel this pull and pull and the damn thing is not coming apart. So we set it again and try again. What's the problem? We don't know; we're not sure. Try it again—it would not work. Ultimately, we never got the suit to work on that night. So we had to go to a green screen and do it again. Even then it didn't work the way they had envisioned.

Season three is also marked by some of the series' most fun episodes, including "Band Candy," in which the adults of Sunnydale all revert to adolescent behaviors after eating the titular band candy due to the sinister machinations of the enigmatic Ethan Rayne, and "Lovers Walk," in which a lovelorn and heartbroken Spike returns to Sunnydale after being dumped by Drusilla.

ARMIN SHIMMERMAN

I'm very proud of "Band Candy." It was great, great fun. Certainly in my career in front of the camera that's the freest I've ever been. I decided I was just going to have a hoot and did. When I came back for the next episode, which was probably three or four weeks later, I remember both Sarah and Alyson just quoting my lines from "Band Candy" at me. To this day, I go to conventions and people ask me to repeat, "Summers, you drive like a spaz."

I consider myself to be an enormously lucky person. My contract with Paramount with *Star Trek* said that I was only allowed to do one other TV show a year. For some reason, the line producer, my fairy godfather, Steve Oster, decided I could do whatever I wanted. And it wasn't just *Buffy*. I went off to do *Seinfeld*. I did *Stargate*, and other shows as well. The true hero here was Steve Oster and the assistant director on *Buffy*, Brenda Kalosh. They juggled their schedules so that they could get me on different days. However, there were two days during the course of my working both shows when I left *Star Trek* in the early afternoon; drove to Torrance, where we usually shot the exteriors for *Buffy*; and then would go to work for *Buffy*. Those two days were enormously long.

In fact, one of those days I remember specifically was a "Band Candy" day. It was difficult as far as hours, but it was enormously invigorating. I cannot explain this to the regular public, and very few actors understand this as well, but it's like doing repertory theater. By doing two disparate characters, doing one made me excited about doing the other, because I didn't get bored with doing the same character three years or seven years straight. It was a chance to get my batteries recharged, because I was doing different characters. It was enormously invigorating, but it also was a lot of time. My wife, Kitty, didn't see me for long swaths of time, because I'd get up early in the morning for either one of the shows and not come home until very late.

Later, when I had friends on *Voyager,* I would say to them, "You know, you really should try to do other shows," but the line producer on that show stuck by the Paramount contract and didn't let them out. So I was enormously lucky.

DAN VEBBER

In "Lovers Walk," we were stuck on this outline with the idea that Xander and Willow were trapped in a basement somewhere and the Scoobies had to find some way to find them. How the hell do they do it? Do they have a tracker on them or something like that? I, at some point, came up with the fact that Oz is a werewolf, so maybe when he gets stressed out he can sniff out Willow. I think that they ended up using that in other episodes as well. So that was a contribution of mine.

"Lovers Walk" marked the return of a series fan favorite, James Marsters's Spike, whose character would grow in importance throughout the remainder of the series, which is surprising given at the end of the second season it appeared Spike was toast.

JAMES MARSTERS
(actor, Spike)

I didn't really see Joss that much. He didn't direct the first episode I was in. It all went very quickly. People were telling me that it was really fun to watch, and so I thought I was really in and then was surprised when Joss walked by me and got in my face—didn't push me up against the wall—but I backed up into a wall and he shook his finger at me and said, "I don't care how popular you are, kid, you are dead! You are dead, do you hear me? Dead."

I was like, *What the fuck?* I've come to realize what was happening was Spike was imperiling the theme of the show. Evil is not cool to Joss Whedon, and I really respect him for that. He thinks of evil as being pathetic, which I agree with. In *Buffy the Vampire Slayer,* vampires are metaphors for the challenges that you overcome in adolescence. And so vampires are supposed to be very ugly and quickly killed off. And that's why we had the vamp face in *Buffy,* so that the moment when we bite people is never sensual. It's always horrific. He once told me, "I don't like that Anne Rice crap; that's not what I'm going for." He had gotten talked into one romantic vampire character by his writing partner, then David Greenwalt, which was Angel, who just took off like a rocket ship. By the time I got on the show, there were already plans that he would have his own show. I think Joss had said, "OK, that's one. We'll do one. No more romantic vampires, that's it."

Then I came along. The character wasn't designed to be romantic—the audience wasn't supposed to respond to me that way. But I think once you made my hair blond and allowed me to have that much mascara on . . . it probably explains *why* the audience thought of me as a romantic character. But that was really dangerous, and this was in the beginning of season two and I think Joss was afraid that the show was slipping away and was just going to become another show about hot, young vampires, which to him is much less interesting.

I am forever amazed and grateful that, in the face of that, he decided *not* to kill me off. To, instead, really engage with the character and this universe and this theme. It speaks to his courage and his talent that he did that. Because, I gotta tell you, I produced theater in Chicago and Seattle: I would've killed me off in a heartbeat . . . probably before five episodes. As soon as the audience said, "Oh, he's romantic," I'd have killed me off after two episodes just to, you know, get it out of the way. So I'm very lucky.

DAN VEBBER

"Lovers Walk" was an episode that was not as heavily rewritten as "The Zeppo." My pitch to Joss for that episode was "we should do a *Rosencrantz & Guildenstern* episode, where it's following a really boring character, and in the background the most exciting, world-ending story is taking place and we just don't even address it." He liked that idea and he ended up doing it. In my draft, the B story was brought to the forefront and the A story was in the background, whereas in Joss's draft of it he had brought up the B story much more. I feel like it might have lost a little bit of that *Rosencrantz & Guildenstern* element, but, for all I know, it wouldn't have been watchable if that were the case.

ARMIN SHIMERMAN

I knew I was going to be gotten rid of certainly when they graduated, so there would be no reason to have me move on to their college existence. None whatsoever. It wasn't as though I was a good friend. They weren't going to use me to solve problems or anything like that. The writing was on the wall. Except for asking to be eaten, I had no other input into my character. Except, one has to say, because I've learned this from years of television work, what the actor brings to the character influences the writing. The actor doesn't necessarily have to say anything. But simply by choices that the actor makes in the course of acting the character in dailies, writers, producers see things and they go, "You know, we can go a little further with that." "Oh, we can see that, you know, Armin has a tendency to go this way as a choice in the character, so we can further that or we can go in a different direction." So I didn't actually say anything, but I'm sure my performance spoke reams to them.

DAVID FURY

There were a couple of missteps, but overall I thought season three was great. It introduced Faith, who was a phenomenal character, and the Mayor was great. I was so happy to be a part of it. We also knew it was going to be the last season of high school, which was going to throw the show into a whole new direction when we got into season four. It's a very different dynamic in college than in high school. Joss first sold the show as "high school is hell."

Everybody gets that. That was the perfect allegory. But college doesn't hold that kind of weight. High school is such a microcosm of society, but college really isn't. College is something more open and more about adulthood and it just didn't have the same clear allegorical signposts that high school does.

Season three was the last year of high school and it was our last attempt to try and tap into them as much as we can. "The Prom" episode is great. The acknowledgment of the class body understanding what Buffy has meant to them. There were a lot of great emotional things in that episode, and Angel was being transitioned out at that point. Overall, it was a really good season and maybe [it was] because I was thrilled to be so much a part of it that it felt so warm and fuzzy. When you're doing twenty-two episodes, they're not all going to be golden, and nothing would ever top the Angelus story at that point. We were in a state of transition. High school to college and Angel to his own show, which had its own growing problems.

HARRY GROENER

By the time I died, I was actually sad, not because of not being able to do it anymore, but because I wanted to know what happened to the kids after graduation. I didn't want to leave that story yet.

THE SPY WHO LOVED ME

"Welcome to the story of the world! Things fall apart, Buffy. Evil comes and goes. But the way people manage is they don't do it alone."

After barely surviving high school graduation (literally!), the Scooby Gang heads off to college sans Xander, who continues living at home. As such, it was a season of major changes, on screen and off. Spike became a series regular after being abandoned by Drusilla, and is rendered incapable of harming humans due to a chip implanted in his head by a secret government organization that fights and studies demons known as the Initiative, its base of operations located rather conveniently in the bowels of UC Sunnydale.

And with the departure of Seth Green's Oz, Willow meets a fellow Wiccan, Tara Maclay (Amber Benson), who will become an important love interest for the series and a groundbreaking lesbian relationship on television. At the same time, Xander begins an unlikely but charming romance with the acerbic Anya Jenkins, the former vengeance demon from third season's delightful episode "The Wish," in which Cordelia found herself in a world in which the Slayer never came to Sunnydale.

DAVID FURY
(producer, *Buffy the Vampire Slayer*)

Joss wanted to get Xander into a relationship, because Cordelia left to be on *Angel*. Anya was not meant to be a character that returned. That was a one-shot deal, but then he hit upon the idea of, What if it's her? It's always great when you can pull from the history of the show rather than just introducing a character. So you realize, "I can use that girl Anya for that," and they were great together. That was a really fun couple. More so than Cordelia and Xander. She was so great. I loved writing for them, and there was a terrific dynamic between the two of them.

More pivotal, however, was the relationship between Buffy and new boyfriend, Riley Finn, played by actor Marc Blucas, a graduate student who is also a top soldier in the Initiative under the guidance of Buffy's professor Maggie Walsh (Lindsay Crouse). The intent of Walsh and the organization is a merging of demons and cybernetics to create deadly supersoldiers, which eventually leads to the reveal of season four's Big Bad, Adam. Domo arigato, Mr. Roboto?

SARAH LEMELMAN

(author, *"It's About Power":* Buffy the Vampire Slayer*'s Stab at Establishing the Strength of Girls on American Television)*

The Initiative is introduced to the show in season four, which immediately follows Buffy's "graduation" from the Council. Buffy gets involved with the Initiative when she discovers that her college boyfriend, Riley Finn, is a rising star of this secret demon-hunting government agency. From the instant she walks into its operations, she is ostracized. Buffy is one of the few females in the facility and sticks out like a sore thumb with the way she dresses and speaks.

When a room of Initiative soldiers and Buffy are briefed on a demon, or what they call "hostile subterrestials" (HSTs), Buffy is noticeably frowned upon by all of the soldiers, including Riley. She asks questions in a childlike and unprofessional manner ("Why can't we damage this poke-a-things arms?"), and when it is suggested that she change out of her bright salmon-colored halter top into the camouflage suits that every other soldier sports, she declines, not wanting to look "all Private Benjamin." Buffy's deviation from the norm is both ridiculed and laughed at, as the camera pans the room of angry and amused faces of soldiers.

JOSS WHEDON

(creator/executive producer, *Buffy the Vampire Slayer*)

Season four was about, How do you keep the group together without being sort of *90210* about it, and believably? The answer is, you don't. By season four, we were into mission statement. Season two was "Spike and Dru"—and then we realized we were doing the Angel thing—and then that became the season. Season three we knew we were going to do the Faith thing and graduate and there was going to be some growing up to do. We didn't come into real mission statements until season four, because things were so different. What we said was this is the first year of college, the first year of college is about being able to do whatever the hell you want, completely losing yourself and trying on new identities and changing and obviously in Willow's case changing a lot. Exploring sexuality, exploring freedom to fuck your boyfriend all day, which Buffy did for a while.

There are periods you go through where it's, "My God, nobody's watching and we can do whatever we want." Giles had been fired and was completely at loose ends. The man had a sombrero on, for God's sake. And the group kind of got torn apart by it. Plus the introduction of Riley into Buffy's life, something that, no matter what, we knew was going to be difficult and strange. Add all that to "Let's play our James Bond fantasies" with the whole idea of the Initiative.

DAVID FURY

It was weird. I remember writing a scene in "The I in Team" where I directly ripped off *From Russia with Love* where it's obviously a training exercise and the lights kind of come on. We think it's Buffy, but it's actually just a training exercise. I'm a Bond fan. If we're going to have a secret-agent organization, I'm going to do a little Bond homage.

JOSS WHEDON

That's pretty much season four. Let's have the cool night-vision goggles. Of course with our budget we had, like, three walls and a shrub—but it was cool in our minds.

DAVID FURY

It was exciting for Joss to challenge himself. For the rest, it became trickier because high school was the perfect allegory for the show. Once we blew up the high school and moved to college, things became less universal. A lot of people don't go to college, so trying to find that allegory in the stories became a little bit more challenging. We were able to latch on to a few things.

One of the things was Xander being the one friend who doesn't go to college and feels left behind. But trying to find what is the commonality in college was trickier.

I got to do a haunted frat house. This was about Buffy and her friends venturing into adulthood, which eventually led to Joyce's death and all these other things that were not part of the show's makeup initially. That said, the creation of the Initiative that Joss had brought to the show, we were somewhat confused by initially. We were trying to figure out what was the allegory. What we came around to believe is there are forces beyond us and as we get into adulthood, we start to understand how complex the world really is and how governments work and it's not about petty little things. It's about a much bigger world. That's sort of what we latched on to.

MARTI NOXON
(supervising producer)

When they read my first script for season four, Joss and David left a message on my answering machine saying my script "didn't cut it," before revealing they were joking and loved it.

Significant additional changes came from the fact that Charisma Carpenter's Cordelia Chase and David Boreanaz had departed the show for the *Angel* spin-off, with the titular hero now seeking redemption on the mean streets of the City of Angels, far from Sunnydale.

JAMES MARSTERS
(actor, Spike)

What changed Joss's mind about bringing me back is he needed a new Cordelia. He needed a character to come in and tell Buffy, "You're stupid; we're all about to die." Cordelia went off to the *Angel* spin-off, so they needed a character to fill those shoes. Joss told me that Sarah actually said, "What about Spike?" Joss thought for a second, "That might work." So, yeah, I was the new Cordelia. In fact, that's why I think I eventually went over to *Angel*, because they lost Cordelia and they needed a new one. I've been following in Cordelia's footsteps ever since.

A major plot point that would reverberate for the rest of the series and set up a far more substantial character arc for Spike in season five was that chip inserted by the Initiative that would prevent him from harming a human (a la Isaac Asimov's three laws of robotics in automatons). Only this chip kept bloodsuckers from biting down on humans like Big Macs.

JAMES MARSTERS

Spike was designed to be a villain, but they decided to keep me around, so they needed to find a way to make Spike a little more recognizable, to put him through experiences that people might actually identify with and kind of take him down off that pedestal of supervillain. It was really important to stop trying to kill Buffy, because if he kept doing that, he was going to either be killed himself or he was going to become pathetic in failing so many times. That was my worry. I didn't see how they were going to fit me in. My fear was that they were going to have to soften him so much that it wouldn't work. But in a way, the situation heightened his frustration and he was even more evil now because he was mad about it.

I was having such a fun time playing the Big Bad, so I was uncomfortable with them taking away my cool. But that's the only way to keep me alive in that universe. In a lot of season four, though, especially the beginning, it wasn't working. You'd see Spike come in in a burning blanket on fire. That was just to get me into the room with the Scooby Gang so I could deliver the line, "Buffy, you're stupid. We're all about to die." It was very cumbersome to get me into the room. It took special effects and everyone was gagging from the fake smoke and I could tell that this just couldn't go on that long. I was not going to be the new Cordelia. I thought, "You know what, they gave me a chance. It's not my fault, but it's not going to happen. I'm probably going to get killed off."

DAVID FURY

Spike was off the show for a while and I don't think there was any intention to bring him back until we wanted to mix things up. To do that, the interesting thing was to put Spike on the side of the good guys, but without selling him out at that time as being a vampire. He's not Angel—he's not the vampire with a soul. How does he become a good guy? So the idea of putting a chip in his head and forcing this creature that wants and needs to kill humans and can't, so he can only get his kicks from killing other demons and vampires, was a way for him to be a reluctant ally and keep him in the mix. It was a very clever way to do that and it provided the means for him to eventually become a domesticated vampire, which would allow him to eventually realize he was in love with Buffy.

JAMES MARSTERS

I didn't like the chip. I recognized that there was a problem to be solved: if you include Spike as a cast member, how do you get him to stop trying to kill Buffy? Because if he keeps trying and you have to fail, that's going to become repetitive and the character's going to be pathetic very quickly. Of course, he can never succeed, obviously. I wanted to have a way that Spike would decide himself to stop trying to kill her for some reason. I felt like the chip was a bit of a deus ex machina, a weak dramatic device and a cop-out. It's an easy way out. I called it "deus ex chip" because there was this machine that was making the decision for us, which I thought was less interesting.

That was the point when I was convinced that it wasn't working and the character was not going to be able to last very long in the show and that they were just cannibalizing him for cheap laughs before he was killed off. I was just in fear and paranoia, so it was horrible. It was all because of my own demons and my own weakness that I was in fear, but I was. I didn't share that with anybody. I was just thinking, this is it. I just didn't see it. It was wonderfully written and part of a great arc and it was all perfect. I was just too scared to appreciate it fully.

But that was a short amount of time, like a month or two. I am an actor who just loves his job. I'm the nerd on the set going, "God, guys, isn't this fun? This is cool, huh?" Other actors couldn't look at me and just say, "We're tired." Whenever they call action, there is a fun to that. So it was never all bad, but it was a little harder to have that fun in Xander's basement.

DAVID FURY

That was not something that Joss knew he was going to do; it's something that sort of came out of a lot of different things, including staff suggestions,

Marti's influence, and things Joss recognized long before things aired that he felt weren't working as well as he hoped. And how do we mix things up? What could we do that would be really cool and surprising? The great idea was to bring back Spike and make him part of the Scooby Gang.

JAMES MARSTERS

My idea was that Spike should fall in love with Buffy. Of course, she never reciprocates because he's way beneath her, but he should fall in love with her and he should try to be good and constantly fail, to comedic effect or to horrifying effect, whichever episode you're doing. But you can go a lot of directions with that, and that will work really well. That wasn't their idea. So, for me it became, How do you do severe migraine without messing up your hair? I stole a page out of William Shatner's book. If you notice, we do "severe headache" very similarly which is we put our knuckles to the side of our head. We don't put our hands through our hair. If you mess your hair up, it's going to take another hour to reset that.

I guess about mid-season, I was hungering for some swagger. I was like, "Spike, is getting really soft here." Even my brother, who is so supportive of everything I do, was like, "Dude, you need to get some balls."

DAVID FURY

The other big change was David Greenwalt was no longer around as Joss's number two. David was a big part of the first three seasons. Joss relied on David very much to be his sounding board for him to test out his ideas. So on those earlier years where I was freelancing for the show, it seemed to be more directed through David and Joss's imaginations rather than the staff. I don't think until season three Joss started to rely on his staff a bit more and started to find some more surprises. Things that surprised himself for the season was through his staff.

So when we got to season four and David had moved on to *Angel,* it was just a different dynamic. Marti moved up into the second sort of position and Marti brought a different thing to the show. She brought a much more emotional angle to it. Often a more romantic angle to the stories that weren't there in the earlier years. All the little heartbreaking things, whether if it was stuff with Tara and Willow or with Xander and Anya.

It was season four that Joss really took Marti under his wing. Joss wanted to mentor Marti into growing into that role. It was a different dynamic where he opened it up more as a staff in terms of relying on them to find some of the ways to get to where he wanted to go.

JOSS WHEDON

We did a lot of things in season four that were different. Some of them met with approval, some less so. Because we get bored. We didn't want to watch the same show every week, and we don't want to make the same show every week. Not having David [Boreanaz] anymore made it easier, because it meant we had new places to go. What had become tough was how could we wring any new changes out of that relationship? Well, we no longer had that problem. Then they were going to college. It was actually an embarrassment of riches.

DAVID FURY

I know it was creatively freeing for Joss. Joss really likes to keep things moving. He likes to challenge himself. The Angel-Buffy relationship had played out. He went to the place where she kills him. That's really more or less what you can do with him. You certainly have the fans and stuff saying this is the love of her life and how can the show go on without Angel? But I'm sure Joss just felt it would open things up in so many different ways.

SARAH LEMELMAN

After Buffy's heartbreak with Angel, it is a long time before she lets anyone in again. It is clear that no other relationship affects her and is as meaningful as her relationship with Angel, but she still strives for some semblance of love in subsequent seasons. Once she graduates high school and enrolls in college at Sunnydale, she meets Riley, who appears to be the perfect all-American boy. They begin a relationship, and it is quickly discovered that Riley is not just an ordinary college boy, but he works as a soldier for a secret government organization known as the Initiative, which hunts down and experiments on demons. Still, he is a far cry from Angel, and Buffy is seen as straddling the fine line of trying to maintain a normal human relationship while still being a powerful Slayer. This puts the two of them in several awkward situations, as Buffy is seen as a stronger and better soldier in Riley's eyes. As a result, a crisis of masculinity is presented where Riley often sees his male status threatened by Buffy.

DAVID FURY

Obviously, the one thing you want to do is make Riley the new love interest for Buffy, but it became kind of clear that the fans weren't reacting. We weren't finding him as interesting a character as we would have liked. Marc Blucas is great, but the chemistry wasn't entirely there. Initially, the excitement of bringing in this cool secret agent to be Buffy's love interest was something Joss was really thrilled with. Marti also had something to do with Marc's casting. I think she just went gaga over him. But the character never quite gelled in the way we wanted.

MARTI NOXON

For my personal taste, and this says a lot about me and my dating history, I liked Riley a lot better once he started to get fucked up. I liked him much better once there was stuff going on with him that I didn't understand or couldn't put my finger on. When he was soldier guy, he just lacked that darkness that is so appealing in our characters. Most of our characters have two sides to them; they're relatively complex. Part of what we were playing with him is that he is presented as the anti-Angel. He was supposed to present kind of a problem to Buffy because he wasn't the scary guy, and could she deal with that? Could she deal with someone who was really there for her and not dangerous?

At the same time, unfortunately, for the audience that was not as interesting. So even though it's a real-life dilemma, it didn't work for some people. Some people loved him unabashedly, as they should have. He's a fine actor and a great-looking guy, but if you're a little twisted like me, it didn't get interesting until he was cheating on her, basically, and going to the dark side of town and getting bitten. That's when I started to feel, "*Now* I want to know more about him."

DAVID FURY

The fact of the matter is characters become far more interesting when they go dark anyway. Riley was such a good guy, a nice, pure, Captain America kind of guy, and it didn't seem to fit in that world. It didn't make us go, "Wow, what a cool guy." It was "What a Boy Scout." Kind of dark was a way to give Marc more to play, to make the character more dimensional. The whole Initiative thing was always a tricky thing to play and the idea of that super-secret-agent monster killer. You take Buffy, which was such an intimate show about friends and family, and you start to make it a little too big. Riley was outside of that world and we were trying to bring him into it, but it just never quite worked.

CHRISTIAN KANE
(actor, *The Librarians*)

Poor Marc Blucas; he's a great guy. I can't say enough about Blucas. He's another one of the nicest guys in Hollywood. He's a dear friend. Nobody in America was ready to accept the fact that Angel was gone. It had nothing to do with Blucas. Nobody was ready to accept that Angel was gone and Angel and Buffy weren't going to be a thing. That's why Blucas got hammered. I don't think that anybody in that role stood a shot. You could've cast Brad Pitt. OK, maybe *that* would work, but other than that I just don't think anyone would've had a shot, because America loved Angel.

MARTI NOXON

When challenged as an actor to go to more dramatic places, Marc stepped up. He's really fine in dramatic scenes. Once he got a little twisted, I was in. The irony of that is we used getting him twisted to sort of launch him out of the show. Ultimately, does the character work? Yes, because we knew where we were going with him and we knew that it wasn't going to go well. I think that maybe there was a long period of time where he was just sort of there, being her sidekick. Some people didn't respond to that and I could understand why. I think people missed him more when he was gone, as you often do in real life when that happens. I felt like in terms of Marc's contribution, he did a tremendously fine job and if there was ever any problem with that character, it was the fault of the writers and not him.

SARAH LEMELMAN

Time and time again, Riley is seen as dented by Buffy's immeasurable strength, from nearly knocking him unconscious in a spar to making him look like a foolish child at a demon bar. When Riley begins to see that the Initiative may not be all the good he believes it to be, he is then faced with not only a crisis of masculinity with Buffy but also an identity crisis, as his whole life's mission is turned upside down. Once again, Buffy is put in a more powerful position, as she is seen comforting Riley while he is sick from the steroids that he had been taking unknowingly from the Initiative. At 6'2", he is seen as utterly helpless, as he is curled in the fetal position, shivering and whimpering.

Buffy's Slayer strength and speed is not the only way in which Riley feels inadequate and emasculated next to her. He also feels that he cannot measure up to Buffy's ex, Angel, and that he does not truly satisfy her physically and emotionally. In "The Yoko Factor" Angel makes an appearance, and the viewers see a huge standoff between the two men. When Angel says he is "going to see an old girlfriend," Riley attacks Angel, but Angel easily knocks Riley out. Despite the fact that the fight is clearly uneven and Angel pulverizes Riley, Riley still comes after Angel to stop him from talking to Buffy. When Buffy, Angel, and Riley all end up in the same room, Angel and Riley engage in what Buffy calls a "display of testosterone poisoning."

JOSS WHEDON

I actually think it was a very strong year. There were things that were difficult. The Initiative, budget-wise and figuring out motivation-wise, you're dealing with a lot of people who aren't your core group. Ultimately, my heart is always with my core group, so that was sort of tricky trying to get the feeling of a huge government conspiracy when we have a shrub and people are saying, "We're going to patrol past *the shrub*!" Eventually you begin to feel that you're just playing dress-up, but we did manage to pull some epic scope on that.

Some people also got kind of twitchy that Buffy was involved in a happy relationship, where she actually gets to have sex. For some reason, that made people very nervous. By and large, the more nervous I make people—as long as they're still watching—the better I feel, because that's what the year was supposed to be about: "We're all redefining who we are, we're sort of falling apart, we're doing what you're supposed to do in the first year of college. We're experimenting." I think some of the best single episodes we've done were fourth season, and we ended so bizarrely.

DAVID FURY

I had to say we sort of stumbled our way through it a little bit. There were some great things that came out of it, but it was a very tricky thing. It did result in some brilliant episodes. We got to do "Hush." Just brilliant stuff in the midst of it. But it was a little bit of a new animal, *Buffy* season four. There was always going to be a little bit of trying to find the right mix.

While few would contend that the fourth season of *Buffy* was one of its best, no one would quibble that a true standout was "Hush," an episode with only seventeen minutes of spoken dialogue over a forty-four-minute running time. In the episode, the enigmatic Gentlemen arrive in Sunnydale and steal the residents' voices so that no one can scream when they cut out the hearts of their victims. Directed beautifully by Whedon, "Hush" is the only episode of 144 to be nominated for an Emmy Award in Outstanding Writing for a Drama Series, as well as Outstanding Cinematography for a Single Camera Series. It lost in both categories.

SARAH MICHELLE GELLAR
(actress, Buffy Summers)

It was one of those moments where I thought, "Oh, this is great! A whole episode with no lines!" I was like, "This is a breeze!" And boy was I wrong.

JOSS WHEDON

Writing it I was terrified. I was more terrified than [I was] with the musical that I just couldn't pull it off. When we were shooting it, everyone knew their action, but there were no lines, there was no rhythm, there were no cues, so everyone would do everything all at once. We had no way to communicate a rhythm.

Making his *Buffy* debut was versatile actor Camden Toy as one of the Gentlemen that preyed on the mute citizenry of Sunnydale. He would return several times to the series including as the skin-eating demon Gnarl in "Same Time, Same Place" in season seven.

CAMDEN TOY
(actor, a Gentleman)

By the time we got called in to audition for "Hush," they still weren't sure what these characters were going to be. I think they were still called "The Laughing Men." Because there was no dialogue, there was talk with the producers, "Well, can't we just get an extra to do this?" Thank goodness Joss said, "No, we need some physical performers to actually bring these to life." Because of that, they were auditioning really last-minute. I got the call that afternoon from my agent, who said they want to see you at 5 P.M. that night. Usually there's a day or two in advance. And I'm, like, "Tonight? What about the script?" And they said, "There's no script; just go." So, I'm like, "Uh, OK."

The casting director and Joss were the only people in the room. They weren't recording any of the auditions. That was kind of what Joss did—he was in the room and he made the decision. They asked me to do an improv where you float in, you cut this young man's heart out, and then you float back out with the heart." I'm like, "What? OK." "Oh, and they're smiling the whole time." So, I do this kind of illusionary thing physically, where it looks like I'm floating. I try to sort of glide in smiling and I cut the heart out.

I finished the audition and Joss kind of starts waving at me, turns his back and goes, "OK, thank you. Oh God, I'm going to have nightmares now." At that point, I thought either I've gotten the role or he thinks I'm a total psycho. I was worried I blew it, but the next day I got a call from my agent saying they wanted me and that's the episode where I met [actor] Doug Jones.

The design for the unsettling Gentlemen was created by Whedon and realized by the series makeup team of makeup supervisor Todd McIntosh and Optic Nerve's John Vulich, a veteran of *Babylon 5,* who passed away in 2016.

CAMDEN TOY

There were six of us actually, all together. Two of them were stunt guys and the other two were Charlie Brumbly and Don Lewis. Charlie was the wisecracking guy on *Baywatch Hawaii.* When we were shooting, he was constantly cracking us up. Don Lewis was well known in the physical community, because he did puppetry and shadow work. He did all the shadow puppetry work in Coppola's *Dracula.* All four of us had a really strong background in physical theater: clowning, mime, martial arts, puppetry. I think that's really why those characters came to life so much.

Interestingly enough, it's only Doug Jones and myself that have our real mouths where we can smile. The idea originally was they were just going to have a plastered-on smile. I remember thinking after auditioning for the role, this is so wrong. They hired me because I scared Joss with my smile. But I thought, "Hey, shut up, it's not my place to say," but as they were getting Joss to give the final sign-off on the design, he was like, "Whoah, wait a minute. We hired Camden and Doug because they both scared me in the room, in broad daylight, with no makeup, with just their smiles and now we're covering them up? No, no, no, you can't do that. You actually have to have their smiles." They were like, "But we're shooting like the day after tomorrow." And Joss said, "No, not for Camden and Doug. You can do it for the other guys, but Camden and Doug, we have to have their smiles."

They made it so they're like little veneers that fit over our actual teeth, so it's our actual mouth and they mostly focused on us, because that's much scarier than a plastered-on smile.

Said Whedon at the time, "I was drawing on everything that had ever frightened me: Nosferatu, Pinhead, Mr. Burns—anything that gave that creepy feel. We got into a lot of reptilian monsters and things that look kind of like aliens, and what I wanted from these guys was, very specifically, fairy tales. I wanted guys that would remind people of what they were scared of when they were children."

CAMDEN TOY

The very first scene that we shot as the Gentlemen was that scene where we knock on the door and the young man opens the door. We float in, cut his heart out, and our—I think we called them "the footmen"—are holding him down. So we shoot the actual door opening later, but the actual scene where we float in, we shot first. And, of course, it's one of the few cases where, as an actor, I don't have to worry about hitting my mark. I'm either on a platform that's on wheels, that's on tracks, that they're pulling or pushing on wires. I remember after the first take the props person or someone went, "Oh my God," after they yelled cut. They said, "I can't believe the dialogue you guys are having and you haven't said a word." That's when Doug and I were like, "I think it's working."

It was also Amber Benson's first episode as Tara, and she thought we were even scarier in person. The cast literally wanted to have nothing to do with us. After the take, they would just sort of walk away. Only Marc Blucas would say, "Hey, how's it going? Great to have you guys." Everybody else was scared of us. Amber Benson's mother told us to leave her alone, that she was really scared by us. We would literally sit with crew or sometimes with Joss to eat, but the rest of the cast would not come near us. It was pretty wild.

In addition to shooting on the Santa Monica stages at Bergamont Stages as well as Westwood's UCLA, which doubled for UC Sunnydale, the episode filmed several days on location at Universal Studios for Sunnydale exteriors as the ominous Gentlemen made their way through town . . . very quietly.

CAMDEN TOY

In the beginning, we shot at Universal Studios, where we were floating down the street for a few days. We were also on a college campus down in Alhambra. The last scene we shot, we were floating down the hall. If you see our feet, we are actually on wires so they had to do that in studio, because they wanted a wider-angle shot. So as soon as they would pull back, we would be on wires—when it's like a headshot or a shoulder shot, that's when we'd be on platforms, because the wires were very difficult. Those were tough. Even Joss talked about that on the DVD commentary. He says, "Oh, yeah, the tall one there is Doug Jones and the shorter one's Camden Toy. The two of them scared me so much, in broad daylight, with just their smiles. So I knew they were going to be great."

One of the season's biggest surprises was the sudden death of Lindsay Crouse's Professor Maggie Walsh at the hands of the nefarious Adam, who seemed destined for a more sizable role.

JOSS WHEDON

A lot of our great shocks come from things that we can't control. We were basically told by Lindsay Crouse's agent that she had to be done by Christmas. We knew that was going to be the progression, that she would create Adam and Adam would destroy her, but we weren't sure how it would completely unfold. Given the situation, we decided to do it abruptly, and that charmed the hell out of me. It's always fun to do something a little startling. To an extent, the characters are telling us what they need, and to an extent the situation dictates what happens.

DAVID FURY

I don't know if Joss has said this, but she is at least partly inspired by his own mother. His mother was a college professor and she was a very big feminist. Very strong-willed. I think she had a huge impact on Joss's life. Certainly the fact that he is an ardent feminist himself. I think his mother can take credit for that, but she was a very strong-willed, very strict woman. But one that Joss respected very much. I believe that Professor Walsh was at least partly inspired by his mother in the sense of being this very good, strong-willed professor that students were scared of. The idea of a mother figure was interesting. She was sort of Riley's mother. She was Adam's mother. When she had scenes with Buffy, it was very much like Buffy was dealing with a mother-in-law character.

Joss was very interested in seeing this girl that he presented in high school who struggles to be normal, knowing that she has to rise to the occasion and save the world, suddenly being wholly terrified of this woman and totally intimidated by her. Lindsey did a good job. It was a tricky character. The whole Initiative thing was very tricky, and, of course, what she represented allegorically might be the most personal thing about it for Joss. I don't think the rest of us could latch on to it as clearly as he could. There might have been some things being worked out there.

Another milestone for the series was the season capper. After defeating the Big Bad in the penultimate episode of the season, Joss Whedon wrote and directed the stylish and surreal finale in which the Scooby Gang confront the First Slayer in a series of dream-like vignettes more akin to an episode of *Twin Peaks* than *Buffy,* providing a remarkable coda for an uneven season.

JOSS WHEDON

It was about combining the totally surreal with the totally mundane. Obviously, things had to get worse at the end of each act—people had to be in peril, because this thing was trying to kill them in their dreams. But beyond that, there really was no structure. I was basically sitting down to write a forty-minute tone poem.

ARMIN SHIMERMAN
(actor, Principal Snyder)

I was very surprised when my agent called and said you have another episode of *Buffy.* I said, "*Buffy*? I'm dead on *Buffy.*" And with all due respect to all the other episodes I did, I think the very best work on *Buffy,* perhaps in my whole career, was in that last episode, "Restless."

JOSS WHEDON

The last episode was all dreams and it's just about as strange as it needs to be. It was a very fun episode and it sort of summed up everything that everyone had gone through, what it meant to them and where it was. It was divided into four acts that are four dreams, one each for Giles, Xander, Willow, and Buffy. It's basically four short stories about how these people feel. We came to realize that we'd taken them to a pretty interesting place.

ARMIN SHIMERMAN

It's a terrific episode, and I'm particularly pleased with my work in that one. There was a note in the script from Joss to me saying, "Armin, have you ever seen *Apocalypse Now*? You need to see this." As a person who lived through the sixties, ironically I had never seen *Apocalypse Now*. So I studied the film and Marlon Brando's performance in particular and I'm really happy with it.

A FIGHT FOR LOVE AND GLORY (AKA DEATH IS YOUR GIFT)

"So Dawn's in trouble. It must be Tuesday."

Foreshadowed in the fourth-season capper "Restless," the fifth season of *Buffy* begins with the arrival of the Key, in the form of Buffy's younger sister. For some, the arrival of Michelle Trachtenberg as Dawn was a welcome breath of fresh air, introducing a bizarre new element into the mythos, while others felt she was a glorified Cousin Oliver (and if you don't know who that is, go look it up—we'll wait). While viewers may have been puzzled over the sudden, enigmatic arrival of Dawn in the Summers residence, the show also introduces the season's new Big Bad, Glorificus, or Glory, played by a scenery-chewing Clare Kramer, and Glory's mellow distaff doppelgänger Ben, played by Charlie Weber.

Glory, a hell goddess exiled from her dimension, is intent on returning home. In order to do so, she needs the Key, which we learn was hidden by a band of monks in the form of Dawn. Unfortunately, the use of the Key will unlock a portal unleashing all the beasts of hell on earth. Realizing the Key would need to be protected, those cagey monks transformed it into human flesh, in the form of Buffy's younger sister, created from the blood of Buffy, knowing she would give her own life, if necessary, to protect it. Which is *exactly* what she does in the moving season finale.

Meanwhile, Buffy was also confronting the departure of Riley, who has come to the sad realization that she will never truly love him, giving Spike the opportunity to pursue his lust, love, and obsession for the Slayer. And, in the most moving and shocking moment of the season, Buffy's mother, Joyce, dies of a brain aneurysm in another of the series' finest hours, "The Body."

JOSS WHEDON

(creator/executive producer, *Buffy the Vampire Slayer*)

For season five, the mission statement was family. When you think you've moved on and grown up and moved out of the house and living your life, family comes back. You realize that they're always a part of your life. Some of that's good and some of that's bad. Also a very strong message with me is you make your own family. Or sometimes it's made for you by monks.

DAVID FURY

(supervising producer, *Buffy the Vampire Slayer*)

Season five was, in Joss's mind, very possibly the last season, because his contract was for five seasons. Every year it was a question mark about whether the show would get picked up. Its ratings were at that time minimal. Right now it'd be a huge hit show, any network would be killing for the ratings we got, but back then it was not a highly rated show. The acclaim was there, but the network would play, as often they do, the political game where they cry poverty. They're like, "We're just not making enough on the show."

This is to a large extent a negotiation ploy, but it was considered a bubble show and Joss was pretty upset with the way they'd play that it just didn't perform well. Forget the fact that it was giving the WB a status it wasn't getting from its other programming. It was hugely successful in terms of promoting the network. But as a last-year-of-a-contract thing, it kind of minimized the value of *Buffy*, which was upsetting to Joss.

MARTI NOXON

(co-executive producer, *Buffy the Vampire Slayer*)

It got harder every season. You'd come from a story meeting where we're saying, "What about this?" "Oh, we've already done that." "What about that?" "Well, we kind of tackled that," or, "We did something like that on *Angel*." Not only do you have almost a hundred story lines on *Buffy* that we've already done, we had another show where you're doing twenty-two stories a year on that. Obviously, we can touch on the same ground, because they're different shows, but you don't want them to be too close. It just compounds the complications. So that in itself makes it harder to break stories—

plus, you know, the exhaustion factor. That's probably the most challenging part of the whole process.

JOSS WHEDON

The introduction of Dawn, the death of Mom, the meeting of Tara's family—all of that stuff was very deliberate. We knew year one of college was freedom and not a lot of Mom. Kristine Sutherland, luckily, was spending a year in Italy, but it was that year, so it was perfect. We were like, "Perfect, then you'll come back and you'll be very heavy in season five and then I'll kill you." So that was the mission statement.

DAVID FURY

We went into the season feeling that we needed to find a way to get to the moment that defined the series and that's what the last couple of episodes dealt with. It was great that in the end Buffy just becomes the girl who's fighting vampires again. The introduction of Dawn was a way to explore that as well. A young girl that turns out to be more than you thought she was.

MARTI NOXON

Some of it was about bringing the Scooby Gang more together. They were a little fractured last year. So sort of "the gang's all here" was part of our mandate, to make the relationships a little closer, a little less estranged. And then we're gunning toward our hundredth episode, which is a pretty big landmark. One of our mandates was just to make it a hell of a ride.

DAVID FURY

That's probably where the Dawn of it comes in, where it became a little bit more rooted in those people rather than something bigger than them. There was an effort to bring it back down to earth a little bit.

STEVEN S. DEKNIGHT
(writer, season five, *Buffy the Vampire Slayer*)

I was on *Undressed* for MTV. Each episode was three different story lines happening in high school, college, and postcollege with young adults in various sexual situations. It's MTV, so it was all very PG-13. Created by Roland Joffé, who did *The Killing Fields,* strangely. I believe I was on my third or fourth season of that. I started to think, I've got a paying job. I have an agent. She was really sweet but kind of at the end of her career, so it would be a perfect time to write a spec and try to segue to another agency before she retires. Two of my favorite shows were *Buffy the Vampire Slayer* and *NYPD Blue.*

I had ideas for both of them. It was a couple of weeks of struggling. Do I write the *NYPD Blue*? Do I write the *Buffy*? Finally, I thought, "Well, I'll write the *Buffy.*" I wrote a spec called "Xander the Slayer" in which the whole story revolves around [the fact that] Buffy's powers are transferred to Xander. It was exploring why men can't be the Slayer.

He becomes very aggressive and non-Xander-like. I wrote this and finished it. Unfortunately, I finished it right in the middle of staffing season, so no agency really wanted to look at it because they were busy with their clients. I had one friend who was repped at UTA. She graciously passed along my script. They read it and said, "Well, we like it, but not enough to rep it." I'm like, "Oh, shit. Well, I've got nothing to lose. I'll give it to my current agent." She was in features. I think she knew like three people in TV. She read it and liked it and passed it along to her TV contacts. I went in to meet about working on the animated series they were developing. They said, "Joss has to read your script first and, quite frankly, he's very harsh on *Buffy* specs." They sent it to Joss, and I think it was like six weeks or something that I hear nothing. I'm just chewing my nails. I finally got a call, "Yeah, can you come over tomorrow? Joss would like to sit down with you."

It's half luck and half having the right material at the right time. I went over and met with him at the *Buffy* office. The *Buffy/Angel* offices were at Bergamot Station in Santa Monica. That's also where the *Buffy* stages were. We talked about comics and movies for about a half hour. At the end, he said, "Look, I know you were talking about the animated show, but do you want to come do an episode of the live-action show?" I said, "Fuck yeah!" They hired me to do a freelance episode and that was "Blood Ties," where Dawn finds out she's not human. That she's the Key. I know a lot of people were thrown by Dawn and confused, even though there's that great scene where there's a room that's obviously used for storage. Then suddenly there's a sister in it, which was obviously a tip-off something odd was going on. For me, I loved that season. Of course, it was my first season, so I had a very strong reaction to it.

JOSS WHEDON

The Dawn thing was off the charts. Michelle was just incredible. The only weakness I would say is that I don't think we had enough time for some of the other characters.

MARTI NOXON

For me, not being a comic book fan, apparently this is not uncommon in comic books: that fantasy characters suddenly arrive. It happens. And it's happened in other stories, but I'd never seen it before. I love comic books, but I mostly read the really twisted ones, the ones about death or suicides. I didn't know there was a precedent. We were like, "How is this going to work?" People were really flipping out, but once we got into the idea that we were just going to leave people sort of disturbed for a while, it was kind of fun. I'd never done anything like that before. I think everybody was concerned that the audience wouldn't go on that journey with us, but Joss just had confidence and that the payoff was going to be worth it. He knew what his role was in the whole season, too. He was just really sure of it, that it might throw people off for a while but it would keep them intrigued as well. My experience is that if he's sure, we should be sure.

JOSS WHEDON

When I started doing comic book movies, people actually had to point out to me that *Buffy* was the *X-Men* and that I'd been making comic book movies since I started doing television. That everything had been designed for that sort of thing. I studied comic books as much as I studied anything else. And by studied I mean read, and tried to convince my parents that somehow this was going to pay off later so they wouldn't tear them up. Every time you turn the page is an opportunity to go, "Oh shit!" Every time. And so you always want something wonderful to happen; instead of just having it be good, you want to be up all the time; you want constantly to have those page-turn moments.

DAVID GREENWALT

(consulting producer, *Buffy the Vampire Slayer*)

I liked *Batman v Superman*. Comic books weren't a big thing to me, like it was to a lot of people I met on *Buffy* and *Angel* who have been real comic book geeks all their lives.

MARTI NOXON

At first she seemed like a traditional annoying kid sister, almost stepping out of another TV show, but that was part of the intention. "What *is* this?" because clearly she isn't *that*. She has conflict with her sister, she has real-life stuff, but there's obviously more to her than this little pesky younger sister. So it was fun to introduce this character you've sort of seen before, but realizing there's something really off about her. That was so inherent in who she was, because she had just appeared, so we could play her a little more traditional and let her emerge as a more layered character. Michelle was just an amazing actress.

DAVID FURY

I thought it was kind of brilliant, actually, because I knew that the initial reaction would be that we were trying to repopulate the show with younger actors. That's the thing networks tend to do after a certain amount of years and just go, "Our teenage characters are getting too old; we need to refresh the show." But that's not what it really was at all. It was just a clever idea about how to introduce a new character in the show and change the history and memories of all the characters, and then *not* explain it for five episodes, which was just fantastic. I loved it when Joss pitched it. He pitched it toward the end of the prior season, because he had alluded to her in the earlier episodes, including "Restless." There were all these clues written about Dawn's appearance, which was a lot of fun.

I did get to name Dawn. We had a little brainstorming session where we're like what do we call Buffy's sister? We were all coming up with different names and at some point I just hit on Dawn. I was just thinking it seemed like a great name for Summers, Dawn Summers and how the dawn is the thing that chases vampires away. I didn't know it was also the name of Joss's sister-in-law, whom I'd never heard of or met.

The fifth season improbably opened with the introduction of the most famous vampire of all time making his first (and last) appearance in the Buffy universe: Count Vladimir Dracula himself. It was an episode that was challenging for the writers and, ultimately, satisfied few fans as well.

DAVID FURY

I can go with a modern Dracula. But it was just the fact that he was somebody else's creation invading Joss's creation. I thought it sort of diminished our rules, our universe. It's like, "All right, let's have Batman come in now and face Buffy." It's the kind of thing you'd go, "No, you can't do that, because Batman is another character from another thing."

MARTI NOXON

The only thing remarkable about that episode is that it's one of the few that we've worked on that just wouldn't break. We had the hardest time breaking that story. Even after it was shot, we had to go back in and reshoot a couple of things. I love the actor who played Dracula and he brought a lot to it, and I thought in many ways it worked, but I still look at it and feel like we didn't quite hit it.

DAVID FURY

I was actually very bothered by that episode. I know that it delighted Joss. It delighted Marti, too, this idea of Buffy facing Dracula. I thought it flew in the face of the mythology of our vampires. It doesn't play in the Dracula playground. The kind of logic I would apply to it is the thing Joss would say,

"Who cares?" Well, I do. I care. We've created these rules and I don't want to break our rules. And Dracula totally broke the rules. We just said, Dracula is some weird anomaly of a vampire, and seeing Xander become Renfield was all fun, but it was an episode I had difficulty embracing. I thought it sort of commented on how Buffy's universe is kind of fictional.

When you start introducing another famous fictional character into our world, to me it bursts the bubble of this universe that Joss created and we created with him. Some people enjoyed it very much. I'm just not one of them.

MARTI NOXON

It's hard to bring a character who's that iconic into your universe; it lent itself to camp. At the same time, we were actually trying to do something deeper than that. We were trying to make it emotional and make it have some resonance. But it was a campy situation, and tone-wise we weren't always sure where we were. Also, that character deserves maybe a longer arc. We tried to do a lot with him in one episode and then got rid of him. So we struggled for tone and we were tired coming out of season four.

STEVEN S. DEKNIGHT

Things seemed to go well. I seemed to mesh OK with the team. The team, they had written some of my favorite stuff. It's Doug Petrie, Jane Espenson, David Fury, Marti Noxon, and Joss, of course, and Rebecca Rand Kirshner were the writers at the time. I had loved all their stuff that I'd seen so far.

They invited me to come to the production meeting. Then afterward, Marti Noxon said, "Hey, can you stick around for a few minutes?" I said, "Yeah, sure." I'm just sitting there all by myself thinking it's going to be they want some kind of rewrite or some scene isn't working. After about ten minutes, a PA [production assistant] pops up and says, "Hey, Joss and Marti want to see you down on the set." I go, "Oh, OK. Great." I go down and it was the Magic Box set, and the heavens opened, the angels sang, and I became part of the show.

To me, that time I spent on *Buffy* and *Angel* was such a defining moment in my career. Not just to start the climb up the ladder, but to get the opportunity to work with Joss and Marti and such a phenomenal group of people.

I can't tell you how much I learned. The great thing about Joss is that he really wanted to train show runners. He had you on set, in editing, in casting, in all the meetings. He really wanted you to know, from the ground up, how to build a show, which a lot of show runners *don't* do.

It was also fantastic because this was the early 2000s. We were shooting here in L.A., both series. That's another thing I feel very lucky about, is that both of the one-hour dramas that I started out on, we shot *Buffy* in Santa Monica and we shot *Angel* on the Paramount lot. To have that, to have it be here, was just such an invaluable experience. It was just absolutely amazing.

Directing her first episode was Marti Noxon, joining the ranks of writers who stepped behind the camera throughout the series' run. "Into the Woods" would be the first of two episodes she would direct that season, the second being "Forever," before her new show-runner duties in the sixth would prevent her from directing additional episodes.

MARTI NOXON

It was really a thrill. It was something I'd often dreamed about doing, and, of course, when you go down to set and you think, "Well that wasn't the way I saw it. It's good, but it's not how I saw it." You know, it's that little voice in your head that says, "I want to rule the world." Joss may have talked about doing it. That year I spent quite a bit of time on, oh, getting married. And before that, I was working on a feature that took a bunch of my time. I kept putting it off, but finally the decks were cleared. It was a really amazing, very overwhelming, and exciting experience. In some ways easier than I thought it was going to be, and in some ways much harder. It was also more collaborative. There's a part of it where you really have to know where you want to go and steer that ship, but on the other hand you also have to be really open and flexible.

Once I realized that there was always someone there you could turn to, and ask a question to or get help from, it stopped being quite so terrifying. It was still terrifying, because the pace is so fast. It's like a two-million-dollar school play; there's no stopping it. We had goals we had to meet every day, and some days it got away from me, but every day I felt like I learned a lot. I also learned what a great crew we had and how wonderful the people we worked with were. It's different when you come down and see people maybe twice a day, or twice a week, than when you're with them 24-7 for eight days. I just learned how lucky we were to have the people we did to work with. And the actors were awesome. It was beyond my wildest dreams. I feel like the episode turned out really well. I was also training at the hand of a master; I think Joss has turned out to be a world-class director, and he can teach me everything I need to know to make a movie some day.

I also wrote the episode. It's pretty Buffy-Riley-arc heavy. It falls into line with a lot of the shows that I've written, which is that it definitely revolves more [around] relationships.

SARAH LEMELMAN

(author, *"It's About Power":* Buffy the Vampire Slayer*'s Stab at Establishing the Strength of Girls on American Television*)

Another reason *Buffy* fans and scholars were so rabidly drawn to the show is the fact that it was one of the first shows ever to normalize a lesbian relationship, as well as to depict a lesbian sex scene on network television. An important aspect of this relationship that the show stresses in the relationship between Willow and Tara is that Tara is a person, and it is about love between two characters, just like any other relationship on the show, instead of the fact that she is a girl, and that it is a same-sex relationship. This emphasis on love between two people, who both happen to be females, was unprecedented.

DAVID FURY

It turned out to be so significant to the fan base that we were presenting this healthy gay relationship for Willow. It's one of the greatest legacies of the show. I don't think we thought about it being that. I don't think we thought we were making some huge statement. I'm not sure Joss was making a huge statement. The fact of the matter is we all had lesbian friends, we knew lesbian couples. It didn't seem that extreme. It seemed sort of appropriate for Willow at the time. Especially as we saw her in "The Wish" and the whole Wicca, female-empowerment kind of thing, it all seemed to fall in nicely having her falling in love with another woman.

ANTHONY C. FERRANTE
(writer, *Fangoria* magazine)

It was a very daring thing. And also, keep in mind, Willow was a witch, not a vampire, so her sexual orientation never had a "vampire" sexuality to it, except when they did the alternate-reality-timeline episode. Joss Whedon opened a lot of doors and broke a lot of taboos with how he handled that story line. He really made it feel organic and not a stunt. And in its wake, you've seen a much stronger, more organic way of integrating LGBTQ characters in mainstream TV shows, both dramatic and genre.

SARAH LEMELMAN

Before the series ended, Whedon was able to actually show a sex scene between Willow and Kennedy, which was the first of its kind on network television. Throughout the entire show, all the other heterosexual couples are seen as having sex, and in some, very explicit scenes—Buffy and Riley and then Buffy and Spike—while Willow and Tara's relationship was forced to be largely subtextual and perceived as innocent. Nevertheless, by the series end, and with the help of UPN, Whedon was able to truly break barriers by his normalization of the relationships between Willow/Tara and Willow/Kennedy, giving fans, scholars, and the gay community another reason to appreciate and study the show.

JOSS WHEDON

The network actually called me and said, "You know, we have a lot of gay this year. We're kind of gayed out. *Dawson's* and this other show . . ." I said, "I don't know. I don't watch those shows. We're going to do this thing. It's what we're going to do." And then they were totally fine. They were like, "Do you have to have the kiss [in 'The Body']?" I was like, "OK, I'm packing up my office." I never pulled that out except that one time. I'm like, "I'm packing up the office" and they were like, "Nope, it's cool."

STEVEN S. DEKNIGHT

It is tricky, especially because it was very groundbreaking, that relationship. I remember Joss had a lot of battles about letting them kiss with the network and the studio. I completely understand about how that would really hurt the viewers who were emotionally invested. Joss always strongly felt that the story comes first. You've got to tell the story that you feel like you want to tell. That was the story he wanted to tell, and I think it was the right story.

DAVID FURY

The greatest controversy was us killing Tara in season six. That was a much bigger controversy than presenting their relationship. That was interesting. And that was the one where we went, "Really, we're killing her?" People's reactions to it were *so* strong. But the actual relationship was very sweet and romantic. We were all down with it.

SARAH LEMELMAN

It's worth mentioning that Joss may have always wanted there to be a gay character on the show. This goes with the theme of Joss supporting the "outcasts" in society, because he's said before that he felt like one during high school and wanted to create a show that would resonate with those who also feel like outcasts/misfits in high school. I think Willow is a perfect character to experiment with, because she really doesn't know what she wants or who she is. In high school, she wants to please others, but it feels like she forgets about herself sometimes. She takes orders from others and forgets to assert herself.

In season four, we have a change, where Willow begins to become independent, and with this independence she understands her sexuality. This all coincides with her becoming a more powerful witch, which is the epitome of feminism and a rejection of the patriarchy. I think Willow's self-discovery really resonated with the audience, especially the LGBTQ community, because it reflects the struggle of introspection that some people in that community have faced. Willow is an especially important character for this community, because it came at a time when America really was not supportive of the community.

AMBER BENSON
(actress, Tara Maclay)

Joss kept Willow as a lesbian, rather than saying, "OK, now she's done." I'm really pleased with how that continued on, that she had somebody else, that she continued to be who she was; she stuck by her guns. She wasn't just a flip-flopper, you know what I mean? I don't think anyone realized how intense the reaction to [Tara's] passing away was going to be. I'm just really pleased that we got to do it. That we got to have that relationship and whether it goes on or it doesn't go on or it ends up in a comic book somewhere or ends up on a porn video somewhere.

Perhaps even more nuanced was one of the most realistic depictions of death ever portrayed in a TV series. Ironically, in a series about myriad supernatural threats, Joyce's death came from a more mundane killer: a brain aneurysm. Written and directed by Joss Whedon shortly after the death of his own mother, "The Body" remains a towering achievement and a highlight of the season and the series.

STEVEN S. DEKNIGHT

I came in halfway through the fifth season. In that first meeting with Joss when he was talking about the season, he talked about how Joyce dies and he wanted to do a whole episode about the aftermath, called "The Body." I'm like, "Holy shit, Joyce dies?" I just loved that. Buffy, to me, is very emotional and also very funny. To take that risk of doing an episode where the main character's mother dies, not from a vampire or anything supernatural, and do an entire episode with no score, that's just really, really gut-wrenching. I go, "Man, this is definitely the place I want to be."

SARAH LEMELMAN

Unlike "Once More, with Feeling," "The Body" is an episode that uses no music at all in order to express a realistic portrayal of death. Throughout the fifth season, Buffy's mother, Joyce, is in and out of the Sunnydale hospital, as she has a brain tumor. However, the viewer—along with the show's characters—is led to believe that Joyce will live on, as her surgery is successful, and she is depicted as a cancer survivor for several episodes, before Buffy comes home one day to find her mother's lifeless body on their couch.

While all the characters are shocked about the loss, Anya, the ex-vengeance demon, perhaps demonstrates the suddenness of Joyce's death best: "But I don't understand! I don't understand how this all happens. How we go through this. I mean, I knew her, and then she's—there's just a body, and I don't understand why she just can't get back in it and not be dead . . . anymore! It's stupid! It's mortal and stupid!"

ANTHONY C. FERRANTE

"The Body" episode, in particular, is absolutely fascinating, dealing with the death of a family member. It wasn't a situation where her mom, who died, came back the next episode through magic. It was finality—and it was handled in a very unique and emotional way. For all the horror, monsters, and vampires in the show, this was probably the most daring thing the show ever did.

DAVID FURY

That was fantastic. That was, again, one of those things where your jaw drops. Joss was very specific that every act was going to be one scene and there would be no music in it. And you're going, "Really?" It's such a heavy episode. And he said, it's going to play more real without any score. So yeah, it was incredibly powerful and brilliant.

Joss was always looking for a different way to tell a *Buffy* story. With "Hush" without dialogue and now with "The Body" doing it without music. Keeping it almost like a stage play and pulling it off in a huge way. It's a classic thing from Superman, which was with all my powers I couldn't save my father. And very much the same with Buffy, you felt like, "I can always protect my mother from things that will kill her," but the helplessness of not being able to save your loved one, your mother, despite all [your] powers—it's a very powerful story.

SARAH LEMELMAN

While critics and fans alike believed that this episode would easily garner an Emmy nomination, it instead only received wide acclaim and was snubbed by the Emmy committee.

CHARISMA CARPENTER

(actress, Cordelia Chase)

I was just disappointed that it was never a Golden Globe winner or that it never got the Emmy, because I thought the themes were so important and I felt Joss and Marti and everyone who was involved on every level deserved it so much. I'm so grateful the makeup people were acknowledged, but it was so high level, in so many different departments. I think the title may have hurt the show in that regard, because you can't take it that seriously. You can't give an Oscar to Julia Roberts for *Pretty Woman* where she plays a hooker.

DAVID GREENWALT

Joss moved forward, and we moved forward every year, and the characters grew and changed. Then one year she gets this sister that no one has ever seen or heard of before. Her mother died in the episode "The Body," which is probably one of the best episodes in television ever made. Joss made these ballsy choices and also shooting weird camera angles, just like an experience of grief with long shots of the dead body, shots out of focus and out of frame and no music. That was a wallop.

MICHELLE TRACHTENBERG

(actress, Dawn Summers)

Being a fan of the show from the very beginning and then being on it was very surreal for me. When I read the episode, it was like I was losing a part of myself, to be honest. I think it really allowed the audience to connect with Dawn for the first time. I wasn't stealing things or whining.

DAVID GREENWALT

People talk about "Hush," also incredibly brilliant, but this show was amazing. And now Joss's own mother died—they had a country place in upstate New York where as a kid there was no TV allowed. You could read, you could do stuff, but there was no chatter allowed during the day, either. She was a really well-known feminist teacher. She was killed when he was twenty-eight driving back from school. So he made this show, "The Body," and it was totally unflinching. You just kept looking at the body over and over again in this weird framing. And the balls to have no music to beg the audience to feel any goddamn thing one way or the other.

We were up in the editing room, and this is to illustrate the kind of relationship we had, Joss and I, and you know, a bunch of the other writers are in there and people are in tears at such an amazing episode, and I go, "God, Joss, what a great episode. It's going to be so great when you show it to your mother. Oh, oops, never mind." He loved me for that. If I could make him fall out of his chair and spit his drink out, you know, that's how we rolled with each other. He knew I adored him.

SARAH MICHELLE GELLAR

The big thing for me with the show was it was always so amazing to be a part of something that was constantly breaking the rules. We were constantly doing things that had never been done. We were constantly challenging both our audience and ourselves.

JOSS WHEDON

When I made "Hush," part of it literally was, "You know, I'm kind of turning into a hack." I felt like I was starting to phone it in and not challenging myself. So I thought, "OK, if I had a story I could only tell visually, that would be much harder." The idea of not using music partially came from what I was trying to evoke, but also partially from me realizing, you know what, I have to take something away from myself. I have to bare myself the same way the actors have to.

DAVID FURY

He just would do things that were always spot-on. How did he think like that? I don't know. Especially when you work in television, there eventually becomes what you think is a formula to what you're doing. It's always like, this is where this is going to happen, and, of course, act four is the big fight scene. Act five is the coda scene. It's all very specific and Joss tried to go, "What if you *don't* have to do any of that? How can I turn this thing on its head?" That's what makes him great.

Introduced in "The Wish," Emma Caulfield, who played Anya, had many scene-stealing moments, perhaps none more memorable than her monologue about the nature of the death as this former vengeance demon ponders the nature of grief. "I don't understand how this all happens," she says. "How we go through this. I mean, I knew her, and then she's–there's just a body, and I don't understand why she just can't get back in it and not be dead anymore. It's stupid. It's mortal and stupid. And, and Xander's crying and not talking, and, and I was having fruit punch, and I thought, well, Joyce will never have any more fruit punch ever, and she'll never have eggs, or yawn or brush her hair, not ever, and no one will explain to me why."

EMMA CAULFIELD
(actress, Anya Jenkins)

I had a real Anya moment and I'm not proud of it. I was asked by a fan, "What were you thinking during your monologue, because I cry every time." I'm like, "Honestly, I was really hungry and I had to go to the bathroom." I was very, very lucky to have that monologue and to be a part of that episode, because it really was a beautifully done episode, from top to finish. Sarah's performance, the writing, and the directing were really flawless and should have won an award.

DAVID FURY

The loss of the character of Joyce the mother is the child stepping into real adulthood. The idea of taking Joyce out of the picture was like the end of Buffy's childhood. We had explored it through five seasons of high school, and with her mother dying and her father being out of the picture, you really feel alone for the first time in your life. You feel like I'm the adult now. It was a significant step, especially as we were preparing for Buffy's death and the end of the season, that Buffy needs to make that transition into full-fledged adulthood.

Joyce's death helped us get there. It came at a completely unexpected and arbitrary time, which is the way death usually comes. We played with her health before, so everyone just went, "Oh, well, that story is over. There's nothing to be worried about anymore." Then suddenly, for Buffy to come home and find her on the sofa dead was devastating, but it's exactly where the character needed to be.

But despite the high-concept appearance of Dawn and later the sudden death of Joyce Summers, the season still needed a "Big Bad," the recurring antagonist for the year, which was epitomized by Clare Kramer's Glory.

STEVEN S. DEKNIGHT

Glen or Glenda. It almost had that kind of thing with Glory where she's really the male doctor. It was bizarre. It was weird. Then you throw in the knights from the old times who were trying to track her down. I thought it was an incredibly interesting idea.

DAVID FURY

Joss had a very clear idea about the whole buildup to the eventual reveal of the Ben-Glory connection and what that meant, which was another brilliant idea. The idea that Ben, who was this new potential love interest, was also our villain [and that] this goddess Glory and they were one in the same was a neat idea. That was transgenderism at its peak. It was a really interesting way to go and we did have lots of discussions about gender identity during that.

CLARE KRAMER
(actress, Glory)

What happened was when I went in to audition for the role, they just had two pages of dialogue, no character description. They didn't indicate that she was going to be bad, even. Or if it was just for one episode. I decided to play her a certain way—the Glory way—and as they went with my story line, they would decide things two or three weeks ahead. So I didn't even know she was going to be the Big Bad until after a couple of episodes in. I certainly didn't know she was going to be a god.

DAVID FURY

Clare Kramer was great as Glory. She relished the part. She was beautiful and she played the evil quite well. It was fun to play this character that all of these people were suddenly coming under the thrall of her, which I introduced. I really got to introduce Dawn in the second episode of the season and that was when she went to the homeless man who is babbling about Glory. I thought it was very interesting.

CLARE KRAMER

I definitely wanted people to like my character, but I remember after my first episode aired I went on one of the message boards to see what everyone's reaction was. Some people hated my character and some people liked my character, but more people didn't at that point, because they were like, "Who is this person trying to fight Buffy? What's going on here?" So I thought to myself, as an actor, I really need to *not* read that people don't like me, otherwise I'm going to try and change my performance and change myself to make me this or that. I knew I had to just trust Joss and the show to deliver the kind of character the audience would want. And so from that day on, I didn't worry about it anymore.

STEVEN S. DEKNIGHT

I remember my first real day of being hired to do the show. We all piled into a Winnebago and went to Santa Clarita, because Marti [Noxon] was directing an episode there. We were talking about Glory. Then there was a lot of talk through the season about: What does Glory want? What's the plan? She wants the Key, but the problem with wanting Dawn as the Key is that basically her evil plan is to go home, which isn't really that horrible. We struggled with that.

CLARE KRAMER

I don't think she was evil at all. She just wanted to go home, and she was just trying to achieve what would get her there. It's not her fault that the monks hid the Key in Dawn, but I also think as the actress, when you approach the character, you can't approach it like, "Oh, she's evil. I'm going to play an evil character." You have to approach it like any role where you don't pinpoint the good or the bad; you just look at the dynamics of that person. Even though she was a god, she was still a person, and it had to be approached that way. So I never saw her as evil; I knew she was the Big Bad, obviously, and she served a purpose on the show and for the season.

STEVEN S. DEKNIGHT

I came up with the idea that when she opens the dimension to go back to her hell dimension, all the dimensions open up and basically bled into Earth. That's where you get the dragons and the monsters that basically destroy the planet. First, I pitched it to David Fury and everybody and they go, "Yeah, you should pitch that to Joss." I remember pitching that to Joss and he goes, "Yeah, yeah. That's a good idea." Then I pitched him another idea that he hated. I got one win that night and one, "No, that's stupid."

MARTI NOXON

I felt like the season was revitalized; there was a lot of energy and we were back where we had Buffy in a really interesting place emotionally. That's always easier to write. The stuff with her mother and Dawn gave really clear emotional stuff for her to play. That gave us a really good, rich season. We started to feel a real updraft; that the show was moving in a positive direction.

Not that we'd felt we had a crappy season, but season four was transitional in a lot of ways. Season five felt like we were into a groove and a lot of the episodes turned out great. It was wonderful to be on a show heading for a hundred episodes and not feeling done—feeling like there was still a lot of life in the show and stories we wanted to tell. Stuff happening to Buffy that year opened up a whole bunch of new possibilities for her. All of that made us feel like we were going into the sixth season with a lot on our plate.

In "Restless," the First Slayer had prophesized to Buffy that "death is your gift." In the fifth season finale, "The Gift," Buffy learned what that actually meant when she sacrificed her life to save Dawn and the earth. And if there was any doubt that this time Buffy's death was for real, the final episode to air on the WB ends with a shot of Buffy's gravestone: "She saved the world . . . a lot."

JAMES MARSTERS
(actor, Spike)

That's the whole challenge of acting; to build an imaginary world in your head that you can release into and play in and seems real. I think Sean Penn calls it "the cage." Meryl Streep calls it "the playpen" or something, I call it "the sandbox." If you build that world in a detailed way, it's kind of like playing house as a kid. You know, if you have a cardboard box it's pretty good. But if you go to a friend's house and they have an actual little house with a skillet with plastic sausages and stuff, and it's more detailed, you can play better. So, you know, acting is about providing yourself with all those details.

When you're in a TV series, you have a long time to build that world. And believe me, in my head there's a little tiny Sunnydale with a very tiny Buffy and very tiny Spike. And little tiny Spike loves little tiny Buffy, and that's all real. And so you just escape into that. So yeah! She was really dead, man. She was dead; she was not coming back; and I was very sad. For real.

DAVID FURY

This was it; this was the end. There was a lot of discussion about how we were going to end this up. Despite the fact that most of us were skeptical that the show could end given its popularity, I think we were still locked into this idea that Buffy will die and this may be the end of the series at that time. We had to build it right and get to the eventual climax the best way we could. If the show did not continue, I have to say it would have been a big bummer. But I don't think we were really convinced *Buffy* would not continue, even if the WB was threatening to cancel us.

JAMES MARSTERS

The biggest challenge was how do we all truly believe she's dead? How do we sell this seriously? She's dead. I think it's only cheesy if you hold back. The answer to that challenge is if we believe it ourselves, the audience can get caught up in that moment and believe it, if only for the time they're watching the episode; they can believe it, too. Then, you know, they turn off the television and say, "Wait a minute! Is this show canceled? No, it's not canceled; she's coming back." But while they're watching it, they get fooled by the commitment of the performance.

STEVEN S. DEKNIGHT

The death of Buffy, that's tricky. When you hear Buffy sacrifices herself, of course, the first reaction is, "That's bullshit. They're bringing her back." It's tough to pull that off and make it feel real. Although the tombstone seemed to have done a major job of doing that, didn't it? It was epic . . . and weird . . . and bizarre. I think it ended in a really interesting place where Buffy sacrifices herself . . . which led into season six.

MORE THAN A FEELING

"So did anybody . . . last night, you know, did anybody, um . . . burst into song?"

The sixth season was far different than any season that had preceded it, since it focused on the personal demons of the Scooby Gang. It begins with Willow casting a powerful spell to bring Buffy back to life; she succeeds and is thrilled to have resurrected her closest friend, only to eventually learn that she didn't free Buffy from a hell dimension but rather pulled her out of heaven.

The season is dark and largely depressing: Buffy is unhappy to be back on earth, Spike attempts to rape her to consummate his obsession with her, Willow wrestles uncomfortably (for herself and the audience) with her magic addiction, Xander abandons Anya at the altar, and Tara is murdered. Sounds fun, doesn't it?

In addition, the Big Bad appears in the form of a troika of supernerds who don't seem all that bad—the Trio: Warren Mears (Adam Busch), Andrew Wells (Tom Lenk), and Jonathan Levinson (Danny Strong, who has subsequently gone on to become one of the most successful TV and film writers in the business as the creator of *Empire*, a screenwriter for films like Lee Daniels's *The Butler, The Hunger Games: Mockingjay,* and the brilliant HBO telefilms *Recount* and *Game Change*). Of course, appearances can be deceiving. . . .

The series also moved from its previous home on the WB to the United Paramount Network following a fierce bidding war. The studio that produced it, Fox, ultimately chose to migrate to a new network home for a larger licensing fee to cover the cost of a series that had grown far more expensive over the years (the show had long gone from filming on Super 16 mm in the early seasons to the traditional 35 mm film stock at the time as well). And with Buffy having died at the end of "The Gift," the WB did nothing to dissuade viewers from thinking that the Slayer was really six feet under and that they should, instead, watch *Angel*. Meanwhile, UPN embarked on an aggressive marketing campaign to let the audience know that Buffy was returning from the dead in a new home across the dial.

DAVID FURY

(co-executive producer, *Buffy the Vampire Slayer*)

Joss was a little fatalistic. He felt he was not going to return to the show. That after season five he would not be coming back. He needed a break, he wanted to do other things, and the network was playing that negotiation game. We had an idea that this might be it. Some of us didn't believe it. They thought it's impossible; they can't possibly let this go. But in essence they did. UPN saw an opportunity, because of the way the WB was playing with the value of the show and wasn't sure they were going to pick it up, so Twentieth Television went, "All right, we'll sell it elsewhere."

KEVIN LEVY

(senior vice president, Program Planning and Scheduling, the CW)

I remember when I was at UPN we had a great marketing campaign for it coming back, "Buffy Lives," which I thought looked great and really did a good job of sending the message that the show was transitioning over to UPN.

STEVEN S. DEKNIGHT

(story editor, *Buffy the Vampire Slayer*)

UPN really took a bath on *Buffy* and the reason they took a bath is that they couldn't come up with any product to launch off of *Buffy*. They had a great lead-in, but they couldn't get the material to get their next hit, and *Enterprise* wasn't really helping them, either.

KEVIN LEVY

We premiered *America's Next Top Model* after the finale of *Buffy* and that was amazing, because that turned into a giant hit for us at UPN. I don't think *Top Model* would have been as much as a self-starter had it not had that lead-in. When we got wrestling it was a big deal; when we got the new *Enterprise,* that was a big deal, but this was a *really* big deal from a competitive standpoint, because it was taking away a major piece from our prime competitor, which was the WB. So not only was it an addition for us, it was addition by subtraction for them as far as our perspective went. And then we got *Roswell* as well. I remember when Dean Valentine, who was our CEO, made that announcement to the assembled company, there was just massive applause when we got it. It was very exciting.

MARTI NOXON

(executive producer/show runner, *Buffy the Vampire Slayer*)

Joss was really clear that resurrection could only come at a cost. That when Buffy comes back, it's not going to be easy. I think that was sort of a genius twist in that we all assumed she had been in some sort of horrible place, and then we discover the reason the resurrection is so painful for her is because she *wasn't*. That was what made it such a great revelation and made Buffy's character a little more interesting.

When Angel came back from hell, he was twitchy for a whole different reason. But I do think Joss's philosophy was right: if you're going to defy the laws of nature in that way, you're going to have to pay a real price. It had repercussions through the whole season.

DAVID FURY

The great thing about a show like *Buffy* is anything is possible. In a show with magic, in a show with dark magic, in a show with witches, bringing someone back to life is not a problem. It's more like you don't want to trivialize that they died. In other words, if somebody dies in an emotional way and then you bring them back and they're fine, it would have been a total cheat toward everything we worked for in season five with Buffy's death. Which is why Joss wanted Buffy to be less than herself when she came back. He wanted her to be damaged and sullen and unhappy. And the secret comes out in the musical where we find out she was in heaven and she was yanked out of it. She was happy, she was with her mother, and this is why I don't know if I want to be back. "I was happier being dead." That's a huge thing to do.

MARTI NOXON

The way she came back was pretty much what people expected. Ultimately, I don't think Joss wanted to waste a tremendous amount of energy in bringing her back. That's not really what people cared about. It's a show called *Buffy the Vampire Slayer,* so they knew she was going to be back. It wasn't like we went out of our way for the audience to say, "Wow, we never saw that coming." At our writers meeting, we simply discussed what would be the most likely thing to have happen now if you were in this fantasy world.

DAVID FURY

When Joss presented that idea and when Marti and I were discussing it when Joss wasn't around, because he was off writing the musical for the first several episodes of the season, we knew this had to be a very painful birth bringing Buffy back, and we had to play into that. That's what people were responding to. They were saying things like, "It's not as fun as it used to be; Buffy is such a drag; it's so serious." That was all intentional. There was a lot of discussion about that. How much of the audience was going to be alienated and when are we going to snap her out of this? Obviously, the key was it's going to be the end of the season when she needed to climb back out of her grave for herself to decide she wanted to live in this world. That was the biggest part.

MARTI NOXON

Once Joss found his hook in the story—that she had been in a good place—he was really committed to the idea that she would not be all cheery when she got back. It's funny, because although the show is not theological in that way, we finally ran out of excuses. Joss has often said that there is no "heaven" as such in the Buffyverse. But if there's a bad place, there has to be a good place. Maybe it's not exactly heaven, but there are counterforces to all other forces, and Joss was finally willing to accept that. A recurring theme in Joss's work and both shows is that life is hard and it's people's actions and relationships with each other that make it livable. He's never said it was a pretty worldview.

JOSS WHEDON

(creator/executive producer, *Buffy the Vampire Slayer*)

Season six was basically about, "OK, now we're grown-ups." You take away Giles, because Tony wanted to go back to England. You see, the recurring theme is that whenever the actors are available, we work around it. But it made sense. We have no mentor, we have no mother, we have no parental figures.

MARTI NOXON

In "Flooded," we were like, "You know, the house is a metaphor for all of the adult problems she'll be dealing with." It turned out pretty well. But we also said, "You know what, not that exciting to have Buffy deal with bills." Because it's not *Buffy the Debt Collector,* it's not *Buffy the Credit Card User,* it's *Buffy the Vampire Slayer.* So we started toying with the idea of adult responsibilities and then decided we probably have to go to nasty sex instead. We tried out a bunch of those in "Flooded" and kind of dispensed with them, because then after an episode we were kind of like, "Well, we probably don't want her worrying about the actual realities of adult life because it got boring."

JOSS WHEDON

We were dealing with marriage and alcoholism and a really abusive relationship. We were dealing with someone who is practically suicidally depressed. It's weird, but people didn't respond to that so much.

MARTI NOXON

We both wanted to reflect the tumult of being in your twenties. Even though the show wasn't as clearly defined by metaphor as it was when we were back in high school, it's appropriate. The twenties are a much more murky period. I think we both wanted to make sure that it felt very real; that when you get to the age that Buffy and the others were, there's supposed to be this really strong conflict between that desire on one hand to be young and taken care of and irresponsible, and on the other to really take charge of your own life. Those two things pull you in really different directions. For me—and I think for a lot of people I knew at that age—it's kind of a war. Sometimes the grown-up is winning and sometimes the kid is winning. That's what we really wanted to deal with.

JOSS WHEDON

Season six of *Buffy* saw a very dark turn for the series, as Buffy herself, recently returned to life, spent most of the year in a very unhappy place and involved in a decidedly unhealthy relationship with Spike.

SARAH MICHELLE GELLAR
(actress, Buffy Summers)

It was definitely tough for me. It's so hard to separate myself from her, so it was tough for me to see these situations and think, "But Buffy wouldn't do this. . . ." And I felt pressure from the force of the fans. I know Joss and Marti both particularly talked me down from a ledge a couple of times, because it just felt so far removed for me at the time. And maybe that was the point—maybe I was struggling in the same way that she was struggling to find who she was. It just felt so foreign to me.

DAVID FURY

The dynamic changes a little bit when you don't have the show runner and visionary of the show around and part of you feels like we're kind of floundering. As much as we're moving forward and we're trying to anticipate and go, What would Joss do here? it was difficult. Marti tried to rely on me a lot for that. I was flattered and appreciative, but I had also been doing a lot of work at *Angel* and kind of splitting my time between the two, so I feel like I wasn't available enough to her, which I felt very badly about. We tried to work together and Marti tried to run the show just as she felt Joss would, but I guess there was always a feeling in the back of our minds, Joss is coming back, right? The show is still going on, he's not just gone, he'll come back eventually. And he did come back. He was living on the East

Coast at the time. He would fly in for a few days and discuss what we were doing for those first couple of episodes and he'd give us thoughts, and then he would go away again.

Marti never really, to my mind, got enough time to really mold into the role of show runner. As much as Joss said he was turning the show over to her, it didn't happen sort of. I was busy writing the second episode, she was writing the first, and when we were writing, we were really not together during that period. So there were a lot of times when she would convene the writers while I was writing or I'd get together with some of the writers while she was writing. We hadn't quite found the way we were going to do it. Joss would come in and give his blessing on certain things, give his notes on scripts we'd hand in, and then disappear again.

JOSS WHEDON

I do remember there was a time when I said to Marti, "OK, I think Buffy's been gone for too long. We've lost her, and it's time now to win her back."

MARTI NOXON

I remember that day, too. It was just a day when everybody kind of thought, "OK, we've reached the bottom of the pool. It's time to surface." Sarah told me, "I just feel like I've lost the hero completely in all this exploration."

SARAH MICHELLE GELLAR

I always looked up to Buffy. I thought when I was younger I would have loved to have a role model like that. A woman who showed you that you don't have to be the smartest and you don't have to be the most beautiful, but you can protect your family and the people that you love and you can be a powerful woman. I think that's what made season six hard for me. For all of us, but especially Joss, Marti, and me, we love her and it was hard for all of us to watch her suffer. I think it was a part of growing pains. It was a tough time, and that's what came through in the end, which was great, because when Buffy herself resurfaced, we all resurfaced and found our voice again.

JOSE MOLINA

(executive story editor, *Firefly*)

I think the show kind of ran its course. The show was designed to be a high school show. And the high school show ended in season three. Then they went to college and the show changed pretty drastically right then and there. So it was evolving, and even season four had some of the best episodes they ever did with, among others, "Hush"; season five is another college season but it had "The Body," which is probably my favorite episode of *Buffy*, hands down. But you can tell, even in those episodes, that it was getting a little grown-up and a little dark and getting a little away from the more fun escapist stories that were there earlier. Of course, the arc of "Becoming" is one of the most heartbreaking arcs in genre TV that I've seen to date. So it's not like the show was ever a laugh riot.

MARTI NOXON

We started to say, "Yeah, we recognize that the season was dark," and now it's what everyone says. I've talked to a lot of fans who really enjoyed the season and didn't have problems with it since, overall, there was still a lot of funny and a lot of good. However, we definitely went to a very dark place, particularly with Buffy and Spike. I recognize that. We took that elevator pretty far down. We got the message that people didn't like a dour *Buffy*, and, you know, we absolutely agreed. You can't stay in that place. But at the same time, it's hard to hear people say, "Yeah, it just wasn't to our liking."

We've had criticism before. Season four also got a lot of hits, so it was a little cyclical. Season four had a great deal of great in it, but people didn't like Riley, people didn't like the Initiative, people didn't like Maggie. It was a loyal fan base, but we heard people wanted stuff to lighten up a bit.

JOSE MOLINA

Marti's sensibilities might have been darker than what the show was used to. And it was really her show. Joss was there, but season seven he was running *Angel* and *Firefly*. So the change of ownership, if you will, was a little jarring. And, as many good episodes as there are in seasons six and seven, the change in tone sort of left me missing what was there before.

DAVID FURY

I will say the show got extremely sexual in the last couple of seasons. It went there. I know Marti and Joss wanted to push the envelope. Joss wanted to make the show darker and he wanted to push standards and practices into letting him do some really twisted things. He wanted Buffy to be self-destructive in a twisted way, and it's hard to convey that in a family show or something that is more network friendly. Marti was very into the relationship stuff; she was into the Spike-Buffy thing and the sort of self-destruction, the idea of Buffy being reckless with Spike and getting into a kind of, like, hate sex. It's kind of sophisticated dark stuff, psychology certainly. That was largely the tone of that season, which was a shift from what we'd been doing on the WB. It seemed appropriate at the time. I think Joss was a little surprised that there was so much pushback, but he never regretted it or thought we made a mistake. He always knew it needed to be that way.

In *Harry Potter and the Order of the Phoenix,* Harry is a cranky teenager. I told Joss that in season six Buffy is Harry. He needed to go through that. It's part of the ritual of growing up into adulthood. It's going through the process of being an asshole who hates everybody, because no one understands them. He agreed that's sort of what Buffy was meant to be in season six.

STEVEN S. DEKNIGHT

Joss knowing where he was going with that, knowing that they would bring Buffy back but she would come back with problems. There's that wonderful moment in an episode I wrote called "Dead Things," where the nerd trio accidentally kill one of their ex-girlfriends, where it turns really dark. Buffy has been carrying on with Spike and she has that wonderful thing with Tara where she says, basically, "Please tell me there's something wrong with me." Because if she didn't come back wrong, then these bad choices are her fault.

SARAH LEMELMAN

(author, *"It's About Power":* Buffy the Vampire Slayer*'s Stab at Establishing the Strength of Girls on American Television*)

Once Riley disappears from Buffy's life, she faces much upheaval, especially since she dies for longer than a couple minutes when she previously drowned in the first season and is brought back to life by the Scooby Gang. This puts her into a deep depression, and she is seen as experimenting with her "darker" self. As a result, she finally gives in to the temptation of Spike, who had been lusting after her for much of the time that Buffy was with Riley. When she proceeds with her "relationship" with Spike, she continues to hold the power, as she had done with Riley, but to a much greater degree. She is certainly no passive female and, instead, dominates Spike to the point where she effeminizes him. This negative and extremely cruel treatment of Spike ultimately leads to his attempted rape of Buffy.

DAVID FURY

The Buffybot thing initially came out of the robot episode "I Was Made to Love You" [in which Spike asks Warren to make a robot Buffy for him]. We were told that Britney Spears was a huge fan of the show and we got word from her reps that she wanted to guest-star on *Buffy*. So the story that was conceived ultimately by Joss, "I Was Made to Love You," was meant for Britney Spears to play the robot. I had a little daughter who was a Britney fan. I took her to the concert and she begins the concert with her face on screen, speaking in almost robotic way, along the lines of, "I want to please, I want to make you mine." And robotically. I think Joss saw it, too, or he heard about it, but he got this idea that if Britney is going to be on the show, she is going to be a robot, a sex-slave robot, because that's what she presents to her audience when you see her.

He presented that to Britney's reps and she balked, because she wasn't looking to do that. I think she was more looking toward being with the Buffy gang as opposed to being some kind of sex-slave robot. The obvious thing that came out of that was Spike making a Buffybot using the same technology from that and having a Buffybot made for him.

I always like when things from the past feed events and ideas into stories. You pull from some other past ideas, because it all feels much more organic that way. It came out of that; it wasn't just random. It was pretty odd to see our heroine Buffy be reduced to that with Spike. But Spike recognizes it is not good enough for him; he is telling us it isn't just external. It's just infatuation, because he was getting that from the robot, but he wasn't getting her real love.

JAMES MARSTERS
(actor, Spike)

That was perfect! That was in the vein of my idea all along of—This is it! This is exactly it! He should be in love with Buffy and just making an idiot out of himself in pursuit of that. The Buffybot is just so much more obscene than anything I could've thought of. It was the most pathetic stalker move imaginable.

DAVID FURY

To me, it's all about a Hellmouth and the things that have come out: the demons, the ghosts, the monsters of your youth that you have to battle. When it become robots, you start going, "Wait a minute, how does that fit into the show?" Joss would say, "You're just way overthinking it. The Hellmouth should be able to provide us with anything we want to do; the energy that comes out of it makes mad scientists out of humans who then go ahead and create something evil."

MARTI NOXON

We had talked about the Spike-Buffy romance toward the end of season five. Joss and I were like, "You know, this is what has to happen. We've got to take this seriously, because he is by far the most sort of screwed-up guy around." We just felt like that's whom she'd be drawn to under the circumstances. Also, you know, he's not unsexy. So we wanted to take advantage of that.

DAVID FURY

It became, "Does Buffy need a love interest?" Of course, it eventually came around to Spike, which was an unusual choice. It was one many of the fans embraced. I was a little less enthusiastic since I knew the vampires were demons essentially. The demons possess someone once they die. So the idea that Spike could love genuinely or Buffy could fall for Spike in any way was tricky for me. We were able to get there once Buffy came back from the dead and she was all messed up. *Then* she could become Spike's love interest, because it was self-destructive. A lot of people still romanticize that. I myself had to come around to it as I eventually started writing episodes about the relationship and I had to believe in it. Those were the challenges that came when we removed Angel. Joss loved those challenges more than he would have loved keeping them together and keeping everything safe and letting the fans dictate, "Oh, don't ever break them up; we love them." He was all about pain.

SARAH LEMELMAN

After Buffy comes back from the dead, Buffy gradually spends more time with Spike, which comes to a climax in "Smashed." She continues her demeaning treatment of Spike by yelling to him, "Look at you, you idiot. Poor Spikey. Can't be a human, can't be a vampire. Where the hell do you fit in? Your job is to kill the Slayer, but all you can do is follow me around making moon eyes." The two engage in combat before Buffy kisses Spike, and after he declares his love for her. This results in a night of hard-core bondage and discipline/sadism and masochism (BDSM) sex between the two, which Buffy rushes to get away from in the morning, describing their engagement as a "freak show."

Spike tries to make the previous night seem momentous, but Buffy downplays its importance and takes on a "man's" role in the conversation, stating it was nothing more than "just sex," because Spike is "convenient." This degrading conversation makes Spike clearly uncomfortable, and he has to assure himself that he is evil and dangerous, which points to the beginning of his confusion over his identity.

In his frustration over Buffy, Spike also became involved with Harmony, now a vampire, whom he remained disdainful of throughout their short and tortured relationship.

MARTI NOXON

A lot of times when we're searching for a character to serve a function in an episode from week to week, we'll think of our cast of characters and see if there is someone from our ensemble who we can use as opposed to someone you've never seen before. Especially if you've had a good experience with an actor and you feel that they can pull it off. And we'll go back and see if we can figure out who that person can be. If we can weave it back into the world, we try to do it. Harmony was a great example of that. So was Anya; she was supposed to be a one-shot; she moved up to that bar and yelled at that bartender about being two hundred years old or something, and we thought, "Oh, that's kind of funny." And she's amazing.

MERCEDES MCNAB

(actress, Harmony Kendall)

He was really nasty and there're times when you are an actor and sometimes you are not really feeling 100 percent committed or whatnot. Every moment is 100 percent genuine. But with those scenes in particular, it felt really in the zone. I felt he and I were both super in the zone and the scenes really translated well and we worked well together. For me, it was just that he was the bad boy, the unobtainable male that every girl tried to turn good, eventually. Which generally never works out.

MARTI NOXON

There was a lot of discussion of how we could get Buffy and Spike to the next phase of their relationship. We had talked about lots of realistic ways it could happen, and Joss was like, "It just has to be epic. It can't be a little thing." The whole notion there was that it was going to come out of the dramatic dynamic they had, which is as much about violence as it is about anything else. In my mind, Spike was always self-centered in his goodness. It's always about his wants and needs. He's not a moral guy and he is good when it serves him to be good. But I don't know if we put enough emphasis on that. He was a little less ambiguous and a little bit more the hero. But he's not a hero. People came to think of him as this softer, more righteous guy, but at least in my mind at his core, he did not have a soul. We still thought of him as a sociopath in the sense that he acts the way he thinks people want him to act in order to get what he wants. But if you've lived in the Buffy universe for years, the dude is just bad. It was the chip that kept him from being *really* bad.

JAMES MARSTERS

What I said to them actually was, "I know at the beginning of the season I was a little bit freaked out because you were taking Spike in different directions. I feel like I'm on a roller coaster, where, like, you get kind of freaked out the first hill you climb. As you start to fall, you start to scream, right? By the middle of the ride your head is back and whatever happens you just go with it." That's where I ended up with Joss, "Just do whatever you want. I'm never going to be nervous. Do anything. Put me in a dress—I don't care. The one thing I ask you is give me two weeks notice if you want to take my shirt off." He kind of got cocky. "Oh, two weeks, huh? Follow me." I ain't like Angel and I certainly ain't like Riley none, so it was very interesting and a whole new thing.

SARAH LEMELMAN

When Riley returns to Sunnydale momentarily, Buffy reevaluates her life, as Riley reminds her that Spike is "deadly, amoral, [and] opportunistic" and that she is a "hell of a woman" who deserves better. Buffy decides to finally end things with Spike, and, for the first time, she treats him like a man rather than an object, when she closes their relationship: "I'm using you. I can't love you . . . And it's killing me. I have to be strong about this. I'm sorry, *William*." Here, she uses his real name, instead of Spike, which puts the two on the same ground for the first time in their brief affair.

MARTI NOXON

It was the beginning of the most divisive story line we've ever had, which is Buffy and Spike boning. I've never seen such a strong reaction on both sides; people either loved it or hated it. To this day, people either truly believe that Spike is completely redeemed and he should be treated a lot better or they truly believe that Buffy was a fool for trusting someone who's been so evil and how could she be so unheroic to let herself be caught up in this really sordid romance? So, you had the total Buffy-Spike shippers or the people who are like, I just don't respect Buffy anymore. And it was fascinating to see.

You know, I slept with bad guys all through college and it was really hot. There were certainly a number of people who were like this who were really hot. I don't even care who's doing it or why. And neither of them are all good or all bad. It wasn't black and white. I've taken a lot of heat from Internet folks, especially because I said stuff like, "You know that that relationship can't work" or "with/without things changing" and other things that make them feel like we're not responsible—or we're sort of comparing it to the Angel-Buffy romance and saying that that romance was really idolized, and this one isn't.

But to me it's much more real. It's like, if these two crazy kids could make it work, it'd be a lot more interesting than kind of a perfect romance with obstacles not of their own making. At the end of the year, Spike went and did something radical, but the violence of it upset people. It's hard to say you're the most feminist show ever and have people beating each other up all the time.

JAMES MARSTERS

I was just terrified. Like, when you do a movie or a play you can read the script beforehand and decide if you want to put yourself through that or if you want to show that part of yourself or if you want to go through the rigors of filming that. Or you can pass. You can say, "I don't want to do that." When you do a TV show, normally once you film one episode, you know what's going to be asked of you, because most television shows are fairly repetitive, which is not a good thing. But when you work with Joss Whedon, all bets are off. You're contracted to do anything that he comes up with to anyone that he wants you to do it to and whatever he dreams up. I started to be terrified of the new script. I'm going to have to experience anything that is thought of. It was scary, but that worked, because I think that Spike was terrified by himself, and it all kind of works. But yeah, it was a horrible realization that all bets were off.

In the fifth season's "Fool for Love," a crossover with *Angel*'s "Darla" episode, it had been revealed the fearsome Spike was originally a meek poet from 1880s-era London named William, who was the object of scorn and derision from his contemporaries and rejected by the love of his life, Cecily. Shortly thereafter, Drusilla sired him and he joined with Angelus and Darla as they traveled the globe on a reign of terror before he killed two Vampire Slayers, a Chinese Slayer during the Boxer Rebellion and a second in New York in 1977.

DAVID FURY

I bucked on doing "Fool for Love." I had an opportunity to do the episode, but because I couldn't buy into it, it went to Doug Petrie and he did an amazing job. He sort of almost kind of convinced me, because he did such a great job with that episode. I went "Gee, I wish I'd done it after all." It still kind of weirded me out that Spike, a soulless creature, could fall in love. I kept saying, it's just an infatuation. It's only external, it's only this, he can't possibly be in love, he has no heart, he has no soul. But I came around; they beat it out of me.

JAMES MARSTERS

What that episode did for me is explain the dichotomy between someone who could truly love his girl and be completely sweet and loving to her and also be a soulless spawn of Hell. That was always to me the most interesting thing about Spike. It was never really addressed. I have thought sometimes maybe it's best not to. I think they did about as well as you could. Spike's progression is the progression of a lot of males, which is early years, not really finding yourself, not really finding your strength, and then finding something that really hooks you and helps you become yourself.

The thing I finally understood when I think about Joss and the way he worked, he and Marti, I don't think the cool is that interesting to them. I think that they can set it up and achieve it effortlessly. I think that it was usually a setup for something much more fallible and much more human and much more goofy and pained and tortured and humiliated. That's what really great writing addresses, the human condition and all its frailty and all its vulnerability. At first, when they started taking my character down from the height of cool that they had placed me, it was a little bit scary. Eventually, I understood why.

And if the show hadn't pushed the limits enough in the sixth season, in the episode "Gone" Xander uncomfortably walks in on an invisible Buffy having sex with Spike.

DAVID FURY

I got to direct my first episode, which allowed Sarah a little break from all the angsty things and to get giddy about being invisible, about the fact that she didn't have to worry about being back in the world, because no one could see her anymore. That was a little attempt to lighten the mood a bit and take us out of being completely somber and to have her having a fight scene with the three invisible nerd villains. It was part of season six which was a definite shift, which unnerved a lot of people. They just didn't understand what we were going for in season six. Buffy was always funny and you're trying to work in the funny, but Buffy is not getting any of the funny. She's not going to be the one quipping. It was a lot trickier to do.

That episode was fun to do, because it was so ridiculous to stage a ridiculous fight with invisible characters. It was a bit of an attempt to find something more fun and to go a little more comic. It was Joss's idea and it needed to be there to cleanse the palette from all the darkness. Her feeling that her invisibility allowed her to be who she was, to be a little bit more lighthearted and reckless, but reckless in a much more fun way.

MARTI NOXON

Yeah, that was something that Joss and David Fury just got all excited about and I was just like, "Ewwwww!" It was disturbing to me . . . and still is. It just shows you that even I have my limits.

JAMES MARSTERS

In a way every year I felt he was so completely different. When they brought me on the show, the two things that I thought were the linchpins of the character was, one, an extreme pleasure in hurting people; and, two, real love for my girlfriend, Drusilla. When they brought me back on the show [in season four], I had neither one of those and I was like, "What are we going to play?" And they found it.

MARTI NOXON

He would've hurt people if he could, in certain circumstances. But, you know, if you've sort of lived in the universe of *Buffy* for years, the dude is bad—and it was the chip that kept him from being *really* bad. This guy is not to be trusted. If I were Buffy, I could trust him with anything sort of related to me, but I wouldn't trust him in the big scheme of things. In my mind, Spike is always self-centered. It's always about his own wants and needs. It's always about Buffy or doing something for Buffy. But anyplace else, he's pretty much amoral. He's not a moral guy. He's good when it serves him to be good. He's not really a hero. He would never eat Dawn. He probably wouldn't eat any of the Scoobies . . . maybe Xander. But, and I feel that this could be the fault of us, people came to think of him as a sort of softer, more kind of righteous guy.

JAMES MARSTERS

I remember one time we were blocking a scene in Buffy's house and Xander was bleeding out in the corner, having been mauled by some demon or something. The cast was gathered around him, gnashing teeth and wailing and keening. I was over in the corner, up against the wall looking bored. The director came up to me and goes, "James, you gotta go over there and care. I know it's early in the morning, but you're a cast member, he's a cast member, he might die. You gotta go over there and express concern." I was like, "No, I don't." And he was like, "Don't you care about Xander?" "Nope, don't care at all. Could live or die—check with Joss. I don't care at all." He was like, "Really? What about the rest of them?" I was like, "Buffy, definitely. Buffy's mother, yes. But the rest of them, no, not at all." So yeah, if you were Buffy or if you were part of her immediate family, then I cared about you. If you weren't, then you were on your own.

Dawn was effectively Buffy's daughter, I think. As far as Buffy's journey, you know . . . her mother dies, and very quickly she gets this little sister whom she now has to take care of. So she's just quickly a single mom. Since I love Buffy, Dawn becomes my stepdaughter, emotionally speaking. I kind of approached it that way.

MARTI NOXON

It got so dark and so intense and then even darker still when Buffy just beats the hell out of Spike. Some people had a real hard time with that and I dig on that one. I understand where they're coming from. It was something that, you know, just went to a real dark place and this is where people started to feel like, "OK, like the episode, like the show, but what's going on?" You know, what's going on with Buffy? What's going on with Spike? I get that. She beats the crap out of him. I can understand why people were starting to wonder. I wouldn't say that we were floundering at all, but I would say that at that point in the relationship we didn't know where it was going and all we had was just her raw emotion. That's what got expressed: just complete confusion and the fact that she kept taking out her pain on him and that he would take it.

JAMES MARSTERS

Every year, I felt like I was playing a new character. I started as the boy toy for Dru. I was cannon fodder and I was going to be done away with and Dru was the main thing. Then I graduated to villain. Then I guess I was the wacky neighbor for a while. Then I was the forlorn man in the corner loving the woman who didn't give anything back. Then I was the lover. Then I was the unhealthy boyfriend.

DAVID FURY

I believe that Spike was a monster even when he was convinced he loved Buffy. He was still a vampire. Yes, he had a chip in his head which kept him from killing, but I think ultimately the vampire's a monster. Unless they have a soul like Angel they can't be anything else. Spike is a demon. There's this demon inside him, so the attempted rape of Buffy. As frightening and awful as that may seem, people were still romanticizing Spike and Buffy, and that was the problem I was having. I don't think their relationship should have been rooted for at that time. At that time, I thought this is a wrong, twisted thing.

JAMES MARSTERS

It all came to a climax in the bathroom in "Seeing Red" when Spike is convinced that if he and Buffy make love one more time they'll come back together and everything will be all right. I don't like those kinds of scenes. If I know that a movie has a rape scene in it, I don't go see it. If something like that comes up on television, I turn it off. It's too upsetting for me. I passed on a lot of roles that have that in it.

But in *Buffy* I was contracted to do whatever they came up with, and that came down the pipes. One of the reasons I think why *Buffy* resonates to this day is that Joss found nine of the best writers in Hollywood and he discovered them all. He found them when they were unknown and young and hungry. He's given Hollywood a whole new generation of writers who are now some of the most influential producers in Hollywood. But what he asked them to do was to come up with their worst day. The day that they're ashamed of. The day they don't talk about. The day that keeps them up at night. And then slap fangs on top of that dark secret and tell the world about it. It was a sustained act of bravery and vulnerability every single week. The writers would not tell you what the life experience was that led to the episode, but we were always guessing.

In that instance, the story was broached by one of the female writers who in college got broken up with by her boyfriend and convinced herself that if they made love one more time, then everything would be fine. She went over to his place and really kind of forced herself on him and he had to push her off and say no. This was a crushing blow to this young woman in her college days and was something she thought about a lot. I think the thought was that since Buffy is a superhero and could defend herself, that you could flip the sexes and it would work. My feeling was that the way the storytelling works is to give the audience a vicarious experience and to have the adventure. You climb behind the eyes of the lead. When anyone watches *Buffy*, they *are* Buffy, and they get to have that adventure as if they're Buffy. That's how storytelling works. And so I was going to try to rape the audience, and *they're* not superheroes. It is a vastly different thing to have a man do that in a scene than a woman, just as an effect on the audience. It was the worst day of my professional career. It was very painful. I remember being in the corner in a fetal position just kind of shaking in between takes.

It led me into therapy, which turned out to be a very good thing. I'm a lot happier having gone through successful therapy than I was before. So it all came out to a good thing for me in the end. But it was a hard day. What I will say is that, as an artist, I don't want to be in my comfort zone and when I'm too comfortable it's probably not as interesting. I was certainly not in my comfort zone at that time. It propelled all the characters in the right way, and it all worked. But it was a hard episode to film.

DAVID FURY

This is a monstrous person who is now obsessed with our hero who is in a very vulnerable place. But don't forget: he is a monster. They went, Spike is so funny, and he quips, and he can't kill anybody; he's so sweet and cute and I want [him] and Buffy to get together. The attempted rape was Steve DeKnight's episode, so blame him for it, by the way. It was an attempt to remind the audience Spike is bad; don't root for this relationship. The people who were for the relationship felt betrayed by Joss and us. It was very specific, because we'd say you shouldn't be rooting for him. It's the typical thing of a girl attracted to a bad boy. An awful wife beater, a guy who is a scumbag and some women go for him and we're not supposed to root for that. That's what this was, so I didn't have the problem everyone had. The people with the problems were the Spike-Buffy shippers who really wanted them to get together.

JAMES MARSTERS

When I got on the show in the very beginning I was told that I was going to die quickly, and I didn't want that. I wanted to live. I wanted to stay around, because they were paying me more than I had ever been paid in my life and I was a young father. As a storyteller, you always have to find the love, whether you're sculpting or painting or telling a story or singing a song. If you can find the love there, you find the gold, as I say. Whether it's love denied, love crushed, love blossoming, wherever that is is where the real power is. So I decided to play Spike with a soul right out of the blocks. I'm like, "Sure, Joss, I'm a soulless vampire. You got it, buddy. No problem," and I immediately went to the scripts like, Where's the love? In the beginning, the love was with Drusilla.

DAVID FURY

That weird incestuous sort of relationship they had was creepy, but I think it was because of his sensitive soul he didn't wholly turn into a monster, which is probably why he loved Drusilla. There was a part of Spike that wanted to love. She was crazy. She was doing anything she could. Spike was creative as a monster, but ultimately we realized there is this sensitive poet inside of him.

JAMES MARSTERS

Some of the scripts read kind of like he was making fun of Drusilla a lot, and I decided to undercut that. I remember there was one scene where she is looking up at the stars, but we're indoors. She's laying on the table. I'm in the wheelchair looking at her and I say, "It's not the stars, love, it's the ceiling." I make some crack about the fact that she's being crazy. I remember being like, "OK, well that's the line of the bad boyfriend that the audience will be glad to be rid of." So instead I just decided to kind of rest my chin on my hands, looking at her adoringly and just saying, "No, that's the ceiling, honey, not the stars," and just undercut that.

DAVID FURY

In "Grave," the episode where Spike is in Africa going through this test and it's revealed so he can get his soul back, because he knew he was a monster after what he did to Buffy and realized the only way he can love her is if he stops being a monster and gets his soul back. I totally bought into it. I understand it from a story standpoint. I'm offended that they were rooting for the relationship *before* that. Maybe we made a mistake in some cases by making Spike so sympathetic at times. But even the worst of us can be sympathetic at times. Even the worst human being can be sympathetic sometimes. Except maybe Donald Trump. So the rape was very controversial and I just don't agree with the interpretation people saw in it. We were not supposed to like Spike's relationship. When he got his soul back, some people didn't like him. I had lots of arguments on the fan boards about it. I said the fact that he got his soul back makes a difference. They didn't see that it did. And they said it's overrated, why do you need a soul? We had these weird arguments talking in theological theory. If we're saying that love comes from the soul, then that's really the only way that Spike can . . . experience real love. People to this day probably still curse my name for making that argument.

Most people didn't care about it like I did. I was the one who was not a shipper of Spike and Buffy, because of the soulless thing. So when he got the soul, for me, I could embrace it now. But what was nice is when we introduce him, he's still pretty fucked up. He's not, "Oh, I've got a soul now I'm a well-adjusted vampire." He's a guy who is pretty messed up and we did that with Angel as well. When we got to do flashbacks or at least part of the lore, it wasn't like Angel got a soul and he's like, "I'm better now, I'll fight for good." It was him living on the streets eating rats and stuff. He was pretty messed up, so it takes a while to make that adjustment from going from soulless vampire to soulful vampire. For me, it at least allowed me to root for Buffy to love him as imperfect and flawed as he was. Then he was someone whose love was more genuine. I always kind of rationalized it that he was more fixated on Buffy than he actually loved her. But with his soul, I went, "It was genuine." It just made it that much more painful, of course.

JAMES MARSTERS

I have to admit I was playing it with a soul from the beginning. Then it was terrifying to get a soul, because I had nothing left. I was like, "What else do I do? I've been doing a soul the whole time. I don't know what I'm going to add now." Luckily, the writing filled all that in. I didn't talk about it. I did not alert anyone to that one. That was going against the show. I didn't feel like I had a choice, though.

DAVID FURY

What I came to justify to myself is that Spike is an anomaly; that somehow that poet that's in him . . . retained a small part of his soul. A romantic part of his soul. And that is from being a very bad poet; someone who was full of all those emotions that allowed him to retain some part of himself that could love Buffy. That's how I rationalized it. I bought it, and I had to buy it because I wrote him in the relationship episodes and eventually in "Lies My Parents Told Me," telling the backstory of his mother and he's just an anomaly. He's the only vampire who could love even though he is almost entirely soulless. I argued that the chip that was in his head was conditioning somewhat and was messing with him. There's so many ways to rationalize it.

JAMES MARSTERS

The thing is, I didn't know Spike was getting a soul. Even filming the scene where it happens, there were three different versions of that scene I had to memorize and the one we finally filmed was a fourth. I didn't know what the hell was going on. I didn't know why I went to Africa. I didn't know if I was going there to get something to kill [Buffy] with. I had no idea. [Spike] kept saying, "I'm going to give her what she deserves." So Joss completely fooled me. I didn't even have the line, "I will give you back your soul!" and they're rolling. It was cut and move on and I'm like . . . James looks around in complete confusion. "Angel 2, yeah!" But that was the immediate problem is you cannot go where Angel has gone. You don't follow up the banjo act with a banjo act.

SARAH LEMELMAN

Susan Brownmiller explains that in most media representations "a good heroine is a dead heroine . . . for victory through physical triumph is a male prerogative that is incompatible with feminine behavior." However, this is not the case [in] *Buffy the Vampire Slayer,* which shows a new version of womanhood, where females can and will fight back and do not have to be [the] victims [of] violent men. Buffy's engagement with Spike is not used necessarily to satiate the desire of viewers to have her in a relationship, but it seems as though it is meant to show the growth and strides Spike makes from his malicious first appearance on the show in the second season. His final act of attempted rape is what triggers him to embark on a quest for redemption, in which he retrieves his soul, but, nevertheless, the time the two spend together is still worth analyzing, as Buffy is able to give strength to females in abusive relationships.

Despite much of the criticism that was leveled at season six as well as the divisive reaction to Spike's and Buffy's sadomasochistic relationship, the season also had its share of standouts, including *The Twilight Zone*-ish "Normal Again," in which Buffy is institutionalized after insisting that she's a Vampire Slayer, which her therapist, played by *Hill Street Blues*'s Michael Warren, insists is a psychotic delusion, also marking the brief return of Kristine Sutherland's Joyce.

SARAH LEMELMAN

Buffy is often seen as yearning to have an ordinary teenage girl life. While this [yearning] is mostly prevalent during her high school years and not openly vocalized once she enters college and beyond, it is perhaps still a wish she desires be fulfilled, as it becomes prevalent in a hallucination after she is poisoned in "Normal Again." This episode does not come until the end of the sixth season, after Buffy has faced much upheaval in her life, including the death of her mother as well as herself, raising her younger sister, and trying to financially support herself, all while carrying out her Slayer duties.

MARTI NOXON

That was the episode that also tripped people out. That was something that was written by Joss's former assistant. It was a pitch that he sold to us and then wrote. Diego [Gutierrez] worked as Joss's assistant for a couple years and he and Joss broke that story together. And it was always something we sort of saw as a stand-alone; it could fit in almost any season at various times. But the idea was really strong and I think the episode turned out really nice and moody and kind of intriguing. The question that seemed to bother people was whether we were actually saying that the whole series was in her mind. I think that we were teasing that, but nobody was coming out and saying, "Don't believe it, it's all fake." It was just a little bit of a tease.

We made a lot of jokes about the snow globe and *St. Elsewhere*. But it's not the truth.

It was a fake out; we were having some fun with the audience. I don't want to denigrate what the whole show has meant. If Buffy's not empowered, then what are we saying? If Buffy's crazy, then there is no girl power; it's all fantasy. And really the whole show stands for the opposite of that, which is that it *isn't* just a fantasy. There should be girls that can kick ass. So I'd be really sad if we made that statement at the end. That's why it's just somewhere in the middle saying, "Wouldn't this be funny if . . . ?" or "Wouldn't this be sad or tragic if . . . ?" In my feeling, and I believe in Joss's as well, that's not the reality of the show. It was just a tease and a trick.

The other fun thing about that is that it was directed by Rick Rosenthal, who was my mentor and boss for many years. He gave me my first big job after [I was] a waitress at a diner in Brentwood. I was writing on the side and he and I struck up a conversation one day and he said, "Geez, you seem like you could have some smarts. You should come pitch on the show that I'm working on."

SARAH LEMELMAN

In Buffy's telling hallucination, she finds herself in an insane asylum, where a doctor conveys to her that her Slayer life and friends are figments of her imagination. Her hallucination shows both her mother and father, alive and together, as wanting to help Buffy repudiate the false alternative reality that she has created in order for her to return home to her loving parents and a normal life. In the end, Buffy is able to fight off the allure of the hallucination, signaling her final rejection of the nuclear family and the securities that it can provide. It may have taken her over six years to realize that she does not need a normal life with a structured nuclear family, but her utterance of "good-bye" to her mother in the hallucination makes Buffy's rejection of familial patriarchy a poignant statement of independence.

But the fatalistic despair of "Normal Again" was positively chipper compared with where the series would eventually end up in its final episodes, which would take the series to its darkest depths yet.

JOSS WHEDON

We were dealing with what [had been] a metaphor, sex, has become very graphic and real sex. What was mystical demons have become three nerds with guns. Very real death, very mundane house payments—the idea was to break down the mythic feeling of the show, because there is a moment at childhood when you no longer get that. Everything isn't bigger than life; it's actual size. It's a real loss. At the same time, the darker side of power and Buffy's guilt about her power and feeling about coming back to the world and getting into a genuinely unhealthy relationship—that was all about dominance and control and, ultimately, deep misogyny.

How lost did we get? Well, our villain turned out to be Willow.

MARTI NOXON

"Wrecked" was the beginning of what was going to be the major arc of the latter part of the season. You know, it seems like it's sort of a resolution, but in fact it's just the beginning. And we all knew that. The part of it that I think is sort of funny is that people were like, "Oh, you know"—that was sort of literal, about Willow being a magic alcoholic. Magic—crawling around the ground and stuff. And it is, in fact, sort of literal, in the sense that we're trying to set up that she doesn't have any control. She's really fucked. But we also knew that this wasn't the end of the story line.

So even though people were like, "Ah, this isn't satisfying. It's just so 'Touched by a Marti,'" you know? But we were like, "Oh, you don't understand." It was one of those ones that was frustrating, because people would react a certain way and we'd be like, "You don't understand. It hasn't even begun." But there's stuff in that episode I really liked. The hallucinations and stuff were really trippy and fun. There was stuff in there I really liked, but I can see why the criticism would be had.

DAVID FURY

It's always fun to start playing people who are damaged or flawed. Actors relish the idea of playing villains and people with character flaws. If you're playing somebody that's just sweet, nice, and great all the time, it can be very boring for an actor. Since Willow had become a witch, the idea of that becoming addictive was an obvious allegory for drug addiction. It was about giving Aly an opportunity to play Willow differently and to have that being something that drives her relationship with Tara and eventually drives them apart. That was more or less what we were thinking at the time.

In "Doublemeat Palace," in the wake of her mother's death and the Summers family's depleted finances, Buffy has to get a job at a fast food restaurant, where she discovers there's more going on than just "do you want fries with that?"

MARTI NOXON

"Doublemeat Palace" is one of the craziest episodes we've ever done. It's just insane. The monster looks like a penis and we knew that. We had to paint it, because initially it was penis colored. It wasn't even a metaphor: it was just a big giant penis. And then we had to paint it brown and . . . it looked like a brown penis, and we just kind of went with it, because the whole episode was so crazy. It was so weird, and I personally really liked it. I just think it's just out there. It was let's try to just have a little fun in a crazy season. And it just got baroque. We tried to go with the feeling of a Coen brothers movie. It was weird and to some degree it succeeded; others not so much. But we got the giant penis.

STEVEN S. DEKNIGHT

I have very fond memories of season six. I know a lot of those are centered around that one episode, "Dead Things," which in a side story is one of the fastest episodes. It was the week before Thanksgiving and it started out I was in the room with the writers and then one writer went back east. Then another writer peeled off. By the end of that week leading up to Thanksgiving, literally, I was sitting in a room by myself. Everybody had left. The story wasn't broken. I went down the hallway and knocked on Joss's door and he was in there with Marti talking about the season.

He pops it open and I go, "Uh, everybody's gone. What do you want me to do?" He goes, "What do you mean everybody's gone?" I go, "They all left for Thanksgiving." He says, "All right, come in. Let's talk about it." We went in and talked about it for like a half hour and had a very loose break. He said, "OK, go off and write it. We need it by Monday."

Literally, I spent I think it was like three and a half days, no sleep, just kind of feeling my way through this episode that it didn't really have an outline on. Came back in Monday all ragged. Joss read it, and, in one of the best compliments he ever could have given me, he said, "You know what? I should have you locked up in a room and every now and then just slide food under the door for you." It turned out to be my personal favorite episode that I wrote, in that kind of fever dream, Thanksgiving crucible. I had a blast on that season. I enjoyed working on it.

MARTI NOXON

"Dead Things" was one of our more chilling, frightening episodes of the season actually. To me, it had some classic *Buffy* good stuff, which was, you know, playing the whole joke of turning Katrina into a sex slave and then that turning out to be no joke at all and not funny. And not funny to make girls your sex slave. In the *Buffy* universe, that's not a big joke. To play it for comedy and then just turn it on its head, I thought was really inspired. That was, again, a Joss pitch.

STEVEN S. DEKNIGHT

It was just so complicated, heart-wrenching, dark, and emotional. I just thought it was a brilliant thing that Joss did, knowing that he took these three nerds from previous episodes.

MARTI NOXON

I was talking to a friend about how to write Andrew and one of the other writers on staff was just like, "Go into Doug Petrie and Drew Greenberg's office, because they love to talk about this kind of stuff." I can talk about *The Partridge Family* and *Three's Company* and *Archie* comics, so I'd have to wander down to their office and go, "What would you say here?" and they'd say something about Han Solo.

STEVEN S. DEKNIGHT

The Trio were kind of goofy, kind of funny, but knowing they were going to do this really horrible thing and go really dark and bad. Knowing that eventually they were going to kill Tara and unleash dark Willow. If you look at that entire season, there's a lot of light and fluffy and fun with the nerds. Then it just all turns sideways, which is something I always loved about the show.

MARTI NOXON

How many times could you go, "It's the end of the world as we know it"? So we tried to do something a little different. We had to come up with a different way to create a threat. I wasn't really party to that criticism. I wasn't really hearing it. In retrospect, obviously, I have. I just was so into them; we just thought they were so funny. Maybe they amused us more than others. But we just thought they were so fun and their motivation was so interesting. You know, what I think people were objecting to was that there wasn't that typical momentum of the season like, "Here it comes, here it comes, here it comes. Here comes the Big Bad."

To be honest, maybe we were being a bit experimental. We were all tired of running that same scenario. You can only say, "It's the worst thing ever!" so many times without feeling like you're just the biggest liar in the world. We needed a break, so we just structured the whole season differently than anything we'd ever done. I just enjoyed that. It was like, oh God, we're faking left and then it's going to be Willow and people may intuit that. But even so, it's just so refreshing not to have to keep saying, "Here comes the apocalypse. Fishes are going to fall from the sky and there's gonna be blood in your bathtub, and boy, it's never been worse than this." It was very nice to not have to ramp up for a whole season.

STEVEN S. DEKNIGHT

Joss had the idea of how it happened and he knew that that was going to incite Willow to go all Dark Phoenix. I'll never forget. He said, "Listen, I've got this one scene in my mind. It's kind of in the coda of the episode. She's in her room; Tara's talking to Willow. There's a gunshot from outside, and Willow's splattered with blood. Tara's last words are, 'Your shirt,' and then she dies." I'm thinking, "Holy shit, that's brilliant. That's awful . . . and brilliant . . . and tragic." Joss would have those cornerstone ideas and a lot of great detail. Then he would rely on his writers to kick it around, flesh it out, pitch it to him. Then he would make adjustments. That's really the way it worked. Joss almost always had the big idea.

DAVID FURY

Clearly people were upset about a beloved character, Tara, being killed. Absolutely. Especially when it's a romantic character. If it had been Angel who had died during the height of the Buffy-Angel thing, that would have been a controversy. But the real controversy was that Joss had provided the world with this wonderful, sweet, and romantic lesbian relationship and killed one of the couple. It's frustrating, because you should be able to kill whoever you want, but unfortunately people read so much into it. Or so much into the fact that, "Oh, you had to kill the lesbian." I'm like, "My God, we killed everybody." We killed so many people on this show, why not the lesbian? Because that's heartbreaking. It needs to happen so Willow can be sent to the dark side. It just made sense story-wise. People are very sensitive about it. They're sensitive when a character of color dies. Well, no, *anybody* can die. And hopefully we'll get to that point where people don't get so bent out of shape, because we're not looking for symbolism in everything; we're just looking for characters we love, of different diverse races or genders or anything else, and we're not going to make a political point of, "Oh, you killed the gay person."

STEVEN S. DEKNIGHT

It's a touchy thing when you kill a character, especially if it's gay, lesbian, trans, or a prominent non-Caucasian character. It can cause a lot of pain, so you have to approach it very, very carefully. Even if you approach it carefully, and reflectively, and with love and understanding, there's still going to be people that are upset. I remember in *Spartacus,* when we killed Oenomaus, played by Peter Mensah, a couple of people on Twitter said I was racist, because I killed the black character. I'm like, "Wait a minute, to start with, Oenomaus historically died sooner than when I killed him and, historically, was white."

DAVID FURY

Joss never apologized for anything. He says this is the story I'm telling. Tara doesn't die because she's a lesbian; Tara dies because it will break our hearts—and that's what he's looking to do. And so nobody should apologize. The fact of the matter is, if that's where the story needs to go, that's where the story needs to go. Stop looking for these characters to be symbols of something. They're just people. And never apologize for it.

STEVEN S. DEKNIGHT

I loved that ultimately the Big Bad was from inside and not an external force. I loved the idea that it was Xander's love and friendship for Willow that brought her back. It also spoke to all of us that grew up reading comics, the whole Dark Phoenix saga in the *X-Men*. I just really, really loved that whole thing and the fantastic way that he had hinted at this darkness in Willow when the vampire Willow came over in "The Wish." It didn't come out of the blue. You saw hints of it in other episodes that she had this capacity to be this very dark person.

SARAH LEMELMAN

The viewer gets a glimpse into Willow's "evil" persona in the episodes "The Wish" and "Doppelgangland" when Willow is shown as a vampire from another reality. Vampire Willow is very telling, in that she is sure of herself and confident in her sexuality. She wears tight, black leather clothes, with a plunging neckline, and bright red lipstick. In "Doppelgangland," the two Willows are contrasted to such an extreme. The lovable "real" Willow is forced by Principal Snyder to tutor a star basketball player and says to her, "I know how you enjoy teaching . . . I know you want to help your school out here. I just know." As Willow is complaining to Buffy that the principle is a bully, Giles enters the room, declaring, "Willow. Get on the computer. I want you to take another pass at accessing the mayor's files," and with no objection, she follows Giles's orders.

While Willow is shown as a doormat for other people to walk all over, vampire Willow is the exact opposite. When the basketball star mistakes the vampire Willow for the real Willow, he says to her, "You're supposed to be at home doing my history report. I flunk that class, you're in big trouble with Snyder. Till we graduate, I own your ass." Not standing for his insolence, she grabs him by the neck and throws him across the room, causing the "stud" to run away in fear.

Not only is vampire Willow cool and collected, but she is also highly sexualized, prompting Willow to describe her as "horrible," "evil," "skanky," and "kinda gay." At this time in the show, she does not understand the implications of her double, but less than a year after their meeting, Willow begins her expedition of identification when she meets Tara.

JOSE MOLINA

Willow was pretty much unrecognizable by the end of the show. It's interesting, because that arc really kicked into high gear when Marti took over. Marti had something to say about addiction that was important to her and she found a way of talking about addiction through Willow and also, you know, about abusive relationships with Buffy and Spike. So most of that I think is in season six and that's more of a reflection of Marti really being given ownership over the show.

MARTI NOXON

When I first started, I was doing a lot more writing and a lot less producing. So I loved it when I got to write a script; that's my first love. But because you do so much more, you've got to stop once in a while and say, "Wait a minute, I'm a writer." I love all this other stuff, but that's what I am first and foremost. That's the thing—you don't want to go too far from your primary purpose.

STEVEN S. DEKNIGHT

There's no way she ruined *Buffy.* I look at that season and there are great episodes. I love the arc of where it goes. Joss was in and out. I've got to be honest, even with *Angel,* it was run by somebody else because Joss couldn't physically be there, but he's always there. I remember when I was on *Angel,* literally going to the set of *Serenity* to talk to Joss about an episode and get notes. Even if he's not there, he's there to some extent.

DAVID FURY

Season six was a tricky season and it's the one Joss envisioned that if *Buffy* did come back, she would not be the same. She will have been lifted out of heaven. That's what he had come to early on so that she would be in this horrible teenage funk. That's kind of what we did and people got very turned off of the show. They said it lost all the fun; they blamed Marti for it, which was incredibly unfair. Marti does like to go to the angst part. She brings the emotional end to the stories that make them so great as well. But when that's all we were doing virtually, it wasn't all hijinks with some emotion. It was just very heavy with ennui and Marti took the brunt of it. To her credit, she embraced it. She fell on her sword and said, "Yep, it's me. I ruined *Buffy*."

JAMES MARSTERS

Oh my God, no! Joss needed someone with as much courage as he had and found that person in Marti Noxon. She is fearless as a storyteller. She can take you to those dark places and then she can make it pay off. She didn't destroy *Buffy* at all . . . *at all*. You know, when you affect people, when you touch them in places that they didn't plan to get touched, it can get a bit touchy [*laughs*]. They can get a little bit defensive. I often think when fans react that way, it may mean that they're actually doing it very well. Joss once said, "I'm not here to please the audience. I just give them something I think that they need and that's not always about wrapping everything up with a bow."

DAVID FURY

Joss hadn't intended on coming back in season six as he eventually did. As far as I recall, he turned the show over to Marti. He really did not want to come back as a show runner per se, but eventually he wound up doing it because we all knew it was his show; it's his vision. That doesn't take away from what Marti brought to the show and was able to do. She manned the ship fantastically. But ultimately Joss just needed the break. And, of course, his break was to go write a musical *Buffy*.

Regardless of how anyone ultimately felt about the season, there's one episode that is clearly a towering achievement for the series that continues to be feted and discussed to this day and is a contemporary television classic. That episode, of course, is the beloved musical episode, "Once More, with Feeling." Brilliantly written (songs as well as script) and directed by Whedon, the episode features the cast breaking into tunes while telling the pivotal and tragic story of Buffy's being ripped out of heaven when Willow's spell resurrected her–all in the guise of a candy-colored MGM musical . . . with singing demons, vampires, and Slayers, along with an unhealthy fear of bunnies.

SARAH LEMELMAN

This episode brings a demon to Sunnydale who causes its citizens to break out into song about their inner troubles and anxieties. It comes at a time when the Scoobies are transitioning to adulthood and highlights this fact, as the audience is able to hear all the characters' secrets. The episode itself was originally broadcast for sixty-eight minutes—breaking from the series' normal sixty-minute time slot. Once again, Whedon took a stab at something he had never done before, and may not have gotten the recognition the episode deserved, but his work nevertheless left its mark, as television in the later 2000s saw a rise in musical episodes, including in the popular *Grey's Anatomy* and *Scrubs*.

DAVID FURY

We knew he was writing the musical and I remember we were probably into the third episode when he came back with the DVD of him and his wife Kai singing on a demo of all the music from the musical and he had the script and we all sat around in a circle reading the script out loud, and then when we'd get to a song we'd put on the DVD and put the song on. We were just blown away. We could not believe that Joss had only taught himself piano a year or so earlier and that he'd written these great songs and we were just staring at each other. Joss was anxious to get into preproduction on the musical and that sort of took over.

JAMES MARSTERS

We used to have these great parties after Joss's Shakespeare readings at his house and we got to know each other really well.

AMY ACKER

(actress, Fred, *Angel*)

The Shakespeare readings were a blast. Everybody had a part. Joss would always have a huge, amazingly beautiful, delicious spread of food and he would do readings. A lot of time he had his brother or someone over who also did the music. They'd thrown some little songs together that would accompany the play. Afterward, it evolved to these little dance parties. It was the most wonderful way to spend a Sunday. I've never heard of another show runner doing it. I guess it helps we were all a little nerdy.

JAMES MARSTERS

I brought my guitar and started playing, because if you're at a party and play guitar, you know, you might as well bring it. After a couple times doing that, Joss started playing piano and other people started bringing their instruments and it became a party/music-making event. At one point Joss said that's where he thought up the idea for a musical, because he realized enough people in the cast could sing.

JOSS WHEDON

Before my dad wrote television, he wrote off-Broadway musicals. My mom had a framed telegram from Moss Hart saying he had a new show coming up and he wanted her to audition for it. And that was a beautiful, perfect little thing for her, and in a way it was like her way of telling us, "I had you three so I don't get to do that!" At Radcliffe, everybody was acting and doing little theatricals, and she directed stuff and starred in it at school or at summer stock or at the Dennis Playhouse, which is one of my earliest memories in Cape Cod for my whole childhood.

STEVEN S. DEKNIGHT

Joss is incredibly funny and quick-witted. I have seldom met anyone that had such a quick wit. Really, I can't even describe how funny Joss is and all of the ideas that just pour out. I'm sure everybody has a "Joss Whedon is brilliant" story, but when I first came in, I know he was learning how to play the piano. I heard rumors, "Oh, yeah, he's learning how to play the piano because he wants to do a musical episode." Then the next year he disappeared to the East Coast for a week or two. After a couple of weeks, we all get a package that's a script and a CD. He had written a musical script in that period of time along with the songs and recorded them with his wife.

JOSS WHEDON

There is a heightened state, particularly in a song in a musical, where if the musical is being done right, this is the moment where it all comes out; this is where everything is building to, and you have this perfect state where not only is somebody articulating who they are and what they need, but it rhymes. Like, it is absolutely this pristine, very structured thing. Everything I do is about that structure and about that moment of somebody going, this is the best version of me that I can explain. You're always trying to hit that feeling, whether it's sad, happy, or scary, whatever that feeling you get when a musical number is in that moment where you're trying to hit those peaks all the time in conversation.

MARTI NOXON

What can you say about old Genius Head? There was a tremendous amount of work and love put into that episode. Joss is a huge musical fan. He spent the majority of the summer writing the music and figuring out exactly how it was going to work. It took a lot more time and a lot more production value than a usual episode but [was] well worth it. It was almost like a vacation for everybody. Joss obviously conceived it and was the mastermind behind all of it creatively, but all of us got into the act one way or the other. Some of us quite literally.

JAMES MARSTERS

I was comfortable singing publicly; I was already doing it in clubs around Los Angeles. Tony [Head] had already come out with an album, so we were comfortable singing, but a lot of the other cast members rightly said to Joss, "You hired me to be a one-camera comedic-dramatic actor. That's my wheelhouse and we're succeeding here, and now you're asking me to do something that I'm not trained for and you're going to ask the audience to be entertained by that? Like, please, no!" I think one actor actually went to Joss and begged to juggle live chainsaws rather than sing, because that would be probably safer for their career than singing.

DAVID FURY

Everybody was excited about the idea, especially the actors who sang. The ones who couldn't Joss assured them they weren't going to look bad: "We're going to record these things and you're going to do fine." I think Aly [Hannigan] and Michelle were probably the most nervous. Sarah, as uneasy as she was initially, rose to the occasion beautifully. She loved dancing, she loved learning the choreography, and she thought she couldn't sing, but I think ultimately what she was able to do was great. There was some anxiety about it. Nobody said I'm not doing it; no one had a hissy fit about it. It was just definitely out of some people's comfort zones. Aly and Michelle were nervous but were given limited things to sing. Joss really protected them. He said, "I'm not going to make you sing huge songs. Just sing a line here, sing a line there." They got very excited once we were doing it. It was all very exiting. There was a lot of energy and buzz around the whole experience.

MARTI NOXON

Everybody felt really energized by it, because they got to do different things and the actors were all really excited. People were going to music lessons, rehearsals, and it was like putting on a show in the barn—only this was a really big barn and there was a $2 million budget. We were all awestruck by the end results. It was a culmination of years and years of stuff that Joss had wanted to do. He's very lucky that he gets to make it happen, and we're very lucky we get to see the end result. Most musical episodes on television are a little more gimmicky than this and don't necessarily move the story forward in a huge way. But this was so important in terms of the season.

JAMES MARSTERS

I thought Joss had gone crazy. I thought that he was absolutely jumping the shark. That he was taking a perfectly good show and just flushing it down the toilet. I mean, it's one thing to watch "Once More, with Feeling" because when you watch it it's just obviously a success and amazing and the music is fabulous. But if you just get the script and you haven't done it yet, it's a big risk.

I think the reason I have such fond memories about "Once More, with Feeling" is that, after a few days of complaining and fear, the cast realized that we were not going to talk Joss out of it and we stopped being so fearful, and we stopped whining, and we got to work. And suddenly people were hiring vocal coaches and dance instructors with their own money. Rehearsing in between scenes—this is the episode before we started filming "Once More, with Feeling." And we got to work. In the face of certain doom . . . guaranteed failure . . . we decided that we would go down swinging and try our best.

We knew we would fail, but we decided to try our best anyway. I was never more proud of us as a company. And then of course Joss edited the first scene that we shot and showed it to us . . . wheeled out a TV onto the soundstage . . . and we crowded around it, and it was brilliant! It was the Xander-Anya dance scene, and it was fabulous. We suddenly realized this thing could actually work. And then from that moment on, we were just flying high. Until the final scene when Hinton Battle came to town. Hinton played Sweet, the villain of the piece. Hinton is a Tony Award–winning Broadway musical stage actor. That man has chops. The *Buffy* cast was just standing in the Bronze staring up at Hinton doing his thing up onstage and realizing, "Oh, *that's* how you do it . . . we're screwed. Like, we can't do that." But luckily through the magic of editing, it all came together.

DAVID FURY

The story is so sound, which is the great part. It's one thing to do a musical episode, and a lot of shows have done it, but they do it as a lark. They do it as a goofy thing, but the songs in the *Buffy* musical and the story are so rich in meaning and emotion. The fact that this is the way Joss wanted to exposit where Buffy had been after she died and the reasons she's being the way she is. Getting under the skin of all these characters in the form of the musical . . . made it so much of a magnificent accomplishment. It was not just, OK, our characters can sing; they sing some songs, and we go back to some silly plot. It was very emotional. It's one of those episodes that makes you cry. It makes me cry when I think about it. It was so beautiful and so well done.

DAVID GREENWALT

(executive producer/cocreator, *Angel*)

Here's the thing that'll really just make you want to quit being a writer. Joss, when I met him, had a keyboard in the office and he did like a few chords. He piddled around on the piano a little bit. He certainly was no musician. The summer before the musical, he went to Cape Cod, where he and [his] then wife Kai had a home, and Tim and I and some of the writers went back there and Joss spent about six or eight weeks working on these songs. He's playing us these songs that are just incredible and then everybody had to sing and dance—even the ones that were shy about singing and dancing. He came up with this great episode, this amazing music. I frankly think it's better than most stuff that's been on Broadway.

JAMES MARSTERS

It was brilliant. It was absolutely wonderful. Everybody was just flying and smiles all over. There is something about music that just taps into emotions more directly than words. I often feel like words have to be processed by the intellect and then accepted or not accepted by the heart. But music bypasses the intellect completely and goes right into the heart. We'd be acting the scene and the time would come for the song. Joss would hit playback, and the big speakers would roar up and this beautiful music would come out and you'd lip-synch, but you'd feel like you were singing, and we were able to go to emotional places that you couldn't just doing dialogue. When a musical is designed, there is a point where the characters can't talk about it anymore. In order to express what they really want to express, they have to sing about it, so it jumps up a level. Then Joss, of course, puts that on its head, and he had people singing things they really should shut up about.

DAVID GREENWALT

I used to go when he was directing it with my then wife and we'd just watch it. It would be Friday night till midnight or two, and it was so beautiful to watch the making of that episode. And then his assistant forgot to enter it in the Emmy nominations, which is a pity because it certainly would've won something.

DAVID FURY

One thing I knew after I heard it was I wanted very much to film the making of it. I want to be behind the scenes, because I thought this is significant and really special, which Joss allowed me to do. By doing that, I wasn't around as much as I probably should have been since Marti needed help, but I got caught up in the musical and wound up going to all the recordings and filming everyone as they were doing all their voice tracks and doing the shooting. It's on the *Buffy* DVD behind the scenes. It was just me and my little camcorder interviewing everybody, asking them to talk about what the experience was like. It was really neat and great to do. But it put me in a weird place when I came back into the room after all this; I felt I'd been away forever. I feel badly I didn't help Marti as much as I should have. But she never complained to me or asked me to stop doing it. She held down the fort and got things done just perfectly without me.

JOSS WHEDON

It was an actual musical where people not only break into song, but they break into songs that I write that are about the story. It's not one of those, "We do a scene, then we do a Motown hit that vaguely fits the scene." It's actually song-driven storytelling that was very connected to the season, because it deals with emotion. I actually think of it as a sequel to "Hush," because singing is like being quiet. You say the things you wouldn't otherwise say. So a lot of the emotions were building over the first few episodes of the season, and then they burst out, literally, in song.

MARTI NOXON

We wanted to do something good and spooky. It was about following the repercussions of what they'd done. There had to be continuing repercussions from what had happened. Obviously, that one has the great scene at the end with the revelation that she had been in a nice place. It was a continuation of the same idea, that you don't get to come back from the dead without some heavy tariffs.

DAVID GREENWALT

I don't know any other executive producer who would be working that hard in year six. Joss would find something that would challenge him, that would actually frighten him a little. "Can I do an episode with no music? Can I do an episode with no dialogue? Can I do an honest-to-God musical and write all the songs?" Him challenging himself like that fired us all up on all of the shows. There was no phoning it in allowed around there; no resting on your laurels. Then *our* excitement kind of fed him and it was a nice little circle. If people were reading Shakespeare at his house on Sundays, he got me writing songs again, which I hadn't done in twenty years. It was all like a little renaissance. A very exciting place to be.

RAYMOND STELLA

(director of photography, *Buffy the Vampire Slayer*)

It was just the show with a little more of a flair. If I was outside, I would make it a little brighter, make it feel a little more dreamy. Adam Shankman was the choreographer, because there's a lot of singing and dancing. Shankman was the director on the *Mystery Girl* thing that I did in San Diego. Gay as a three-dollar bill. Not that there is anything wrong with that.

KEVIN LEVY

The musical episode was a big deal for us. We did have a party for the musical episode. I remember we screened it on the Paramount lot in that big theater that they have, and we invited a lot of the cast. That was the first time any of us had seen the final cut of it. It was great. It's just amazing to see that years later people still do all those sing-alongs.

STEVEN S. DEKNIGHT

His musical talent is vast. You can see his love of music and musical theater just shining through in that and *Dr. Horrible.* I long for another Joss Whedon musical, because I think he's so damn good at it.

DAVID GREENWALT

We all went and watched it. It was just amazing. Joss went from knowing five chords when we met to writing that episode in five or six years. That's a talent that's not visited on everybody. You combine that with the hard work ethic and you can't go wrong.

JAMES MARSTERS

By the time we got to "Tabula Rasa," which was the one after the musical, we were like, "Oh, this sucks. There's no music! It's boring." And in fact, "Tabula Rasa" was one of the most delightful, where we all lost our identities and it was complete farce.

MARTI NOXON

It was Joss's notion that they all lose their memory. I thought that was just brilliant, because that way we can have a fun, lighthearted episode and then in the end, you know, reality comes crashing back. And it's not good. So, that was really the goal there; to do something where we knew there were going to be repercussions, but we also knew wasn't going to be so serious and sad. And we found a way with Big Genius Head's help. I was really into that one. You know, we got to really poke fun at ourselves. It was farcical and turned out really well.

STEVEN S. DEKNIGHT

I love humor. One of the biggest things I loved [about] working on *Buffy* was just what Joss had set up. That you could have a deeply serious scene and somebody can say something funny, like in real life. It was never one or the other. The show does have so much great, great funny dialogue. I was surrounded by incredibly funny writers. David Fury, Jane Espenson's hysterical, Doug Petrie—just everybody was so much fun. In that sixth season, Drew Greenberg joined us, who was also just absolutely delightful.

MARTI NOXON

I would have done things differently if I had to do things again. But at the same time, overall I felt like it still was compelling. It may have made you mad or nervous or frustrated, but it was always interesting. We also had some really lovely episodes in there. I was just invested in the whole Spike-Buffy thing and the whole Willow thing. Those story lines really worked for me. I don't know how we could have done another "Here comes the Big Bad." We'd done it so many times and very successfully, but I just feel like you had to shake it up and that was probably what was going on. Joss was just interested in trying some new stuff and we were all for it. Season seven might not have been as successful if we hadn't had season six. We needed to do some downbeats in order to get back to doing the show with the same enthusiasm.

LEAVING SUNNYDALE

"What are we going to do now?"

After five years on the WB and two more on UPN, it was clear to the *Buffy* brain trust that the show had run its course. Most of all, its star, Sarah Michelle Gellar, was ready to move on. Despite rumors that the series might continue with Faith or one of the other Slayers created in the finale, season seven would bring Buffy full circle and end the series with a suitably epic conclusion. While *Angel* would continue for another year on the WB and Dark Horse would extend the series in comic books ad infinitum, this would be the last year Sarah Michelle Gellar would wield Mr. Pointy, and rumors of a feature film resurrection, which Gellar quickly dismissed, have sadly never materialized.

JOSS WHEDON
(creator/executive producer, *Buffy the Vampire Slayer*)

The fact is most of the cast not only knew it was the last year but were very glad of it. However, some of the crew did not know, which was totally my bonehead mistake. The actors did know and they kind of sucked up some energy from the crew. They just felt an official announcement should have been made before it was [on] the cover of a magazine, and they're not wrong. I just was like, "We've known this from the beginning of the year." It was just about paying respect.

MARTI NOXON
(executive producer/show runner, *Buffy the Vampire Slayer*)

I definitely feel like we left before we jumped the shark. It really felt right and was the right time. People were glad to be out of the dark pit of despair, so that's good. Everybody was very positive about the final year, so it felt like a good time to say good-bye. I actually feel we could have gone on. There were fresh ideas. I do think that it would have been harder and harder to make it feel like we weren't treading over the same territory, but do feel like we could have gone on. I don't know if it would have been the same people leading the troops, because, speaking for myself, I was ready to do other things.

JAMES MARSTERS
(actor, Spike)

Season seven was a bitch to film. They were trying to convince Sarah to come back for an eighth season, and Sarah would have none of it. We were known as "Buffy the Weekend Slayer" around Hollywood. Most shows film twelve hours a day and not a minute longer than twelve hours, because after twelve hours you have to pay the crew double. Twelve hours was a minimum day on *Buffy*. It was fourteen, sixteen, eighteen normally. We went up to twenty quite often. So, we would start at 4:30 in the morning on Monday and we would end when the sun rose Saturday morning. There were a lot of people in Los Angeles that would not work on *Buffy*, because they knew the long hours. And nobody got toasted more than Sarah Michelle Gellar; she was in almost every scene. When you do that to an actor for seven years straight, there's a good chance that they're going to want to marry Freddie Prinze Jr. and make cookies after it's over. No amount of money was going to change that. She was the consummate professional. She was on time all the time, had her lines down without fail, never missed a beat. That woman is a machine; she's amazing, and she carried that show for seven years.

JOSS WHEDON

The seventh season was a return to girl power stuff, a return to high school, a return to the mission statement of the show. A little less questioning of the meaning and possible evil of her own power and all of their power, and more in their reveling in the usefulness of it. I wanted to see more of a proactive Buffy. She was very reactive season six, though I disagree with people who say it sucked. Our mission statement season six was let's make things difficult for them, and seventh season it was let's show them in charge. The grown-up world sort of hit them in the face [in season six], and now let's see what happens when they hit back.

DAVID FURY

(co-executive producer, *Buffy the Vampire Slayer*)

Season seven was nice in that we got to get out of a little bit of the darkness of six, which was entirely about Buffy recovering from being dead. It was a little bit of a downer. And seven marked a chance for us to kind of lighten things a little bit. When we were talking about season seven, trying to figure it out, what I remember was we didn't really have anything to begin with. We all kind of got together and Joss is looking for what the Big Bad should be and eventually we landed on the First and then tried to figure out what the First's plan was. I believe I was the one that proposed this idea of, for better or worse, the Potentials.

The seventh season's nefarious Big Bad is the First, the oldest form of evil in existence. It has no corporeal form, and instead it can take the shape of anyone who has died. Throughout the season, it takes the ghostlike visage of Buffy with the intention of destroying the entire Slayer lineage, which includes Buffy and a reformed Faith as well as all Potential Slayers; ordinary girls next in line to be called to become the Slayer. Once the First destroys the Slayer line, the scales of good and malevolence will be definitively tipped toward evil, so that the First can become all-powerful once more and walk the earth.

DAVID FURY

In Joss's construction of the mythology of the show, it was very clear—and we had to discuss this—there can be only one Slayer, but obviously when we had Kendra come on and we had Faith come on, there had to be other girls who were aware of the fact that they may be called to be the Slayer and were trained. A lot of the girls wouldn't know. They'd go through life never knowing they were that. Then there were some who Watchers recognized as being a Potential and "I'm going to train her in case that day comes." That was not part of the show's mythology until that point.

Joss works from the point of whatever is serving the story he wants to tell in the moment. Bringing Kendra in was more important than figuring out the logic of how could she suddenly come in and be a Slayer with having to have a Watcher, since she talks about being trained for years. It didn't quite line up, but he never really gave it much thought. But we had to address it in seven when I made the suggestion, "What if we do a plot that's kind of like a spy thriller, where all the spies are being murdered all over the world?" The idea of Potentials, any girl that might become the Slayer, being eliminated. That was what we landed on, and I got to write one of the early episodes; I got to introduce a lot of the Potentials who became regulars for the season. For better or worse, because some people didn't love the idea. Some people felt it took the smallness away from the Slayer to suddenly have all these girls in there. But Joss embraced it when he recognized there was a great statement to be made that all of you have the potential to be Slayers. All girls, all women, have that potential. So the idea of bestowing that and Buffy sharing her powers for mystical reasons to the others, and them all being elevated to Slayer status, was, I think, a very wonderful, empowering message, regardless of whether or not the sticklers for the mythology thought it was good. As a co-executive producer of the show to suddenly give this whole idea of an army of Slayers was fun.

Among the First's allies are Caleb, a sadistic "priest" played by Nathan Fillion (*Firefly, Castle*), and the murder of Potentials leads Giles and Willow to seek out the remaining Potentials to bring them to Sunnydale, where they will be trained by Buffy and Faith to battle the First.

JOSS WHEDON

Everybody was tired of being depressed, including us. It was the last season, and we wanted to get back to where we started. Let's go back to the beginning. Not the word, not the bang, the real beginning—and the real beginning is girl power. The real beginning is, "What does it mean to be a Slayer?" And not to feel guilty about the power, but, having seen the dark side of it, to find the light again. To explore the idea of the Slayer fully and perhaps to see a very grown-up and romantic and confusing relationship that isn't about power but is actually genuinely beautiful between two people, Buffy and Spike. We were very focused on that.

ELIZABETH CRAFT

(executive story editor, *Angel*)

At the end of *Buffy*, they won. They closed the Hellmouth. *Angel* ended with a loss—the apocalypse.

DAVID FURY

For a while we didn't know it was the last season, so it was not one of those things where we immediately knew what the end would be, but I think it made for a great climax of the series to just eternally close up the Hellmouth and essentially Sunnydale being swallowed up. I thought it was great. And the whole question of Buffy, saying, "What's next?" She now had choices that she didn't have before. I thought it was a wonderful way to end the show.

SARAH LEMELMAN

(author, *"It's About Power": Buffy the Vampire Slayer's Stab at Establishing the Strength of Girls on American Television*)

Before the First Evil's plan is even set in motion, Buffy realizes that it is important to share what she has learned over her years as a Slayer. She first does this with her younger sister, Dawn, telling her, "It's about power—who's got it, who knows how to use it." In this instance, she is finally training Dawn how to fight vampires, something that Dawn had been desperate to learn for so long, but Buffy believed it to be something that her baby sister should be guarded against.

Buffy guides both Dawn and the show's viewers to one of the most important teachings of the show: "Power. He's got it. He's going to use it. It's real. It's the only lesson . . ." This interaction is more than the power of vampires—it is about the power divides in society, and even though power might be naturally gifted to men, Buffy demonstrates that women can wield it, too.

JAMES MARSTERS
(actor, Spike)

Plan B, in case Sarah could not be wooed into more episodes, they were searching for a replacement for her. They had the idea of the Potentials. I don't know if there were five or seven wonderful young actresses that they were looking at to see if one of them could be the new Buffy.

DAVID FURY

Not true at all. I love James, but he has no idea what he's talking about. Potentials was not a network decision. It was my idea that I pitched to Joss, and he wound up buying the idea. I will say there was always talk, I think, from the network of Dawn being somebody, initially in the inception, but I don't think that ever became serious. It was just a thought in the beginning of, like, "Oh, maybe if Sarah doesn't come back we can keep Dawn." But Dawn never landed as strong as a character as we'd hoped. As great as Michelle was, she just didn't seem to be the character to carry the show. If there was going to be a spin-off, I guarantee you it was always going to be Faith. There's no reason at all to look elsewhere than Eliza, because Faith was an awesome character. So trust me, the Potentials was not a network plan to spin off the show.

JAMES MARSTERS

It was tough, though; every scene that had the Potentials in them, you had to do coverage on all those actors. So when you're doing a scene with two people, you do the master shot and then you do the close-ups on each actor, and it takes a certain amount of time. If there's three people in the scene, it takes a lot longer because you have to do coverage on the third person. If you do a scene with seven people, it takes a long time to finish that scene because you have to do close-ups on *everybody*. And so with the Potentials you have to do seven extra shots in addition to the regular cast. You'd have like twelve people, and those were long days. Those were backbreaking days. My memory is, "Oh no! A Potentials scene; we're gonna be here all day." They were all lovely people, they were all really nice, and they were excited to be doing the show, but it was a lot of shots.

FELICIA DAY
(actress, Vi)

I was a baby actress. I had moved to L.A. two years before. I was just learning what the acting world was like. I had done *Bring It On Again* and commercials and a few guest stars and was really green. I went in and had auditioned for Amy Acker's role on *Angel* the pilot season before. They had liked me for that, but clearly Amy Acker is amazing. But I got called back the next year for this guest star, and I went in and it was an Asian role. I don't know if they couldn't find the actress or I actually went in for the guest star of the girl who died in that episode. She was a blond girl who turned out to be a demon posing as a Potential. I read for that and they were like, "OK, can you go out and read these other sides for this other part?" They didn't even say what it was. It turned out it was supposed to be an Asian girl.

Fortunately, I'm a better cold reader than auditioner, because I get nervous. I'm kind of a bomb in audition rooms until I have to improv or cold read. So it was actually to my advantage. They gave me three monologues, this long audition piece. I came in and was flying by the seat of my pants and that's what I do the best. I went out thinking I'm never going to get this, and then they called me the next day and booked me, and I was working the day after that. It was a real surprise. They renamed the part Vi, and then they ended up bringing in a girl who played the Asian Potential from Shanghai, Chao-Ahn, but she didn't speak English. It was a really twisty, weird, windy way to get the role.

SARAH LEMELMAN

In the tenth episode of the season, entitled "Bring on the Night," Giles arrives to Sunnydale and introduces the first of many Potential Slayers. Along with this, he tells Buffy the First Evil's master plot to eliminate the Slayer line, and Giles, continuing to stick with what he knows—books—says to Buffy, "I'm afraid it falls to you . . . We'll do what we can, but you're the only one who has the strength to protect these girls and the world against what's coming."

Here, it is believed by Giles that Buffy must follow her preordained path and face what is to come, alone, once more. It is the arrival of Kennedy, a new Potential Slayer (who states, "That's it? That's the plan? I don't see how one person—even a Slayer—could protect us") that prompts Buffy to change her approach in tackling and making decisions. These lines by Kennedy are the commencement of a togetherness and unity for each and every female on the show, despite the differences of being a Slayer, Potential Slayer, witch, or even a human. Each has their own strength, even if it is not physical, and each can contribute in a positive way. No longer will Buffy stand for her life, or the other girls' lives, as being the pawn of destiny and fate.

It is at this point where the viewers see that although women may have their backs against the wall in society, as Buffy and her army of girls are depicted as in this season, these roles do not have to define who they are as people. There is always a point of fighting, and being fearless, despite all the difficulties and limitations placed on women and girls. It is possible to break out of society's clutches and create one's own power. There may be barriers and men who have more power, but working as a single unit can begin a movement for change.

JOSS WHEDON

The seventh season, more than any other, has a lot of single episodes that I'm very proud of, but at the same time we were never more concentrated on putting everything in place to get to the last episode, to really feel as though we've wrapped things up. Without ending everything, we wanted to really get the sense of closure. This was always the message.

FELICIA DAY

I had heard about *Buffy* in college. I hadn't really watched the show, although I love fantasy and sci-fi and I was obsessed with *Star Trek* as a kid. But I never got to watch any of these shows, so I didn't know who Joss Whedon was. One day at lunch when a lot of the Potentials were there, this dude sits down at the table with us Potentials and starts talking. He didn't introduce himself. I was like, "Who is this guy sitting at our table?" He starts talking to all the actors, and somehow he says, "Well, most actors just don't have a college degree." I, of course, took this as a personal insult. Because I'm very uppity and I was homeschooled, my social skills are low. I said, "Well, I have a music degree and a 4.0 GPA." I really sounded like an ass. At the end of the meal, I asked one of the girls, "Who is that guy?" They told me he was the creator of the show. So I expected to get killed off. I honestly did, because we were dropping like flies throughout the season anyway and I really laid a poop on the table there. But I think it worked to my advantage, because he does like smart-mouth girls. Thank God he has good taste like that.

SARAH LEMELMAN

The final season of *Buffy* steps away from the idea that Buffy must grapple with the weight of the world on her shoulders, completely alone. A larger picture is shown, where the First Evil is introduced, with the master plan of killing the entire Slayer line—including all Potential Slayers, who have not yet been called upon. For once, Buffy sees that she is no longer alone and that there are girls across the world who are scared like her, as each of them may one day face the burden of being the Slayer, a life that, as it is written, means death. This bond that Buffy begins to recognize in the final season draws many parallels from the Riot Grrrls of the late 1980s and early 1990s.

Returning to don prosthetics again in seventh season was Camden Toy, who had last been seen as one of the Gentlemen in fourth season's "Hush." This time he would play Gnarl in "Same Time, Same Place."

CAMDEN TOY
(actor, Gnarl)

They were so excited by the Gentlemen that they kept saying we're definitely going to have you back, but as time went on they realized if we bring the Gentlemen back, what do we do with them? It was such a complete standalone episode, so that never happened, but I stayed in touch with casting. I constantly was going, "Hey, I heard you're casting this 'blah bitty blah' role. Can I come in and read for it?" and they'd go, "Nah." They weren't having me in, and I was wondering what was going on. It wasn't until seventh season when my acting career had really slowed down and I had gone back to editing that I got a call from casting. They told me they had a role they were having trouble with and she said, "You're really thin; that's our memory." And I said I was, and then she asked how tall I was, since they were looking for short people, which I'm not. She goes, "OK, hmmm. Well, we've got this role and we're really having trouble casting it and we were looking at really short people and nobody is getting it. Would you mind coming in and reading for it?" And I said, "I don't mind." And it was Gnarl, the skin-eating demon. He's literally the Hannibal Lecter of the demon world.

For whatever reason, people would come in and audition as though this was for a normal role. He's a demon from another realm, so you kind of have to use your imagination in a way that you don't have to do with a lot of television acting. I don't think they fully understood what they wanted until I brought what I did and all these different layers kept happening. When I finally got the role, they rushed me into makeup and they had to take a mold of my head, my feet, my teeth, and my hands. They eventually gave me finger extensions to play with as well. I got the teeth ahead of time, which usually doesn't happen; so often with roles that involve teeth, they would have to postdub the lines, because you put the teeth in and you can't really understand what they're saying. I had so much time ahead of shooting with the teeth that I was able to practice and actually able to say all that dialogue with those teeth in. They were shocked. The producers couldn't believe it. That never happens.

I was very lucky. Rob Hall's company, Almost Human, were very generous. They made an extra pair for me to take home and they made me an extra pair of the finger extensions, so I was able to really wrap my lips around the dialogue in a way that I would not have been able to if I couldn't rehearse with the teeth.

At this point, makeup maestro Robert Hall and his company Almost Human had replaced Optic Nerve as the vendor for the show's many prosthetics as well as for *Angel,* where Hall and his team, which included Jason Collins and Elvis Jones (now the owner of their own makeup and effects shop, Autonomous FX) created some of the show's most memorable creatures.

CAMDEN TOY

Up until about the middle of season six it was John Vulich's company, and Todd McIntosh was the key on the show. Rob [Hall] was already working on *Angel,* and they really liked what he was doing on *Angel,* so they decided to say, "Hey, would you mind doing one character?" So he did Sweet, Hinton Battle's character from "Once More, with Feeling," and they really liked what he did, because he didn't do a typical demon. It was different than usual. And, of course, Rob is unusual in that he has a shop, but he's also in the makeup guild. He can come on set and apply the makeup. I don't think that that sat well with Todd, since he was the key in makeup and he wanted to control that. He eventually left the show, and Rob took over the entire thing. Rob was actually applying that makeup, but with his shop designing and building it as well, which is unusual.

RAYMOND STELLA

(director of photography, *Buffy the Vampire Slayer*)

We had our problems lighting makeup prosthetics so more is left to the imagination and keeping it from looking like rubber. It was a big show, so they had good people working. They had a lot of good prosthetics and a lot of different characters on that show. Once it started taking off, they started putting more and more money into it. That's the problem when you become a hit show: it becomes harder and harder, because you have to be a lot more innovative than you were in the start. It's like being number one; it's harder to stay there than to get there.

DAVID BOREANAZ

(actor, Angel)

The difficult part is taking it off. You can't just rip it off, because you'll rip all your skin off. And that hurts. So it's difficult. But we had a great crew who did a wonderful job. It's exciting to see them create stuff. I'll look to my left and there's a Frankenstein monster. In one episode I was turned into a demon, so I had to wear a full prosthetic. It's tedious depending on what you're in.

One *Buffy* actor with plenty of experience in masks was Armin Shimerman, whose day job was still across town in Hollywood on *Deep Space Nine* on the Paramount lot at Melrose and Gower.

ARMIN SHIMERMAN
(actor, Principal Snyder)

They didn't come to me with advice, but I gave advice. Whenever I'd see the vampires or any of the other monsters in prosthetics, I would just smile, thinking, "Thank God I don't have to do that today." And tell them to drink a lot of water.

Toy, knowing it was the final season, was ready to say good-bye to *Buffy* after making his mark again as Gnarl before he got a call to take on the recurring role of the Ubervamp, Turok-Han, who serves the First.

CAMDEN TOY

At that point I thought I was done. Then I got a call from Rob Hall, who says, "You didn't hear it from me, but they're talking about bringing you back." It was the original Ubervamp that shows up for four episodes before they actually have an army of Ubervamps to show up. They were thinking originally if this is just a killing machine, we can cast a stunt person. It was Marti Noxon that said, "We really need an actor to bring it to life when he's not fighting. Like a Camden Toy." And Rob piped up at that point and said, "It's funny you should say that, because we have all his molds. We could actually start building the makeup on his molds today." I think that seed was planted then.

JAMES MARSTERS

My final scenes were done on second unit with David Solomon, who was one of our best directors. He did some second unit as well as directing some of our better episodes. There had already been tearful speeches made about how we began and how we got through it, but that was all in the scene with the Scooby Gang, so I didn't have that. But there was something that was kind of right about that, because I never really fit into that gang on screen and that had a reflection in life, too. So there was something kind of apt being in second unit again except the toys were just massive. Oh my God! They pulled out the stops—there was some money there.

ALAN J. LEVI
(director, "Sleeper")

I enjoyed the show. It was a different kind of a show for me. I enjoyed the girls and working with them. James Marsters came to me and said, "This is an unusual script in that it revolves around me. I don't get many like this. Will you help me through this? Will you watch me?" I said, I'll be happy to. I spent a lot of time with him in molding that performance. He cried in a couple of scenes and was very involved in the entire show.

Unfortunately, I spent too much time with him. I went way over almost every day in scenes with him, and so I talked to the producer afterwards and apologized and he said, "We're at the end of the run and everybody's tightening down on the budgets," and he said, "You performed a good show and you did James a good favor, but you didn't do me a good favor. They came down on me for going over. If I get another show, I'll be happy to hire you, but I can't ask you back for *Buffy* because somebody's got to get the blame." He was honest because I was. They would call down at seven o'clock at night and the AD would say, "We have another two hours to go." From that standpoint, it was not a happy situation.

CAMDEN TOY

Those final episodes were tough, because there was so much fighting and so much choreography that we were constantly running behind. On television, you can't stop and not start the next episode, so literally we would be coming to the eighth day where we're supposed to be ending that episode and we're not done. The next day we had to start shooting the next episode, but then periodically throughout that day the ADs would ask us to go over to stage five, where David Fury would be directing our B unit. Or David Solomon or whoever. In fact, in the episode where Sarah finally takes the Ubervamp's head off, they actually got in the editing room and realized they hadn't gotten enough coverage for that last fight scene. They actually had to create that scene again that was shot on a construction site in studio. There was no way we could go back to the location, so Sarah and I filmed with James Contner, who directed all the second-unit stuff that day. James was a focus puller on *Jaws*. He was lovely and has great stories.

He was one of the few directors where when you got to set you would start working immediately. Usually, I'd often be sitting on set for a good forty-five minutes or longer before they'd actually be shooting. Not in James's case. James would be like, "OK, get Camden ready." I'd walk on set, and he took me to work immediately.

JAMES MARSTERS

I tried to get as many stunts as I could. I always had to argue that I come from stage where you don't get a stuntman, so I can actually do more than you think I can.

JEFF PRUITT
(stunt coordinator, *Buffy the Vampire Slayer*)

One thing that Joss and I talked about when I first started was he said, "I don't want you to do *Power Rangers* stuff. It's not like that." "No, no, no. Just let me gradually start increasing the fights and you'll see, we'll have our own style. It will be like, a girl goes down a dark alley, and this little hundred-pound girl starts fighting vampires. It will be cool, but it won't be flying around on wires like *Power Rangers*." I remember Joss had shot the pilot for *Buffy*, and some executive said they wanted to make an after-school *Power Rangers*–type show. Buffy would be like Amy Jo Johnson going to school by herself, and she would be the one doing the action. Joss was like, "It's *not* that kind of show." He was trying to convince them to do the kind of show he wanted to do, which they never quite got right with the movie.

Sarah actually recommended me for the job. I met with Joss and he would say, "How would you do this? How would you do that?" I'd jump up, demonstrate, and explain how you'd shoot that. But he said, "I learned from the first season that Buffy can only throw one punch and one kick and that's all we have time for. We don't have the budget to do a second unit." "Trust me, there are techniques we can use. I can shoot three close-ups of Sarah and then do the whole fight with Sophia [Crawford]." I showed him tapes of me fighting in different movies and he said, "That's the style of Buffy; that's the style I want. Can you do that?" "Yes, we can," and then he hired me.

SOPHIA CRAWFORD
(stunt double, Buffy)

At some point Joss decided he only wanted me to double Sarah, whereas at the start there had been three of us. He offered me an exclusive contract to be Buffy's double and not work on any other show. It was a surprise to me; I'd had no indication that anything was going on, but basically what he told me was that he favored the way I moved, and he had a vision of Buffy and how she fought and her style and her energy, and he just felt I fit the character better. I continued for the next three seasons, having done four seasons all together.

JEFF PRUITT

We had a great time working with the actors. David Boreanaz had actually tried to get on *Power Rangers*. I met him at a party and he had been an assistant in the prop department on one of the Best of the Best movies. Some of the girls who worked on the movie with him told me that he wanted to get into acting, and since I was directing *Power Rangers*, they wanted to see if I could get him on the show, because he didn't have a SAG card yet. So I put him in touch with the casting people and everything. And then later, when I came to *Buffy*, there was this Angel character and he right away recognized me. Right then I said, "Okay, does your character do some kind of fights?" He said, "I help out sometimes, but then Buffy saves me." This was in first season.

I could talk to Joss about any Japanese anime I may see, but the one that you don't mention is called *Devil Hunter Yohko*. This is the scenario—it starts off like this, unto every generation is born a Slayer. The Slayer goes to high school—Yohko is the Slayer—and she has a Watcher. She has a best friend who's this nerdy girl who does computers, and the computer girl has a best friend who's a guy and she has a thing for him, but he has a thing for Yohko. And then there's this other guy who's a mysterious demon vampire guy who watches them from the side and brings them information about the underworld. She has to train, through her Watcher, because she's going to have to pretend to be a high school student while she fights demons. Only her two buddies know she's a Slayer. I mentioned that to him and he said, "No, no, no, it's not like that." I said, "Well if it's not like that, then that means Angel is not that guy. Angel could be, like I did on *Power Rangers*,

I could make him anything," because on *Power Rangers* they wanted to do the cliché thing of the girls falls down, twists her ankle, and the guy saves her. Billy is the nerd who can't fight as well as the other guys, but pretty soon I started making Billy able to fight as well as anybody. Make the girls fight as good as the guys. Everybody was a team. When I added Kimberly and Tommy fighting together, the fans went crazy over that. So I said to Joss, I know this is a different show, but can't we do a version of that where I let Angel kick some guys in the head?" "Well, Angel doesn't kick guys in the head." "Can't I try it just a little bit?" "Okay, I'll let you try it a little bit and we'll see how it goes."

So I got a stunt double to slow kick a guy in the head, and they started dressing David Boreanaz in black all the time. Then he and Buffy were a team and they were fighting side by side, and the fans loved it. After that, that's when everything took off. I said to David, "See, I made you a Power Ranger."

SOPHIA CRAWFORD

Initially I knew very little about the show or what it was. After being there a little while, and watching Sarah on the first few episodes—and the entire Scooby Gang—doing their dialogue, I was listening to it and said, "Wow, this is actually pretty funny." Then I started getting the scripts and would read them and follow along with everybody else. But it kind of evolved with me.

The fighting became more prominent as the show went on than it was in the beginning, and I think it was also in part too the fear of it taking too much time to shoot what we were sort of planning, because we came in there and initially most of the process was slow. Choreography, getting things done. Maybe from Jeff's experience of working on *Power Rangers*, everything having to go *so* quickly, Jeff was very quick, so we were able to get a bigger amount of work done in the same time. Nothing really changed timewise.

We weren't really given more time to shoot scenes in the beginning, but as they saw what the stunt guys were capable of, not just me but the terrific stunt team, once they started seeing their skills, Joss was the one who was like, "I want more of this!" Like I said, everything kind of escalated. They saw more, they wanted more. We were very happy to give them more. In the beginning we were told it wasn't to be in a *Power Rangers* style, no wire gags. More than anything it was about gymnastics and Buffy's fighting power.

CAMDEN TOY

Ryan Watson was my stunt double. He's just an amazing martial artist. There were things he could do that I couldn't do. I also have a background in martial arts and I did have to learn all of the choreography, but Ryan was the one who told me, "He's really a killing machine. He's an ancient vampire—he's like a Neanderthal, so we don't want him to be a typical chop-and-kick vampire. He really needs to be more like an animal. The script says, 'He's the vampire that vampires fear.'"

The way I sort of thought of them in my head was sort of Taz, the Tasmanian devil. So Ryan and I kind of worked on that and we kind of came up with a number of things and I was able to learn all of that choreography except for a few minor things here and there that Ryan had to do—it was pretty wild.

JAMES MARSTERS

There's a scene where Spike is drunk, because he's depressed about Drusilla leaving him and he passes out outdoors and wakes up in the morning because the sun is lighting him on fire. The scene started with the close-up on the hand igniting and Spike opening his eyes and realizing he's on fire and going to put it out in some water. I was like, "I can do that. That'll be great." They told me, "James, no. This is one of the most dangerous gags in all of stunts; it's an unprotected fire gag." Usually when a character's on fire in film, they're clothed and it's not their skin on fire; it's their clothes that are burning and the actor has many layers of protection underneath so that they don't get burned themselves. But with an unprotected gag, you dip your hand in a protective gel and then you dip your hand in fuel and they light you on fire. The gel burns off *really* fast, so you only have about four seconds before you have to put it out or you get really mangled. But idiot James Marsters decided that I wanted that gag to go a little longer, because there was this wonderful moment where Spike's eyes wake up and he's looking at his hand on fire and it takes him a while to realize this is not a dream; this is real. And I thought that that would be funnier. Not even thinking about the fact that every second is precious for a television show, especially something like *Buffy*, that's so jam-packed with good dialogue that they can't afford four more seconds of just me staring at my hand.

So I let it go long. We did two takes. I thought that I got away with it the first take, but when they lit me for the second one it was hell. Luckily it was the last shot of the episode and I remember thinking, just get off the set. Don't let them know that you blew the gag and that you're hurt, because if they find out that you're hurt, they'll never let you do another stunt. And just go to the hospital. Don't go to the medic on the set. Just get out as quickly as possible and drive directly to the hospital. I just remember walking to my trailer and everyone's like, "Great job, James! So, glad you were back." I'm just grinning my teeth as these blisters are forming on my hand. "Thanks so much, so good to be back." Meanwhile, my entire hand was covered in quarter- and dime-sized blisters all over. It was really bad, but I went to the hospital and got it taken care of. They didn't find out about it. I guess they will now—too late, though.

RAYMOND STELLA

You could always tell when our stunt double was running compared to Sarah, because she ran more like a girl. I'm not sexist or anything, but they had a different gait. So Sarah would have her gait and then when you see the other one you can tell pretty easily. They did a pretty good job covering the faces and doing the stunts.

FELICIA DAY

It was challenging. I'd never really done stunts, although I was a dancer and I did martial arts lessons as a kid. So that was really fun for me. But it was really taxing, and I remember one of the last episodes, there's this big monologue Sarah had to do and she didn't generally come in to block, she would just come in to shoot, because she'd done this a long time. It was a long monologue where she had so many fight moves where she had to throw a weapon up. I'm talking a page monologue. We were like, "Wow, she didn't even come in for rehearsal." She came in, and the stunt person showed her one time what they were doing and she nailed it on the first take. I was astonished. I haven't seen anything since where an actor is just like, boom. Technically precise, but also it was emotional and just really impressive. It was very rigorous, and being on that show really was similar to being on *Supernatural,* which I was on for several seasons, in that you'd always go to a location and you'd have fans waiting outside, because they found out where you're shooting and because they love it, *and* it always becomes a Fraturday [Friday-night shoot that goes into Saturday morning]. You're shooting until two or three A.M. and yet you're just loving it, because you know that you're making something that a lot of people are going to appreciate beyond just the moment.

JAMES MARSTERS

It took me a long time to learn the lesson that stunts take a price on the body. Doing stunts is like playing football; you don't necessarily have to go to the hospital after every game, but it's hard to get up out of bed. Some Monday mornings are difficult. If you do that for enough years, your body takes a whack. I didn't learn that lesson until *Angel* stopped filming, the show came down, and about a week after that my back just froze up and I couldn't walk. I just completely broke down.

DAVID FURY

The First afforded us a great opportunity to see all the villains of the past. Knowing at that point that this was it for *Buffy,* having the First was a way to bring back a lot of characters from the series and being able to see the Mayor, or seeing the Master, or seeing Glory was a perfect way to do that, because it kind of takes the form of anything it wants to and taking those forms was a fun opportunity. I'm of the opinion . . . things [pulled] from the past of the shows are much richer. Instead of inventing a whole new villain for the season we haven't seen before, now it's pulling something from the past. I thought it was a good idea. It gave a lot of faces to evil and that's what made it work.

HARRY GROENER
(actor, Mayor Richard Wilkins)

Long after Mayor Wilkins is destroyed and gone, it's the last season and my wife and I got back from New York when we were still living [there and in L.A.]. We're at a coffee shop having breakfast, and she says, "Why don't you call and tell them you're back in town; maybe they'll put you in a episode." I said, "They're not going to do that." She said, "Don't be an asshole. Give him a call." So I call my agent and said let them know. And they indeed did that fantasy with Faith and put me in the episode. It was good to see everyone. It was like old home week.

JAMES MARSTERS

I do have to say one [of my] favorite memories of doing the entire series was doing "Lies My Parents Told Me," which was an episode I cowrote with Drew Goddard and directed in the latter part of the season. It was a Spike-centric episode. Principal Wood's mother was killed by Spike, and it was a whole revenge story, but it was just a really fun, glorious experience for me. I had so many different great experiences working on *Buffy* and *Angel,* but my last meaningful involvement in *Buffy* was that episode.

CAMDEN TOY

When I came back to play the Ubervamp, Sarah and I had long nights between takes when we would just sit and chat. We'd certainly worked together before that, but that was the character where we really got to bond and get to know each other. And suddenly that night, she said, "Oh my God. I don't have any idea what you look like." So I went, "That must be creepy."

Sarah was a little bit like the Jewish mother on set, and I mean that in the best possible way. She was like, "Have you got enough to eat? Are you warm enough? You comfortable?" Literally, one night we were shooting one of the Ubervamp episodes, and we're going way into overtime and it's really late. They're serving the second meal in, and she's like, "They've got fried chicken over at craft services." But I had the teeth and the hands in and I couldn't eat. I told her I had to wait since we're shooting the scene right now, and she's like, "No, no, no. If you don't grab it now, it's gonna be gone." She literally grabs me and kind of drags me over there and starts serving me dinner. She's like, "What do you want? Do you want a wing? You want a thigh? What do you want?" So she's preparing this plate for me, because I can't hold anything with my vampire hands, and she said, "Now we have to hide this somewhere so that you can eat after this scene." The star of the show was serving me dinner. She was very sweet. She and I had a great time together.

SARAH LEMELMAN

Since season seven is so largely focused on the Potential Slayers and Buffy's empowerment of them, it is easy to overlook the other women on the program and feel that maybe this message of empowerment does not necessarily apply to everyone or is even relatable at all to viewers. *Buffy* continues to tackle this idea of enabling women, making sure that the empowerment it advocates can be applicable to all.

FELICIA DAY

I really didn't understand what was going on. I was so new. They said you were recurring, but I didn't know how many that meant. Every week, we would get the script and this was back when you got scripts on paper delivered on your doorstep. So you'd grab the script and you'd look at the last page and see if you were alive or not. Many Potentials died over the season and no one would tell you anything. So I always assumed I would die or piss somebody off and get killed or whatever. I was just so incredibly grateful to even get a script every week. It was really formative in my life, because seeing the fandom and the family on set, it really showed me what I wanted to do with my life as an actor. I didn't want to just show up to work; I really wanted to be on a show that meant something more to people.

SARAH LEMELMAN

The episode "Potential" crushes any doubts that *Buffy* may not be relatable, as Xander tells Dawn, who falsely thought she was a Potential Slayer, "It's a harsh gig being a Potential. Just being picked out of a crowd. Danger, destiny . . . They're special, no doubt . . . They'll never know how tough it is, Dawnie, to be the one who *isn't* Chosen, to live so near to the spotlight and never step in it. I saw you last night. I see you working here today. You're not special. You're extraordinary."

It is a touching message that brings Dawn to tears, and defends the idea that any seemingly ordinary girl in the world is important, in her own way. It reminds the audience that even though *Buffy* is a supernatural show, its characters can still be relatable and have been relatable, all throughout its run, even though the final season overwhelmingly revolves around Buffy and the Potential Slayers. The episode "Potential" gently communicates that a girl need not have powers to be great.

In the series capper, "Chosen," written and directed by Whedon, the scope felt like a movie with thousands of Ubervamps, the death of some of the series' most beloved characters, and the destruction of the Hellmouth–and, unfortunately, Sunnydale.

JOSS WHEDON

I feel that I wrote the perfect ending and wrapped everything up exactly the way it should be and really sort of hit the final chord of this beautiful symphony. That, unfortunately, was in season five. So with season seven, I sort of had to shut the door on this was the last episode a little bit, because the weight of that was crushing me. I was terrified. But I so very specifically knew what I needed to say and what I needed to have happen. That was all in there.

JAMES MARSTERS

The finale was fun, but it wasn't cool. Spike has no idea that he was going be the big hero. He just wanted a freaking necklace. He just didn't want Angel to have that necklace and he was just proud that he got it and not Angel. It was just very petty on his part and the thing starts glowing and he lights on fire and he's like, "What the f . . . oh no!" I played it as it wasn't a big heroic act. It was a wonderful scene, though, between Buffy and Spike. He could proclaim his love before he was gone. But I don't think of him as the heroic savior in that; I think of him as the guinea pig hero.

FELICIA DAY

We got along with all the series regulars, who were very friendly to us. But we had our own little clique, because there was, like, seven of us. It was really great. My fondest memory was when Alyson came in one day to the makeup trailer and she was knitting. I was like, "Oh, you're knitting. That's really stupid." I literally said that to her like a little snot. And then a week later I came in with my own knitting needles, and she was like, "Oh, really? You're going to knit now?" I was like, "Yeah, I'm sorry." Clearly. I don't give great first impressions, but we were good friends after that. It spread throughout the other Potentials. Most of the times on set we would sit around at like 2 A.M. on a Friday shooting and we'd all just be sitting in a knitting circle, like fifteen-year-olds knitting. It's really funny. Believe me, I learned more dirty stories from those other girls than any set with guys on it.

JAMES MARSTERS

One of the things that happened at the beginning of a lot of seasons was Joss would come to me and say, "I have no idea what to do with you. I know what the basic arc is for the show; I know how all the other characters have arcs within that. But I just have nothing. I don't know what to do." I was like, "Well, you always figure it out, dude. You're paying me anyway. I'll be here waiting." I was never that worried. I think what he did was he kind of plugged the character in as necessary to serve the other characters' arcs. So I was the disposable bad guy at first. Then I was the whacky neighbor. And then I was the wrong boyfriend. And then I was the guinea pig hero. On *Angel,* I was the jerk friend who promised to only be on your couch for one week but just won't leave.

Because the writing was so good, it was stitched together into a journey that makes sense. But because it wasn't one thought-out arc, it doesn't have the smooth lines that a normal character trajectory has. It wound around, took a lot of surprising detours on its way, and it's just this wonderful happy accident. Spike had a very interesting journey, because it was kind of made up on the fly. In lesser hands that would be very haphazard and not very satisfying at all. But in really talented hands, that all stitched it together, and it becomes something that you respond to.

JOSS WHEDON

When you get into actually writing the finale, you're just like, "Oh God, it's not good enough." Then you're like, "Dude, you've got to chill," because it's unbearable pressure. You want it to go out with a bang; you don't want it to dribble out. You want the last episode to mean something that no other episode has. It was fucking large. It was so hard to shoot.

RAYMOND STELLA

That final episode was another fourteen-to-fifteen-day shoot. A lot of characters. A lot of visual effects. But by then I was pretty much going, "I'm out of here. Let's get this thing done."

SARAH LEMELMAN

Buffy the Vampire Slayer seems to recognize this oppressive nature of love and romantic relationships and appears to pose the question of the fundamental meaning of love, and if it truly is needed. This occurs with the exploration of its hero's complicated love life and her involvement with Angel, Riley, and Spike. Each male she is embroiled with has her investigate what relationships mean for a female in a man's world.

Buffy very clearly strives for this bliss in her relationships throughout the seven seasons of the show, but in the final episode of the series, she points out to viewers that, "I always feared there was something wrong with me. You know, because I couldn't make [relationships] work. But maybe I'm not supposed to . . . because I'm not finished becoming whoever the hell it is I'm gonna turn out to be. Maybe one day I turn around and realize I'm ready. Then . . . that's fine. That'll be then. When I'm done."

It may have taken her 144 episodes to realize that she needs to choose herself and continue to grow, but it is an important lesson to the viewers, many of whom are girls with insecurities about their true worth because they cannot find love. Despite that fact that she is hurt giving up these men, she is better for it in the end. She presents a stronger version of a woman to the world and demonstrates that there is nothing wrong with independence and an uncertain future in love.

DAVID BOREANAZ

We shot [*Angel*] on a soundstage in a big studio, and going back to *Buffy*, where they shoot in these little warehouses—that was interesting. The biggest thing for me was the height of the ceiling: it's really low. As far as getting back to work with Sarah [Michelle Gellar] again, you know, she's great. We just kind of stepped into the shoes, the characters picked up where they left off, and we kind of rocked it.

STEVEN S. DEKNIGHT

Here's the thing that pissed a lot of people off is that David was very gracious to go and do a cameo on *Buffy* toward the end of their series. He didn't make a big deal out of it and try to extort anybody for a lot of money. He wanted to do it, and I guess he expected the same consideration back, which we did *not* get. Which is unfortunate, because it would've been nice and it would've helped our numbers on *Angel*, but what can you do?

One of the biggest surprises in the finale was Spike's sacrifice to save the world. However, not unlike a certain pointy-eared Vulcan, audiences already knew this fan favorite would be back since it had already been announced that James Marsters was joining the cast of the WB's *Angel*.

DAVID FURY

I don't know why these things happens. Publicists do it, or networks do it to get people excited about it, but it ruins it to know when you're trying to give a great emotional death scene to go, "Oh, he'll be back on *Angel*." It's like, you just ruined it for everybody. I don't love that, but it *is* a business. It's more important to them; they don't care about spoiling things as much as if they'll get a few more viewers to watch something because they're teasing you're going to see James Marsters as Spike on *Angel.* That's more important for them than whether or not they're destroying a story.

JAMES MARSTERS

Joss was incensed that the WB let the cat out of the bag that I was coming on *Angel,* because he wanted to break the audience's heart on *Buffy.* He was like, "No one's gonna be sad now; they know you're gonna come back." But at that time *Buffy* was on UPN, and *Angel* was on a different network, and so there was no loyalty to each other. *Angel* had no loyalty to *Buffy,* so they had no reason to keep the secret. I was just like, "Light me on fire, OK? I'm fine."

SARAH LEMELMAN

For the first time on the show, Buffy is no longer alone in the fight, as she has been for the past 143 episodes. Buffy's power is now a shared power, as there has been an awakening of girls across the globe. Even though there are causalities in the final fight, and not every Slayer survives, the First Evil is defeated, and Buffy once again rejects the fate that has been laid out before her, just as she had done when she was a young sixteen-year-old, destined to die at the hands of the Master. The show ends on a high note of female empowerment, as Buffy smiles, knowing she has truly defeated destiny and created a feminist revolution. Women and girls alike are free to orchestrate their own future and should not be afraid to do so. Thanks to Buffy Summers, viewers across the world have been graced with one of the greatest activists of girl power, serving as a role model, icon, and source of inspiration for young women.

As *Buffy* proves time and time again, patriarchy is ever present, but it cannot prevail. The seven seasons of the show depict a world in which institutional, familial, and individual-level patriarchy oppresses and disadvantages women, but it is something that can always be overcome. The fight to end this domination is no easy feat, as there is always a struggle to gain equality and independence. *Buffy* shows a realistic version of an ideal world: men may try to control women, but their efforts can and will be beaten.

JAMES MARSTERS

I'm a subversive artist by nature. When I produced theater, we did a lot of subversion, which is not about trying to make the audience uncomfortable or angry, but when it happens you know it's working. One of the things I loved about *Buffy* is that we were divesting the audience of the idea that women can't defend themselves. Right up in their face about it. I never thought that I could be part of a subversive art when I came down to Los Angeles, because I didn't know about Joss. I didn't know that Joss Whedon existed yet.

ARMIN SHIMERMAN

When *Buffy* was shooting its last episode and I was long since dead, they called me up and said, "Armin, we'd love for you to come down to the set and shoot a picture with the cast and crew on our last day of shooting." Because I'd always watched the show before I was on it, while I was on it, after I was off of it, I knew that there were hundreds of reoccurring characters. So I assumed it was going to be a large party, a ton of people.

I got to the set, only to see three other people besides myself invited to take the picture. I was really surprised by that. We took the picture, I caught up with some old friends I hadn't seen in a long time, and when the picture was done and we all said good-bye, I was talking to Joss Whedon. As I was walking back to my car, I posed to him the question "Why were there only four of us?" And he very nicely said, "Armin, the four of you are the only four people that all of us liked." So, my weaselly character on *Buffy,* which was my on-camera persona, was not my persona off camera. We got along really very well.

ELIZA DUSHKU
(actress, Faith)

Faith is my girl. She's always been good to me, and she's been a good friend to me. I love that character, this show, the places we've gone, and all the different emotions we've experimented with. I feel like she's a part of me. It was good to be back on *Buffy.* Sarah is such a doll. We were like reunited high school friends.

SARAH LEMELMAN

As Willow says in her final line of the show, the future of American television was truly changed after the production's completion. Not only did shows about teenage feminists begin to sprout but also television programs began to utilize concepts like the normalization of lesbian relationships, long story arcs, and new slang that *Buffy the Vampire Slayer* both laid the foundation for and helped popularize.

Buffy empowers females on the show, as well as its viewers, who are taught to embrace girl power. By giving its viewers a new female model to look up to in a time when girls were not always taken seriously, *Buffy* stepped into the limelight and defied traditional depictions of women on television. Vampires, and even the experiences of high school students, may not seem like "serious" topics, but the show demonstrates that a fantasy/action/drama has the ability to both teach a lesson about feminism and be wildly popular and influential, to this very day.

ELIZA DUSHKU

I've gotten letters from girls who have said, "I was being abused for six years. Your character came on, and I realized that if Faith could stand up to these guys trying to bring her down, so could I." That stuff is really intense—cool success stories from people who just watch this character.

SARAH LEMELMAN

What began as a passing thought of an amateur writer became a hugely successful reality and overturned the doubts of critics that young women could hold a commanding presence on screen. *Buffy the Vampire Slayer* is truly a feminist and popular culture landmark.

FELICIA DAY

Joss gave me some amazing, really great lines, action, and scenes in the finale. In the comics canon, I'm the head of the New York Slayers. We worked together on several things since then, and I will always attribute it to my smart mouth. He invited everyone to the Mutant Enemy strike day during the Writers Guild strike. When I was walking around, I was like, "Hey, did you see my Web series?" In 2007 it wasn't as annoying, because they didn't really exist. It was before that. Old-school. He told me, "Yeah, I'm thinking about doing a musical myself for the Internet." And I'm like, "That's amazing!" And then two months later I got an email about *Dr. Horrible.* Then I got to do *Dollhouse* as well with him. I don't think there's another person whose work resonates with me soul-wise in a way, and I'm just really lucky I got to work on so many different things with him.

DAN VEBBER

(co-executive producer, *Futurama*)

Buffy gave Warner Bros. a network. It certainly gave some actors a career. Now you don't even think about it anymore when you have a strong female protagonist, but back then it was the only game in town. It's the type of thing where some pop culture television show or movie will create an idea that then becomes so cliché over the years that when you watch the original thing you think, "Oh, that's *so* cliché." But you have to remember, no, this thing created the cliché. That's how I feel now watching those *Buffy* episodes. They feel really charming and retro and '90s to me—and a little simple in some ways. When you think of it in context, it was a big deal. They were the first one to try it. I'm really happy that I got to be a part of that.

SARAH LEMELMAN

It is perhaps fitting that Xander (a male) believes the Scooby Gang and the Potentials have saved the world, while Willow (a female) corrects him and asserts that the group *has* changed the world. They may have defeated the First and destroyed Sunnydale's Hellmouth, but the most important feat the group accomplished was the sharing of Buffy's power to all Potential Slayers throughout the world. After seven seasons and 144 episodes, *Buffy the Vampire Slayer* concludes with its most potent message: girls do not need to be afraid but, instead, should be confident in who they are and always stand up for themselves.

JOSS WHEDON

The fact of the matter is that I've always identified with female heroes and had trouble finding them. It was great the first time I was watching and realized, "Buffy, she's my hero." That's how I want the show to be remembered. As for some of her sillier outfits and cheesier effects . . .

KELLY A. MANNERS
(producer, *Buffy the Vampire Slayer*)

When a crew latches on to a show that's successful, they never want to move on. Because you're not out looking for your next show and shooting thirteen episodes and getting canceled and it's a revolving door. When you create those relationships with the crew, it becomes a great big family.

My dad did *Route 66* and my brother, sister, and I traveled with him the first season. By the second season it was twenty-seven kids from the crew traveling from state to state with that show. And then with Nora, who was Shirley Temple's tutor, we'd go to school three hours a day in bars and that was another real family. Same thing with *Buffy* and when I did *Dukes of Hazzard*. That was a family. Now the new thing is if you get a second season, you're lucky, it seems. With the new cable season, it's ten and out. It's not the same. The business has changed.

SETH GREEN
(actor, Oz)

I actually miss arriving at my trailer every morning to find that David Boreanaz had already pooped in it, without fail. It was always that funny thing where I would arrive, and he would be coming out of my door and be like, "Left something for you, buddy!"

JOSS WHEDON

I do have visions of spinning the show off into a Star Trek-kian film franchise, but I also have visions of invading Poland, so we'll see which one I'll do. I want the show to be remembered as a consistently intelligent, funny, emotionally involving entertainment that subtly changed the entire world—or a small portion of pop culture. Enlightenment is the slowest process this side of evolution. Three steps forward, nine steps back. It's very hard to have come up in the '70s, to be raised by a feminist and then live through the Reagan era, and now God help us.

Feminism, which hopefully will become an obsolete term by the time I'm dead, is a really important thing. Not just feminism, but antimisogyny. Changing the way that people think about women and the way they think about themselves is what I want to do with my life. There are other things I have to say, there are other things I want to do and stories I want to tell, but that's the most important thing to me. If *Buffy* made the slightest notch in any of pop culture in that direction, well that's pretty damn good.

PART TWO

ANGEL

"Fangs, don't fail me now."

BACK IN BLACK

"He's a shadow, a faceless champion of the hapless human race. . . ."

Spin-offs have been a part of television for decades, producers and networks viewing them as opportunities to expand a brand or franchise. Norman Lear made a staple of it with spin-offs of the popular CBS sitcom *All in the Family,* including *Maude, Good Times, The Jeffersons, Gloria, Archie Bunker's Place,* and, later, *704 Hauser;* while Garry Marshall used *Happy Days* as a launching pad for *Laverne and Shirley, Mork and Mindy,* and *Joanie Loves Chachi,* among others.

Sometimes, these shows exploit the original by attempting to wring a few more dollars out of a successful idea (*AfterMASH,* anyone?); other times, a combination of commerce *and* creativity, the desire to keep a good thing going, works hand in hand with an attempt to offer viewers something that is new yet redolent of the mother-ship series.

Angel falls into the latter category, taking a popular supporting character from *Buffy the Vampire Slayer* and giving him a series of his own. At the time, this particular spin-off was greeted with some skepticism; more than a few fans wondered how exactly this vampire with a soul was going to serve as the centerpiece of his own show, given that he had mostly served as a love interest for Buffy for three seasons of vampire slaying.

In the end, *Angel* turned out to have a lot in common with two other spin-offs that *did* connect with the audience. The first was *Frasier,* spawned from one of the most beloved sitcoms of the 1980s, *Cheers*. Kelsey Grammer's Frasier Crane was a supporting character in an ensemble series, and, with all due respect to the actor, there was nothing that seemed to scream that this character needed to branch off on his own. In fact, *if* there was going to be a *Cheers* spin-off, a more likely one would have been focused on Cliff Clavin and Norm Peterson, the barflies who arguably provided even more laughs than Frasier ever had. Of course, anyone who doubted the possibilities were ultimately surprised as Frasier became a fully fleshed-out character on a show that had the same eleven-year run as its predecessor. In that regard, *Angel* was in good company (despite only running five years compared with *Buffy*'s seven).

The other close cousin to *Angel* was *Star Trek: Deep Space Nine*, the cult spin-off of *Star Trek: The Next Generation*. That Star Trek series, the first to take place on a space station rather than a starship, was in a very different setting (just as *Angel* took place in Los Angeles as opposed to *Buffy*'s demon-infested Sunnydale). Additionally, both *Deep Space Nine* and *Angel* were originally designed to be stand-alone shows, each episode expected to have a beginning, middle, and an end to make it easier for an audience to tune in at any point and not feel lost. But both quickly discovered that there was an inherent creative need for serialization and began to embrace that means of storytelling. The resulting growing tapestry gave birth to two series that predicted the very nature of binge television *and* that creatively equaled if not surpassed the shows that gave birth to them—a fact not always recognized by the critics or the larger audiences that viewed the shows that spawned them.

As a character, Angel himself represents the sympathetic vampire, member of the undead with a conscience, whose existence is haunted by reflections of what he is and the misery he has wrought over the centuries. At the time of the show's original run, he was far from the medium's first such representation, following a long road of the vampire's evolution from genuine creature of the night to the more broody, angst-driven variety.

LEO BRAUDY
(film historian; professor of English,
University of Southern California)

In film, all of the other genres—from Westerns to musicals—come and go, but horror seems to have a perpetual life, despite, or perhaps because of, its focus on the dead. The images (of horror), the motifs, the characters, and the plot structures have a greater metamorphic variety than some of the other genres. They can be refitted to new historical situations.

STUART FISCHOFF
(media psychologist)

When Universal made *Dracula*, [the] character had a certain human element to it, an element that would remain throughout the 1930s and '40s.

What you find is that the monsters pre-1950s always had a reason for their monsterness. They always had a side of them that was sympathetic. They murdered for life-serving or life-saving reasons. Dracula had to take blood to live. Frankenstein was misunderstood. Wolfman was tormented by his demons.

In the '50s I think you hit all of the nuclear concerns—the effects of the radioactive fallout—and then from the 1960s and beyond the monsters are killing for no other reason than they wanted to kill. I think there was this major shift in how monsters in general and vampires in particular were seen prior to the '70s and subsequent to the '70s. I think that reflects the change in sensibility of our culture. It may well come out of the post-Holocaust, Second World War idea that human beings can be so awful and death can be so inexplicable, random, and capricious.

Then, of course, when you get into the '70s and '80s, we lived with drive-by shootings, gangs, and things like that. You might make the point that in earlier times, vampires and their ilk were seen in the background of a just world and that subsequently the world was chaotic, death could strike you at any moment, and life was unfair. Vampires in that era reflected that. They just killed.

GUILLERMO DEL TORO
(executive producer, *The Strain*)

I am fed up with vampires being tortured Victorian heroes. I just don't like the whole concept. I think vampirism is essentially sucking someone else's blood, which can be dealt with as an addiction or in so many other ways which are interesting. I just want vampires to be scary again; the concept of being drained of your blood by something to be scary again, as opposed to a romantic interlude.

With that Victorian era, where the westernization of the vampire myth occurs in the nineteenth century, the scariest part of this was that they would rob you of your life and turn you into something not human. I think that most people imagine vampires in a romantic way, and most women fantasize about being drained by Angel or Tom Cruise or Brad Pitt, but nobody is going to fantasize about being drained by creatures.

I am fascinated by the several ways that you can read the same phenomenon [vampirism]. It can be a sexual, erotic thing. It can have a purely addictive element to it. There is a political element in it. There is also the more basic, more fun elements of the monster. There are so many takes you can have on that myth that are fascinating.

STEVE NILES

(creator/writer, *30 Days of Night*)

The appeal of vampires for me is that I can't stand them. It had just gotten to the point where vampires and Dracula and the whole thing had just been turned into something silly, which is a tendency of people in general. We like to tame our fears, so we start with Nosferatu and we end with Count Chocula. And then on TV you've got *Buffy* and teenage girls dating vampires. The romanticized notion was taking over vampires, and they were just becoming human, really. They were like humans who had to drink blood once in a while. And so basically they were just not scary to me at all. So we thought we needed to figure out a way to make them scary again, and I said, "There's nothing more frightening than an intelligent creature who looks at you as nothing but food," so we started with that. And then I started to think, "Land sharks," and I thought that was where we wanted to get back to. There it is, no argument. It's all about food, and the vampire would look at us with as much mercy as we look at cows.

JOHN BADHAM

(director, *Dracula* [1979])

If you look at the character of Dracula as an extremely evil person, it doesn't mean that he has to be ugly. When you think about many of the so-called evil temptations of the world that we face, they are quite often packaged in extremely attractive ways. That's one of their appeals; a successful evil is the one that we think is terrific. You can say, for instance, cigarettes are in this category. "I smoke because I want to be cool and I want to be admired and people who smoke cigarettes look cool. Oh yeah, it says I'm going to die, but I don't take that seriously." Alcohol; drugs; wild, wild women—you can pick your poison. But, usually, any evil that is successful comes in a very attractive package. *That's* the seduction of it.

LEO BRAUDY

The romanticized vampire was implicit in the beginning, because the vampire was always a kind of Byronic figure. The vampire myths really start long before Dracula and start to become popular in English and German fiction at the beginning of the nineteenth century. And the figure of Byron pretended to be himself and wrote about the solitary person on the moors with this horrible hurt inside. That just went right into the vampire myth. So a romanticized element has always been there as a potential part of it.

JONATHAN FRID

(actor, Barnabas Collins, *Dark Shadows* [1966–71])

I loved to play horror for horror's sake. Inner horror. I never thought I created fear with the fang business of Barnabas. I always felt foolish doing that part of it. The horror part I liked was "the lie." There's nothing more horrible than looking someone in the eyes who's telling you a lie and you know it. Somehow that scares me more than anything. In terms of the theater, I liked the inner drama rather than the outward manifestation. An inner conflict or emotional confrontation is more of a drama to me.

That's why with Barnabas there were many scenes I was thrilled to do and why the show came alive so many times for me. Barnabas's lie, that he was pretending to be something that he wasn't, motivated me. That pretense was something that the actor playing Barnabas had to remember all the time. He got the lust for blood every once in a while, but always what preyed on his mind was the lie. And of course it played right into my lie as an actor. I was lying that I was calm and comfortable in the studio, just as Barnabas was lying that he was the calm and comfortable cousin from England. He wasn't at all. He was a sick, unbelievable creep that the world didn't know about.

LEO BRAUDY

That lie is appealing and certainly appealing to teenagers, who always feel they have that secret self inside that nobody appreciates. It's an empowerment thing. What makes me unique, is it the dark side or something else?

RON SPROAT
(writer, *Dark Shadows*)

Part of it is because Jonathan played a duality and had kind of a lost quality as well. He said originally, and I think he was right, "Don't write the evil; I'll play it that way. I look that way." He also said that he'd done *Richard III* and he was astounded by the reviews at the time, because they said he was the most evil Richard. He said, "I was playing for sympathy." So he suggested that we write against the evil and he would play against it, which would make it more interesting. That's what we did and I thought it worked.

BARRY ATWATER
(actor, Janos Skorzeny, *The Night Stalker*)

I just figured Skorzeny was a guy who *needs* blood. I figured he can't be very different from a guy who needs heroin, who's an addict. I've never taken heroin and never intended to, but what I heard about it is that a guy has to have it. If Skorzeny didn't have blood, what would happen to him? It must be really hell *not* to have blood. It's not a question of being immoral or cruel. It's a question of, "I've got to have it. It's too bad if people die because of it." I felt the people who were chasing me were my enemies. *They* were the "heavies," the "villains."

FRANK LANGELLA
(actor, Dracula)

I never wanted Dracula to strike terror from the first day of rehearsal of the play to the making of the [1979] film. I didn't see him as a character who went around with long fingernails and hollow eyes and fangs and all that stuff. It didn't interest me to play him that way, because it would have just been repeating a tried and true genre, which everybody knows works. I wanted him to be somewhat vulnerable, hopefully somewhat neurotic, and occasionally not sure of his territory.

I wanted him to be some kind of man who had come to some relative peace in life with his circumstances. He had to exist for blood, but he didn't necessarily spend all his waking hours in pursuit of it or in some kind of horrific guise. So I wouldn't be upset if people said I changed the character, because that's why I wanted to do it. It would have been absolutely of no interest to me to have done it in the Hammer way with fangs and snarling and all of that stuff. I just decided to play him as a mortal man for a very long time, and slowly began to add the curse. I found it fascinating to work on him in this way instead of as a predator.

JOSS WHEDON
(executive producer/cocreator, *Angel*)

For my generation, before David Boreanaz, there has been one truly vulnerable vampire, and that was Frank Langella. He was the standard as far as I was concerned. He was younger; he was cooler. I saw him on stage before I saw the movie.

That, plus *Interview with the Vampire,* which really laid it home—the alienated human and how he deals with life as opposed to the bloodsucking thing in the shadows—and really brought it up to date. I don't know if there's any stopping it. They lend themselves to *The Wild Bunch* with *Near Dark,* and they lend themselves to futuristic movies as well. They fit. There is always a dark corner with a beautiful and frightening person there.

BEN CROSS
(actor, Barnabas Collins, *Dark Shadows* [1991])

I think one of the first things that might be appealing about vampires is that the way women might view a vampire and a vampire tale is somewhat different from the way a man would. We reached a certain point in the series where we simply had to go back to the past and find out exactly what went on. And so we did go back and saw Barnabas as this really nice guy. Very, very happy family. And it was really like a cautionary tale for married men. He actually had a fling with the wrong person. And the phrase of hell having no fury like a woman scorned was absolutely true, because, in fact, she came from hell. And so, in a sense, he makes a human mistake that a lot of people, if they're honest, have actually made. He regrets it and then becomes a victim and a vampire. So, in a sense, he was as much a victim of his own condition in the same way as the people he found himself biting.

MARTI NOXON
(consulting producer, *Angel*)

Part of the reason that someone like Anne Rice is so popular is that she was coming up about the same time as our awareness of AIDS and blood diseases grew, and fears of sex and blood were intermingled. It probably gave her work a little more poignancy and gravity. But because the myth has been around so much longer than that, the appeal has so much to do with our longing to escape death, and so much to do with our knowledge that that can't happen, because the cost of this would be to be some kind of monster.

At the same time, we have a desire for some kind of loophole and are also drawn to the idea of a romantic soul who finds his life mate, or who will die trying to find the life mate that he will be able to live with for eternity. It's one of the genres where women and men can watch and get into it on different levels. Guys are looking at it as pure horror and most of the women look at it as a sexual and romantic metaphor. To be taken and made eternal—*that's* pretty hot.

MELISSA ROSENBERG
(writer, The Twilight Saga)

The vampire genre means different things to different people. First of all, on a completely surface level, vampires are always beautiful. And it's also very sexual, the undertones, so that's sensual if nothing else. In the case of *Twilight*, for Bella it's "this guy wants me." Here's this incredibly average, gawky, uncomfortable girl, very normal and someone we can all relate to, and here's this god who knows she is special. I think that fills a fantasy for us. And you still have the titillation that this is someone who, ultimately, is unavailable, so you have the unrequited-love part of it. And there's also the fantasy of the ultimate connection—you are one, through fluid. I think there's the romantic tragedy of it, but there's also the fantasy of it. It's attractive to be that connected to someone.

CHARLAINE HARRIS
(author, the Southern Vampire book series)

Most people hope that vampires, having had so many years to practice sex, have become super good at it. Everybody, or especially women, I guess, want to be the *one*—the one that makes a vampire love a human for the first time for a century or decades or however long they've been alive. The one that pulls the vampire out of his world and into yours. You want to be that important to somebody, to make them cross boundaries like that.

LEO BRAUDY

The vampire myth is concerned with the relationship between the undead and the living, and the need for blood to survive, the sense of this past world that feeds on the present. These are all very general fears that don't go away very quickly. Also, of all the monsters, the vampire is the most human, and therefore represents human potential. Nobody is going to become King Kong and you have to be dead to be put together to be Frankenstein. If you're Dr. Jekyll and Mr. Hyde or the Wolfman, you have no control over your transformation. The idea that you have a secret self inside that you call on in times of danger is really only suitable for the vampire myth.

LAURELL K. HAMILTON
(author, Anita Blake series)

Humans have a tendency to be fascinated by and attracted to what scares them, and nothing scares most people like death. Vampires are dead, but they're still people, walking and living. Even as a bloodsucking monster, you're still alive. I think people find that comforting.

CHRIS SARANDON
(actor, Jerry Dandridge, *Fright Night*)

The thing that appealed to me about playing this vampire, Jerry Dandridge, is that he was totally contemporary. He wasn't the count of legend or Bram Stoker, but a guy who everybody knew and couldn't believe was being accused of being a vampire. He isn't the personification of pure evil that vampires are known to be. Just think about this guy's problems. On the one hand, you've got somebody who's got something everybody would probably love to have, which is eternal life.

Also, he's tremendously powerful physically and attractive sexually. What he does, people are, for some reason, attracted to. But at the same time, how would you like to know that if people found out about you, they'd be terrified? That is to be eternal, but spend eternity shunned by any normal kind of society, not being able to form any kind of normal human relationship. To be, in a way, damned to eternity. There was a sense of this guy's tragedy as well as his attractiveness.

GERAINT WYN DAVIES

(actor, Nick Knight, *Forever Knight*)

The vampire genre allows things to be explored in a way they frequently aren't. *Forever Knight* dealt with big issues. It wasn't about the fact that the guy was a vampire. It was about the choices that he had to make *because* of that. It would be the same thing if he was a drug addict or anybody with an addiction. And he was addicted to this lifestyle, this blood—the idea of somebody else's life so that you can live. It had much more the inner struggle of the individual, so it wasn't so much about biting people and eyes flashing. It was about the inner turmoil and about growth for someone who had been around for eight hundred years.

TIM MINEAR

(co-executive producer, *Angel*)

These days vampires are viewed as noble, tortured creatures that are somehow above us. That has a lot to do with Anne Rice. People can relate to feeling apart and sometimes above, yet somehow not part of the rest of the world. I think that's pretty much a universal feeling, particularly for people going through adolescence. There's something romantic about not dying. It seems like a way to give a character this huge gift, but then makes it ugly because they don't really deserve it. It has something to do with alienation. That's what it is for Angel. Here's this guy who really wants to be a part of the world, but he can't be yet.

JULIE BENZ
(actress, Darla)

Vampires are very sexual, very sensual, and they have amazing freedom. The essence of them all is very dark and sexual. They're sexual, hungry beings. I think everybody has a dark side, and vampires are living the dark side. So we seem to enjoy watching these characters live in the dark without the restraints of society.

STUART FISCHOFF

Certainly the vampire legend has been infected with sex and romance. The whole notion of biting as penetration maintains its sexual allure. With female vampires you get a lot more of the sex connection, also the attraction men have for dangerous sex. Plus the myth of the female using sex to destroy. It has an approach-and-avoidance quality to it. The vampire also interacts with the idea of infection and the transmission of disease. The connection between bloodlust and sex lust is very, very strong, so every time you get some kind of plague, whether it's AIDS or some other sexually transmitted disease, it kind of feeds right into the notion of infection and from being bitten by the vampire.

STEPHENIE MEYER
(author, The Twilight Saga)

We love to be scared—the horror industry is doing great, but most of the monsters are disgusting. They're oozing or something, but vampires are the only ones who are dangerous and scary, but at the same time they're hot. That's why they're so popular—there's both sides to that.

JOSS WHEDON

Any great fantasy has to contain your greatest wish and your darkest fear. The idea of a vampire is someone who is cut off from the rest of humanity, which I think everybody feels like sometimes. He is cut off and shunned, and at the same time exalted. Of all the creatures—and we need our creatures—we've created, he is the most exalted. The Phantom of the Opera? Yeah, he can play the piano, but you don't want to kiss him. The vampire is the person who sees everything, who's above everything, who's completely alienated from humans but looks human, can interact with humans, can love like a human. People just relate to that. It's a myth they want to see themselves in . . . to a degree. Obviously, *Buffy* is more about Buffy than it is about vampires, but I think there's a tinge of that there that people can't get enough of.

The initial setup for the *Angel* series is that Angel has relocated to Los Angeles, mostly to put some distance between him and Buffy Summers. There he finds new purpose in his life when he meets the half demon Doyle, who serves as a conduit for the Powers That Be and, as such, informs Angel that he's there to help the helpless. Once *Buffy*'s Cordelia Chase enters the picture, this new "family" launches Angel Investigations, which has to represent television's first vampire private detective.

JOSS WHEDON

I saw *Angel* as the second half, somewhat-more-adult version of the same metaphor as *Buffy*, which is personal demons as actual demons with horns. But it's not a high school humiliation, alienation kind of thing. It was more of an adult, "I'm walking in a grown-up world," twentysomething-thirtysomething setting. We dealt a lot with addiction as a metaphor, because *that's* Angel. He was sort of a reformed drunk, so he was fighting his way back to something resembling humanity and helping others do the same. We knew it would be a little darker, but it wouldn't be one of those relentlessly all blue-colored, angsty, "I track a serial killer every week" shows.

MARTI NOXON

We talked a lot about Angel's mission. Would the setup be something like, "If he saved a hundred souls, he'd get to be human," or would it not be that literal? Would it be a little looser? We talked about it endlessly, right down to, "Where does he live? What does he drive?" At one point there was some possibility of a car company doing some advertising tie-in and they wanted

Angel to drive an SUV [*laughs*]. So we were saying, "Angel doesn't drive an SUV, does he?" "No!" "Even if we got free SUVs?" "No, he still doesn't drive an SUV." Those are the *temptations* we faced daily. So there was definitely a struggle, and there were things in the original *Angel*, the original conception of the show, that were darker than it became.

TIM MINEAR

When you look at the pilot—and I know this was a seminal moment for both Joss Whedon and David Greenwalt—there was the fact that Angel does *not* save the girl. There's this big twist where she actually ends up dying like two-thirds of the way through the story. I think *that* set the tone for the show.

MARTI NOXON

That was absolutely the point. In this world and this universe, there was a greater mystery, and Angel's place in it wasn't always going to be clear. But then he had to sort of trust that he was doing the right thing and that there was a greater good he was serving. In fact, he did stop the evil vampire in the pilot and helped Cordelia, who probably would have been killed by him. That was one of the places where Joss and David were thinking in a fashion that made people so intrigued with what they did, because you really didn't know what was going to happen.

TIM MINEAR

The thing you *didn't* see was written in the script. Angel goes in, finds her dead body, cradles her, and sees her blood on his hand. He lifts his hand and, I think, he actually put his finger in his mouth. Originally that was, for Joss and David, the point of the episode; that this guy is really on the edge. He's struggling. But that moment just didn't work, and we ended up cutting it from the episode. It was dark enough that he didn't save the girl. I don't think you needed him licking her dead body. It was very cool, but that's often what happens. The thing that you thought was the point of the story ends up excised at the end.

DAVID BOREANAZ

(actor, Angel)

In the beginning, *Angel* was an analogy to everyday living. I think when you wake up in the morning and look at yourself in the mirror, you see yourself, but in there are these fears and these demons that somehow are sleeping or hidden in your past. When you walk out that door and face people, you don't really know how people are, they're touch and go, and those demons and fears will come out. So the idea was that I would be fighting those demons and it would be a fight for humanity; how many souls can I save in order to save my own? And Angel as a character is very complex, because he does have the opportunity to delve into dangerous personalities at times, but he knows how to keep that at bay; he has a soul.

MARTI NOXON

What's interesting to me about Angel is that it's *not* just a perfect moment of happiness that trips him up and he's bad again. One of the things we wanted to explore on the series was the idea that there's a part of him that's very dark, and if those impulses get triggered and pushed too far, he's capable of going back to the dark side. That was always real interesting to me.

STEVEN S. DEKNIGHT

(supervising producer, *Angel*)

There are a lot of elements to *Angel* that are appealing. One is the brooding antihero. You've got a vampire with a soul trying to atone for his crimes. That's just one of those mythical stories that people love. That you almost *crave*. Luke Skywalker standing on Tatooine, watching the twin suns set . . . God, if only there were a scene that approached that kind emotional resonance in any of the Star Wars prequels. But it's that kind of mythical storytelling that I think really resonates on a subconscious level. Besides that, it's a show that has humor, action, horror. It's got a blend of everything. And deep painful drama, and at the time it was hard to find another show on TV that had all of those elements and that could shift gears in the middle of a deep, emotional scene where you'll suddenly have a funny line, and vice versa.

TIM MINEAR

In the episode "She," there's a moment during a party at Cordelia's apartment when a woman asks Angel to dance and he imagines himself doing the dorkiest dance anyone could imagine and gracefully declines. Joss had been talking about Boreanaz's funny dance. Actually, I put it into the script for "Sense & Sensitivity" at one point where he said, "I feel so deeply now, the only way I can express myself is through interpretive dance," and I had him do this thing. It was really funny, but Joss thought it was too much. Plus, we wanted to save it until it was just right. So we put it into "She." Here's this guy who looks like this, and he's a complete social retard. We had a lot of success playing that aspect of the character.

DAVID GREENWALT
(executive producer/cocreator, *Angel*)

We'd wanted to do the dance for years on *Buffy*. It was like, "Maybe this is Xander's imagination of the way he sees Angel dancing," but Joss just filed the idea away. When we were writing "She," he said, "Do a party scene, have a girl ask him to dance, and do his fantasy of what it would look like." To me that's pretty terrific writing, because it's fun and entertaining, but it also makes a point about why Angel doesn't mix with people. The normal reason is because he doesn't want to drink their blood, no happiness and all of that shit. But also he doesn't want to look like a goofball. You don't expect to see your hero even in a fantasy doing that, yet it's on point. It's emotionally correct *and* funny as shit.

KELLY A. MANNERS
(producer, *Angel*)

I think it was much easier to sell *Angel* than *Buffy*, because the characters had already been established. The network knew what they were going to get. Of course *Angel* went a different direction. A vampire with a soul opens up a detective agency—it's kind of humorous to think back. We shot our presentation in three days, and it sold the show. We didn't spend a lot of time and money on it. It was a twenty-minute quickie, and that's all the network needed to see, and we were on our way.

DAVID BOREANAZ

I didn't see the *Buffy* connection as either a burden or a problem. I just saw that they were going to be compared, because *Angel* came out of *Buffy*. There was really no way to control that, and I didn't look to control any of that. I saw it as a blessing to be able to have the show when *Buffy* came out and had a character evolve into its own show was remarkable, and very fortunate for me.

THOMAS P. VITALE
(executive vice president, programming and original movies, Syfy and Chiller)

What made *Angel* so fascinating is that at first blush it seems like a very straightforward spin-off from *Buffy* . . . just take the general premise of *Buffy* and some of the recurring characters, add in some new people, change the city, and have a new show. But *Angel* was much more than that. *Angel* was a show that stood up on its own. Although *Angel* probably won't be considered "important" like *Buffy*, it was a very good show. In terms of audience appeal, I think that *Angel* ultimately appealed primarily to a core genre audience, whereas *Buffy*'s appeal transcended audience distinctions between genre and nongenre viewers.

KEITH SZARABAJKA
(actor, Holtz)

I actually liked *Angel* better than *Buffy*. I thought it was darker and more interesting, you know? I always thought *Buffy* was a little tongue-in-cheek, whereas with *Angel*, while there was this certain sort of winking quality to it, it still felt that if vampires were real, Angel would have been real. It was sort of like *The Equalizer* with fangs.

JOSS WHEDON

We didn't have to do an actual pilot, because we had an order for thirteen and because David Greenwalt and I were both making *Buffy*, there was no way we could shoot something for pilot season. So the idea was always just to shoot the presentation and then go straight into production.

DAVID GREENWALT

Buffy and *Angel* were among the best things that ever happened in my paltry life. I came to TV late, in my '40s. I had been sick of movies and determined to make it in television. This was the first really successful thing. Well, I was on *The Commish*, but *Buffy* changed a lot of things anyway. And three years or so into that show, Joss walks into my office one day and he says, "What do you think about spinning off Angel into his own show and doing it together with me?" By then I was smart enough to say, "Uh, yes, please."

JOSS WHEDON

We were terrified pretty much 24-7 during that time; we just kept working and working. David worked the most on *Angel*, I worked the most on *Buffy*, and we sort of supported each other. We were constantly going back to each other's office and stuff. But in terms of the breaking of stories and the editing and all that, that all happened together. The staffs from both shows knew each other, and so there was a lot of crosscurrents. We just kept it one big concept instead of two totally separate ones.

KELLY A. MANNERS

We didn't mind being the child of *Buffy*. *Buffy* was mother ship and we all realized that. We had the same show runners, so we knew what we were in for. I can't tell you there were huge hurdles. The only huge hurdle was every time we accomplished an impossible show, Joss would see it was accomplished and he'd raise the bar on the next one. I'd say, "Joss, pretty soon we're not going to be able to pole vault over it." "Well, you said that on the last one and you guys got it done."

JOSS WHEDON

One of the ideas we had pitched the network for *Angel* was the idea of creating a mythos for twentysomethings, because there is none. Adolescence is very charged in American mythos, middle age is very charged in American mythos. Twentysomethings? Nobody cares. We said it would be interesting to investigate the fears and growth and the things that happen to you in your twenties, which are just as important as any other decade in your life, but doesn't really exist, mythically speaking, in American fiction. What we realized is that there is this passage in your life during which you create the person you're going to be. When you're a teen, you're in a structured environment where they're telling you what to do. When you're in your thirties, you're dealing with the choices you made, but it is in fact in your twenties when you've made a lot of important life decisions. It's when you first learn how to be a grown-up.

MARTI NOXON

Joss and David Greenwalt spent a tremendous amount of time talking about creating the show, as did I with them. You were creating a whole new world, and they were always really clear about things that they wanted. At the same time, it was about how do you morph this character who has been so broody and solitary into a guy in a whole new universe? So we spent *a lot* of time talking about what the metaphor was. *Buffy* had a very strong central metaphor: high school is hell, which we were able to generalize that more into young adulthood is hell. The monsters were oftentimes standing in for real-life situations. There was a lot of talk about that and what the metaphor on the show is. The WB wanted a lot of twentysomething kind of story lines; you know, take the *Buffy* audience and go a little bit older.

DAVID FURY

(writer, *Angel*)

There was a struggle early on of, exactly what is this show? *Buffy* was very clear: we knew what the allegory was; we knew what the crux of the show was. *Angel* was a more difficult show. To simply say he was a vampire private detective in Los Angeles didn't really tell us anything. Eventually Tim Minear decided it was really about trying to stay moral in an immoral world. The struggle, you put in the context of men, is how to be a good man in a bad world. Stay on the straight and narrow. Some of the allegory was addiction, alcoholism, and that kind of thing. We kind of covered a little bit of that with Willow and her magic on *Buffy*. But with Angel it's about a guy who had fallen off the wagon, basically becoming Angelus, and now it's like, "I've got to atone for that and make up for it. How do I be a good man?" That was the best we could come up with at first.

TIM MINEAR

What I like about the whole idea of *Angel* is the concept of redemption. And this idea of recovery as well. You look at the show on its face and wonder how anyone can relate to it. It's sort of about twentysomethings, but the lead is 240 and change. The truth is, here's a guy who's *choosing* to be good. He's got stuff in his past that he's got to make up for. One of my favorite experiences was writing the episode where he "eats" his family. To me, that is *so* interesting. You don't see that on television every day. The lead character has not only got a past, but he's got a huge past and it's *horrible*. So the darkness appealed to me. Actually, the Joss Whedon sensibility combined with that darkness is right up my alley.

MARTI NOXON

Early on, there was a real focus on the addiction. Early on we had him *really* struggling with his desire to drink blood again, and that's hinted at in the pilot. At one point it was going to be much more of a story line, born out of the season-three finale of *Buffy*, "Graduation Day," where Angel has to drink Buffy's blood. From that, we were positing that his addiction, his need, was really heightened. But the whole drank-from-Buffy was too far away, and it wasn't part of the story enough for people to relate to what was going on there. But I think his drinking from Buffy was part of it and that the addiction had really been reawakened. The desire to feed was back, and it was really eating away at him. But that connection wasn't clear enough, so it didn't really play.

JOSS WHEDON

Part of what we wanted to say with this show is that redemption is difficult and it takes a long time and there isn't always a goal in sight. You just have to keep trying to do right and trying to make up for what's gone before. And if you make it easy, if you say, "Find the golden key," that's kind of a false hope. And the thing about a hero is that even when it doesn't look like there's a light at the end of the tunnel, he's going to keep digging, just because *that's* who he is.

JOSE MOLINA

(former assistant to Howard Gordon)

I was a little skeptical that this dark, brooding, mirthless guy dressed all in black could really carry a show that would be fun. And I read the pilot script and I was *still* skeptical. I remember thinking, "This is fine, but it's no *Buffy*. It's missing the greatness of *Buffy*." And I was there working on it and scripts starting coming in and there were some problems right away. Like I remember the network threw out the second script. Like completely threw it out and they had to come up with a different story. So I wasn't the only skeptic, and then we started shooting and then the dailies for the pilot started coming in and, oh my God, they were fucking fantastic! This was Batman as a vampire. And I ate my words immediately. As soon as I saw the first cut of the pilot, I went to Joss and I was just gushing about how good it was.

JOSS WHEDON

Inevitably you look at one guy and say, "Oh, we'll use him again," and you never do. Or you go, "Oh, the dynamic between these two is what works," and it doesn't. Or there's a different dynamic that you never expected. That being said, it was clear to me when I first sort of devised the *Buffy* pilot that Angel was the one character who is bigger than life in the same way that Buffy was. A kind of superhero. And I knew—as the dark, mysterious love interest—that he had the potential to be a breakout character, but I also knew he had the potential to go away after three episodes. *Then* we found David Boreanaz.

MARTI NOXON

The audience reaction to Angel kind of made it a necessity for a spin-off. But one of the strongest reasons is David Boreanaz emerged as a true leading man, and one whom I feel had a kind of energy and bearing that very few guys on TV had. He's a man, not a kid, and there wasn't a lot of competition out there for a manly, funny, versatile leading guy. So the WB was itching for a vehicle for him.

DAVID GREENWALT

So Joss comes to me and says, "Let's do this *Angel* spin-off." I think we got a guarantee of twelve episodes on the air before we had really done anything, which was terrific. We weren't just going to make a pilot and wait. *Then* David Boreanaz's agent called and said they wanted a new price for him on *Buffy* and they didn't even want to talk about what we were going to pay him on *Angel*. This is a great Joss story. Everybody's in an uproar and we're in his big office and people are pacing and we're like, "What the fuck are we going to do? We've got this twelve-episode guarantee," and blah, blah, blah. So his agents are asking for all this stuff. I remember Joss just sitting like Michael Corleone, very quietly, plotting his death. He says to me, "David, I'd like you to call Mr. Boreanaz's agent. I want you to tell them that, in fact, we're going to spin another character off. His name is Bob Fenuti, Demon Hunter, and we're going to make him up and spin him off." Of course I did that and they came back like, "Oh no, no, no, no. We didn't mean anything we said." So he totally flipped it back to [David's] agent with this one really simple idea. That's what I love about Joss: he can think under pressure.

MARTI NOXON

The other thing is that we were in danger, on *Buffy*, of getting into a rut. The relationship between Buffy and Angel had served the show so well, and for that reason you keep trying to extend it beyond its natural possibilities and people start getting tired of it. Yet at the same time you don't want to let it go. It was a bit like the *Beauty and the Beast* TV series from the late '80s, or even *Cheers*. That show survived the departure of Shelley Long beautifully and the producers brought in another quirky leading lady. Basically, spinning Angel off served both shows, to get him his own series while giving Buffy a new world of possibilities.

SARAH MICHELLE GELLAR
(actress, Buffy Summers)

I can't say enough amazing things about David Boreanaz. In the three years we worked together, we never had so much as a disagreement and, I mean, that's unbelievable. We worked so well together. We could gauge each other's moods. So for me it was very daunting to be without him and there was the concern that, you know, part of the reason that *Buffy* worked was Angel, and you got this feeling of, "What if I can't do it on my own? What if I need David?" But it was a very exciting time for him as well. And luckily, I thought it was a good challenge for me.

CHARISMA CARPENTER
(actress, Cordelia Chase)

What's funny about David is by his very nature he's a very giddy person, and silly, and it always surprised me, because he has sort of—and I mean this as a compliment, but it isn't going to sound like that—a Cro-Magnon strength, "I will pummel you" kind of image. He looks like he could break you, but he's so silly and really good-natured and easy to smile, so he carried the responsibility through a difficult time—having to do with his marriage—with such grace and a lot of love from his family. They came out a lot. It was a good point in both of our lives. I mean, we were going through stuff, but it was beautiful.

TIM MINEAR

I had had an experience before where I'd be on a show and the leading man was, let's say, only OK. What I learned was that if you had a star, a guy who could really carry the show, then you could probably have a success, and I thought David Boreanaz was just that guy. A lot of people weren't sure, based on his role on *Buffy*. He sort of played this one-note thing, but I thought he could do a whole lot more.

I also thought that he was a lot like David Duchovny in that this guy is a guy you *want* in your living room. Television is very tricky. You can go to a movie and you can see somebody like John Malkovich. You could go specifically to see that guy, but do you want him in your living room every week? I think David is sort of a classic leading man, action-star-type guy; he's definitely got the charisma for it and he's got the chops for it, as he proved year after year. No attitude at all. He totally set the tone on the set, and the crew loved him. A real workhorse. He had to be, because he was in practically every scene.

JOSS WHEDON

The biggest surprise—that's not the right word—was David, who just came out of the gate swinging. Not just with the brooding, handsome, dark-guy stuff, but with the comedy and with a real sort of humanity to him—a real openness that we didn't get to see on *Buffy.* We all had confidence that he could do that, but to see him sort of take center stage and completely hold his own was really gratifying and cool. *Frasier* from *Cheers* was exactly my analogy for this, because not everybody would have picked Frasier as the guy to spin off, but look what happened.

DAVID BOREANAZ

I remember we were working on an episode of *Buffy.* I was wearing a terrible wig and speaking in an even worse Irish accent. Joss called me and said, "I'd like to talk to you tomorrow." I asked, "Am I getting fired?" "No, it's a good thing." I said, "I still think I'm going to get fired." Went into his office the next morning and he said, "We're thinking of doing a spin-off series. David is going to run with it; I'm going to assist with it." "What do you mean you're going to assist with it?" "I'll be there, but I won't be there." "OK, what does *that* mean?" "It means he'll run it, pass on the scripts, and I'll read them and comment on them." I think I was so focused on what I was doing at the time, so I didn't really get a chance to absorb it. I left the office, called my dad and said, "They offered me my own spin-off series. This is amazing!" But I was *still* concerned about the bad accent I was doing. But that's kind of how I operate: I don't think too much about what's going to be coming, just the here and now.

MARTI NOXON

One of the things we discovered as we went along was that the shows could be much funnier than we thought the genre would permit when we started. We'd done a couple of episodes that kind of were big, funny romps in the same way that *Buffy* could be, and that was a real surprise. David just had the chops. And we discovered more and more ways in which we could take advantage of that. We began doing a wider variety of episodes and the characters were continuing to expand. A lot of times the way a story arc altered had so much to do with what the actors brought to the table; we suddenly realized not to depersonalize them and recognized that they were instruments that could be played in many ways. Suddenly you had a lot more options. We learned how versatile the characters were, because the actors were so strong.

TIM MINEAR

I went to the preview where they ran the pilot of *Angel* for a sample audience sitting there with the knobs to vote for what they did or did not like. There were fans of *Buffy,* male and female; there were people who didn't watch *Buffy,* male and female; and across the board the one thing they agreed on was that they all loved David Boreanaz. The men thought that this guy was really cool; they didn't feel threatened by him and felt that he was somebody they could relate to. And, of course, the women were in love with him. That's really special because he doesn't come across as someone you can't relate to, because we can all understand what it's like to fumble and not get out what it is we're trying to say.

DAVID BOREANAZ

I kind of took the character for what he was and I think every day there was something new and exciting about him that I learned with every script. Joss and David were always like, "Well, we're going to do this in episode six, we're going to do this," and I said, "I'm working on episode two now. I'm not concerned about episode seven or eight." Within each episode I learned something different about him. Yes, he has a tortured soul and he has a guilty conscience, but at the same time, he was trying to rebuild that and make amends for his own true sanity, to make himself a better person. I think we saw that happen slowly but surely.

Early on, people kept talking about the pressure of my headlining the show. Pressure is something that everybody can understand. I think that pressure is something that you bring upon yourself, and I was fortunate enough to have two great parents who instilled a lot of confidence in myself and also a lot of humility. So at the same time I learned just to take things for what they are, work hard, and be loose with it. And with those ingredients, along with great cast members and a great support team, and being part of the whole rather than being part of the given, then I think it works out.

Initially, there was a bit of a challenge in finding exactly what *Angel* would be as a series as opposed to *Buffy,* and that situation came to a head during production of the second episode, when everything came to a crashing halt.

DAVID GREENWALT

We wanted to do a darker, more urban show. We set it in L.A. to make a more noir kind of show. We had all these exciting ideas and we wrote the pilot and Joss directed it. Having a twelve-episode guarantee doesn't always mean it's going to be smooth sailing. David Fury had written another script—I think it was going to be the second episode—and we were *really* going dark. For example, in the second script Angel not only doesn't save the girl, he gets down on the floor and licks up the blood, because we thought we'd do a whole alcoholic metaphor for him. We also had a gal cop, the Kate Lockley character, who'd gone undercover and had become a real hooker and cocaine addict. The WB read that and completely fucking freaked out. There was a big meeting and we shut down.

DAVID FURY

I broke the story with Joss and David, which was a little dark. It introduced the character of Kate Lockley, the policeman and undercover cop, but it went to darker places. There were some pretty awful things in there. It dealt with some kind of prostitutes who were ripping people apart. Anyway, she was a cop who was going undercover with a prostitution ring, and it was actually based on a movie called *Report to the Commissioner.* That's where the name Lockley comes from. There was a great twisted thing in the movie that he was an undercover cop that realized that this prostitute or criminal's girlfriend is another undercover cop. He winds up inadvertently killing her, and the whole movie is told in flashback. So in putting Angel in with somebody he didn't realize was a cop, I was trying to get that same sort of thing. David and Joss—and maybe more so David—wanted to set it apart from *Buffy.* He didn't want it to be *Buffy 2,* so he wanted to go to a much darker place. He wanted to be pushing the envelope. That's what I went for and a couple of weeks from production the studio just balked.

TIM MINEAR

Obviously, we were still trying to figure out what the show was at that point. This was the first episode after the pilot, and it was written before the new staff arrived. They just went incredibly dark with this thing and decided at the end of the day that it was a little bit *too* hopeless, a little too grim. After that episode was written and was actually being prepped, the network, too, had some concerns about it.

DAVID FURY

This is a studio from which there were virtually no notes that they ever gave on the *Buffy* scripts. We'd get on the notes call for a script and they'd just go, "This is great. Keep doing what you're doing." That's generally how they went. *Angel,* because it was a new entity, may have had more scrutiny on it. When they recognized this isn't as fun as *Buffy,* it's far more dark . . . they kind of put the pause button on and shut down production.

DAVID GREENWALT

You know what? The network was right. It would have been too much to ask of an audience too soon. We were kind of off there, and were out there a little bit. We just adjusted it to not be so dark. So we fixed it and it turned into a really good show that went to a lot of interesting places over the years. People have frequently come up to me and said, "Oh, I like *Angel* better than *Buffy*." In the beginning, part of the problem is that the metaphor in *Buffy* was so clear. It was a little harder in *Angel*, because people in their twenties just are not that interesting. I also think part of the problem is that we were suffering a little *Buffy* fatigue and wanted to do something quite a bit different as opposed to something just a little bit different.

DAVID FURY

We had to scramble and I had to work with Marti Noxon on another story, which became "Lonely Heart." It did include Kate Lockley, but it was very different. So we turned out another version of the second episode and Marti was a huge help on it. She graciously allowed me to take solo credit. The shutdown for the darkness of the script needed to go lighter and the show did veer a little more into *Buffy* territory. It lightened up a bit, but it always remained a darker version of *Buffy*. We had to earn it, I guess. The second episode was most scary to them because it was so dark, but the show went to some *very* dark places later.

TIM MINEAR

At the time, the Internet ran rampant with rumors that the WB had shut down the show for retooling. You can't really call it a shutdown, because we hadn't really started. We just pushed back the shoot date for the first episode a week or two. It's not like alarms went off and we had to pull the plug on everything. I read where people were saying the network freaked and they told us to shut down, and that's not true at all. We were still creating what the idea of the show was going to be, and basically we decided to rethink the first episode. The other thing people didn't realize is that a lot of the other episodes we'd done that first year were written earlier and did not change significantly. It was really that first episode where we went back, rethought it, and were lucky we had the luxury to do that.

DAVID FURY

This is obviously true of a lot of shows, but I think it's true of Joss organically that these shows have to grow into themselves. A lot of shows aren't allowed to. So he had that wonderful benefit from the WB at the time that the shows were able to find themselves; they weren't quick to just say, "You know what? It's not gelling, so we're going to take it off the air." Because it's not like either show lit up the ratings. It never did. It was more of a cult phenomenon. It was just highly regarded by critics. Of course, it had some attractive people who got to be on the covers of magazines, but both series took some time to find themselves.

KELLY A. MANNERS

It was just a retooling of the show. I don't think it was just the network that shut us down. I think Joss Whedon thought, "You know what? This isn't the way I really want to take this show," so I think Joss went to the network and said, "Hey, let me have a couple of weeks to really figure out which direction I want to take this in." They rebuilt the story arc and it was much better than what we had for the first thirteen, yet we could use the material we had previously shot, so it wasn't going to be cost prohibitive. It was just the cost of carrying a few people. It was a really important time for the show.

DAVID FURY

Early on, there was always a frustration of, "I don't know what this show is. I don't know what I'm doing. How do we come up with a story?" Whereas *Buffy* was like, "We had so many avenues to pull from," but what's the universal truth in *Angel*? There was no truth of a private detective in L.A. everyone can relate to. It was a harder show to write. That could be frustrating.

JOSS WHEDON

The shutdown really didn't mean anything except that we took a little time to rewrite the second story, because the second episode is really pretty important in terms of a mission statement. It tells you where the thing is really going, because you throw everything you can into a pilot and that's fine. Hopefully it tells you what the show is, but with the second one you get a sense of where the show's really going; these are the elements they took from the pilot and will be continuing with. It wasn't like, "Oh my God, it's the end of the world." It was the network telling us that we needed to make an adjustment, and David Greenwalt and I saying, "Gee, we wished we disagreed with you." In truth, it helped us a lot. I'll always take a note if it's a good one.

When any series is gestating, it falls to the show runner to bring together the writing staff capable of bringing the vision to life. In its earliest conceptual stages, it was believed that the staff of *Buffy* would be able to handle all the script writing for *Angel,* but this proved untenable, and it proved necessary to bring on additional writers for the spin-off. (Whedon attempted the same thing with *Firefly,* initially planning to use the writers from *Buffy* and *Angel* to write all the episodes until realizing this, too, was untenable.)

In the first year, the writing staff included, from *Buffy,* Jane Espenson, Douglas Petrie, David Fury, and Marti Noxon, in addition to Whedon and Greenwalt. New to Mutant Enemy was producer Tracey Stern, staff writer Jeannine Renshaw, and consulting producer Howard Gordon (who had served in a similar position during *Buffy*'s second season). One of those new hires, and in hindsight the greatest strength Whedon and Greenwalt could have found, was writer Tim Minear, who in many ways came to define the voice of *Angel.*

Born in New York City on October 29, 1963, Minear, before joining the staff of *Angel,* wrote for *Lois and Clark: The New Adventures of Superman, The X-Files,* and *Strange World.* He worked on *Firefly* alongside Joss Whedon, and subsequent to *Angel* his writer/producer credits include *Wonderfalls, The Inside, Drive, Dollhouse, Terriers, The Chicago Code,* and *American Horror Story.*

HOWARD GORDON

(consulting producer, *Angel*)

If I can take credit for anything, it's introducing Tim Minear to Joss. I knew Tim and I knew right away that he would be able to speak Joss's vernacular. It was almost like setting two people [up] on a date; you just had a feeling. This was Tim's idiom, his voice. Or he would be able to complement Joss's voice.

TIM MINEAR

I was at *The X-Files* and I was *very* unhappy. It was kind of be careful what you wish for sort of thing. I had written an *X-Files* spec, and that's what got me on that show. I was there for a year, and it wasn't great. The people were great, just not the experience. I used to hang out with Kim Metcalf, who was an assistant to Ken Horton at *Millennium*. I was sort of whining about feeling underused or whatever, and at some point Kim says, "I want to show you something," and she took me into the conference room of *Millennium* and put in a videotape. It was the *Buffy* episode "Surprise." I didn't really know what it was. What she said to me was, "You shouldn't be here. You should be working with Joss Whedon." That was probably two years before I ever ended up at Mutant Enemy. That was literally my first exposure to *Buffy*, from somebody who was telling me that I should be working with Joss, whom I didn't know. She was weirdly prescient about that. Then everybody knows the tale that I was working with Howard Gordon on *Strange World* after I left *The X-Files*. I was called by my agent that I had a meeting with David Greenwalt and Joss Whedon and that I should go in and pitch some *Buffy* ideas.

I hadn't really watched any *Buffy*, save for the brief moment in Kim's office. I borrowed a bunch of videotapes of episodes and kind of crammed on them. I think I came up with four or six pretty-well-worked-out pitches, at least three of them were *really* well worked out. I pitched close-ended episodes, like Xander loses his virginity because Druids are coming to Sunnydale and they're looking for a virgin sacrifice. Literally, if he doesn't lose his virginity, it's a matter of life and death. That seemed like what it feels like when you're a boy in high school, and so it seemed to me that it was taking a metaphor of what he was doing with horror and making it about the stages of growing up. I think that's what he responded to in terms of, "Boy, this guy gets it. It's too bad he's so angry that I can't be around him."

See, when I had met with Joss and David and pitched them these ideas, Joss subsequently said they were the best pitches he had ever heard but that he found me to be the angriest man he'd ever met and didn't think he'd ever be able to be in a room with me.

DAVID GREENWALT

Tim Minear came to *Angel*, and Tim is one of the best writers I've ever worked with. Also a very funny, sarcastic guy. To be insulted by him is a pleasure, you know? As a matter of fact, the first year of *Angel* he's sitting around the table of all the writers and he wasn't very friendly. They were saying, "Why aren't you more friendly? Why don't you get to be friends with us and go out with us?" He says, "Well, none of you will be here next year. Why would I do that?"

TIM MINEAR

I probably *seemed* angry because I was coming off of a not great year at *The X-Files*. I think they maybe asked me how it went and I may have told them. Joss just didn't know how to take me. Later, when *Angel* got spun off, Greenwalt, who I guess had been sufficiently impressed with me in the room, went back to Joss and said, "Can I hire him for *Angel*?" Joss was like, "Well, it's your show. You're the one running it, so it's up to you, but I can't be in a room with him." So that was my start at Mutant Enemy.

David Greenwalt contacted Minear's agent to see about hiring him for the show, but Minear turned him down. Five times.

TIM MINEAR

I was pretty young at the time. You have to understand, I went from *Lois and Clark*, which was my first real job, to *The X-Files*. I was there for a year and they were actually going to pick up my option and bring me back for another year. I think I was the first person in the history of *The X-Files* to say, "Nah, I don't want to." It's not like I was being offered something else; I just knew that I wasn't happy and that I could probably do better someplace else. I had no fear that I would end up not getting work, which was probably naive of me at the time. So I took a vacation, then worked with Howard Gordon on *Strange World*. At the time, there was actually a possibility of doing a Tim Burton syndicated show, *Lost in Oz*, and I was supposed to meet with him in London.

Howard Gordon actually said to me, "Your problem is that you're usually the smartest person in the room. You need to be in a place where you're not. You need to be with Joss, because he's smarter than you and you can actually learn something." So my agent and Howard were telling me to take

Angel. This was a show that was going to go for sure, and it was a spin-off of not just a good show—*Buffy*—but an important show that was kind of right in the zeitgeist of what was going on. So I said yes.

By that time, I'd started becoming more familiar with *Buffy.* Angel had already turned evil. I think all of that stuff was around the time that television critics were writing about the most subversive television is being made on this kids' network, the WB. It talked about *Buffy* and how people thought this was some campy horror thing. They thought of Scooby-Doo, literally. They were completely missing the subversive nature of this, as Joss was saying, in that format. It wasn't camp. In fact, it was drama. It was, in fact, *great* drama.

HOWARD GORDON

I said to him, "Tim, I promise you that this is going to be a long-term and incredibly productive relationship." I sort of threw myself under the bus and said, "It probably won't be for me, but I know your voice and you're going to learn stuff here and become"—I may have used the phrase—"Crown Prince." I just felt it was going to be a good match, so I encouraged him. I said he would thrive there, and he did.

JOSE MOLINA

Because of his difficulties with the voice, Howard was a little hesitant to do it, but he was friends with David Greenwalt, who was running *Angel,* so the stars kind of aligned for him to go over there as part of his deal at 20th. From day one, before the pilot was even shot, when it was just a script, he went on board as consultant on *Angel* and I went with him. I desperately wanted the staff writer job on that first season, and one of the things that I still give Howard shit about is that he never submitted me for that job. Like, "C'mon, man, you said you couldn't tell my voice apart from theirs—let me have that gig."

DAVID GREENWALT

At the time, Joss was really running two shows. I certainly was running *Angel* and didn't do all that much at *Buffy,* but I was always fascinated by what was going on there and what was happening to Buffy. But people like Marti Noxon, David Fury, and Doug Petrie were pretty involved with *Angel,* particularly in the early year or two.

JOSE MOLINA

I think Joss knew the show was still finding itself. The first half of the first season was pretty uneven; toward the end, Tim Minear was writing a little bit more and Tim would become the voice of the show. Joss let it grow, but the staff that they had on season one was a very small staff. Joss wanted to have the *Buffy* writers write *Angel*'s scripts, which is something that he would try again later when *Firefly* started. He didn't want to hire a staff; he wanted the *Buffy* and *Angel* writers to write all those. Needless to say, he was wrong. But because the *Angel* staff was so small and because he was split between two shows, nobody quite had a handle on what made the show work.

TIM MINEAR

I have to say that the first several months of working on *Angel* were horrible. *Buffy* was going into its third or fourth year, writers were brought in on *Angel,* and yet they did the easiest thing they could: they had the *Buffy* staff write the first batch of episodes. It made sense, but we felt like we were the red-headed stepchildren at *Angel.* We were completely shut out. They had already started working on stories for the show and scripts with some of the *Buffy* writers, which in truth made perfect sense. This was a group of writers that Joss and David had taken years to cast, to find out who worked and who didn't. By the time *Angel* started up, you had the varsity version of the *Buffy* writers' room. They felt, David and Joss, more comfortable, I think, working with those people that they'd been working with for years and that they knew as opposed to this new group.

DAVID GREENWALT

I know the writers were very pissed off. We used to go to Joss's house and watch *Buffy* occasionally live and you couldn't speak during the show, which

I wish people would follow now. He invited all these people to the *Angel* premiere, but he didn't invite any of the *Angel* writers. He didn't do it on purpose, but people were insulted they weren't invited.

TIM MINEAR

The new group started being worked in a little bit. We would meet, we would talk about stories, and we would pitch ideas. I pitched something . . . actually, maybe Joss and David pitched the idea of a vampire that Angel made coming back to haunt him. That was the first thing I wrote, which was "Somnambulist." The idea was originally called "The Killer I Created." I took the idea, wrote an outline, then wrote a script, and Joss really liked it. Now what was interesting is [that] even though each of the new writers is working on a script, those were not the priority scripts. In fact, I think "Somnambulist" was like episode nine or ten of the first season, but it was the very first thing I wrote. It's not the first thing even with my name on it. We wrote these scripts and put them in the bank. By the time we got around to shooting those scripts, the show had sort of found its identity and they had to be revised.

An important moment in Minear's career on the show occurred when a script came in that simply didn't work and he was asked to rewrite it. After that, he started getting more responsibility, including being asked to write the script for "Hero" with Howard Gordon and turn it around in twenty-four hours. In the script, Angel's colleague and friend, the half demon Doyle, dies. The script nearly severed Minear's relationship with Mutant Enemy because Greenwalt expressed his opinion that half the script was "pretty good" and the other half suitable for "wip[ing] his ass with."

TIM MINEAR

I was pretty clear with my response: "When you wipe your ass with it, keep the brads in." And then I went to my office and started to pack up my stuff, which wasn't much. I wasn't going to be talked to that way, particularly when I hadn't slept in two days because of that script. I simply decided that I wasn't going to stay for a second in a place where I wasn't appreciated, not that I expected to be treated with kid gloves.

DAVID GREENWALT

Tim and Howard Gordon wrote a very early script together, and I insulted the script. It needed some work. Howard had the same experience on *Angel* that I did on *X-Files* in that it wasn't really in his wheelhouse, so we kind of helped each other on each other's shows. Anyway, I insulted this script and I was a little more insulting in those days. I'm back in my office, and my assistant comes in and he says, "You might want to talk to Tim Minear." I said, "Why would I talk to him?" He says, "Because he's packing up his office and he's leaving." I went and actually begged him not to go.

TIM MINEAR

That night I really thought about what had happened and pretty much had a panic attack. I thought, "I really said some things to my boss today and he's probably stewing right now and is going to fire me tomorrow." But that's not what happened. The next day he was incredibly nice to me. He said, "Some of the things you said to me were great. Do you know who my best writer is here?" I said, "Yeah, it's goddamned me! You don't treat me that way, which is why I'm leaving." He said, "Don't." Then he added, "They were going to pick up your option on *The X-Files,* which is a very high-profile show." I said, "Yeah, but I don't care." "There's a lot of money to be made there." "The two things I don't care about is the prestige and the money." He said, "That's what I'm afraid of." After that we were the best of friends, and I think Joss really respected that, too. When people see that you're not afraid to leave, they don't want you to.

DAVID GREENWALT

Tim and I became fast friends. Tim would turn in scripts that were just so beautiful. I'd tell him, "This is a really good script," and he says, "It better be, because it's all I have." He would stay up writing night after night after night. Another really hard worker—and I have tried to work with him ever since, but the son of a bitch has belonged to Fox all these years. Every show I've ever done since, I couldn't get him.

JOSE MOLINA

I'd known Tim Minear on *Strange World* and we became friendly, because I was Howard Gordon's assistant and his conduit to Howard. He let me read a draft of his script and even let me give notes and listened to my notes. He was really open to me as a writer and one of his legacies at Mutant Enemy, and still . . . is that he does not pigeonhole assistants as assistants. It's been through him that a lot of writers who were former assistants, starting with myself and Mere Smith, were able to write on those Mutant Enemy shows.

Among additional crew members hired for *Angel* included Kelly A. Manners as producer, who was "in the trenches" during production and describes himself as the show's "money man." He served as coproducer on *Buffy,* and after *Angel* went on to *Torchwood* and *Powers*. Also hired were first assistant director Ian Woolf (*The X-Files, Criminal Minds*) and production designer Stuart Blatt (*Dollhouse, Quantico, Criminal Minds: Beyond Borders*).

KELLY A. MANNERS

Angel was my first show as line producer, and that's a *big* jump. It was my show, so I loved that. The fact that Joss entrusted me with it was an honor. I was very excited to move on. David Greenwalt and I skipped off the *Buffy* lot together knowing we were going to create something new and different and have a good time. As to my responsibilities, I had final say on the entire crew. I do get a vote when it comes to the directors. If my production manager brings me an early one-liner of an episode and it can't be shot, I do a little thinking and I call up the writers and say, "Hey, instead of blowing up these three cars, why don't we just run one car into a light pole? We can still tell the same story, but we'll save a lot of money." The trick of my job is I'm the conduit, the hub, between the studio and the creatives and my job is to give them everything they want or as close to everything they want and yet keep the studio off their backs.

IAN WOOLF
(first assistant director, *Angel*)

I've done so many different shows that it's really just standard operating procedure for me. I mean, I knew coming in as first AD that it's all about the scheduling of the project and getting the day's work done and helping the director get what he needs on the screen. I wasn't a fan; I was just doing my job.

KELLY A. MANNERS

We stole some of the crew from *Buffy*. The production designer, although he wasn't my production designer, oversaw season one of *Angel*. We had people in place to keep the Whedon franchise going in the same direction and bringing Joss's vision to the screen, which is what it was all about. Every show's got its challenges going in, whether it's not being able to get the correct makeup artists or the correct visual effects house. We kept the same visual effects house as did *Buffy*. We stole a prosthetics makeup artist from *Buffy* and brought him over to *Angel*. Those would have been the biggies, but we had most of that in place going in. I got a leg up and kind of cheated.

IAN WOOLF

As the show went on, the cast became less a fan of the makeup. David Boreanaz didn't like it especially. The moment you were done with a sequence where you knew that was the last part of the vamp sequence, he would literally stand there waiting. I'd say, "Wait, David. Wait. Let me make sure the gate's clean before you do anything." The moment I said the gate's clean on the camera, he would basically just rip the vamp makeup off his forehead. He hated it *so* much. He wouldn't wait for the makeup guys to put the right solvent on to take it off nicely, he would just rip it off.

Stunts were an integral part of both *Buffy* and *Angel*, and Woolf remembers well a near-climactic moment in the series' premiere episode, "City Of . . ."

IAN WOOLF

In the first episode we had the most impressive thing we had ever done, because we shot it off at 1100 Wilshire, which is this huge office building, and we did two double descenders. One stunt guy was on one descender, falling, and above him about twenty feet was our stunt coordinator at the time, Jeff Cadiente. He was free-falling down on this descender rig. About halfway down, the actor, who is a stuntman, obviously, hits a switch and self-ignites himself on fire, because he's supposed to be a vampire. When we get to the bottom, we had to put him out with fire extinguishers. Like I said, it was one of the most impressive things that I've done in a long, long time.

DAVID GREENWALT

Whatever else we faced in season one, I would say "The Ring," in which Angel ends up captive and fighting other creatures, was the hardest episode of television I'd ever done up until then. Think about that episode. You've got twenty-three guys in makeup, you've got fight upon fight upon fight, and *then* you have a riot in that place. So physically it was the biggest show we ever did by then, and it was just a hundred hours in the editing room. There was never an easy moment in that show. Maybe it wasn't something people hadn't seen before, but we kept raising the bar. From a production standpoint, it was a hell of an achievement.

Serving as production designer of *Angel*'s pilot, including the creation of the office for Angel Investigations, was *Buffy*'s Carey Meyer. For episode two onward, he suggested that a friend of his, Stuart Blatt, who had been working in low-budget features, interview for the position. Blatt did and was hired, staying with the show until the end.

STUART BLATT
(production designer, *Angel*)

I loved Carey's design for it. I loved the fact that in the downstairs, Angel lived in this sort of janitor workmen's closet area, so that was kind of gritty and mysterious and played into his vampire qualities of it being dark and mysterious and somewhat like a tomb. The other great thing is they had built a real working elevator that, even though we built the whole set on one floor, it insinuated it was two floors. In other words, they built the set on one floor, so the upstairs, the Investigations part of it, was one floor, and you get into the old cage elevator and it would start to move down in a pit in the ground. Then, cut, and you'd pick it up on the other side, where they raised the elevator up and they'd bring him to the next level, as if there was a transition from one floor to the next. It was very clever, although it was very slow moving. One of the things Joss said was, "To the Batcave!" and then it was like the calendar turning, because it was such a slow-moving elevator. It was a great visual, but not with any kind of momentum. In a practical sense it worked, but not if you were trying to heighten the tension.

When it came to casting *Angel*, the one given was, naturally, David Boreanaz. Joining him from *Buffy* was Charisma Carpenter's Cordelia, who has moved from Sunnydale to Los Angeles in the hopes of furthering/starting her acting career, when she inadvertently bumps into Angel and ends up working with him. Additionally, Glenn Quinn, best known at the time as playing Roseanne Conner's son-in-law Mark Healy on *Roseanne,* was cast as Doyle, the half-demon Irishman who serves as Angel's connection to the Powers That Be.

Unfortunately, because of problems he had with drug and alcohol addiction, Quinn was let go with the ninth episode of the season, "Hero," in which Doyle sacrifices himself to save a number of demons (the good kind) from being destroyed–and passes his visions on to Cordelia through what became a good-bye kiss. Added to the show in his place was Alexis Denisof as former Watcher Wesley Wyndam-Price, who arrives, somewhat comically, as a "rogue demon hunter" but gradually evolves into something much more. Additionally, in seasons one and two Elisabeth Röhm played Kate Lockley, a police detective and frenemy to Angel who can't cope with the demon-filled reality around her and tries to ignore it as best she can, but nonetheless does end up occasionally working with him on certain cases.

TIM MINEAR

Building an ensemble definitely gives you more places to go. It's like the difference between a combo and an orchestra. Oboes are great, but you don't want *just* oboes. You want to have the full complement of the sound so you can create what you want. You can see that Joss did that brilliantly in *Buffy.*

He just kept adding characters and you're thinking there's just no way he can service all of them, but he did.

DAVID GREENWALT

We learned on *Buffy*, and I wished I'd carried it through to *Grimm*, to start with three or four characters and add one a year. As opposed to starting with seven or eight characters.

TIM MINEAR

Each character that you add brings something interesting to the dynamic and changes it in some fundamental way. I just think he was really right in doing that, and each character is so specific. That's certainly the approach we took on *Angel*.

JOSS WHEDON

In the narrative of *Angel* at the beginning, Cordelia comes to L.A. to be an actress, which didn't go as well for her as it did for Charisma. When I first was developing the idea, David Greenwalt's first comment was, "We've got to bring Charisma along, because she doesn't belong in this world at all, and she would have no patience for it." And so the juxtaposition of those two characters just seemed like a natural.

CHARISMA CARPENTER

Joss and David were very aware of my anxiety issues, and I really appreciate them really saying, "OK, we have this spin-off and you have to be a part of it. So how can we put our best foot forward, because we really want you for this thing?" And to basically say, "We know the devil, we know what we're dealing with, what are *you* going to do to help us? And what can we do to help make this work? Because you are what we want; we want that big smile to work off of David, who is dark and moody. We want that bright light; we want you to come over and join us, but what can we do?"

I could have cried. Like, "Really? You want me? OK!" And it was just such a moment, and I think it's because they saw that my character resonated with people; they saw that I cared; they loved the character and whatever it was I brought to it worked for them. So it was win-win . . . But I had my acting coach there and we worked on my anxiety happening less and less.

DAVID GREENWALT

I wanted to bring Charisma Carpenter to *Angel,* because I knew Angel would be dark and brooding and somewhat humorous sometimes, so he needed this big ditzy dame to really bring it to life.

CHARISMA CARPENTER

The funny thing is, I didn't really work with David Boreanaz much on *Buffy,* which is kind of interesting. We barely worked together, and if we did it was a group thing. When I did *Supernatural,* James Marsters was on the show and we had never worked together. So there we were, ten or eleven years post our shows and it's like, "Nice to meet you."

JOSS WHEDON

With Cordelia, we knew we were going to have to bring her down a peg by taking away her money and waking her up to the real world while still keeping what was great about her, which is her bluntness and lack of tolerance for brooding.

CHARISMA CARPENTER

At the same time, initially I was very concerned. I wanted to make sure that the writers were the ones that were involved with *Buffy* so as to ensure quality. Knowing that Joss and David—who happened to be my biggest fans—would be a big part of the show, I was immediately relieved, to say the least.

DAVID GREENWALT

I *am* Cordelia.

CHARISMA CARPENTER

He's not kidding. There's an element in there. He's in touch with his bitchier self.

TIM MINEAR

Cordelia—off the charts! I love that character. I love Charisma. She's like a savant. She's just so good. When she taps into her Cordelianess, it's amazing. And it was the easiest character for me to write, because I could just hear that voice because of Charisma. Honestly, who would have thought that Cordelia could be *this* interesting? On *Buffy,* Cordelia was played for laughs, so what we found we could do was bring in characters who had been comic relief to some degree and give them arcs, give them a trajectory, give them a place to go, deepen them and have them become more three-dimensional. That worked to our advantage a lot, actually.

CHARISMA CARPENTER

Spin-offs, as they go, aren't usually very successful, so of course I asked if there would be an open door if things should not go well. I wanted to make sure that I could come back to *Buffy* if I had to. Joss said, "I would never put you out there without a net. Of course, I don't know if logistics will back me up on that, but sure." I *think* he was kidding. He loves to make jokes that make actors insecure; he thinks it's really funny. He loves to say, "By the way, you're fired," and then he gets a chuckle out of it. Then he says, "Every time I say that to an actor, they never laugh." That's because it's really *not* funny, Joss.

What was *great,* though, and I know this sounds silly, is we were actually going to shoot at Paramount, a real movie studio. So there was all sorts of goodness happening left and right. It was a really happy time, exciting. The whole thing felt very new and different. It was actually really special, because it was the same character, so there was no sort of panic or scrambling to make it work or discovering who she is and how to play her. All of that stuff had been fleshed out, so it was a well-oiled machine going in and doing something that was the same, but more. I was literally *The Jeffersons'* theme song, "Movin' on Up."

TIM MINEAR

I always liked the character of Kate, thought she was useful and I used her as much as I could. There was a lot of consternation amongst fandom, because they thought we were trying to create a love interest for Angel, which maybe we were, but that was never the sole intent. We just felt like we needed to expand the cast of characters for this to be a show. Plus, it's always good to have a character that is from the outside. Obviously, it is always helpful on a show like this where he is a detective, that he has a contact within the police department. That just sort of made sense as a way that you do these things, and then you get to play the reality of how somebody outside of the supernatural world, once they are given a peek behind the curtain, might react to that.

ELISABETH RÖHM
(actress, Kate Lockley)

In a way, I've never had as exciting a character as I had on *Angel*, because of how well-developed she was. Her anger toward her father, her interest in the dark side of Angel and being able to see that he was good. And just the pain about her mother, her attempted suicide, and getting booted off the police force.

TIM MINEAR

Like I said, there was a lot of consternation in fandom and eventually we sort of phased her out. In the end, I think she served her purpose, and what *really* happened is that Elisabeth got *Law & Order*. The truth is that a lot of these people we don't "own," because they're not regulars on the show, so if they get another offer or they get another show or something, potentially you will have to figure out a way to write them out, because they just won't be around to shoot anything.

ELISABETH RÖHM

I'm pretty much grateful for everything. I was lucky to get that job and to be working with awesome people. They were busy writing what they were writing, and I thought what they were writing was interesting. But then I got my own show called *Bull*, and I was lucky, because Joss was like, "I'll keep you as a recurring character." But I had my own show that I was a lead on, so I would work on this regular show from five in the morning until ten at night, and then I'd have to go over and do vampire hours with the guys and Charisma and be there until six in the morning. *Then* I got *Law & Order*, which moved me to New York, meaning that all that L.A. stuff was out. In a way, I wish I had just gotten on a jet plane and come there twice a week and continued doing it until the end of *Angel*. I would have loved that.

DAVID FURY

The Kate character didn't pan out as well as we hoped it would. She was definitely used several times, but we were hoping that she was going to become part of the unit, but you try something and it works or it doesn't. Maybe the chemistry was off? Maybe we just couldn't feel it.

ELISABETH RÖHM

I felt we had chemistry. Outside of the world of *Angel*, you look at something like Drusilla and Spike, and it's awesome. You see the chemistry between Juliet and James, and that's how it was between David and I. It was great chemistry.

DAVID FURY

Maybe the character didn't have enough going on. She wasn't supernatural; she basically would just be providing police work, which is what you want your characters to do. To be trying to find things out. I don't know. She was lovely, but it just wasn't gelling into that she would be part of the crowd. Forgetting the whole Cordelia thing, there was no real need for a love interest. The whole point of Angel is his loneliness. The fact that he gave Buffy up, the fact that he's come here basically to atone for a lot of things—you didn't want to see him with another person. And Lockley was devised to be that romantic interest, and I just don't think people wanted that at that time. They wanted to cling to the idea of the lost love. That's why Buffy got brought in in the middle of the season, to remind us of that loss in the *Superman II* moment.

"Doyle is a lunatic, basically," the late Glenn Quinn related at the time of the show's first season. "That's obviously why they hired me. He's like a gambler, hustler, Irish half demon, half human. And Angel meets Doyle in Los Angeles. Doyle knows Los Angeles like the back of his hand. And he kind of steers Angel around toward the lost souls. Doyle gets a vision–a name, a place–and passes them on to Angel and they go out and see who they can treat, who they can help."

As to the Buffyverse mythology, he added, "When I was first cast, I got a few episodes sent over to the house, but I'm a pretty avid fan of vampire movies and Celtic mythology and whatnot. Being from Ireland, I kind of grew up with all that kind of stuff. So I'm just really excited to actually walk in Doyle's shoes and basically have fun with him. It's going to be really interesting." He died of a drug overdose on December 3, 2002.

RANDALL SLAVIN
(actor, Male Oracle)

It's a very small world. I was probably one of the first people Glenn Quinn met when he came over from Ireland. I grew up down in Long Beach, California, and one of my close friends was his cousin—this guy named Damien, who worked at a paint store in Long Beach. One day he told me his cousin Glenn was coming in from Ireland that day, and I remember us hanging out and waiting for Glenn to come in. And this was years before he was an actor. When I met him, he had this huge hair, like Bono from the second U2 album—all mullet and incredibly huge '80s hair. So then years later, doing the show and talking . . . Glenn was a sweet, sweet kid and it was just funny that all those years later I would guest-star on his show.

DAVID GREENWALT

When it came to Doyle, we did something pretty outrageous in this business. By then I talked to Steven Bochco, who trained me that you never suffer a misbehaving actor. He taught me how to look an actor in the eye and say, "Look me in the eye. I'm a serial killer; you're going to die. You're either going to behave or you're going to die." I was determined that I was not going to take any shit from any actor under any condition, because life is too short. We loved Glenn. He auditioned and was great. The three of them—David, Charisma, and Glenn—made a great cast for the show. I didn't know until later the full extent of Glenn's problems, but what I experienced on the show is he would have trouble remembering his lines. I don't recall him showing up late so much as screwing around on the set and laughing.

Look, I totally support actors laughing and talking right up until the call of action. Except when they're laughing at their performance and their lack of professionalism. I took him into my little motor home; we were in downtown L.A., and let's say this was around episode four or five. I said to him, "Look me in the eye. I'm a serial killer. You're going to die. You may not come to my set not knowing your lines. You may not come to my set and laugh over not knowing your lines. A lot of these people are driving a long way here to work, and they have eighteen-hour days. They work very, very hard for a hell of a lot less money than you're making, and I will not stand for it. Do you understand me?" And he began to cry.

So I assumed he understood me, but then of course absolutely nothing changed and we ended up killing him, heroically, in episode nine. But think about it: we've got a twelve-episode order and to kill one of the three main characters nine episodes in, it just creates the feeling of, "Watch out, folks, anything can happen." It was a bold move, but I was pretty adamant that I was not going to spend my life dealing with that kind of crap.

CHARISMA CARPENTER

Working with Glenn and David, it was impossible to get any work done, because they were so rowdy and really bonded early on and were total boys. It's really precious to reflect on, but working with Glenn was so much fun. Not many people know this, but Nicky Brendon from *Buffy* has more talent in his pinkie than most people and just gets away sometimes. That's a struggle, but when he works his magic it's amazing. That's how I felt when I was with Glenn; I felt the same kind of thing in terms of getting in his way. He got in his own way with other stuff; he had some demons. It's a weird industry, especially when you have extreme talent and some trauma in your life, and it can be really challenging to reconcile all that money and adulation and work demand. "How do I have a personal life? How do I work nineteen hours a day? How do I balance all that stuff?" And you're young, so it's a lot.

Nicky is probably one of the smartest people I know; he's very witty, he has a lot of issues, but he's amazing, and when we worked together it was always magic. When I went over to *Angel,* that was going to be one of the things I was going to miss the most. When I met Glenn, it was sort of like that familiar love, brotherly love, great affection for him, but just in awe of his talent. And the chemistry between David and Glenn was palpable; they were peanut butter and jelly, and I miss him very much.

TIM MINEAR

I thought Glenn was great. He was charismatic *and* troubled. His sort of personal demons came out through some of his performance. The problem was he had *real* personal demons, and it was really a problem on the set. David Boreanaz was always so incredibly supportive of Glenn and tried to help him through in any way he could. They were truly friends. David really understood him and wanted him to get better, but when someone has a problem like a drug addiction, there's really nothing you can do for them unless they decide they want to do something for themselves. I know this personally.

KELLY A. MANNERS

It was a terrible thing to watch. He came in with a horrible drug and alcohol problem. It was amazing the work he did for us, because I thought it was pretty good. Poor Glenn, he had a tiger on his back; there was no doubt about it. That poor kid didn't stand a chance. Listen, I came up in the '70s and '80s. I did the *Dukes of Hazzard,* where everyone was on blow. I've seen it. A lot of us crossed that muddy field. Most of us didn't get out, and those of us who did are very, very fortunate. And he definitely affected production. Lateness and hungover, not being able to get his lines out. It was very, very tough.

CHRISTIAN KANE
(actor, Lindsey McDonald)

Glenn was going through a bunch of shit. Me and Boreanaz would pick him up and we'd go out and have a cocktail . . . I didn't know him well. I knew him well enough to know that he was quiet, but the only person that can answer what was really happening would be Boreanaz. Boreanaz and him were very tight.

DAVID BOREANAZ

Glenn is a tough thing to discuss, because he was such a good friend of mine. I kind of keep that unanswered. It's still tough to talk about. But God bless his soul; it was a big learning experience for me working with someone of his talent.

DAVID GREENWALT

I felt bad about the whole thing. I don't feel guilty, because what I offered was tough love, which was his only shot. But it's a horrible, horrible chapter. I knew there were drug issues with him, but not the extent. God rest his soul, he overdosed two or three years later.

CHARISMA CARPENTER

When I found out he died, I must have fallen to my knees. Alexis was the one who told me. I was on set and he said he had something to tell me. He told me Glenn passed away and he took me in his arms. It was *so* painful, because you see someone trying to figure it out a little bit and think it's going to be OK, and then it just hits you sideways. It makes no sense.

DAVID GREENWALT

I have no idea if Glenn was having a negative impact on David Boreanaz, as some people were saying. My experience with David was never anything but stellar. Showed up, did the work. I never had a problem with him ever. I think the two times he complained about a script, he was right. Other than that, he behaved extremely well. On *Buffy* he understood that she's the star and his place in that universe. I never saw him misbehave in any way on any of my shows with him. He has really good parents from Philadelphia. I used to say to him, "If you misbehave, I'm calling your mom and dad."

TIM MINEAR

We also looked at the impact the death of Doyle would have on the show as a whole. Again, you look at the pilot and the story where Angel *doesn't* save the girl. You look at episode nine of a twenty-two episode season, and the guy who is in the main titles, the sidekick, dies. The reason for that is that it proves anything can happen. And there was some feeling, too, that David's and Glenn's characters were very similar. They were both half human and half demon, they both had a past, they both were brooding-type characters, and they were both searching for redemption. It just seemed like the same note to some degree.

HOWARD GORDON

If the death of Doyle was in Joss Whedon's head from the beginning, I honestly don't know. While he didn't say, "We're going to kill him," he *did* say, "We *could* kill him if we want to." It was more of a fluid understanding that this character was a tryout in a way. In the end, I think they felt how much more bold it was to develop this character and then kill him. What it does is create a way of handling the fact that, generally, in television you know that no one is going to die. It has this wonderful effect of saying that nothing is safe, which is kind of cool. At the same time, I can't say I take any pleasure in killing a lead character.

KELLY A. MANNERS

I think by the second episode after we let him go, everybody realized that the decision made was the right one. Before that, people thought it was a shitty thing to do, but then everybody just got back on the train and realized it was really good for the show. And, you know, even if Glenn had been a model citizen, the way things went after his departure, I think helped the show. That's my opinion. And we certainly got a lot of mileage out of it, absolutely, in the sense of him giving his gift to Cordelia, his prophetic visions. Which changed that character, too, and gave her more to do.

CHARISMA CARPENTER

I didn't know when the evolution of Cordelia began, but there is no question that there was major character development. And they kind of had to, because at that point I was the only female in the regular cast and what's the point of my coming over if they weren't going to?

JOSE MOLINA

"Hero" turned a curve for the show. Or the show turned a curve with that episode in that all of a sudden it *wasn't* a guest-star-of-the-week show. You were really telling stories about your characters and how their relationships affected each other. Doyle leaves Cordelia with part of his gift. That the Powers That Be are now in *her* head, Doyle remains a part of Cordelia and is there for a part of Angel's life. Would they have killed him off without Glenn's issues? I think they might have by the end of the season anyway, because that trio of characters just wasn't gelling as well as it could have.

DAVID GREENWALT

It actually did hurt the show a little bit in that I would get letters like, "Dear Mr. Greenwalt, if in fact that is your name, how dare you get rid of Doyle?" He was a great character and he was terrific, but I said to him, "This is not a game," so we ended up killing and replacing him with Alexis Denisof, who had appeared on *Buffy*, as the Wesley character. Alexis stayed with the show and became a very good friend of mine to boot.

TIM MINEAR

We had always planned to add characters throughout the season, and the idea to bring in Wesley came after the decision to kill off Doyle, but it came shortly after. In fact, my script "Somnambulist," which had been banked early on, had to be revised, because the first version was with Doyle. By the time we got around to making the episode, Doyle had been dispatched. I had to revise it and turn it into Wesley, which weirdly made more sense that Wesley would have all this knowledge about Angel's past. Also that he was suspicious and not quite on Team Angel at the time the story takes place, so that actually made perfect sense.

DAVID GREENWALT

When Wesley joined the show, you know on *Buffy* he was more comic relief. It was interesting to bring him onto this and try to evolve him into something more serious. I love humor, but you have to be careful that it doesn't go into camp. *Buffy* was never camp, but a lot of directors didn't know that in the early days. The same with *Angel*. The humor has to grow out of either tragedy or the drama of the show. One time I wrote this thing for Wesley about a massage parlor somewhere, and he sort of knew exactly where it was. The implication was that he went there, and Joss and Alexis were like, "Uh, no. Can't say and do that." That would've been too far with his character, although it would've been funny. He did some good slapstick for me. I remember he was flipping and falling down on these newspapers. Alexis is pretty versatile, but, you know, him going so dark and then Angel comes in and tries to smother him in the hospital with a pillow in season three? Great stuff. You could go there in those shows; you didn't have to protect people too much.

TIM MINEAR

Alexis was fighting an uphill battle. People hated him because they loved Doyle. They were absolutely dead set against him; they didn't like him in

Buffy. But he wasn't supposed to be likable in *Buffy*. You could say the same thing about Cordelia. You know, "This character in *Buffy*, I don't know how she's going to work in this show." Well, you bring them into this show and suddenly you get to see more sides of them. Eventually Alexis won over a lot of the fans. Some of them begrudgingly, some of them wholeheartedly. And, for the record, Wesley was not supposed to be a replacement for Doyle. Cordelia was the replacement for Doyle, which is why she was given the visions.

DAVID GREENWALT

The thing about Alexis is that he's a pretty tremendous actor. He'd been on London's West End, choreographed fight scenes for a fairly famous production of *Hamlet* there. This guy really knew his stuff, and he's very subtle and very precise and I liked what he brought to the show. We gave him more of a life separate from Angel; we didn't want him to just be the guy coming in to read from a book. The character wasn't a total buffoon, although a guy who can fall down on coffee beans always has a place in my show. But you have to balance him. The whole thing that attracted me to the Joss Whedon universe as a former movie guy is that I could do humor and drama in the same shows. I like the tragedy and the comedy.

JOSS WHEDON

On *Buffy* we had a great time just having Alexis be as dorky as possible, but there comes a point with every actor where they say, "Can I be cool now?" Alexis was like, "How can I be dorkier? What can I do to be sillier? How can I fall down more? Let's think this through." When we brought him on *Angel*, we knew we would want to find what made that character tick. It really is fun to see exactly how he evolved. When somebody becomes a regular on a show, they can't be a caricature. You have to find out what makes them behave in such a silly fashion. In Wesley's case, it had a lot to do with the way people perceived him and a lack of self-confidence and a lot of naïveté, much of which he lost.

TIM MINEAR

Later in season one we did an episode called "I've Got You Under My Skin," about a possessed kid, and the group tries to help the family. This was one of the very early scripts that we wrote before Doyle was killed. The thing I pitched to Joss was the parallels between this family and our little family. My idea was that Angel should accidentally call Wesley Doyle, because it should be about these two men who lose a son. At the end of the story the father loses his son, and at the beginning of the story Angel has lost a "son," sort of. These two men are desperately trying to keep their family together, and through no fault of their own they can't.

Once we sort of hit upon that, the theme became much clearer. If you can find the emotional resonance with your character in a plot, then the thing starts to fall into place much more easily. It's not just a bunch of moves, which is what it was before. We went in a million different directions in the development process: Angel lost this youth, Angel was possessed by a demon, Angel understands this kid. That's kind of there, but not really. Then it became about that moment where the kid speaks in Doyle's voice and Angel grabs the towel, wraps it around his hand, and grabs the cross. The idea of a vampire having to perform an exorcism is just too great.

Originally, in an earlier version of the script, there was a priest who was brought in and got locked out of the game and Angel took over. Joss at some point said, "Do we need this priest? Can't it be Wesley?" Suddenly it made perfect sense, because Angel's problem at the beginning of the story is, "I let Doyle die. Things got too dangerous and I let him die, because he did something that I couldn't do." Now you have Wesley saying, "I can perform this exorcism; you can't." And you have Angel saying, "I can't let you do that." He finally agrees, but at the end of the day he really saves Wesley's life. So he's sort of atoning for the Doyle thing, even though that really wasn't his fault. That's why we could keep going back to episode nine and say, "It was absolutely right to kill Doyle," because it made the second half of the season that much stronger.

Like *Buffy,* one of the big struggles of *Angel* early in its run was the practice of stand-alone storytelling versus serialized story arcs, and initially the writers intended to focus on the former. Somehow, though, the show itself seemed to demand serialized story arcs, resisting every attempt by the writers to tell self-contained stories.

DAVID GREENWALT

In those days, and even up until when we started *Grimm,* networks were *terrified* of too much serialization. Even back on *The X-Files,* they said that a regular fan is seeing every second or third show. Only the rabid people are seeing every episode. But the serialization was so natural on *Buffy,* because we were so into the emotions of all the characters. We could do stand-alone episodes, but that still had all these great character conflicts. We did a lot of that kind of stuff. I can't remember if the network was pushing for one thing or the other, but when you're first showing off your wares, usually that first twelve or thirteen, you want people to just really come to the show and enjoy it.

KELLY A. MANNERS

I think the reason they were trying to do the case of the week is, back then, before DVRs, on demand, and streaming, with a lot of those series we found that if people missed an episode or two, they got lost and then they were done. So Joss thought case of the week would work on *Angel,* but it was obvious that it *had* to be serialized.

CHARISMA CARPENTER

Season one was probably the most frustrating for me, just because they were really wonderfully written one-off shows, so they weren't continuous, but they were wonderful for the guest stars. Anybody that would guest-star on our show then was going to get a juicy role with amazing writing. And good for them, but I was annoyed. I mean, I don't want to offend anybody, but I wanted to get into the relationships between David, Glenn, and I, and then David, Alexis, and I.

It's obvious in hindsight, and you never know when you're in the middle of it, but I remember feeling at the time that I wanted more to do and how lucky for these guest stars, that they get to be vulnerable, they get to laugh, they get to do all this great stuff. I think we kind of found our groove in season two, where it started to be about us as an investigative group and our inner workings and our relationships with each other, and how we cared about each other and how we supported each other. That's when *Angel* really resonated and went to the next level with the audience.

TIM MINEAR

If you watch the early episodes of the series, you can see where we thought the show was originally going to go, which was in the direction of an anthology with the client of the week, and the emotional stakes would be with the guest character. Sort of like *The Fugitive*. We decided that the emotional action is with our people. You can have an interesting plot and an interesting client, but it's difficult to create sympathy for someone you're introducing for one episode. Season one's "Eternity" is a good example. Originally this actress had a problem and it was dealt with from her point of view. But if you look at how the episode ended up, it's really about our core people, and by the end of the episode the client's gone. So the way the story originally broke is that it was about this actress and the entire second half of the story was still about this actress. Joss came in one day and said, "You know what? This is wrong. What needs to happen is Angel needs to go bad." Suddenly that element was added and now that's what that episode was absolutely about.

You can see, in that episode, Joss and David and me and everybody else saying, "Let's stop doing these closed-ended detective stories and start making it about Angel." I remember Joss saying, after watching the cut of the episode, "We have to start making it about Angel and his friends, in the way that *Buffy* is about Buffy." Whenever they would break an episode of *Buffy*, if it would start to become too much about the machinations of a plot, Joss would always come back to the question, "What's the *Buffy* of it? What is the story we're telling? What is that saying about her? What is it doing to either further her character, or how is this a roadblock to her character? What does she learn about herself? Why does this story need to be told about this character?" Often, whole stories would be thrown out, and we'd start them from scratch, because we didn't have the *Angel* of it.

DAVID GREENWALT

When we started the show, we thought, "Well, this will be an anthology show. We'll solve a case every week." And then we fell in love with our characters and we actually became more interested in what happens with the people. We wanted to know what's going on with their lives. So we sort of reverted to a little bit more of a saga, I think.

TIM MINEAR

Once we used *that* as a guiding principle, we could always come back to what was important. We took that into *Firefly,* too. People loved the few episodes that we made of that show. Part of it was because Joss was absolutely fanatical about saying, "Every minute of air time has to do something to make the audience love these people." It can't just be about some wacky hijinks or some wacky story. Every moment that we have is precious in order to have the audience connect with these characters. That's a lesson we learned on *Buffy.* It's a lesson that we actually knew from *Buffy* that we learned on *Angel* by spinning our wheels for the first nine episodes of season one. Then when you get into season two, things become much more about the mythology, much more about story arcs and character arcs. The danger with that, of course, is that when it starts to become *just* that, then the snake starts eating its own tail. In a way, it starts to become about nothing because it all becomes about Phlebotinum and ancient scrolls, and [deus] ex machina devices. It's easy to get lost in that stuff, too. For the most part, I think we avoided that.

JOSE MOLINA

Joss from the get-go knew that in order for a show to work, it lived and died with the characters. If you can't tell a story that emotionally involves and engages the characters, you're not going to engage the audience. He knew that the way to do that was to have a soap opera backdrop to all the weekly shenanigans. You could have your monsters of the week, but your monster of the week only really served to enlighten what was going on with the characters in the soap opera. The monster of the week with the serialized story became the norm, and it still kind of is twenty years later.

DAVID GREENWALT

If you're a deep fan, you're going to get more layers of the thing with serialization, and that's really what we did on *Buffy* and *Angel,* and I've tried to do on my other shows. Particularly *Grimm.* Some people wouldn't remember that guy was in year three or whatever, but for us it makes it seem more real.

TIM MINEAR

The living nature of the show is not always conscious, but it's what happens when you get a certain amount of hours of the show under your belt. The things starts developing a life of its own.

And that life was developed even further, thanks to the use of extensive flashbacks, which served to illuminate Angel's backstory, particularly when people from his past have survived into the present and reenter his life. It was something that the network wanted jettisoned, but the writers continued to embrace far more than *Buffy* ever did.

TIM MINEAR

I definitely loved the idea of going into his past. At the time the Internet board said that we were ripping off *Forever Knight,* which I think is funny, because they're both vampire detective shows. So you're going to go certain places with a guy who has a couple of hundred years under his belt and who has a violent past and is trying to redeem himself. Obviously, there are similarities. But if you looked at our flashbacks over the course of season one, they were sort of a piece. In "The Prodigal" the flashbacks took place before he was turned into a vampire and up until that moment. And then in "Five by Five" it was after he got his soul back. Actually, right before and right after he got his soul back. So we were telling the progression in the flashbacks, but in separate episodes, and I thought that was interesting.

In the first season we did the episode "Hero," and I wanted to do an origin of Angel. I had a big hard-on for that. When I pitched it to Joss, I said, "It's Angel clawing his way out of his grave and Darla standing there." And he just said, "It's *so* important." To me, my favorite scene in that episode is when he comes back, confronts his father, and then kills him. And also, if you pay close attention to the episode, you find out how Angel got his name. His father says, "You can't come in here. A demon has to be invited in," and Angel glances over to the door and says, "I was invited," and you see his little sister, dead. He looks at his father and says, "She thought I was an angel returned to her."

IAN WOOLF

Flashbacks were expensive and there was the money crunch of it all on a first-season show. It was Fox producing it for the WB, so it had to be done on budget. There was a constant pressure of being able to come in on budget every episode. Kelly Manners was the element producer, so he kept an iron fist on that. There was a little bit of that tension about money, but I think we all had a great time that first season. We all enjoyed working with Joss, the cast was great, and the flashbacks *did* add a lot to the show.

STUART BLATT

The flashbacks were *great*. We did 1930s Chicago on the Universal back lot. We did Transylvania. We shot European streets at Universal, which became a go-to for us. We did Rome there—we took all the cobblestone streets and covered them with dirt. We had horses and carriages, and old fire engine carriages pulled by horses. One of the most fun things was building one wall of a giant ship. It was a flashback of Angel coming to Ellis Island in 1908 and on one stage we built an enormous wall of the ship, with a gangplank and hundreds of extras coming off in period costumes. We had horse-drawn carriages on the stage, and it really was kind of a spectacular vision.

DAVID GREENWALT

We'd always intended flashbacks to learn a lot about Angel's past, but some of those were our more exciting shows. The guy's been alive for a long time—there's lots to reference about him, lots to learn about him. They were really fun to do and the exciting thing was figuring out how they reflect on the modern-day story. Obviously, the flashbacks in the Faith episode were about what happened to him the day after he got his soul back. This is sort of in the place that Faith is about to be in; she's sort of got the chance to *have* a soul. So his journey is interesting while at the same time it reflects directly on what's happening to her in her story.

TIM MINEAR

Here's how they worked for us: the flashbacks throughout season one were there to tell us more about Angel, but at the end of the day we've told you who Darla was. When she appears in that box in the season finale, we understand what it means. And that in turn gave us some fertile ground for interesting stories in year two.

IAN WOOLF

As an assistant director, you've got to be a chameleon, because every episode that you're out there on the floor AD-ing, you have a different director with you. Those directors roll in and roll out. It's always a challenge as the first AD to sort of mold yourself to whomever you've got to be working for that particular episode. Some of the directors were very experienced and make your life easy, while others were neophytes and look like deer in the headlights when they showed up on the set. It was a constantly evolving situation as the first AD on that kind of show. Lots of elements to deal with. A lot of elements to schedule—all those fight sequences and the wire work that we would do, and the vampire makeup. It was a giant jigsaw puzzle every eight days that you had to deal with. That's what I spent my whole life doing. Now I'm a producer, so I still have to do it, but on a larger scale.

Not helping the situation was the fact that the show's exterior filming mostly shot at night, which wasn't always easy. Added to this is that there were plenty of instances throughout the series when the vampire Angel is in uncomfortably close proximity to shafts of sunlight–for instance, in the police station.

TIM MINEAR

Believe me, our backs were all up about the sun thing. It made Joss crazy and [was] something we tried to get a handle on, especially when Angel was in the police station. We never wrote that he should be in the light; it just turned out that way. The truth is, the schedule was punishing; they had to light it very quickly, and we had to shoot an episode in eight days. We actually went back and reshot stuff that was particularly egregious.

At the end of "The Prodigal," for instance, when Angel is watching Kate at her father's grave, the first version of that he was clearly outside in the sunlight. We went back and reshot it very close and very dark, and left it more ambiguous. There's actually a scene in that episode between Kate and Angel where she says, "It's the middle of the day, how did you get here?" and he explains, "Well, I came up through the sewer." She remembers she was dragged down there in a previous episode.

IAN WOOLF

It was a really tough show, because, obviously, vampires don't come out during the day, so we would spend a lot of time shooting the grungy alleys of downtown Los Angeles at night. Typically, your Monday would start out with a 7 A.M. call, and by the time you got around to Friday, you were in for a 5:00 or 6:00 P.M. call, working all night long, and then the sun would be coming up Saturday morning when you'd wrap. It was a grueling process for the crew and cast. I know that there was, at one point, an episode where there was the Ring of Amara, which Angel could wear and he could come out in the sun. At the end of the episode it got destroyed. For a couple of months after that, there was a chant from the crew about bringing back the Ring of Amara.

DAVID BOREANAZ

Oh, *the ring*. I was able to walk out in the sun with the ring. Every crew member was pissed, because I had the ring and that meant they had to work until four or five in the morning.

That episode, "In the Dark," has James Marsters guest-starring as Spike, who battles Angel over the ring that renders vampires invulnerable. At episode's end, Angel has the ring, experiences a day in the sun, and then destroys it, a move that many compared to the end of *Titanic,* when the elderly version of the Rose character (played by Gloria Stuart) throws a priceless diamond into the sea. Humorously, the episode also began with Spike on a rooftop, narrating a moment between Angel and a woman he's just rescued.

JAMES MARSTERS
(actor, Spike)

Working on *Angel* for that episode felt very much like working on *Buffy.* My biggest memory of that, however, was that I was still at that point jealous of David, so I could not stand going on his show and being so much shorter than he was. I remember I put lifts in my boots for the first time that episode. It worked, but I had to hide it; I didn't tell anybody. I remember doing the stunts with lifts, which is a little harder. It's like doing it in high heels. When I got on the show for real in the fifth season, I remember thinking, "Oh, that's just too pathetic, James. You can't wear lifts the whole time. Just admit it: you're shorter than David." By that time I wasn't jealous. But when you watch that first episode, Spike is unnaturally tall.

And with Spike's commentary—that was a very brave piece of writing to just undercut your lead like that. Just merciless. I'm not sure a lot of shows in the beginning would have the balls to do that. If you're really confident, then you can get away with that and still hold the audience's interest and still make the lead character inspiring. But you have to have that confidence *and* you have to be able to back it up.

MARTI NOXON

If I was Angel, I might just put the ring away rather than destroy it. You never know when you might need it. But I understood why he did what he did, better than Gloria Stuart in *Titanic.* I wanted to slap her. Give that diamond to somebody.

TIM MINEAR

That's *not* the problem I have with the ending of *Titanic*. My problem with the ending of *Titanic* is that she throws it in the water as if that means something about Jack [Leonardo DiCaprio]. It's got nothing to do with Jack. It was the other guy's diamond, and I have no idea why she's throwing it in the water. But in this episode, it makes perfect sense for Angel to destroy the ring. Can he be trusted? *That* is the point of the series. If he has the power to be invincible, what would happen if he spent eternity as Angelus? It's too dangerous. Was there any other vampire in the history of the Jossverse at that point that has a soul? No, so the person that could possibly wear that ring would be Angel, and Angel knows that he can't be trusted. Think about Jenny Calendar. In that light, the ending makes perfect sense to me.

Early on in *Angel*'s run, there was a dependency on crossover elements from *Buffy* to help build an audience for the new show. Not only did James Marsters appear in "In the Dark" along with Seth Green (Oz), but Sarah Michelle Gellar came to the show as Buffy Summers in "I Will Remember You." The first full-fledged crossover, it has Buffy travel to Los Angeles as Angel, splattered with a demon's blood during a battle with it, suddenly finds himself human. The two lovers come together, believing that they've found true happiness with no chance of Angelus returning, but learn that Angel must become what he once was to save the planet. The price for being allowed to do so: no one but Angel will remember the events of the day.

And then there was the two-part "Five by Five" and "Sanctuary," which saw Eliza Dushku reprising the role of Faith. In the former, she's hired by the evil law firm Wolfram & Hart to kill Angel, but by episode's end, as Faith and Angel battle in an alley, she's pleading with him to kill her, which he refuses to do. In the latter, Angel has begun the rehabilitation process with Faith, complicated by the arrival of Buffy and a militant group of Watchers intent on capturing Faith. An intriguing moment between Buffy and Angel occurs when, hurt by Angel's defense of Faith, Buffy comments that she's found happiness with someone (Riley), for which Angel rebukes her, noting that she has the fortune to have such an opportunity, but he doesn't.

TIM MINEAR

A lot of people have issues with the resetting of the clock thing in "I Will Remember You," but I personally love it. For me it's all worth it, because of the scene where Sarah is saying, "I'll never forget; I'll never forget; I'll never forget," and then, boom, she forgot. Oh, man, it just kills me. And then Angel and Buffy having sex—never a bad thing. The one thing that I would say about the episode is that we discussed the idea that the entire situation was a test by the Powers That Be.

It was supposed to be sort of the *Last Temptation of Angel.* In *The Last Temptation of Christ,* his whole fever dream when he's on the cross is that he comes down off the cross, he gets to live a normal life and grow old, and at the end he chooses to make the sacrifice. That was sort of the idea, and something that got lost there was the idea that they were trying to see if he was worthy. There were no scenes of this shot; I think the idea just kind of fell out of the script naturally, but it was one thing we had discussed during the breaking of the story. But then, as would happen, it became about the emotional aspect of it instead.

DAVID GREENWALT

That episode was their last time together, and their "perfect moment," but I don't think it would have lasted even if the Powers That Be hadn't intervened. It would be like getting back with your first wife, you know? It would be a nightmare.

ELIZA DUSHKU
(actress, Faith)

I was kind of this really hard Boston chick. That worked well for Faith and for the creation of that character Joss really zoned into that, and we worked with it. But as the years go on, and you start recovering and repairing from high school, I became less defensive, less hard. My friends and I were saying to each other, "OK, we don't have to be such haters. We don't have to be so terrified. We can start evolving." I don't want to say that I've softened up, but I've definitely lost some of that anger and fear and defensive nature that I had when I was seventeen, eighteen, or nineteen years old.

When I returned as Faith, I said to Joss, "When I get to *Angel,* do I get, like, really soft?" He said, "I wouldn't say soft, but you've definitely changed. But the ways you've changed—art definitely imitates life." It's not so hard to draw these parallels between the characters and the real life people when we're always growing and changing. Even Sarah Michelle Gellar's character evolved in so many different ways.

TIM MINEAR

The episode "Five by Five" really was something. Faith was hired by Wolfram & Hart to kill Angel, but she ends up putting a wedge between Angel and Buffy in her quest for redemption. It's a story that just fell into place. It was just so clean and simple that I loved it. She's supposed to be the assassin, but she has a death wish. It's just that simple. The turn doesn't come until the very end, and it's just beyond powerful. The way they played it, it gets me every time I see it.

ELIZA DUSHKU

It was at first a little intimidating, but that was in the first two days. At the time, I was in those scenes with David Boreanaz, whom I love to pieces. He's so much fun to work with, and I can see that even he was going through changes, and his character had turned into something else. I thought, you know, we're trying to make a little bit of reality in this world of these hugely fictional scenarios and scenes. That's reality. People change, and the characters are going to change with us. What I've gone through is kind of what Faith has gone through, too. It was good to be back.

DAVID GREENWALT

In the episode "Five by Five," written by Jim Kouf, there's a scene where Faith and Angel have this big fight in an alley in downtown L.A. We say to Kelly Manners, our great line producer, that we've got to have rain and a lot of it. He's just like, "No, we can't afford it, can't do it, not going to happen." Well it rained for real that night. Just crazy, and now you have this great fight in the rain.

TIM MINEAR

It *poured* while we were shooting. It was the first night of a big torrential rain storm that we had for several days. It started that night, on the set of *Angel*, while Angel and Faith were fighting.

The challenge of "Sanctuary" is that it was Faith as we had never seen her before. It was sort of easy when it was just Faith, which was a lot of fun. The problem was trying to make her turn realistic.

JOSS WHEDON

That moment between Buffy and Angel, where she talks about Riley, was a very important scene for me, because we all assumed that they were going to resolve it; that they were going to get into an argument about Faith and at the end of the episode they were going to resolve it and it would be nice and pretty. I was working on that scene and was having trouble writing it, until I realized that it was because they *can't* make up. He has to cut loose at her. As soon as I started to write it, I realized that it was the defining moment when he basically said, "I have a show and it's not just an offspring of your show; it's something different." And at that moment, the training wheels came off. That, to me, in a very different way, was as powerful a moment as "I Will Remember You."

A significant moment in Minear's relationship with Joss Whedon, which reflects his creative influence on *Angel*, occurred during the season one episode "Sense & Sensitivity."

TIM MINEAR

The first script I had written for the show that got made was "Sense & Sensitivity." Joss felt that the director had kind of air-balled it, because it wasn't funny the way it was on the page. He just didn't like the way that it came out. I remember sitting in David Greenwalt's office watching the cut with Joss on the Avid, and Joss saying, "We can't air this; it's so bad. This is the worst thing that this company has ever produced." I'm like, "Great. That's just great." I felt somewhat responsible. What I said to him was, "Look, let me go in . . . I don't like the way this was cut. If you'd let me go into the editing room, I think I can make it better." He kind of said sure. I went in with the editor, and I reset the whole thing. When I showed it to him, he was hugely relieved and thought, "OK, it's improved enough that we can at least put this on the air." I think the fact that he hated it so much and that he ended up liking it OK after I went into the editing room told him that I was valuable to his show. After that, they would bring me the scripts that they didn't think were working. I did a lot of rewriting in the first year without my name on the scripts.

Two other elements of the show introduced in season one were the conduit between Team Angel and the Powers That Be—a cosmic force that seems to be guiding everything—and the law firm Wolfram & Hart. The former was represented by the Oracles, as played by Randall Slavin and Carey Cannon, from whom Angel would occasionally seek guidance and who, in their arrogance, could barely tolerate his presence.

And then there was Wolfram & Hart, which on initial introduction seemed to be merely a law firm for supernatural creatures but very quickly became the representation of evil itself in this world. Indeed, what's revealed in season two is that the firm's often-referred-to Home Office is actually Earth and that the firm exists in direct response to the evil that lies within every human soul. The human workers at the firm, including Christian Kane's Lindsey McDonald, Stephanie Romanov's Lilah Morgan, and Sam Anderson's Holland Manners, work to ensure that Angel, whom the prophecies claim will be a key player in the coming apocalypse, is on their side. For Angel, that apocalypse is particularly significant in that it's been foreseen that, after it, the vampire with a soul would be made human again.

In the season one finale, "To Shanshu in L.A.," Wolfram & Hart looks to bring Angel to its side by tearing him apart from within, notably by taking out his crew. In the episode, a Vocah demon blows up Angel Investigations, nearly killing Wesley, who's hospitalized, then affecting Cordelia's visions so that instead of getting them one at a time, she's assaulted by all of them at once, plunging her into a catatonic state. Angel goes to see the Oracles and finds they've also been killed by the Vocah to cut off his ties to the Powers That Be, though the female Oracle does reach out to him spiritually, pointing him in the direction of Wolfram & Hart. He interrupts a ceremony involving five vampires being sacrificed around a large crate, kills the demon, severs Lindsey's right hand to obtain the vital scroll Lindsey was about to burn rather than let Angel get his hands on it, and, with the scroll, Angel is able to cure Cordelia.

At the very end, Angel, Cordelia, and Wesley are drawn together, stronger than ever, while the contents of that crate are revealed: Wolfram & Hart has resurrected Julie Benz's Darla, the vampire that sired Angel.

CHARISMA CARPENTER

My coach and I did a lot of research for the scene where Cordy's mind is overloaded. She went out to the library and checked out a couple of books, because I was working so much, and we were very specific in what we were looking for. Then we got this amazing book of *Life* magazine's top photographs from around the world, and we were looking at images from the Vietnam War, Hiroshima, fire victims—photos that captured in the moment what disaster is on a personal level, what it looks like on a human face. I took those images and expanded on them with my imagination. Sometimes when you're acting you worry that your well will be dry, and that was a day that a concern like that would be completely valid and justified, because it was basically eight hours of that one scene.

Also, in that episode David was grabbing me and trying to restrain me and I told him I really wanted him to restrain me. I know this is so incidental, but I was wearing a mesh-type shirt and the fabric was very coarse, so I had the worst lesions on my shoulders from where he grabbed me, which just helped the moment, of course. When I was having the seizures, it was a really great moment for me artistically, being able to experience a moment like that. Self-satisfaction is very difficult to attain for anyone. You know, "Are you pursuing what your life's work is meant to be? Are you happy and fulfilled?" That was one of those days where you go into a scene scared shitless and you walk out going, "Yeah! I did it!" It felt good in my heart, so I could walk away from it happy.

TIM MINEAR

The fans called the Oracles the "Glitter Twins." I understand. It's a little bit Star Trek-y in terms of the look.

CAREY CANNON
(actress, Female Oracle)

When I went in to audition, I remember thinking that it was really smart. I only got two pages—you get six or seven lines—and I understood that the principal character in the series would be in the scene, and that's always exciting when you're an actor. And I got an idea of who the character was, how they were imagining these Powers That Be, and it just seemed sort of arch and smart. I thought the writing was really good. It was fun to audition for it, and it was a nice change from hamburger commercials.

RANDALL SLAVIN

I had no idea what *Buffy* or *Angel* was. Most jobs you just sort of go in wondering, "What am I doing here?" I have to be honest, it was sort of the end of my days as an actor. Acting was a miserable experience for me, honestly. I had no desire to read these scripts or understand what was going on, or to know the story. It's why I went into photography.

CAREY CANNON

Being painted gold and wearing the toga for the character was so fun. It's always interesting to get to talk to the technicians who make that stuff happen, and these people have been doing this for a long time now. The makeup trailers had any number of latex monstrosities and beautiful creatures in and out, and they had lots of creatures they'd make and paint. It took several hours, as I recall, to spray all that gold on. Plus I had tattoos—I remember they cut out these templates and used an airbrush to spray in, but it was fun. Their work was interesting. They liked to talk about the different vampires and demons.

RANDALL SLAVIN

I'd known Charisma Carpenter before I did the show, and I remember sitting in my little dressing room in my stupid purple toga and painted gold on the Paramount lot, and I didn't want to run into Charisma because it was so fucking embarrassing. Once I snuck out to eat lunch and ran into her and she was like, "Hey, I've been looking for you. I didn't know where you were." And I'm like, "Ugh, I'm trying to avoid you."

CAREY CANNON

It was pretty clear what the writers thought these Oracle characters were, and they were sort of declarative, so there's not a lot of area for doubt, right? You just say the things as if they were true. I work in a Shakespeare theater and we do a lot of Greeks, and you're not looking for Apollo to shift. You just sort of say the thing.

RANDALL SLAVIN

The whole experience was awful. It's sort of like an actor's dream in a sense, because they'd call me once in a while and say, "Hey, we need you next week," and it's great, because you don't have to audition anymore. You go and just do your thing; it should have been a dream and it was miserable. Every time I'd go back, I'd have to stand in my underwear and get painted. And it was always a different person, so there was no sense of any familiarity. So every time you go back, you get a stranger standing in front of you and you're in your underwear and they're slobbering paint on you. Miserable experience, and no fault of anyone, but it probably would have been a miserable experience on any job I was doing. Let's just say my passion had waned.

CAREY CANNON

David Boreanaz was unfailingly kind as was everyone on that set. I'd actually done very little before this; this was the only episodic TV I'd ever done before I left L.A. It took a number of people to make the couple of scenes happen, and one of them involved a rigged watch that had to fly across the space, so there were all these people standing around to make this little gimmick happen, which felt like stage magic. It wasn't CG'd in; they just had to make this happen. So David was a distance from us—he introduced himself and he was gracious—which I think stars tend to be when they have to welcome people all the time, so he did that.

I also remember not being able to tell when it was my turn to talk, because he was so far away and he was used to TV—he'd been doing this for a while and he knew the mic was an inch from his mouth. I'd been used to working in theater, and I literally didn't know when it was my turn to talk, because he didn't move his mouth much. He was speaking so quietly. He was not an emoter—very stoic, and he was at his most stoic in those scenes. There was not a lot he had to do with his face, and so I think I screwed up a take or two because I was looking at him and didn't know it was my turn to talk. That's the part of the anxiety that stands out. But he didn't react badly at all. It took a minute for them to reset the gimmicky thing.

RANDALL SLAVIN

David was an asshole. He was just unpleasant, whereas on other shows you'd guest and they're really warm, because they know it's an awkward thing to walk onto an established show, and they know it's an uncomfortable situation for everyone. Some people you work [with] on a show and they're really warm and you feel like they're welcoming you there, and other people definitely make you feel lesser than. David fell into that second category. He was just dismissive and unwelcoming, just playing at the hierarchy of set life, because there's definitely a hierarchy.

I remember I had this stupid line, which I couldn't remember for the fucking life of me. I was having some sort of family issues, and there was this one stupid line, and as an actor sometimes you can get stuck on it, and the longer you're stuck on it, the harder it is to get out. And as a guest star it's a really uncomfortable experience, and David was *really* fucking frustrating, and he had it in for me. It was this stupid line; I couldn't remember it. I couldn't get it out, now, however many years later, I can tell it to you without question—I must have done twenty takes on this stupid-ass line—"That which we serve is no longer that which you serve. You are released from your fealty."

JAMES MARSTERS

This is why you never pay attention to critics. I remember doing plays and you'd have these things called previews before you'd open the play and sometimes you would talk to the audience after the show about their impressions. Sometimes the audience would fill out questionnaires and you'd read them together as a company. You would be amazed. You would read one person who said, "This is the most amazing piece of art; I was transported, thank you so much; I learned a lot; hats off to you." And then the very next one would be, "This is the biggest piece of shit I've seen in my life. How dare you waste my time?" These people could've been sitting right next to each other, watching the exact same performance, and they would have radically different impressions. And I came to realize that a critic is just one more view, and they're human beings. You don't know how they're gonna react, but their opinion is not more important than others. So I'm sorry that the guy had a difficult time. I find that when you have a high social position, a lot of people want a lot from you. You can give that to some people, but you don't have time to give that to everyone and people can get angry about that.

CAREY CANNON

Wasn't it terrible that the Oracles were killed? We were not very good at reading the future, were we? I mean, really not great Oracles. Again to reference the Greeks, the Oracle of Delphi would have said, "Bad day. You guys should go out for lunch or something." What's funny is they ended up killing us rather abruptly, and my agent thinks it's because Randall's agent asked for more money. I remember being surprised when I got the script and I was like, "We're dead? How can we be dead?" So I'm repeating a sixteen-year-old rumor from my former agent who may no longer be on the planet. But I remember her saying, "I think they were looking for more money, because they originally wanted to bring the characters back."

RANDALL SLAVIN

I *wasn't* happy they killed us. As miserable as I was, you're still like, "I'm going to do it." Apparently I couldn't see the future for myself, because I was very upset that they killed us and then I was having trouble with other things I was inquiring about. The industry was kicking me out in a lot of ways.

DAVID GREENWALT

The idea of Wolfram & Hart came from Mr. Whedon, of course. Obviously, it grew over the course of the season. It was just a good representation of nefarious interests and power in the show.

DAVID FURY

When you're doing a show about evil and vampires, the closest thing we have in life to evil and vampires are lawyers. I'm sure most people would agree with that, with the exception of most lawyers. I don't think that, early on, they were expecting to lean into it as much as they did, but all of that stuff was *so* rich. And it was an opportunity to get great actors in there, like John Rubenstein and Sam Anderson. All of these great actors as corporate lawyers who were basically minions of hell. It just lent itself to it, and those characters became very important in the show.

TIM MINEAR

With Wolfram & Hart, I think Joss had a pretty good idea of an evil law firm. It always stood for Wolf, Ram, and Hart, which are three mystical animals that were sort of representing the Senior Partners on Earth, the darkness. That was clear right from the beginning. As far as it becoming so central of a corporate villain, that seed was planted early so that we could do that. And, of course, Wolfram & Hart gave us a character like Lindsey, whom Christian Kane played. He's great, which is why we kept bringing him back. He does appear in the pilot, and then we started writing for him specifically.

CHRISTIAN KANE

I was familiar with *Buffy* and I'd seen Boreanaz; we'd worked out at a gym together and were actually friends. Me and David had been friends before *Angel*, and later on he became one of my best friends. I auditioned for the part of Riley in *Buffy*'s fourth season. I lost the role to Marc Blucas, and Joss called and said, "We want to hire you for Lindsey." I didn't audition for the part; they just hired me because I'd already auditioned for Riley. David Greenwalt actually created my character. There was a show he did called *Profit*; a great show that didn't find an audience, but he gave me episodes and said I should watch it. Lindsey was loosely based on *Profit*.

DAVID GREENWALT

I love Christian. I actually wanted to build a show around him, an entirely other show. Also, Christian can sing, as you know. I actually wrote a couple of songs he sang in the show, which was part of the fun in working with Joss—we could do stuff like that. I really dug him and his character. We had that nightclub where you could sing to reveal yourself, and one of my favorite things was Angel listening to Christian and saying, "He's not *that* good," as Cordy is taken by his singing. A great guy. I was very intrigued by the fact that he was a pretty self-taught actor. He would stay home from school, watch TV, and just practice acting while watching movies.

JOSS WHEDON

Season one was definitely figuring out what the heck the show was going to be. Actually, all of the seasons have been about that, but in season one we really came in with a mission statement of what we referred to as "Touched by an Equalizer." We used a lot of guest stars and a lot of stand-alone stories, but really figured out about halfway through the season that we couldn't care less about those things. We were more interested in the characters—when Angel turned into Angelus and Faith turned up in the next episode, those were really the best shows of the season, and they were the first ones that absolutely concentrated only on our characters. We realized that *that* was the paradigm.

The show would be coming from emotion and from the evolution of the characters we had not been getting from the monster of the week. That discovery about the show also led to the decision that we had to increase our ensemble—that this was not going to be a stand-alone show or a *Wiseguy*-like show with only three characters. We were going to have to mix things up a bit, so we got J. August Richards as Charles Gunn and we did something we'd never done before: we put him in for a little arc to see if he could stand as a regular in season two, and, of course, he did.

MARTI NOXON

Comparing the two series, one of them, *Buffy,* was definitely coming from a young woman's perspective, and the other was definitely a more masculine point of view and a more masculine tone. The *Angel* show, especially in the beginning, had more of a noir flavor, a bit of the private eye genre, which we were twisting a little bit. We were still trying to draw the same kind of metaphors: the way that, on *Buffy,* we would use moments to kind of metaphorize—that's a Marti word, by the way—the situation that teenagers and young people encounter. Certainly on *Angel* the monsters were metaphors, too, but for a slightly older audience.

DAVID BOREANAZ

Getting the show off the ground was a lot of hard work, and a lot of frustration and a lot of great energy and a lot of crazy stuff happening in my life. I was just really bombarded with tons of stuff and didn't know what was going to happen. You were kind of on the pulse of anxious anxiety and that energy of kind of grasping it and letting it slip away. It was really kind of intriguing and fresh.

JOSS WHEDON

At the end of season one, we realized that there were still so much that these people could go through—so many life experiences. And because we had the added benefit of being a fantasy show, we were in arenas where it didn't feel like there was any sort of sameness or fear of repetition of ideas.

In the season finale, the office building housing Angel Investigations was destroyed, which was precipitated on camera by Wolfram & Hart and behind the scenes by the show's unhappy crew.

TIM MINEAR

The destruction of the Angel Investigations office was done for a very pragmatic reason: the set was incredibly hard to shoot in. It looked cool, but it was hard to move the camera around. It was hard to stage scenes on that set, so that's why we blew it up.

STUART BLATT

It *was* limiting, especially as the cast was growing in size. There was very little room to move around, so it was great looking, but it had worn out its welcome at the end of the season. So we built a whole episode around the building exploding and them having to flee, which felt like a fitting end to it.

TIM MINEAR

We just got tired of it, which is why we went to the hotel in season two, because we wanted something that was big and expansive and would be easy to shoot in. We went from little cavernous rooms with that middle elevator, that sort of storefront feel, to something that was grand.

KELLY A. MANNERS

It was the last night of shooting and David Greenwalt's directing. The front of Angel Investigations was actually a wall, stage fifteen, I believe. We had done everything with the studio and cleared what we were doing.

DAVID GREENWALT

We were going to blow up the exterior of Angel Investigations. First off, it's our first year, which was on the Paramount lot with an exterior set. It wasn't on a soundstage. Well, we blew the hell out of that thing, which was fun, because it was a good ending, too. Not that everything went smoothly.

KELLY A. MANNERS

Everybody signed off on it. As you can recall, that was a pretty massive explosion. I see the parked cars; they have planks under them. I go up to my effects man, who I don't realize is dripping wet, and I go, "Don't tell me you put rubber cement on these fucking cars." I'm madder than hell. He goes, "Kelly, in a minute you're not going to care," and when we blew that, it blew a water main and flooded the set of another Fox show. Well, he was right. I didn't care about the rubber cement on the cars after that.

OUT OF THE PAST

"If nothing we do matters, then all that matters is what we do. . . ."

By the time *Angel* had gone into its second season and *Buffy the Vampire Slayer* into its fifth, the secret was out and the Whedonverse had become a darling of the critics and certainly the audience. Both shows were considered to represent a new wave in the television medium—despite appearing on the relatively low-rated WB network—where the show runners were becoming almost as famous as their creations, and where storytelling was becoming bolder, riskier.

For season two of *Angel,* David Greenwalt remained primary show runner, though Joss Whedon was executive producer as well; Marti Noxon was consulting producer, with some scripts written by *Buffy*'s Jane Espenson, Douglas Petrie, and David Fury. Tim Minear became co-executive producer midseason, Mere Smith moved from script coordinator to staff writer, Jim Kouf became a consulting producer, and Shawn Ryan joined the staff.

The season kicked off with an episode called "Judgment," in which Angel kills the wrong demon—a protector in its own right—and finds himself having to protect the demon's charge. For the series, it was deemed an important installment. The same could be said for "Are You Now or Have You Ever Been," which was born out of the fact that the decision was made to change the home base for Angel Investigations in season two from an office setting to a hotel. The latter was first seen, in dilapidated condition, in "Judgment" and followed up by this episode in which Angel, despite his first impulse to ignore the situation, comes to the aid of a young woman in the 1950s and ends up being "murdered" for his troubles by a McCarthyesque mob of people being manipulated by the paranoia demon Thesulac. In the present, after freeing the one person who still lived there—the now elderly woman he had tried to help, whose guilt kept her a prisoner for all those years—and dispatching the demon, Angel decides to buy the hotel and turn it into his new base of operations.

TIM MINEAR

(co-executive producer, *Angel*)

First episodes back are always difficult; it's more or less a mission statement. You want an audience to start the show off fresh and get what the show is. It had all of the elements that were required. It introduced everybody again, and it demonstrated that this is an action show with really, in many ways, a traditional action hero lead and what his relationship was to the people around him. It also dropped some hints as to the coming continuing story. I thought it worked. I liked that Angel screwed up. We also felt that ending the first season with the "Pinocchio's going to be a real boy some day" prophecy was something we had to complicate. Which is really the idea behind the episode in terms of the series. Once there's a prophecy that everything is going to work out, it sort of takes the tension out of the story that you're telling. So what Angel learned in that episode is that it was not about the prophecy, it's not about the end of the tunnel, it's about the tunnel and the journey through it. Nothing is assured, which is another thing we kept trying to hit in the stories we told over season two. Something that appears to be good news could turn out to be terrible news. Something that appeared to be bad news could be something good.

In season two, we also really wanted to delve in to Angel's mythology. It was a bit of a trick to create the mythology for this show, and what I would always do is go back to *Buffy* episodes where there had been a little bit of his backstory and always try to do the math so that it would make sense. You may not have suspected that he lived in a hotel in the 1950s in Los Angeles, because the first time you saw him on *Buffy* he was in the '90s when he showed up at her high school with Whistler. So I was telling the story from before he was a vampire to after he got reinsouled by the gypsy curse, to his trying to get back together with Darla when he had a soul, to his kind of wandering the Earth. You know, he's not always going to be living on the street. Sometimes he's going to be living in a hotel. The episode in the hotel—"Are You Now or Have You Ever Been"—was to say there was a part of him that tried to be a hero, who tried to help, and when it went wrong and he was disappointed by the people one more time, that sort of sent him down a darker path until he found his mission fifty years later.

DAVID GREENWALT
(executive producer/cocreator, *Angel*)

There's no denying that *Angel* grew out of *Buffy*, but when we spun the show off originally, our notion was this will be a really dark, gritty urban show, and then we got really bored with that, because the sets were ugly and brown and stuff. That's why we had to blow that office up the first year. So it was always clearly, to me, its own show.

KELLY A. MANNERS
(producer, *Angel*)

I don't think Joss was ever happy with the first set we put up, Angel Investigations, so he thought it would be much more interesting to have more space to roam around in and spend time in, and that was the purpose of the hotel set. And it was a gorgeous set. The exterior played on a condo in West L.A. I don't remember what street it's on. No matter where you pointed the camera, there was a great look. That's my memory of that set. In season five when we changed the location to a law firm, I *really* shit.

STUART BLATT
(production designer, *Angel*)

I remember a lot of sets over those five years, but the hotel was a biggie and a joy. One of the great things with Joss and David Greenwalt is that they gave me and us pretty much carte blanche once they signed off on something. "OK, I see where you're headed with this," and they let us take the reins and run with it. One of the great things about the hotel is that for the exterior we used the Los Altos Apartments on Wilshire Boulevard, with the garden in front of that, and then we elaborated. We built a beautiful lobby and beautiful garden outside and the upstairs stairwell. We had elevators in there that didn't work, but then we built a whole series of upstairs hallways, literally very reminiscent of *Barton Fink*. We were motivated by the spookiness of that, and how the walls would come alive with the old wallpaper and carpeting.

DAVID GREENWALT

The hotel was actually more appropriate than the first year's thing, which was meant to be more like a private eye, film noir kind of L.A. thing to make it look different than *Buffy*. *Angel* is more Raymond Chandler than *Buffy*. Also, for me, I grew up in the small-hotel business, so I naturally took to that. And it just made more sense; you could have a lot more people and it still functioned kind of as an office for people to come to and look for him and get cases and stuff. It just looked a lot cooler to me.

IAN WOOLF

(first assistant director, *Angel*)

Changing to the hotel was certainly a learning curve for all of us, because it was a completely new lighting rig—everything was new so everybody had to relearn. People get sort of comfortable in a standing set. You have to learn how to light it. Once you do that, you can light it fast, because you're there all the time. Then when you start to build a whole new permanent set like that, again, it's a bit of a learning curve for everybody, from the cameraman on down. Just how do you get into the set? Where do you stage everybody and what's going to be safe for picture and all that?

DAVID FURY

(writer, *Angel*)

We found the original office was just kind of dull and dark and difficult to shoot in the way it was designed. The openness and idea of living in a hotel seemed more appealing, much more cavernous, more depth. From filmmaking points of view, the directors didn't love the old space, so getting a little bit more grandeur in the hotel provided the opportunity for all sorts of rooms, ballrooms, or individual hotel rooms, or office. They just made the decision that they wanted something more inviting for the audience. And for the network, the literal darkness of the show was always an issue, and this was designed to help with that. We had to keep explaining to them it's a vampire show; they only go out at night. I know we're also dealing with demons, but when you're dealing with Angel and your hero is a vampire, you can only operate at night. It's going to be dark. But we wanted to get some light, and that's where the hotel came from.

STUART BLATT

The episode "Are You Now or Have You Ever Been" was one of the most fun episodes, because we got to really explore the hotel, and we built a fantastically huge basement for it.

TIM MINEAR

We wanted something that had some scope to it, that was different. Actually it was Rebecca Rand Kirshner, a writer on *Buffy,* who suggested an abandoned old Hollywood hotel, and that just clicked with us. And at the end of "Have You Been," Wesley says, "You know better than anyone that this is a house of evil," and Angel says, "Not anymore," because he's exorcised the demon from this place. I think the hotel represents Angel himself. If you take the scene at the end of the episode and apply the conversation that Wesley is having with Angel, I think the metaphor is pretty clear. This is a place that has seen the worst side of demonic influence as well as the worst side of human action, and Angel is saying that that has changed. So the hotel represents him, and the idea of coming into a place that was once a house of evil and making it a force for good is a metaphor for Angel on the show. And also just a really cool place to shoot.

In the season one episode "War Zone," J. August Richards was introduced as Charles Gunn, leader of a street gang that spends its evenings hunting vampires. In the end, Gunn and Angel form an uneasy alliance, which leads to the character becoming a series regular in season two and, gradually, a part of Team Angel. More recently, the actor, born August 28, 1973, has starred on such series as *Agents of S.H.I.E.L.D.* (he played Deathlok) and *Notorious.*

J. AUGUST RICHARDS
(actor, Charles Gunn)

My uncle from the time I was a little boy always was amazed by me, because he didn't understand how I was born knowing what I wanted to do. Probably before I knew what an actor was, I knew that I wanted to be inside the television. I thought that you literally could open up the back and get in it. It wasn't something I had to figure out I wanted to do. It's just who I am.

I was really supported by my parents to explore anything that I wanted to, and encouraged by them as well. That was 90 percent of it. I think also, not to sound arrogant or anything, but I was born with a certain ingenuity. My first big job was on *The Cosby Show*. The way I did that was I noticed on every TV show that I was watching at that time that they had these lists at the beginning and end of the show, and I gathered that those were the people who helped put it together. I kept noticing something called a casting director, and assumed that meant that person was in charge of putting people on the show, so I wrote down his name because I felt like I belonged on *The Cosby Show*. I called his office and [I told] the person that answered the phone . . . that I wanted to be on the show, and she said, "You and everybody else," and hung up on me. Then I called back and asked for the casting director by name. I told her my name, and he picked up the phone. I explained that I wanted to be on *The Cosby Show*. He was like, "Do you have an agent?" "What's that?" "That's who would get you on *The Cosby Show*. Get an agent." "How do I get an agent?" He was kind and patient enough to talk me through the process.

That same casting director was a speaker at a New York acting camp that Richards attended, where he caught his attention, which eventually led to that role on *The Cosby Show*.

J. AUGUST RICHARDS

Obviously, I've done a lot of this genre, and I do honestly enjoy it. I feel like my theater training comes in extremely handy in this world, because when I was in theater school we'd have to find a way to personalize the experience of people who lived way in the past, whether that was Chekhov or Shakespeare or Gibson. We'd have to find a way to learn about what was going on in the world at that time and find a way to personalize it and make it mean something to ourselves. I'm very drawn to that, and in this world you have to do the same thing. Also as an actor, I have a lot more of a fighting chance in this world, because it's not easy to make the circumstances of these characters personal. I know that the genre is something I love to do, so I feel like when it comes down to the auditioning process, I have a fighting chance, because oftentimes you have to do scenes with a green screen or you have to be looking at a dot and imagine that it is a massive outer space being, and that work is what I love to do.

TIM MINEAR

The idea behind Gunn is that Gary Campbell, a freelancer, came in and pitched the idea of these street kids battling vampires that nobody notices. That was sort of the genesis of that idea. I know that Joss wanted to introduce another guy who would be very different from Wesley and also very different from Angel. Gunn is a character that shoots from the hip. He's a little bit hardened by his experience, and he doesn't have any sympathy for people who act like victims.

J. AUGUST RICHARDS

I'd heard about *Buffy* but had never seen it. I remember reading in the trades that David Boreanaz was getting a spin-off. At that point in my life, I was obsessed with being on the WB, because I noticed that all of the actors on there were going on to have film careers. I thought if I could get on the WB, then I'd have a film career, too. I auditioned for a few other shows, then got this audition for a show called *Angel* to play a character called Day, a vampire hunter. Day as opposed to Night. They were seeing all ethnicities. Ricky Martin was a big thing at the time, so there were a lot of Hispanic and Latino actors there, and a lot of white actors there, and a few black actors. That was my first step into being on *Angel*.

TIM MINEAR

The other thing is that we were actively trying to bring some diversity to the show. It was an incredibly white show. We also wanted to not just show the glamorous sides of Los Angeles; we wanted to say maybe in the rougher sections of town, you take the metaphor of the vampires and the demons and the otherworldly things under the surface of L.A., and so it is not just sort of the storefront-detective vampire and the fancy law firms but also the kids on the street in the gangs. It was a way of doing *The Lost Boys* a little bit. They were sort of the anti–*Lost Boys,* because they were fighting vampires as opposed to being vampires.

J. AUGUST RICHARDS

Auditioning for the show was definitely one of those magical moments in my life and in my career. It was interesting, because the sides that I received, the audition material, was not from an episode. It was a stand-alone piece of writing for this character. Basically the scene was three pages of this character called Day talking to Angel, who was a vampire, and telling him how much he hated vampires and would never work with a vampire ever, because his job in life was to kill every vampire he's seen. "You might say that you're different than other vampires, but I hate all vampires and I know vampires are horrible people." Three whole pages of basically the same thing. What was I going to add to that?

On my way to the audition, I heard the voice of Meryl Streep in my head. I saw her on *Inside the Actor's Studio*, and she said, "Always examine the opposite of what your character is saying." I thought about that literally as I walked through the door, and said to myself, "Oh my God, I actually *do* want to work with Angel, but because my parents were killed by vampires and I'm a street kid, I've essentially been orphaned and orphans often have a hard time asking for love. The way that they do it is to push a person away until that person proves that they're worthy enough for them to be let in." For the first time, I did the scene with that. By the time I was done, the casting director asked me to come back a few hours later, when Joss Whedon and David Greenwalt were present.

DAVID GREENWALT

J. August Richards came in and knocked the hell out of that. Later we got that little triangle between Wesley and Gunn and Fred. We got *a lot* of mileage out of that. But in the beginning, there was a certain reckless abandon about the character, a certain, "I love the hunt and the thrill and I kind of like killing vampires," which at the same time there was also, "I protect a lot of people." Angel as a vampire should be killed by him and his gang, but Angel does some good things, so they're a little confused if they should kill him or not. Gunn certainly wants nothing to do with Angel, but there is a point where Angel is saying, "You may not want anything to do with me, but I may need your help some day."

TIM MINEAR

J. is just charismatic and great, and he got the part. I think we struggled a little bit to try to figure out how to incorporate that stuff into the show, because if there was one thing we were kind of bad at, it was writing something that felt [like] real L.A. street gangs or any of that stuff. It was hard for us; we just weren't very good at it. The episode that I wrote that I'm the least fond of was called "That Old Gang of Mine." It was the story of Gunn severing his ties permanently with his gang, and I just had so much trouble writing that. Not because of Gunn and not because of J., but I just didn't feel comfortable writing that world for some reason. It was hard for me to make it feel lived in and real. We eventually conquered that; Gunn was definitely an important member of the ensemble by the end of the series.

J. AUGUST RICHARDS

Everyone was just so warm and welcoming, and it just made me feel really comfortable and really at home very quickly. Obviously, I've made some lifelong friends from that show and from *Buffy*. We're all as close as we can be. Everybody's got their own lives, their own families, and things going on, but the admiration and the love is still there. Everyone on the crew was amazing. I'm still friends with so many people and have worked with them again. It was a really tight-knit family. Some sets are not like that at all. A lot of people say that, but not every set is what I experienced on *Angel*. I've experienced the opposite since and before.

DAVID FURY

Every new character is going to bring a different dynamic. The fact that you brought in Gunn, who is a street fighter but with a chip on his shoulder about vampires, was a way of bringing a different dynamic. What was great about Wesley was when he came onto *Angel*, he was not the same guy as he was on *Buffy*. He refashioned himself. He had his own midlife crisis and stopped being auspiciously British and suddenly tried to become something a bit more. It helped to have familiar characters coming on, like Wesley, but bringing Gunn [on] was something more specifically to add to the mix and create a bit more of a fighting force. A bit more of a dynamic between everyone. It was just a way of creating their own gang that they just didn't have. It was a slow build finding the right mix of people, and J. was great, but there was always that trick of, like, now what do we do with him? But, again, the growing pains of once you figure that out, once you give them your own agendas, they become an interesting part of the mix.

DAVID GREENWALT

With *Buffy* we began asking, "Who of our characters can we bring back?" At one point they had something like forty-one people in the *Buffy* pantheon. We had a lot fewer people on *Angel*, but as time went on we began adding to the list. The idea was we wanted to get a great big mix that would give us more people to draw on and more arcs to build.

Another charming new character "tested" on the series was Krevlornswath of the Deathwok Clan, who was first introduced as "The Host" and then as Lorne. Whatever name he goes by, he was the owner of the demon karaoke bar Caritas, who had the innate ability to "read" a person's feelings through their singing and thereby to get glimpses into the future. The green-skinned, horn-adorned Lorne was played by Andy Hallett. Born August 4, 1975, in Osterville, Massachusetts, Hallett was actually an assistant to Joss Whedon's then wife Kai when he came to the attention of Whedon himself.

ANDY HALLETT
(actor, Lorne)

I used to drag Joss into karaoke bars, and I think he was stunned by that whole scene. He got such a kick out of them and I think somehow, some way, he saw this vision of Lorne in there somewhere. So he asked me one day if I wanted to audition for this role. He said, "It's inspired by you, but you still might not get the part." He said he wanted me to audition for this part of the karaoke demon, and what did I think. I was like, "Oh my God!" I thought it would be a couple of times, but I did fifty-one episodes as a guest cast member before he asked me to be a regular. That wasn't until season four, episode fourteen. He called and said, "We want you to join the team. What do you think?" Luckily, I can say that I already felt like a team player, . . . like I was part of the family. So of course I accepted instantly.

DAVID GREENWALT

When Joss created that character of a guy who ran a nightclub, I mean, the character *was* Andy. *Totally* Andy. So as a lark, as we began to read and test people, we tested Andy, and, lo and behold, he was the best. I think he may have had some theatrical experience. He certainly was a theatrical personality. So we cast him.

ANDY HALLETT

The thing that I'll never forget was when he said, "None of us know what the future holds, and who knows what will happen with the show. I just wanted to have you have the opportunity to say that you were a series regular in case the show doesn't get picked up next year." I thought that was really wonderful on his part and really considerate, to think of me and my résumé and so forth. Having that on your résumé holds a lot more weight than saying you were a guest star. So I just thought that was spectacular.

TIM MINEAR

With Andy, it turned out he was great. We all just felt that he was so fun and so easy to write, so in a lot of ways the part just expanded and became less of a device and more of a character. And the truth is, I don't think it took Andy long to get where he needed to be. He was pretty great from the beginning, especially for someone who had no experience and who had to act in all that crazy makeup.

ANDY HALLETT

It took three hours for makeup. Dayne Johnson also became a real dear friend of mine. He was head of the makeup department. He used to be on *Buffy*; then he came over to head the staff of *Angel,* and obviously he has a lot to do on the show. He did my makeup, and we got along great. I couldn't imagine spending that much time in the makeup chair with someone you can't stand. Getting up at 4 A.M., traveling to the studio, and then sitting for three hours without being able to move or do anything makes it hard to stay awake. It could be pretty boring. But Dayne went out and bought a DVD player, a TV, and a VCR, and it was wonderful, because then I could watch movies in the chair. I never used to watch movies, so he got me watching movies.

DAVID GREENWALT

He *hated* the makeup. I mean, passionately. It made him claustrophobic and he was *not* happy. Did we expect him to become as prominent as he became? I think you can apply that to any of our characters who became more prominent. You know, why not use people you've already cast and know? So when you're breaking stories, you're like, "What if Andy did this? What if so and so does that? What if Christian Kane does this?" You use your stable, because you know them, the audience knows them, you can depend on them, and the fun of TV is you're not writing short stories like you are in a movie; you're writing big sprawling novels. I'm always happy to see people grow in a role in a show. It's fun.

TIM MINEAR

In the second season we did an episode called "Happy Anniversary," and what I liked about it was that it got Lorne out of the bar. Basically, it's a buddy movie with Angel and Lorne, and I think it was really interesting that those two characters, wherever you put them together, are an intriguing pair. They're so different, but Andy and David really complemented each other when they were on screen together.

In the season one finale, Wolfram & Hart brings Julie Benz's Darla from the afterlife. (Darla had been dusted by Angel in the first season of *Buffy the Vampire Slayer,* when it was revealed that she was the one who had originally turned him into a vampire). In *Angel* she is unexpectedly brought back as a mortal, with a soul, and is completely disoriented. Wolfram & Hart, largely through Lindsey, uses her to manipulate Angel, who thinks he's losing his mind.

TIM MINEAR

The return of Darla gave us an opportunity to dig deeper into Angel. In the episode "Dear Boy," we had a flashback to Angel's first encounter with Drusilla. There's a moment in the episode, during the flashback, where Drusilla's cowering in the convent and Darla is saying, "I thought you were going to kill her." Angel says, "No, I decided to make her one of us." Darla says, "She insane," and Angel responds, "Yeah, eternal torment. Am I learning?" There's a look on Darla's face that says, "This guy's much worse than I am right now." That's the whole point of that. He's the student up until that point, and after that he overtakes the teacher and becomes something that even she can't quite grasp, which I think is interesting.

CHRISTIAN KANE
(actor, Lindsey McDonald)

I loved working with Julie. She's such a talented actress. I looked forward to going to work every day when she was there. I loved that the fact that her story line brought me more into it. You've seen Lindsey confused and you've seen him have morals, but you never saw him with a heart, and that's what I thought was so smart with the writing, was that when Darla showed up, you saw that Lindsey had a heart. He actually wasn't a bad guy. He just worked for a bad guy. He actually loved this woman so much, and there was nothing he could do to ever make her fall for him.

DAVID GREENWALT

Julie Benz came back as Darla, and what a great actor and person. I had so much fun with both her and David; I directed them quite a bit. But you never know; you put a person in, they do one little thing, and later on you're thinking, "What if that person came back and did *this*?" It just grows kind of organically, and that's always fun. We've done that quite a bit on *Grimm*, and when it works, it works.

JULIE BENZ
(actress, Darla)

I was actually a little worried coming back. I was afraid that maybe I had lost Darla. I'd done a lot of work since *Buffy* and I thought my work had grown a lot in those four years. But what that did, I think, was enrich the character more, and I'm glad I had the opportunity to play her at that point rather than being given the story line back then. I don't know that I could have handled some of the things I was required to do as an actress four years earlier.

TIM MINEAR

We brought Julie back as Darla as a human, and my feeling was, "What does that mean for her?" The best way to explore that would be to look at what she was as a human four hundred years ago before she was a vampire and do an origin piece of her. That's what "Darla" was. You can only do that so much, because it should really be her story with Angel throughout the 150 years that they were together. But I wanted to show her as a person and what that means.

JULIE BENZ

Having a soul is like a cancer to her. To Darla, having a soul is the most disgusting thing in the world and for a while she is in denial of it. It's really hard to live with a soul when you've been alive for four hundred years. She didn't walk Angel's path. Of course, with a soul you start having feelings, and she has very strong feelings for Angel because they were together for 150 years.

TIM MINEAR

I realized, "That's a big fucking romance is what it is." A hundred and fifty years of being with somebody, that's what I call having a history. But at no time was I trying to play this as being Angel's true love. It's more like the play *Who's Afraid of Virginia Woolf?*—this troubled old married couple with secrets. I wasn't trying for her to take Buffy's place in his heart by any stretch of the imagination. But here's a guy who's been around for a couple of hundred years before he ever met Buffy, and certainly he was shaped in some way. Having Julie allowed us to explore that a little bit.

JULIE BENZ

The revelation that she never made him happy kind of screws her up. I think if she was a vampire, that wouldn't have bothered her that much, but as a human that rejection is real human pain. That's something she's never experienced before. She's always done the rejecting. I think that was very hard for her. As a human you have more feelings and emotions, and she was having a hard time dealing with the fact that Buffy made him happy and she didn't. He and Darla were together for so long, but Buffy was only with him for three years. There was also the disappointment that he's not the man she loved anyway. He's Angel and she loved Angelus. It's this epic story, and when you get past the whole vampire thing, it really is a classic love triangle. I think that's why the audience could relate to it. Darla was the jilted girlfriend or the ex-wife.

TIM MINEAR

What we needed was sort of the anti–Angel/Buffy relationship, and a lot of that actually made it into the episode "Guise Will Be Guise," where T'ish Magev is talking about Darla and his relationship with Darla and he suggests that what Angel should do is go out and find another powerful small blonde and break her heart, and then he'll get over Darla. Which is sort of me, with a nodding wink, saying, "Maybe the entire series of *Buffy* was about Angel not being over his first love. Maybe it is more about Angel and Darla than it is about Angel and Buffy." Which I think is a perfectly reasonable point of view to take when you are writing a show called *Angel*.

Indeed, there comes a moment in season two when Angel puts his life and soul on the line: he attempts to give Darla, who is dying from the syphilis that was killing her before she was first turned, another shot at life by participating in a series of deadly otherworldly tests. Although he ultimately passes these tests, the revelation that Darla has already been given a second life through Wolfram & Hart negates the possibility of his saving her.

In the end, Darla, moved by Angel's willingness to sacrifice himself, accepts the fact that she is dying and takes Angel up on his offer to be with her until the end. *Then* Lindsey appears on the scene, using a Taser on Angel while Drusilla enters the room and bites Darla, turning her back into a vampire.

The following episode, "Reunion," has Angel desperately trying to locate Darla's body before her vampire resurrection can take place so that he can stake her, but Drusilla interferes, allowing the final transformation to occur. From there, Dru and Darla go on a killing spree. Angel, blaming himself for what's happened to Darla, seems to go off the deep end, firing his crew and going this-side-of-Angelus dark, ultimately allowing the not-so-dynamic duo to feast on a bunch of Wolfram & Hart lawyers.

TIM MINEAR

Back at a lunch I had with Marti, Joss, and David where we came up with the idea that Darla was going to be human, the moment I mentioned that idea, Joss immediately came up with the scene. He said, "Later in the season, Drusilla will walk in and re-vamp her in front of Angel." We knew that was going to happen. What I find amazing is that some of the fans didn't care for the Darla arc and complained that it was Darla all year and was boring. I disagree, and in fact in almost every episode she appeared, something new happened. There was the big reveal, "Oh, she's human"; then there was the big reveal, "Oh, she's dying"; and then, of course, Drusilla walked in and she was a vampire again. So Darla—*not* a static character for us in season two.

And with Angel going dark, the card you *don't* always want to play, that you want to save, is him going evil or losing his soul or becoming Angelus, so we were looking for a way to give him a dark night of the soul while he still had his soul. It's often referred to as the beige Angel arc: he's not exactly dark, he is not angelic, he is not evil. We felt like we wanted to explore sort of existential despair, because that is always fun, and it just made for more interesting stories. I mean, it is certainly my favorite thing on the show. And it's actually better than him being Angelus, because he is making a moral choice, so that when he locks lawyers in a wine cellar with vampires, you completely understand it. This was before the war on terror and before waterboarding and that sort of thing, but it kind of falls into that category where it's sort of like, why should I have a responsibility to *not* lock up these people in there with the things they have brought on themselves?

DAVID GREENWALT

We always had that darkness in us. We terrified the WB, and they were right at that juncture. But that's what's interesting about that character: he's got a soul, but he has this other side and he is such an old soul, if you will, and such a tormented guy. The more evil he was, the more fun for us and for the audience. It just made him deeper and deeper, really. Then you'd do these flashbacks and you'd understand all the different things that had happened to him and how he came to be how he was. Just a lot to draw on. The metaphor for Buffy will always be the strongest, which is adolescence. There isn't much of a metaphor for your twenties; it's actually a bunch of wasted time until you decide what you're doing. But because this guy was so old and had been through *so* much, you could do a deeper, darker arc to the stories with him. You could go *anywhere.*

TIM MINEAR

It's not something we hesitated over. Not even a little. He doesn't kill those people, though he certainly is complicit and aids what happens to them by not only shutting the doors but locking them in. What's cool about Angel is that we can do that. Sometimes there are two different things at work in terms of whether or not he should take certain steps. Your character might do a certain thing, but the actor playing him may want to protect that image. David didn't do that to us. He happens to be the kind of actor who's game for anything. He allowed himself to look goofy, he allowed himself to be beaten, he allowed himself to do dark and heroic things, and I think for David it was more interesting to go to those places.

DAVID GREENWALT

One could say that in that arc we went just south of Angelus, but it was scarier in some ways because he still had a soul during all of this. My answer to how dangerous it was for the image of the character is that I hope it was pretty dangerous, because *that* makes interesting drama. I would further comment that what is interesting about Angel is that he contains the good and evil that you and I have inside of us, except that he is a very extreme version of it. He's sort of a naturally dramatic form of it. It was necessary for him to go dark, first of all from a structural level of we didn't want to repeat ourselves where we're a formula show of Cordelia has a vision, we solve a crime; Cordelia has a vision, we solve a crime. I was getting bored with that formula when Joss said, "What if he locks lawyers in a room with the vampire girls, and afterward he goes home and his people are like, 'We're all that's standing between you and darkness,' and *he* says, 'You're right. You're all fired.' "

The way he went dark was when you watch the show unfold, you discover that he knew that he had to go to a place where he had to kill Darla and Drusilla, although he in fact set them on fire. Killing is bad, but burning them is pretty dark, too. He knew he had to go to a dark place. It's like those tunnel fighters in Vietnam—what they would have to do to their mind and soul to go into a tunnel that's probably filled with mines and people with knives and having to try and kill people. So Angel was, in fact, trying to protect his people; at the same time, he was doing something that was very harsh to them.

DAVID FURY

For *Buffy* you understood what it was about. It was initially about high school is hell and surviving that. But then when we started doing *Angel*, the question was, what is the show *really* about? It's about trying to remain a good man in an evil world. So the struggle of Angel to remain good is very much part of the show. It's very much a struggle we all have to some extent. We always take the shortcut, or maybe do underhanded things, but we try to be moral creatures. We try to do the right thing. That's kind of what Angel's struggle is. There's a little bit of an angel and devil on his shoulder, and pushing him toward the devil is definitely a cool thing to do.

DAVID GREENWALT

Look, the darker the better, if it's justified. If there's some kind of emotion involved. The thing we had to keep in mind is [that] nobody is a villain. Nobody is evil. Nobody thinks, "I'm evil; I'm bad." They think, "Oooh, this is a great day," or whatever they think. A hero who is all good and who only does good things is A, boring; and B, I don't believe it. I don't know if there would be a C or not. The C would be when I was a kid, my favorite shows were things like *Maverick* and *Rockford*. These sort of heroes were like, "I don't want to get hurt, I don't want to fight. I'd like to get a lot of money for what I'm doing." I could identify with *that*. Somebody who is just square-jawed, never does anything bad, is always good—is bullshit. So, you know, the darker the better. And the truth is, some things you cannot bring a character back from.

DAVID FURY

They were trying to do a very different show than *Buffy* at that time. It was trying to separate itself and be the much more adult version, the dark version. They were pushing that envelope. Remember, that first episode I wrote for season one got thrown out because it was way too dark. The network was scared of it. So we backed off and said, "We'll start here and make it a little bit darker as we go." I could have done that episode, "Corrupt," in the second season, but it wasn't going to fly as the second episode, because they weren't ready to go that dark. But the darkness kept sneaking in more and more, and eventually it snuck in *so* much that we had to pull back on it.

TIM MINEAR

Then, when all of that was over, we didn't just hit the reset button. It took him a while to regain the trust of his crew, but he had to learn something. And then they got to go and learn something about themselves in his absence, and when he came back he said, "I don't want to run the team; I want to work *for* you guys." It altered the dynamic, even though he still sort of ran things. The show is *not* called *Wesley.*

You know, we were ahead of the curve on a lot of things. What I mean is, we did things like Angel locks lawyers in a wine cellar with vampires, turns his back on them, and lets people get killed. Or when he fires his crew, or when he takes a particularly dark turn. That was absolutely thrilling at the time. It was so exciting to do that stuff, and even to the fans just how shocking and great that was. You have to remember, this is before FX. This is before *The Shield. The Sopranos* was around, I think, but that was really the beginning. This is before serialized storytelling was happening on cable. Because we were on the WB, we could get away with things like Angel's existential crisis, and throwing Darla around the room, and having hate sex with her, because he's in a moment of existential despair.

That stuff was not happening on television. At least not that I recall. In a way, the WB was a forerunner of the kind of storytelling that you now see with *Game of Thrones* and *Breaking Bad.* Obviously, *The Shield* was the real beginning of that, but, you know, Shawn Ryan came out of our shop. Shawn Ryan was on *Angel,* and working with me on that show before he went off and made the pilot for *The Shield.* I'm not saying *Angel* influenced that script or anything. I'm just saying that we were doing it before anybody else. I don't want to make it sound like we were reinventing the wheel, because there was *NYPD Blue,* and there were other adult network shows where main characters had dark nights of the soul. I'm just saying that what we were doing on the WB was, I think, really a forerunner to the things that now live on FX and Showtime and HBO and places like that.

Moving from strength to strength in season two, the dark Angel arc came to a close with "Reprise" and "Epiphany" and his discovering the truth about

Wolfram & Hart's home office–that the Home Office is Earth–and that the evil in the souls of humans fuels them. In total despair, Angel finds Darla and gives himself up to her sexually, a moment set up in such a way as to duplicate the moment that cost him his soul on *Buffy* in "Innocence."

Shockingly, it has the opposite effect in that it makes him rediscover himself and his purpose. He leaves her, saying that if he sees her again he'll kill her. Later, he's confronted by Lindsey–enraged by jealousy over Angel and Darla–who runs him over with his truck and attacks with a sledgehammer, though in the end Angel gets the upper hand, smashing Lindsey's false one to pieces.

TIM MINEAR

I remember when we were talking about it, that this would be the episode where he had an epiphany. I said to Joss, "Look, he slept with Buffy and lost his soul. What if he sleeps with Darla and metaphorically gets his soul back?" Like at one point he has a moment of perfect happiness, so he loses his soul. But here it is an echo of that—we shoot it the same way; we make it *seem* like that is where we're going—but really he has a moment of perfect despair and he realizes what he must do. Everyone sort of understood that I was riffing on that. And the truth is, it wouldn't make any sense for him to have a moment of perfect happiness with Darla. That was another thing that I was trying to point out, because everyone kept thinking, if he has sex, he is going to lose his soul. The truth is, that was *never* the point. I mean, if he had the perfect chocolate soda, would *that* turn him evil?

CHRISTIAN KANE

That whole sequence in "Epiphany" was a huge moment for me. To see the guitar in the closet and not be able to play it; it's dusty. Then I put my hand on to go to work. It was an unbelievable moment for me. The night before we shot it, David Boreanaz and I had hung out and we were very hungover the day we shot the scene. We were both really hurting that day.

TIM MINEAR

That fight was probably the most violent thing we'd done. David Greenwalt wanted me to tone it down a little bit. He left it up to me, but he said, "I feel like this is too violent." I felt it wasn't, and he was like, "OK." It's so funny that we didn't get a note from the network about that. The note I did get was about the end of "Reprise," when Angel drops the ring and says, "Do you want this?" and Darla grabs for it.

We filmed an extra slap which had to be cut. It's all about context, because he's about to take her and it does start to look a little bit like rape. The funny thing is, they didn't give me a note on this throwing her through the doors. He throws her through the doors, and she lands on her hands and elbows on a pile of broken glass. They didn't give me a note on that, but the little face slap they insisted on cutting. Then with the Lindsey-Angel thing, I didn't get a note at all, and that was incredibly violent.

Christian Kane was doing all his own stuff in that scene. He was *really* into it. The fun thing is that Christian for a year and a half complained about the shirts and ties. Hates them, doesn't want to wear them. And I had to be very explicit and say, "He's got his tie on in this scene; it's very important because later he's going to pull off his tie and it's going to mean something. Therefore he needs to have his tie on."

CHRISTIAN KANE

Look, man, in a world of superheroes I was a *lawyer*. Everyone had a sword and I had a *pen*. I didn't know that that pen was going to be that mighty, but it was no fun for me. Then they cut my hand off, and I'm sitting here in a suit and tie—while everybody else is dressed in leather, flying around the set—without a hand. I was miserable. I remember directors coming in and they would be like, "So, Drusilla's here and Julie Benz's character, Darla, is here . . . Oh, Lindsey's here. Let's have them punch Lindsey." I'm like, "No!" He's like, "They've got to punch somebody when they walk in, so you'll just be the guy." "No, man, stop having girls hit me!" And remember, I'm right-handed and they cut off my right hand, so I couldn't even eat lunch. My hand was in a plastic surgical glove. Then there was a brace put on; then there was another surgical glove taped on that, and then it was painted. That was twelve hours a day. I used to have to ride home with my hand out the window, because it smelled *so* bad. One time I was sitting next to Tim Minear at lunchtime and I said, "What are you doing?" He said, "I'm writing the next episode," and I looked over at him and said, "Fucking kill me." He didn't.

TIM MINEAR

Wherever you put Angel and Lindsey together it's interesting, and the idea of them working together, which happened in "Dead End," certainly sparked everybody's imagination. The idea that Angel had had this epiphany and was more easygoing would infuriate Lindsey all the more, which just made it so much fun. They really have a great chemistry. Actually, Lindsey is a perfect fit for the show, because here's this morally ambiguous guy who is seeking his own kind of redemption. So he fits right into the universe.

Although she wouldn't recur until season five,"Disharmony" saw Mercedes McNab reprising her *Buffy* role of Cordelia's old friend Harmony, who shows up in L.A. Harmony's behavior leads Cordelia to think, humorously, that she's a lesbian, but then Cordelia discovers that Harmony is actually a vampire. She tries to redeem Harmony, but that proves impossible as Harmony nearly betrays the group to a vampire cult.

MERCEDES MCNAB
(actress, Harmony Kendall)

Being called for *Angel* was very shocking for me. By that time I had moved to New York. My run with *Buffy* was over, but then I got the call when I was in New York and they asked me to come back for *Angel*. That was completely out of the blue.

TIM MINEAR

That was one of the few episodes where we did get to do the "metaphor" on *Angel*, which is "my old high school friend shows up in town and we've both changed." And she happens to have changed into a vampire. I thought Charisma was hysterical in that episode. But more importantly, it put Cordelia in a situation where she ends up doing the same thing Angel did with Darla, because she needs to forgive him and this kind of puts them on the same moral level to some extent.

MERCEDES MCNAB

I think Harmony was always trying to find her way. She would try to be whatever person she thought she was at the time. Inherently, she is selfish and evil. And out for number one, which always supersedes all else.

JOSS WHEDON

(executive producer/cocreator, *Angel*)

As well as things were going in season two, we had our guest stars drop out after episode eighteen—Julie Benz and Christian Kane. We couldn't get them and here we were with four more episodes, and the two people who had sort of driven the entire season were gone. So we sort of looked at each other and scratched our heads.

TIM MINEAR

We had assumed we would be continuing the Darla story, that either Angel would have to kill her by the end of the season or there would be some ultimate confrontation. But because Julie wasn't available, we couldn't do that.

JOSS WHEDON

As much of a problem [as] not having those actors was, after "Epiphany" what we wanted to do with the last four episodes was have an unbelievably grand adventure where we sort of comment on where we've come as characters.

DAVID GREENWALT

We were like, "What the fuck are we going to do for the last four episodes?" Joss just thought and thought, and he basically spat out the idea for these last four episodes. You just didn't see Pylea coming. It was a really fun twist and an interesting way to go, and having to be rescued from that world where Cordelia had the experience of being a goddess.

JOSS WHEDON

I said, "Can we just go to Oz? Can we just be ridiculous? Are we allowed to do that?" And everyone seemed to like that, so we decided to go and make a really strange comedy—a real fantasy comedy. Those are the Pylea episodes, which I think are among the funniest things we ever did on *Buffy* or *Angel*.

If you substituted the simians from *Planet of the Apes* with demons, you'd have a sense of Pylea, an alternative dimension where humans are viewed as animals and the more demonically inclined reign supreme. It also happens to be the home world of Lorne, which he was desperate to escape from–the reasons for that quickly becoming obvious.

This world, which can probably best be described as medieval, is one that Cordelia accidentally goes to, resulting in the rest of Team Angel having to follow and rescue her. Once there, it's a pretty topsy-turvy ride; for a time, it seems that Cordelia doesn't need rescuing. In Pylea they meet Winifred "Fred" Burkle, also from Earth, who has been there for five years and is *definitely* in need of rescue. While there, Angel can walk around in the sun and see his own reflection, the downside being when he "vamps" out he becomes a demon that threatens to eclipse his humanity permanently.

Also added into the mix during the Pylea arc is actor Mark Lutz, who portrayed a warrior from that realm, the Groosalugg, ultimately nickamed "Groo" by Cordelia. Half demon, he's a character who would return in season three when Groo came to our world.

MARK LUTZ
(actor, Groo)

If you talk to a lot of actors, a lot of them will tell you the same thing: a fish out of water is one of the most fun things to play, which was particularly true when Groo came back to L.A. with the gang—there was an opportunity for comedy there and a silliness that I loved. Nonsense is the route to my very soul, so it was fun to play the dichotomy of Groo being this champion that has all these great, wonderful qualities on paper, but all this naïveté. A lot of people characterized him as being dumb, but I don't think he was. He was naive and earnest and meant well. An innocent in a lot of ways. And besides being a fish out of water, he was also the pivot in the love triangle between Angel and Cordelia. You get to play the fish out of water *and* the guy who comes between the hero and the girl? Great, sign me up.

TIM MINEAR

We knew we wanted to do Pylea, and the question was whether or not we could afford to. It was incredibly expensive to do. Think of all the demon makeups, first of all. Shooting on location; creating a place to shoot it; creating a castle—all this stuff was expensive. We actually ended up going to this little Mexican village that's not a real village. It's sort of a back-lot thing out in the boondocks where film companies shoot sometimes. If you look closely, you may notice that Pylea is also China from earlier in the series. Same exact village but redressed. So that was a lot of location shooting and a lot of day shooting, which we didn't normally do.

STUART BLATT

To make it Pylea, we put half timbers on the houses, which gave it a somewhat medievaly, English countryside look. We cobbled together whatever we could to convey the image of a sort of medieval storybook land. We built a stock in the middle of town, where their heads were put through a chopping block.

J. AUGUST RICHARDS

It was *fun* to shoot outside during the day. It had a totally other feeling for us, because everything we did was usually late at night. But by the end of the week, we were always working until about 6 A.M. Thursday and Friday were always late calls going to work at five or six P.M. and be out by six A.M. the following day, so it was just nice to be able to shoot during the day.

MARK LUTZ

Pylea had that Old West feeling in a way, and that was the nature of the buildings there, which had probably been there since the '30s. So there was a nice ring of authenticity. And I remember shooting the fight with David Boreanaz; it was like two or three in the morning. This was back in the day when it actually rained in California—I know it's hard to believe—so it was pouring rain, and we were basically rolling around in it. It wasn't warm. Not Canada cold, but it wasn't warm, and I felt like Conan or something, going mano a mano with the main guy in the show.

When I came back in season three, we were running through Echo Park and I'm still in the full Groo garb. There's crowds of people around that aren't on set, just the public, and it was funny to see the looks when you're running in your Conan outfit, with this broadsword, on a street. The passersby are like, "What's that guy doing?" Kind of a fun moment.

KELLY A. MANNERS

Pylea sounds like a gum disease. Those episodes were really challenging. The funny story about that is that we're in a van and Joss was the character who did the dancing in Pylea. He's all in his green makeup and his long red wig sitting in the van, and a stunt guy sits down right next to him and turns to me and goes, "Whedon's lost his mind. This script is the biggest piece of shit I've ever read." I think the Host character was part of the Death Walk Clan, and we called this stunt guy the Dumb Fuck Clan. He's sitting down next to Joss Whedon and doesn't know it. Well, he wasn't back the next season.

TIM MINEAR

What we wanted to do was basically give each of the characters an opportunity to live out their fantasies; they kind of get to express the part of them that is important to them. So Angel gets to be in the sun, he gets to be a hero, but then that has a flip side. Cordelia wants to be a princess and she gets to literally be one, but there is a dark side. Wesley gets to be a leader, but he has to lead people to their deaths in order to win the battle. And Lorne is like a classic story of a guy who is gay and is rejected by his family and has to go off to the city to create his own family.

We never said specifically that the Host was gay, or that Lorne was gay, but that was definitely the way we wrote him. When we went to Pylea, the idea was to make it the dimension that he escaped from. It gave him something to do; he had to go back and kind of face the family that rejected him and realize that he had made the right decision to leave. So everybody gets to express their most primary color.

DAVID GREENWALT

From a structural standpoint, Angel went dark from episodes ten to sixteen, but by sixteen he had begun to make his amends. He came back and worked *for* his people on a whole new footing. So it wasn't the last part of the season in which he went all dark, but, instead, we went to Pylea for a romp in this *Wizard of Oz*–like place, but still a place where he turns into a horrible beast and had to, again, confront this whole, "I don't want to be this thing that wants to kill my friends." You have Wesley saying to him, "You're not a demon with a man inside, you're a man with a demon inside. You need to remember what you are." We were always looking for ways for Angel's dark side to come out and get a little out of control; that's what made him interesting.

BEN EDLUND
(supervising producer, season four)

From Pylea we get Fred and had already gotten Lorne, important parts of the universe. To me, something like the Pylea arc has the breeze of standalone, because it's omnivorous, it'll go somewhere and eat that little delicious lighter fare of being in Pylea where you don't have to weigh as much for at least a portion of it. But then you also get these profound characters that come out of it, profound in terms of they each have their own angst and their own plight and their own need. And they fold into the larger mythos. It's like, why the hell does Gilgamesh go out into the woods to meet Enkidu? Why? I don't know. Maybe he wants to fight and fuck a hairy man [*laughs*]? He's a real pain in the ass around town, but is it episodic or is it serialized? It turns out that after three thousand years it seems serialized, but it's pretty fucking episodic.

TIM MINEAR

The fans were divided about Pylea. They were saying things like, "Where's Darla? Where's the angst? What's going on?' We brought in Darla and instead of Angel staking her and saving everybody and they're off for pancakes and eggs together at the end of the season, Darla was demoralized and just went away. I think that people weren't sure what to make of that. It didn't seem like a resolution to them, and in fact it was not, as they—and we—would discover in season three. What people had to remember is that the season was about Angel, not about Darla. If you look at Pylea, and what we did there, it's sort of a metaphor writ large for what all our characters had been through in the second season.

JOSS WHEDON

Pylea also gave us the opportunity to introduce what would ultimately be the final piece of the puzzle in creating an ensemble: Amy Acker.

TIM MINEAR

We felt that we needed another color for the show, and that was a character that Joss had been considering before we'd ever written an episode for her. He was actually reading actors for the part when Amy came in. He saw her and immediately saw the star potential there, and I totally agreed.

AMY ACKER
(actress, Fred)

I had had a pretty big awareness of *Buffy*. My college boyfriend, his roommate, and his roommate's girlfriend, they hosted "*Buffy* night" at their house. Everybody came over and ate pizza. I was a theater major so wasn't always around, but whenever I had a free night, I would see them and wonder, "Why are they so obsessed with this?" Then I got into it myself.

A native of Dallas, Texas, she was born Amy Louise Acker on December 5, 1976. Graduating from Southern Methodist University, she made some television guest appearances prior to *Angel* but subsequently was either recurring or a regular on such shows as *Alias, Drive, Dollhouse, Happy Town,* and *Person of Interest.*

AMY ACKER

I had been a dancer and mostly done ballet growing up. I ended up having knee surgery and I had to take a credit in school for arts, where I had this amazing theater teacher in high school that was so good that when I got to college, I felt like, "Oh, I already know all this." She just really pushed everybody in her classes. You read Stanislavski and about all of these people . . . we did *The Crucible,* and Tony Kushner, and these great plays that were not dumbed down for high schoolers in many ways. I had always been super shy, but I found out that if I said words that other people wrote, and got to be characters other than myself, that it was sort of this amazing thing that I couldn't imagine doing anything else after it started.

I think that's part of the reason I'm drawn to this genre. I mean, all of my favorite roles that I've gotten to do have been in genre TV. Those roles really allow you to transform—sometimes from a human to an alien—but it also gives you a journey as a character that a lot of other shows don't really always have. When I look back at *Angel* and think about the role of Fred, it was almost like I had seven different parts on the show. I had been to the crazy alternate dimension in a potato sack, and then head of the lab, then Illyria . . . there's just so much room for a character journey.

DAVID GREENWALT

I knew Joss was going to love Amy Acker from the time we tested her. We were shooting something in a library downtown, a little scene with her, and right from the start she was like a Joss Whedon character. She's a doll to boot and really talented and well trained and, of course, makes it look easy. You see Amy and she's sort of a sweet Audrey Hepburn, but she has this whole other level that she can play with that sweet face and you really want to use all that if you can. We used her in *Grimm* and she was like a soccer mom who also was a spider woman who sucked out people's innards. She was great and can do two sides of the coin really well.

AMY ACKER

I had moved to New York and then to Los Angeles, and I had only been there a month when I got an audition for the part. They were looking for this little three-episode part on *Angel*. So I went in and met the casting director, auditioned, and got a call back. I went and got to meet Joss, and then all of a sudden, when I was about to start, they said, "Well, actually we're thinking of maybe having a new series regular," and they were toying with the idea of characters that had already been on the show or introducing a new part.

TIM MINEAR

Joss wrote these very funny scenes that were not part of a script, just as audition pieces, and I remember how great she was in that stuff.

JOSS WHEDON

As we did with J., we brought her in for a little arc-let to make sure she would register and then brought her in as a regular.

TIM MINEAR

I don't think it's a mystery that the character of Fred is very much a Joss Whedon type; he likes those cute, frumpy, brainy girls who end up becoming knockouts. She sort of falls into the Willow mode of a brainy girl.

AMY ACKER

Joss, before I actually started filming, wrote that little *Midsummer Night's Dream*–inspired scene that's on one of the DVDs that Alexis and J. and I did.

J. AUGUST RICHARDS

That screen test was when we first met her even before she got the role. It was awesome. Joss really put her through her paces. He had a lot of notes, and she took everything like a champ. He was just trying to see how much he could play with her, and he can and he could. As you see with her ultimately becoming Illyria, he had great faith in her ability to change. It was awesome. Her being added to the show. It's hard for me to even think of a time when she was not on the show.

AMY ACKER

When I started, I found out that I was actually going to be a regular on the show. And I was ecstatic! It was my first real TV job, so I was terrified, excited . . . all of those things. Looking back at it after so many auditions from that point to now, it just seemed like it all went *way* too easily. I guess it was just meant to be. Usually there are so many more hoops to jump through—it spoiled me for future auditions. There were definitely aspects of Fred I could easily connect to. I don't know that they were even necessarily there to begin with, but being from Texas and a little awkward and shy . . . well, that didn't take too much acting on my part [*laughs*].

For J. August Richards, season two represented an important turning point in his career and his life–*and* represented the first year he had ever spent as a series regular.

J. AUGUST RICHARDS

In that season we were all finding out how to incorporate Gunn into the group and we found him, slowly but surely, what his purpose would be and how he would interact with everyone. One thing I remember was having a really great off-camera rapport with Alexis and us bringing that on camera. We invented a handshake that the characters would have, because we liked the idea that they were so different but they could be so close. Consciously I made the choice that Wesley was Gunn's best friend.

I also think over the course of season two, it was about Wesley, Cordelia, and Angel becoming members of *Gunn's* family. I feel like's Gunn's super-objective throughout the course of the five seasons never changed, which was to protect his family. Because he'd already lost his parents, every kid on the street, and ultimately Angel, Wesley, and Cordelia would become his family, so it never changed. He would die for the people he loved. That was really the essence and the core of the character for me, that he was just someone [who] would give it all for the people that he loved.

JOSS WHEDON

In season two, again we sort of figured that our strength lay with the people we knew, so we started to have more fun with Lindsey and, of course, Darla. Darla was our big shocker at the end of the first season. Season two also aired at a point when we were still matching *Angel* up with *Buffy*, because they were on the same network and the same night. For example, we had an arc in season two that I love where Angel just got very, very dark and very into beating the bad guys. We deliberately set it up so that his epiphany—his return to grace, if you will—was aired the same night as the death of Buffy's mom. We knew we could not do a depressing *Angel* after showing "The Body." People would be killing themselves, including us. So the series still sort of matched.

TIM MINEAR

Season two took Angel to his own personal existential dark place that he crawled his way out of. He was able to be happy for a second in Pylea, and then the shit hit the fan when he got back to see Willow waiting for him, which was our way to tie in to the season five finale of *Buffy* when Buffy died. So we definitely go off on a cliffhanger. I will say the Pylea arc in and of itself had a beginning, a middle, and an end. That story gets resolved. And then when we come back to the real world, it's a little bit like when you come back from vacation and you're like, "I had a great vacation, but now I have to go back to real life." That's kind of where we leave you off.

HERE COMES THE SON

"The father shall kill the son . . ."

By its third season, *Angel* had clearly differentiated itself from *Buffy the Vampire Slayer*, *Angel*'s depth of storytelling, characterizations, and, in many instances, scope allowing it to go places far beyond its progenitor.

Behind the scenes, Joss Whedon's time was divided between *Buffy*, *Angel*, and the then in-development *Firefly;* David Greenwalt remained show runner, Tim Minear became executive producer mid-season, Marti Noxon remained consulting producer, and Jeffrey Bell, who had served as a writer for *The X-Files*, joined the staff as a coproducer.

JOSS WHEDON
(executive producer/cocreator, *Angel*)

Going into season three, we were dealing with that thing in your twenties when you're waiting for your life to start, and you suddenly realize that it has. It was everybody sort of taking stock of their lives, and being sort of conflicted about where they are. The idea was they would stop and deal with who they are, where they are, how they deal with each other, what they're doing, and at the same time they fought evil things. Also, seasons three and four, more than anything else, represented *Angel* at its most turgid, and therefore was the most beloved by me. Dark and strange and fabulous.

TIM MINEAR
(executive producer, *Angel*)

By the time we got to season three, I think we finally realized what *Angel* was in some ways, although we always knew to some degree. I mean, people would say, "The show's just now finding itself," and they were saying that since the second half of the first season. The secret about *Angel* is that it was constantly changing, so it was whatever it was at any particular point. It wasn't like *Buffy* with the hard, fast, very clear metaphor. It worked best as a Douglas Sirk–like giant melodrama. The other thing is that people would ask, "Why can't Angel ever be happy?" and the answer is because it's tedious when he's happy. And the *other* thing we learned is that pain, if it's earned character-wise, makes characters compelling. After season three, Wesley's no longer a guy who slips on coffee beans; this guy's had his throat slit, and it makes him incredibly compelling even though he's not a bad guy.

BEN EDLUND
(supervising producer, *Angel*)

Oh my God, look what happened to Wesley. That was actually very impressive, I thought, to go from *Buffy* to get that kind of tweed, sort of coded dude as hard-core as they got was amazing. And for Alexis to be as strong in running both ends of that portrait was *great*.

DAVID GREENWALT
(executive producer/cocreator, *Angel*)

We really didn't give Angel a break, nor, in some ways, *should* he have one. As these shows go on, you have to keep conflict in the characters' life and give [them] new stuff to deal with.

As the third season began, Amy Acker's Fred had become a full-blown regular, and the actress felt that she fit right in with the rest of the cast.

AMY ACKER
(actress, Fred)

You know, maybe I was so inexperienced and young at the time that I didn't know that I should be worried that there could be dynamics that I was interfering with or anything. But everyone was so great. I mean, David, Charisma, J., Alexis—it immediately felt like they were happy I was there. And we were a super tight-knit group. There was never any real weirdness with anything on the set.

I had this sort of little-sister relationship with David. He was always playing jokes, and if he was off camera, he would be trying to make me laugh (which wasn't very hard to do)—teasing me and that kind of stuff. Charisma was just so sweet and nice, always just working so hard to do good at her stuff. She would run lines with you if you wanted, which was just super-helpful. J. and Alexis . . . any show I could do with J. and Alexis would be my dream job. Alexis, obviously, I love, and that's part of the reason getting to do *Much Ado About Nothing* with him was so special. I just think he's such a wonderful acting partner and makes everything come alive and elevates your performance. And J. is probably the most positive person that I've ever met in my life. You can't be around J. without smiling, and that's just a wonderful person to be around. And then he's supertalented on top of that.

J. AUGUST RICHARDS
(actor, Charles Gunn)

I knew what it felt like to be the new guy in the cast, so I tried to be the most welcoming person that I could. It wasn't difficult, because everyone loved Amy and she's so easy to love, and quickly.

TIM MINEAR

Here's what Fred brought to the mix—and this is just my opinion. Besides the fact that Amy is wonderful in a scene, tears your heart out, and is gut funny, there is a scene in season two's "Through the Looking Glass" where she's with Angel and she's very worried about Cordelia. Angel says, "Oh no, they made her a princess." She just stops and says, "When I got here, they never did that . . . That's good for her." Then we cut to Cordelia on that throne, going, "Maybe I should just leave." Back-to-back gut funny performances from our two actresses. The fact that we could have two funny women on the show was a good thing. But I think the thing Fred brings to the party is this: Angel doesn't owe her an apology. She is somebody with whom he has a clean slate. I think it's important to have somebody in his life to whom he does not owe an apology, that he hasn't hurt. That was an important element for the show. The other thing I think she brought to the show is the science, so she was valuable in that respect. Also, it wasn't a bad thing to have another female character for all of them to play off of. No-brainer.

AMY ACKER

Shooting on the Paramount lot was one of the most fun parts of that job. Paramount has this amazing old-Hollywood feel. You can just kind of "see" all the people that drove through those same gates, making all of these wonderful movies that you've watched forever. We would park next to the big lot where they fill it with water and have the big sky mural painted on it so they can use it for filming. It's probably my favorite lot that I've ever worked on.

Integral to season three was the character of Daniel Holtz, an eighteenth-century vampire hunter and a constant obstacle to Angelus and Darla. The conflict seemed to culminate with them slaughtering Holtz's family, being sure to leave his turned daughter to greet Holtz, a sequence that, after Holtz spent the night holding and singing softly to her, sees him thrusting her into the morning sun, thus destroying her. All of this set him on a path of what some would call vengeance but he referred to as justice. An incorporeal demon known as Sahjhan–in an act of self-preservation–brings Holtz to the present to unleash him against Angel.

Added into the mix was the return of Julie Benz's Darla, who, after having had sex with Angel in season two, is now pregnant–which is supposed to be impossible for vampires. Thus, Angel suddenly finds himself an expectant father.

Cast in the role of Holtz was Keith Szarabajka, an American-born actor whose credits include playing Mickey Kostmayer on *The Equalizer*, Harlan Williams in Stephen King's *Golden Years*, and Charles Henry "Chaz" Gracen in *Profit*, created by John McNamara and David Greenwalt, who thought the actor would be perfect as Holtz.

DAVID GREENWALT

Keith has got the *greatest* voice. An aside about *Profit*: Adrian Pasdar has a low voice, Keith has a low voice—all these people have these incredibly low voices—and on *Profit* they were all trying to outdo each other at who could talk lower. But Keith was great.

KEITH SZARABAJKA
(actor, Daniel Holtz)

I'd worked with David Greenwalt on the show *Profit,* probably five years earlier, and it had been a wonderful experience. It was one of the greatest shows I'd ever been in. Unfortunately, it was ahead of its time and we were infinitely disappointed when it crashed and burned. David called and asked me if I wanted to do *Angel* and I thought it would be great. I was originally signed for eight shows and I think I ended up doing eleven. I was told that his name was Holtz and that he was a Van Helsing type of character, so I thought maybe they would want me to be Dutch or German. We went through a whole bunch of different possibilities and he said it was really England. "OK, so we'll give him an English accent." We didn't make it too Northern, just a standard British accent. And I just loved doing it. I mean, what's not to love about it? I got to ride a horse; I had a sword, a crossbow; I wore a duster; I got to speak with an English accent and do all these sort of pseudo-Shakespearean sort of riffs.

The season-two episode "The Trial" featured a flashback with Angelus and Darla making their way to a barn to escape the vampire hunter who is seeking vengeance for the fact that the duo murdered his family.

TIM MINEAR

We knew. Sometimes we would go back and say, "Hey, why don't we explore that?" But in this case it was definitely a plant. The Holtz character is an interesting Big Bad, because he's a very righteous man. It's not only that he believes in what he's doing, but he's right. Angel did terrible things. Angel murdered his entire family. This is a guy who has a legitimate beef, and he's not going around killing innocent people. Ted Bundy reforms—so what? He still killed all those people. Hitler reforms—so what? He's still guilty. So it creates an interesting dilemma. This is a character who believes he's on a quest from God, and in fact he may have been.

KEITH SZARABAJKA

Holtz was brokenhearted, and he wanted justice somehow for what had happened to him and his family. I mean, I challenge you to think about this: Angel, when he was Angelus, killed my wife, ate my baby, and then turned my eleven-year-old daughter into a vampire, forcing me to dust her. And *I'm* the villain? At the same time, I think there was a sort of begrudging admiration that Holtz had for Angel and vice versa. They knew they were enemies, but they were *good* enemies in a way. He was an antivillain in the same way that, in many ways, Angel was an antihero. That, at least to me, is what made it interesting.

JEFFREY BELL
(producer, *Angel*)

With each season, it's really the material leading us. What I mean by that is in season three, the decision was made that Darla comes back pregnant, which makes it very much about Angel. The hotel became very much family. Angel became not so much a vampire but an expectant father. In a supernatural world, that brought very real, very understandable emotions to a genre of show. I think once we sort of did that in season three, the show got interesting in kind of an arcy way. The emotions of Angel and him losing his son, and his son coming back and hating him—to me, that all came out of Angel's relationship with *his* father and all the angst that comes with that.

CHARISMA CARPENTER
(actress, Cordelia Chase)

Julie Benz is a wonderful actress, and whenever her character was on the show, nine out of ten times I wasn't in it, because it was in flashback and I wasn't in those scenes. It was until season three that there was more interfacing. For the first time I got to know her better and I remember her behind the scenes knitting me a scarf, which I still have to this day, and it has a little label in it, "Made by Julie." So she is a wonderful addition to any set and a wonderful talent. As far as the story line goes, I remember she tried to fight me, which brought Angel and Cordelia closer, so that was good; he got protective because of her reappearance.

TIM MINEAR

We knew season three was going to be in three pieces: revealing Darla's pregnancy, involving Angel with that pregnancy, Darla's death/the birth of Connor . . . all of that threaded throughout. Then Holtz stealing Connor and Connor returning as an angry adolescent. So, yeah, I think the show changed enough in the course of events that it kept things interesting.

JOSS WHEDON

Here's an interesting tidbit: at that point we had five players, which were enough for an ensemble and stories that are created from within, and conflicts and romance and all of that stuff. But we felt, "Great, that's our season." But it wasn't enough. We loved it, but we hadn't really finished it yet.

TIM MINEAR

We brought Darla back in that box at the end of season one, and it is sort of a famous story in the Whedonverse that I made a dirty joke. Joss said, "What can we do in season two?" and I said, "Well, we brought Darla back in a box, maybe we bring back something in Darla's box," which is where he got the idea of impregnating her, so that was the idea that came up early. I remember him saying that she comes back as human, and once she finally accepts being human, Drusilla can come in and resire her and turn her back into a vampire. So we knew that that was going to happen early on. We had some great kind of orange cones set down along the road of season two, and we wrote up to those big moments, which of course led us to season three.

JOSS WHEDON

Tim Minear and I were attempting to figure out what unknown quantity was missing from the show. While we were talking, we reflected on the fact that we'd already done "Darla in the Box." Then Tim made a dirty joke, and that dirty joke actually made me stop and say, "Darla's pregnant!" And it literally came from his twelve-year-old humor. Of course she's pregnant, and then we did the math and we realized that, yes, she'd be a couple of months away from giving birth based on the fact that she and Angel had had sex when they did in the second season. At that moment we had our third season; everything mapped out of the idea of fatherhood, the idea of what the pregnancy meant to Darla.

JULIE BENZ
(actress, Darla)

When I showed up pregnant, I had to wear a leotard that was stuffed with a pillow and it was pretty uncomfortable, but I think the biggest challenge during all those pregnant scenes was being on camera without any makeup on. That's pretty much a challenge when you're an actress, just to go on camera completely raw. But I felt that Darla was pretty strung out by then, so it worked.

TIM MINEAR

The reveal of Darla's pregnancy was the first episode post *Buffy* and *Angel* being on the same network. And instead of just pretending that that—Angel having sex with Darla—never happened, we had to deal with it in some permutation. We've also played the trick before where Angel finally comes to some peace about an issue, but it doesn't last—in this instance it's that you can't live in the past. But we discover that sometimes the past comes back, 'cause here comes Darla. You know, just because *you* decide that it's OK now doesn't mean that the people that you affected will agree.

In season two, part of the reason we went to Pylea was that we had scheduling problems with Julie Benz. So instead of having a giant resolution with her, we just wanted her to kind of fade away, because it became not about her. But some fans felt cheated, that it seemed like we were building to something, because the Darla story was not over. I remember David Greenwalt, Joss Whedon, and myself were walking down by the beach near Santa Monica, talking about the third season. We knew we were going to bring Holtz in, because we'd set that up in season two in "The Trial" with just a mention of him—the idea being that Angel's past would come back to haunt him. Holtz would appear, and somehow Wesley would either fall in with Holtz or be corrupted by Holtz, but we knew that something like that was going to happen. It still didn't feel like enough, so I made the dirty joke about Darla. That's where that idea first took root, but immediately we knew it was the right thing to do. It was just so mythic. *And* impossible.

The episode "Lullaby" represents the culmination of the first part of the season's arc, as it ends with Angel and Darla trying to escape from Wolfram & Hart and other factions who want to get their hands on this miracle baby—destined for a key role in the impending apocalypse—before it's born. It all ends tragically with Darla staking herself in an alley, leaving behind a crying baby that Angel scoops up.

JULIE BENZ

Darla's whole world was rocked. She never thought she could get pregnant and then all of a sudden she's carrying this child and experiencing this soul for the first time in four hundred years. She recognized that as soon as the baby's born, the soul's going to go away, and it's the first time she really experienced true love, so she was going through *a lot*.

JOSS WHEDON

One of the most beautiful things we've ever done was Darla's speech about how—because she has a baby with a soul—she loves it, and once it's out of her, she knows she won't be able to feel that again, and she can't stand it. It's one of the most beautiful things I've ever seen on the show. And when she stakes herself to save the child, it's a beautiful sacrifice.

JULIE BENZ

I was up in Vancouver working on *Taken* and I got the script sent to me and I just sat in my trailer and cried. I thought, "What a beautiful exit to a great character." I just felt that it was such a great gift from the writers to Darla, to be able to go out in such an epic way.

BEN EDLUND

What I think happened is that someone came up with that image of Darla staking herself, and no matter what it took, and no matter where it went, they *needed* that.

STEVEN S. DEKNIGHT
(producer, *Angel*)

When Darla stakes herself to give birth to her baby, not only was it magnificently filmed by Tim Minear, but it's one of those moments where you're like, "I can't believe they just did that." *That's* the kind of TV I love. That's the *Twin Peaks* of it for me, when you sit there with your mouth open saying, "I can't believe they just did that."

DAVID GREENWALT

My mouth hung open *a lot* during those years. You know, working with Joss, breaking story with Joss—I compare this to playing music with Mozart, which is just that that guy is incredibly good at what he does and works harder than everybody else, if you combine those two things. Most of these stories were broken by Joss; Joss and me; Joss, me, and Tim; Joss, me, and Marti—whatever the combination. Knowing Tim, Darla staking herself *was* his idea. I loved it. Joss used to say, "We don't give people what they want; we give them what they need." I always like the crazier pace, but it still had to be emotionally true, because it has to be inevitable but surprising. And that was just an amazing film school for me during those years.

KEITH SZARABAJKA

To me, the best episodes that we did were "Lullaby" and "Benediction." Those are my two favorites in that there was just such remorse and regret at the same time that Holtz had to do what he was going to do. It was much more evident in "Benediction," because "Lullaby" was where everything kind of happened.

TIM MINEAR

The episode is Angel's face-to-face confrontation with Holtz. Basically, since everything had been playing in real time for the last episode or two, when we came into "Lullaby," act one, it actually plays like act four. It's not so much a setup as it is a resolution of the previous episode. This is also the revelation that Angel and Darla just didn't kill Holtz's family, but they turned the little girl and Holtz had to come back and find her, then throw her out in the sun. Once we got that, I kind of knew what to write. I mean, I knew that this was about Angel starting to allow himself to believe that he was going to have a son, or a child. But then juxtaposing that with this other man's family that he had destroyed, all of which built to what I thought was a really cool moment in the alley in the end. After Darla stakes herself and Angel's holding the baby in the pouring rain and Holtz steps aside to allow him to pass.

KEITH SZARABAJKA

That *wasn't* a change of heart on Holtz's part, just a piece of the plan. I don't think Holtz ever really believed that Angel could ever *not* be Angelus. Even in the show there was always the possibility that he could change. So while Holtz recognizes that he's been "in-soul-ated," I don't think he ever really trusted that Angelus had become Angel and was going to be Angel permanently.

TIM MINEAR

When we're watching the episode, it feels like Holtz has found within himself some measure of understanding and, I don't know if I would say forgiveness, but compassion. And then when he says to Sahjhan, "I told you I would show no pity and I won't," we realize it's much worse than that. In fact, he's not ready to just kill Angel, because he sees a way to make him suffer the way he has had to suffer. And that moment of letting Angel pass plays out for the rest of the season until Holtz grabs the kid, then brings the kid back as a teenager and seems to have forgiven Angel yet again, and fucks him over completely.

DAVID GREENWALT

Losing a child is the scariest thing in the world. I don't know a worse one than that. Luckily, it's never happened to me, but I do know quite a few people it's happened to. You don't ever really come back from that, you know? You go on, and if you have other kids you go on well, hopefully, but you don't get over that.

As things played out, Angel brought the baby–named Connor–back to the hotel and began mapping out plans on raising him. At the same time, Holtz (along with Sahjhan) develops a plan that convinces Wesley–via an altered prophecy–that Angel is destined to kill his son. In response, Wesley steals the child; heads to the park, where one of Holtz's minions, Justine, slits his throat; and gives the child to Holtz, who, following a shoot-out with members of Wolfram & Hart, is actually allowed by Angel to leap through a portal to a hell dimension that Sahjhan has opened, hoping it will give Connor a greater chance for survival. What he doesn't expect is that a couple of episodes later, Connor would return at the age of eighteen, ready to take down his father. Holtz, now elderly, manipulates his "son" against his actual father.

JOSS WHEDON

Angel having a son brought out a lot of colors in him that we would never have seen. Then, of course, we had set up Holtz in the season before and him stealing the son and the son coming back as a teenager who hates nothing more than, oh, say, his father. There was just a huge amount to play with and the show was firing on all cylinders. So you could say, "The show is about a bunch of twentysomethings with emotions" and it's like, "OK, good." But if you say, "I'm a vampire and I've created a son," your response is, "OK, better." A lot to be mined there. I only regret that that season was two years before I had my own son, because when we were breaking this story, I was going, "Yeah, I guess Angel would like this." I couldn't feel an emotion toward it. Then when I had my son, I was like, "Can we do that season again?"

DAVID BOREANAZ
(actor, Angel)

Having a baby on the set was interesting. We would do rehearsals without the child. When we were ready to roll, we would get the kid and it would change the whole dynamics of the scene, because there are laws that there are only certain times that you can have a child work on the set. It was so time-consuming, but very calming, because when you have a baby in your arms, it's eating off your energies. You have to be kind of in tune with the child and still do your work as the character on a show. It was difficult. But it was very good practice for me, though. I'd been living vicariously through my sisters, with my niece and my nephews. When I had a child of my own, it definitely enhanced that practice.

TIM MINEAR

"Sleep Tight" is where Wesley takes the kid to give him to Holtz but realizes that he had to get out of town with the kid himself, which is exactly what Holtz was hoping for, putting Wesley in a very vulnerable position while he's keeping everyone at the hotel busy. Then, of course, Justine cuts Wesley's throat and takes the baby, and Holtz jumps through a dimensional portal with Connor and there's pain for *everyone*. With "Forgiving," we were really trying to figure this fucking story out, because, basically, what we had was Cordelia's out of town, Angel has just lost his son, and Wesley is lying in a field someplace, but we knew where we wanted to end it. We wanted it to seem like Angel has realized why Wesley did what he did and has gone to make some kind of bridge between them at the hospital and instead tries to smother him with a pillow. *That* we knew. What we didn't really have was an engine for the story to keep it going, which is why we brought back Sahjhan, because we knew we had to play off his character in some way.

Things build up to the episode "The Price," which is the setup for Connor's return. Because Angel had gone through all these extreme measures to try to get the kid back, we wanted to answer the question of, Did he do the right thing? And our answer is, in fact, he did. Even though Angel messed with things he probably shouldn't have been messing with, when it comes to certain things, you have to try whatever you have to try in order to know that there's no hope.

That whole story is about how we think that this dimensional thing that he opened to get Sahjhan back, is the terror of these mysterious slugs that's appeared in the hotel when, in fact, it is not. It is something breaking through from the other side, which is Quor'toth. And, at first, we think it's these little slug monsters that are escaping, and, in fact, they're running away from something that's even scarier, which turns out to be Connor, who's now seventeen or eighteen. When Fred is possessed by the slug creature, she says, "The destroyer is coming," and then in the next episode, "Benediction," Holtz says to Connor, "It was brilliant the way you found the cracks and a way to get out," and Connor says, "I scared the slugs into fleeing and they went straight to the holes and I followed them."

"A New World," which Jeff Bell wrote and I directed, is something we wanted to do kick-ass action in. You know, the minute that kid comes back we wanted to do kick-ass action. We wanted to show a complicated fight scene that we don't usually spend enough time on. I wanted to come into a fight that was so big that there wasn't an opening credits until well into the first act. The very opening of the episode is those CGI stakes with the CGI axe, and then we come back in and there's a big fight, and *then* Connor runs outside and jumps on the back of a bus and is driven away. You know, we'd gone to Pylea and then we wanted to show what it was like for someone who came into this world from another place and didn't know it. Part of the story we were following from Connor's point of view, following him into the dirty underbelly of Los Angeles. And it all culminates with Angel and Connor confronting each other. It was Angel trying to be a dad.

BEN EDLUND

Being born in an alley after Darla stakes herself makes Connor, in a sense, the bastard child of his own gestation. What came afterward was this thing of how trackable is that? How much can you understand about that as a person trying to understand the plight of Angel? How much better do you understand your main character because he's had a son who's disappeared, went to hell, was born from vampires, and returned in his teenage years as a troubled "child," because he was raised on a demon plane? So Angel went from being a parent to being the parent of a teenager. It's like an illegitimate child story, basically.

TIM MINEAR

In "Benediction," Holtz is back, looking terrible in a rubber face. Had we known it was going to look like that, we would not have done it. But we ended up using foam or whatever that crap is that makes him look like he has a giant rubber face. But, thankfully, Keith is so good that he acts through all that crappy makeup and I start to forget about it. But the story is about the resolution of Holtz, and if you look at the episode you'll see that he never lies. He never says a single lie in the whole episode, even though he is completely tricking Connor into thinking that Angel murdered him. Everything he says is true. He realizes that Angel and Connor are destined to somehow be together. That the kid found his way here, and if that's the case, they have some kind of a destiny. That he really has to let the kid go. The only thing he cares about is the fact that Connor loves him. And the only way to ensure that is to make sure that he hates Angel, and so he does what he does.

KEITH SZARABAJKA

All of that is, I think, tied into the fact, again, that he never really trusted that Angelus was completely Angel or that he was going to remain Angel. And then he felt that he owed something to his murdered family. He had to do *something.* And from Holtz's point of view, this was more justice than vengeance. This was a man who could articulate his feeling and his emotions, but I think that the loss of his family was something that was almost too deep for him—I think it would be too deep for *anyone*. As a father, I don't know how I would cope with one of my sons being murdered or both, God forbid. My vengeance might know no bounds. You don't know how you're going to respond until that actually happens to you.

TIM MINEAR

The final moments between Angel and Holtz have Angel pinning him against a wall, and when I was writing the episode, it was all about that moment. It was all about Angel accusing this guy of kidnapping his son and then the guy saying, "And you murdered mine." There's *nothing* Angel can say to that. The whole notion of Angel saying, "You want me to say I'm sorry, but it would mean nothing." And the guy whose family you murdered, saying, "It wouldn't mean much, but it would mean a little. So I think you have to say it."

KEITH SZARABAJKA

Sometimes when I find a script is poorly written, it's difficult to memorize, but I never had a problem with any of the scripts for *Angel,* and I had some long speeches in that show. It was so good, and the character always made sense to me. There were a couple in the middle there where I went, "OK, we're sort of into a jogging mode here as opposed to really doing something," but that happens in episodic TV. I think that there was a good character arc all the way through the thing, and it followed up and landed. It started somewhere and landed somewhere else, which I thought was great.

Cast as the teenage Connor was Vincent Kartheiser, a Minneapolis native who trained at the Guthrie Theater there. When he was six, he performed in a number of stage productions, including *A Christmas Carol*. Other stage roles followed, and he also appeared on an episode of *ER*. After *Angel,* he went on to his critically acclaimed role as the obsequious Pete Campbell on Matt Weiner's brilliant *Mad Men*.

VINCENT KARTHEISER
(actor, Connor)

The project was sent to me by my agent. Originally, he wasn't even called Connor and he wasn't even Angel's son. I was actually just booked as "street kid." So I went in and they told me it was a good role, but they couldn't quite tell me what it was. They did say that it was going to be three episodes and the end of the show's third year and that they might pick me up for season four. So I went in and auditioned with a very basic script. Nothing too special, nothing giving away the identity of my character, and I got the part. *Then* they told me who the character was, and I was excited.

At the same time, in those kind of circumstances, I'm rather shy, and I was really, really nervous. I showed up and there they all were, seven actors all sitting round the couch, telling inside jokes with one another and laughing. Amazingly, within a couple of weeks I really felt welcomed by quite a few of them, and really part of their family. Halfway through the next season, I was one of the gang. The cast was extraordinarily nice and there was such a great ambiance on the set.

DAVID GREENWALT

Angel was *that* kind of show, where a baby can go into another dimension and come back out and is suddenly nineteen. We got to play out some great father-son stuff with him. God, he was so good on *Mad Men* and he was great on our show. He comes out of the Guthrie Theater out of Minneapolis, and he was pretty damn well trained for a young person. He did such *amazing* shit on *Mad Men*. He brought a lot of oomph to our show.

VINCENT KARTHEISER

Doing *Angel* was very different to film. The process is very different. On film you have much more time, there's much more collaboration, and you know what you're getting yourself into. You read the script and that's the script you're going to do. Whereas on TV you get a new script two days before you're shooting, so you don't know what your character's going to do until you get the new script, and then there's really no rehearsal. Collaboration is there, but, depending on the director, it can be a lot of collaboration or it can be very minimal. I have a lot of respect for people who do it well. I have a lot of respect for David Boreanaz, for the amazing job he's done for years and years. I take my hat off to anyone who can continually work those kind of hours day after day and still come out with amazing performances.

KEITH SZARABAJKA

I didn't actually have a lot of scenes with Vincent. I actually got to know him better after going to conventions. He's a nice kid. A little diffident, and I think he's changed now that he did *Mad Men* for so long and had a lot of success with it. But on *Angel* he was a late adolescent. I never had a problem with him.

VINCENT KARTHEISER

There's some of me in that character, but I'm a very lighthearted person in most circumstances. I should say, on the exterior I'm a very light person. I tend to like to make jokes and I'm sarcastic, and I'd like to think I'm witty and funny and don't take myself seriously. But I also have that other side of me when I feel I've been improperly treated, or if I feel I'm not happy with something I've done and I'm not happy with myself. I think everyone has more than one side to him.

Proving that not everything was dire in season three, some humor (and pathos) was worked in with the return of Mark Lutz's Groo, who came to this world from Pylea to be with Cordelia, whom he had fallen in love with, and who, they both believed, had developed feelings for him as well.

MARK LUTZ

There came that moment where Groo, trying to fit in, dressed like Angel and had his hair cut the same way—oh my God, that was so much fun. And that was the thing about Charisma: we had a funny rapport going between us. As an actor, doing those scenes [was] easy; it didn't even feel like work.

CHARISMA CARPENTER

Honestly, I hated that relationship between Cordelia and Groo. I don't know why; I just didn't think it worked. I suppose it served a purpose for the story; obviously, it had to be sort of that level of hero to compete with Angel, so it made sense on that level, but I didn't like it. I guess as a character sometimes you have to go away and have a certain experience to bring you back to the right place.

In the season finale, "Tomorrow," Cordelia, having broken up with Groo, is on her way to a meeting with Angel to confess her feelings for him but is elevated to a higher plane of existence, while Connor and Justine–in what they believe is a final act of retribution for Holtz–are in the midst of sealing a tasered Angel in a waterproof box and sinking it to the bottom of the ocean (ironically, a cliffhanger that was identically co-opted by *The Vampire Diaries* years later).

CHARISMA CARPENTER

I liked the fact that a relationship was building between Angel and Cordelia. I thought that a relationship that grows out of friendship and loyalty is probably the best relationship to have, and so when that occurred it sort of made sense. As she grew and she got deeper, they're fighting the big fight and they'd been through so much, and seeing everything they see, and having visions and knowing who he is, it made sense. His love for Buffy was a love of passion and it was a great, great love. Like a first love, it's never going to go away and it's always going to be special. But first loves always end, so I feel with Cordy and Angel it was a mature love, a love born out of friendship and circumstance, and it was really beautiful. When she goes to her ascension, it's like, "How can the Powers That Be take me *now*? Like, I have to have this conversation. I have to tell him how I feel; he has to know I love him." I get emotional just saying that, because I can't imagine just discovering that, oh my God, this person who has been here all along and I didn't realize it . . . and *then* you can't go to him and you can't tell him how you feel.

DAVID GREENWALT

One of my favorite things with Charisma was that bit where she ascends, which I directed. She was really game, because she went up probably sixty or seventy feet on that thing. I was always a big fan of hers.

CHARISMA CARPENTER

I wish I knew what they originally had in mind with this whole ascension idea. I don't know if it's bullshit or not, but they said they didn't know what to do with the character; how to service her, but I don't think that was it. I think I was having some personal issues and they were feeling like I was a wild card, and they didn't know how to cope with it or deal with it, or how to make it work at that juncture.

TIM MINEAR

"Tomorrow" was our first cliffhanger. I mean, we generally went out on something that set up the next year, but we just decided it would be cool to leave things the worst possible way they can be. So that's what we did. We wanted some real questions and it worked, because, deep down, it's terrific. It means that season four hits the ground running; there was no revving anything up and it was just about touching it to the ground and letting it go.

At the end of season three, both David Greenwalt and Tim Minear left *Angel,* but for two very different reasons. Greenwalt's was contractual, while Minear was moving over to Whedon's new space opera, *Firefly*.

DAVID GREENWALT

I left *Angel* after the third season due to a major contract dispute. I had gotten a couple of nice overall deals with Fox, first to do *Buffy* and then to do *Angel,* and things were very copacetic, but then Fox was like, "Nobody's getting a raise. As a matter of fact, everybody's taking a cut." I remember going to meet with Dana Walden and my then agent, Bob Gummer, saying, "Look, I don't know that you understand what I've given to *Buffy* and *Angel.* I would be there at 7 A.M. on a Sunday figuring out all my stuff if I was directing. I gave a lot of blood to those two shows and gracefully, given nobody squeezed it out of me. I'm perfectly happy to not take a raise. I understand tough times; we cut the budget by 2 percent. But I will not accept you actually taking away some money."

Joss was deep into *Firefly* and a bunch of other stuff, and he kind of missed this whole thing that was going on with me. It was kind of a sad chapter in our story together, because I kept saying, "Joss, they're not making the deal and if you don't call somebody . . ." He was deep into stuff and by the time he got around to it I finally made my move, and also the show *Miracles* had offered me a pretty lucrative deal, which I really liked. I didn't really want to leave, but I was sort of offended about this whole idea of taking money away as opposed to not getting a raise. So I had to leave, and Joss kind of woke up and it was just too late. At that point he said he could cobble money together from *Buffy, Angel,* and *Firefly,* but it was too late. It really was not about money anymore. And so we kind of parted ways. But we stayed close.

Those three years of *Angel* were good. I would've been happy to stay, and in retrospect maybe I should have stayed, because I went off to do a bunch of other shows that didn't succeed, like *Jake 2.0* and *Miracles*.

TIM MINEAR

I have to say that Mutant Enemy, bar none, was *exactly* what Howard Gordon said it would be. I learned so much working with Joss and David, and for me that's going to be the highlight of my career. I don't even know how to describe what it was like to be at *Angel* while *Buffy* was on the air, and then on *Firefly. Angel* may have been the highlight for me. I was intimately involved with every aspect of that show. I got to direct episodes, which brings everything full circle. From the time I had my 8 mm camera to this moment, I wanted to get behind the camera and I wanted to not just write the stories, but tell the stories and make the stories and direct the stories and edit the stories. As a writer/producer in TV, you get to do all of those things. The fact is that the writer/producer conceptualizes what's going to happen, gets the costumes, talks to the production designer about what the thing is going to look like, interacts with the director of photography, sits in the editing room with the editor, sits with the composer and spots the show and says, "I want Wagner here, and I want this to sound like Bernard Hermann." You get to do *everything* in television and this was the best film school ever.

BEAUTY AND THE BEAST

"Angel's just something that you're forced to wear. . . ."

Of *Angel*'s five-season run, it was the fourth that was the most in danger of running off the rails creatively, for a number of reasons. For starters, there was a behind-the-scenes shake-up. David Greenwalt was gone, having departed over a contract dispute with production company 20th Century Fox; Tim Minear, although involved creatively for part of the season, was serving as a show runner along with Joss Whedon on the sci-fi series *Firefly*; Marti Noxon was focused fully on *Buffy*'s final season, with David Fury taking her position as consulting producer; writer Steven S. DeKnight came over from *Buffy;* Elizabeth Craft and Sarah Fain were brought in as staff writers; Ben Edlund, following the cancellation of the aforementioned *Firefly,* joined the show as producer; and, while Jeffrey Bell would eventually end up serving as show runner, early on writer/producer David Simkins was brought in from outside by Mutant Enemy to guide things. His credits prior to doing the show included *Dark Angel, FreakyLinks,* and *Roswell,* and after Angel he moved on to such shows as *Charmed, Blade: The Series, The Dresden Files, Warehouse 13, Grimm,* and *Powers.*

STEVEN S. DEKNIGHT
(supervising producer, *Angel*)

After spending two seasons on *Buffy,* Joss came to me at the end of season six and said he wanted Tim Minear to run *Firefly,* but he didn't want to take Tim away from David Greenwalt and leave him with a hole in his staff—obviously this was before David left the show. So Joss asked if I could help out and move over to *Angel.* I'd always expressed an interest in the show, because I watched it every week. I always came down to the *Angel* office, which was right down below the *Buffy* office, [to] talk about the episodes each week. And then I'd come back up to the *Buffy* office and say, "Did you see that fight on *Angel* last night? Why aren't we doing fights like that?" I was always talking about how beautiful it looked and it was letterboxed, and why weren't we letterboxed? *Buffy* was my first love and the show I wanted to be on when it ended, but I just couldn't resist coming down to *Angel*. Plus, you know, there was a promotion and raise and opportunity dangled in front of me, which didn't hurt at all. In true *Godfather* fashion, Joss made me an offer I couldn't refuse.

BEN EDLUND
(producer, *Angel*)

In 2001, I ended up doing the *Tick* live-action show, which was many things. In addition to being a nightmare, it was also a good thing. It was really hard, so I needed to take time off. Then I had no money and I needed a job, and I heard *Firefly* was being done. My agent told me "this spaceship show" was being done by the guy who did *Buffy*. I was sort of out at that point, just body surfing and trying to write a feature, so I went in. Actually, I remember, I did not know who Joss was. I went to a meeting for *Firefly* and I ended up shaking Tim Minear's hand and calling him Joss. You're supposed to *not* get the job after you fuck up that bad, but we had a fairly good meeting. And as I understood it, I think Tim Minear was a big proponent of mine, maybe because [*laughs*] I might have amused him. But very much, as I understood it, he was a champion of mine in the hiring process and I'm quite grateful to him. He had a quasi-mentor energy, which I appreciate to this day.

That was a really good camp to get in. So we worked for the twelve episodes of *Firefly*, it got canceled, and I was really fortunate to have been in the situation where I was able to distinguish myself, and Joss wanted me to transfer from *Firefly* to *Angel*. They brought me on and I was writing on the last part of season four. I was kind of like this bubble of investment being dragged along by Mutant Enemy for the next season. And then I did the full fifth season.

STEVEN S. DEKNIGHT

I agreed to go to *Angel*. We wrapped *Buffy* and everybody's taking a hiatus. I pop in to the office during a hiatus, if memory serves me correctly, to start clearing out my office. I go into David Greenwalt's and he goes, "Hey, how you doing?" "You know, starting my vacation." He says, "OK. You're writing the first episode of next season." I found out he was supposed to be writing it, but he was in negotiations with Fox to renew his deal. It wasn't going well, so he decided to leave the show. As a result, whereas I thought I would kind of ease into the season, write an episode around six once I got my feet wet, that wasn't the case at all. So I got to do the first episode of season four. I spent my vacation working on that episode. Then wrote it again, because it had such a loose break. That was part one of my most painful memories working for Mutant Enemy. I had written a script and Tim Minear really liked it, and Jeff Bell really liked it. Tim Minear was consulting, I believe, and they'd enlisted Jeff Bell to help oversee the show while they were looking for a new show runner. There were a lot of things about the script that didn't work, because we didn't dot the i's or cross the t's before we dove into writing it.

My note session was tortuous in my mind. It was, like, a two- or three-hour note session. I was in the room with all the other writers and Joss was being shadowed by a reporter—I want to say for *The New York Times*. The reporter was in the room as I was basically dismantled, having given up my vacation to write this. I can chuckle about it now, but it stung at the time. The bigger picture is, he was absolutely right. The episode needed to be re-broken, no doubt about it. But that was my auspicious start on *Angel.*

David Simkins at the time was under an overall deal with Fox, and, with Greenwalt leaving, it was the studio's suggestion that he become part of the show, an idea he rejected when first broached by his agent. It was his feeling that the writing staffs at Mutant Enemy were fairly insular and it simply didn't seem like the right fit. Ultimately, though, he was convinced to go in for an interview.

DAVID SIMKINS
(executive producer, *Angel*)

I was familiar with *Buffy* and *Angel* in terms of the zeitgeist of it all. I'd seen them both and liked them very much, but I was *not* a die-hard fan. I respected them and loved what they were doing in terms of opening the door for a different, better, more fun kind of storytelling that TV had not been exposed to before. Those two shows were incredibly groundbreaking in terms of approaching material and doing something with the vampire genre that was unique and fun.

DAVID FURY

(consulting producer, *Angel*)

In season four, *Angel* needed a little more help. I was working on the show concurrently with season seven of *Buffy*. This was the year that David Greenwalt left, and Tim Minear, who was going to be the new show runner, went to run *Firefly*. So suddenly the two main guys from *Angel* were gone. I was a senior writer on *Buffy* and they wanted me to come on. I came on as a consultant and it was a difficult time initially, because we were trying to acclimate. And they brought in a show runner who struggled.

DAVID SIMKINS

The meeting was very unusual for me in terms of how most of these interviews go. Usually when I'm being interviewed for a job like this, the questions run the gamut from what you're watching on TV, what you like, how you work with writers in the room, do you like to break off and give the writers an idea and let them come back to you with it more fleshed out? Usually it's kind of specific, because room work when you're writing for television can be a bit of a crucible of sorts. A lot of emotions come out in the room, a lot of jokes, a lot of good stuff. But the interview with Joss was different in that Tim Minear was there as well. The interview was such that I was *not* asked a lot of questions. The sense that I'd had—and it had happened before—is that in between the meeting being set up and the meeting actually happening, another player is being offered the job. So you're sitting there in this interview, not really being interviewed. The suspicion was that there's somebody else waiting in the wings and they're just waiting for the deal to close. So I sat on the couch, I listened to Joss and Tim crack a lot of inside jokes about actors and Fox executives. I did my best to laugh along, but I really couldn't follow the thread, having not been a part of the clique. The meeting ended, and, driving home, I called my agent and said, "That was interesting, but I'm not going to get the gig." I was already moving on mentally to the next thing.

But later that afternoon I received a phone call that I had gotten the job. I was floored; I didn't know *how* I got the job. I just wasn't sure what was happening there. But, again, I told my agent that I was going to pass, because it didn't feel right. I respected Joss and Tim and loved the work they were doing, but it just felt with so many seasons behind *Buffy* and three behind *Angel,* I would be coming into a situation where it was already a well-oiled machine. And to be perfectly honest, I wasn't sure why they weren't hiring from within. I was a little confused by that, and then I thought what was happening was Fox was paying me since I was under contract, and it's very common for writers or producers to be put on another show so the cost can be written off. I told my agent it felt like I was being put into a position just to make Fox happy, but he told me I was overthinking it. So for the second time, against my better judgment, I said, "OK."

STEVEN S. DEKNIGHT

You can't just bring anybody onto a Joss Whedon show to run it. You've got to get his sensibilities; you need to understand him. They brought in a guy—David Simkins—who was very nice, but he just didn't mesh. It just wasn't a good fit.

DAVID SIMKINS

One of the first things that happened after I got the job is that Joss and Tim and I all went out for dinner, ostensibly for what I thought was to explain the ins and outs, or tell me what the ropes would be that I'd have to learn. But then Joss told me that the first two scripts for the season had already been written and—and he used this exact expression—they had been "Simkins-proofed," which he laughed at. I kind of laughed at that, too, but what I understood that to mean is that the first two scripts had been written in case I was going to screw up the start of the season. It *was* a bit disheartening, I have to admit, to know that I was already being seen as a bit of an interloper and a bit of a nuisance. But I understood that. I knew that Joss's relationship with the studio was a bit tense and that he was having some problems on *Firefly,* that they weren't happy with the way things were going there. *Buffy* was wrapping and they wanted *Angel* to stay on. It's something that, if I was in Joss's position, I would have considered if I knew that someone like David Greenwalt was leaving. I would want to get a head start. I don't think Joss meant it maliciously; it was just that sometimes Joss says things that are truthful, but there can also be a bit of cruelty in that truth.

That's what makes his writing so good is that he's honest in the stories he tells and the characters he writes.

But I buried all that and got a hold of the first three seasons of *Angel,* watched every episode, and absolutely fell in love with the show. So I felt I was ready when we opened the room for real and I met the writers, sat in the writers' room, and was eager and on board and happy to be a part of it.

DAVID FURY

David Simkins couldn't quite acclimate to our way of working. He didn't quite understand the show and he didn't quite understand Joss's sensibilities. And we did. We were much more in tune. The people that Joss hired and kept were people whom he basically mentored in the way of doing things, the way to tell stories, and the way to break those stories. And it was an odd experience, because to get someone from outside the family to run the show was a bit of a feeling of them abandoning their show. I was there as a consultant, but at some point it became very difficult to help. We weren't talking the same language. You realize, "Oh, we have a problem here," and we're not going to be telling the kind of stories that meant something or work for us.

DAVID SIMKINS

Usually when you're hired as a show runner, if it's for your own show or a first season you're coming in on, you have a certain autonomy. You're definitely filling out a list of requirements a studio or network has for the show. If you're hired for a detective show, you don't make it a musical . . . *unless* you're Joss, and then it's great. In this case, I was very aware that there was a specific language to this show, a shorthand and a familiarity that all of the writers had with these characters and this concept. My initial thought was to sit down, shut up, keep my eyes open, and just make sure that the trains ran on time. To do that, I had to let these trains be driven by people who knew how to drive them. I was there to watch the narrative arcs in terms of where the characters were going and [make] sure things were carried forward. I had no inclination to come in and redefine the show or say we're going to do this, we're going to do that. That *wasn't* my job. I was basically hired to make sure the stories, outlines, and concepts got to Joss in a timely manner. And when he approved or disapproved of those ideas, to make sure that all got relayed to keep things running as smoothly as possible.

DAVID FURY

Joss was very focused on *Firefly* and they didn't seem to want to think about *Angel*. They said, "Good luck with it." The feeling was almost they couldn't care less; just let somebody else run it. I don't know if that's the case, but it felt that way at the time. I would seek out Tim and Joss; I would go to the set of *Firefly* to try and talk to them about, "Here's where we're at with my story to the third episode," and I would be going to them directly, because I wasn't getting what I needed from David Simkins. Everyone was kind of struggling and morale was down. It was a very tricky time. I just wanted us to be able to do good work. I wasn't looking for anybody to get in trouble or leave. I was just concerned that the show was going to fall apart, and that's exactly what was happening.

DAVID SIMKINS

Having the first two scripts written, we had a bit of luxury there where we could take some time to figure out what the third and fourth episodes would be. We had some continuing stories and arcs that we had to honor, so that was included as well. I would say to Joss or Tim, "What do you think of this?" or, "How does this work?" Jeff Bell, bless his heart, one day I was sitting with him at the table in the writers' room and was sort of noodling on an idea, and Jeff leaned over and very sweetly whispered, "That's not this show," and I was very thankful, because *that* was the kind of thing I was needing to know coming into a situation that was new. I looked to Jeff for that; he was very good at that sort of thing.

DAVID FURY

To some extent I separated myself. I would basically use Joss as the de facto show runner and go to [him] and Tim for notes rather than going to David for my episode. And David seemed at that point fine with that. I was more like, "Let's wait and see when David tries to write the show if he grasps the way it's done." Sometimes until you actually do it, you *don't* really understand why you're doing it this way. But he never got the chance; they just kind of moved on anyway. I had actually proposed that Jeff Bell would be an ideal choice to run the show, because Jeff had worked closely on it in the last year and was already a producer there anyway. I said, "I think you need to promote somebody from within who knows the show and knows the Mutant Enemy way of doing things, and I think it should be Jeff." In the end they agreed.

DAVID SIMKINS

The details of what went down is that we were looking for our third script idea. I'd gone to Joss and pitched a concept about a villain who was trading futures. Not in a stock market sense, but this character had a way to identify the potential in someone's future abilities. Like if you were going to grow up and become a world-famous surgeon, he would know this, take your future, hold on to that mojo from you, and sell it on some kind of black market to the highest bidder. It was kind of an odd concept. David Fury got the nod to write the script, and I remember clearly one day in the writers' room, we were trying to break the story.

Now I'm very much the kind of person where you just keep going wherever the story goes. You know it's going to end up in the weeds at some point and you'll pull it back. I'm sure David is that way, too, but for whatever reason on that particular day he turned to me and said, "I don't get this. I don't understand what this story is about." I said, "Well, David, I don't think any of us do. That's kind of the point of why we're here, trying to break this." But then I realized later that there was a bigger issue going on. I got the sense that David was not particularly happy with my presence there. I could be completely reading into that, and I have nothing but respect for David—he's obviously a very accomplished and talented writer—but for whatever reason, there was an issue there.

STEVEN S. DEKNIGHT

I remember I was on set for the first day of shooting on that season premiere. David Simkins and I were on set. Then he left to go back to the office. A couple of hours later I got a call that he had been let go. They had Jeff Bell step in as kind of an interim show runner, although, of course, in classic fashion they wouldn't give him the title until the next season. I can't say enough good things about Jeff Bell. Gracious, calm, good humored, just really lovely. He got everything dumped on top on him and just executed the season wonderfully in my opinion.

DAVID SIMKINS

So David wrote the outline for episode three, which got approved. Then he wrote the script and delivered it. It was the first script coming in under my tenure, so I was very nervous about it and was already predisposed to be very hypercritical of the draft. I'd never worked with David before, I didn't know his writing process, and I just wasn't sure about it, so I gave the draft to a couple of veteran *Angel* writers on the sly to read and to come to me. I just needed somebody to give me some kind of barometer. The reading I got from them was *not* positive. It concerned me to the point where I went to Tim and said, "I'm not sure about this. What should I do?" Tim and Joss were up to their eyeballs with *Firefly* and I felt terrible about bringing them into this question, because it wasn't your job to do that. It was my job to make that decision, but I thought out of deference to David I needed to go a little higher up the food chain and get an opinion. And the opinion I got was that the script was fine. That's what I needed to know.

The next day at the office, I got a call from my agent and was told that I was being let go. It was shocking. I was not prepared for that. Joss called me later in the day when he had the time to tell me he was sorry, and he apologized for the situation, but added, "I just don't have time to teach you how the show works." I was like, "OK." I hung up the phone, packed up my stuff, and left.

DAVID GREENWALT

(consulting producer/cocreator)

I happen to know Simkins before and after that. A great guy and good writer, but not a Joss fit. Or not an *Angel* fit. I remember he had a few issues with something we were breaking, and he goes to talk to Joss about his issues. Next day, he's gone. I left and it fell to Jeff Bell's very capable shoulders. For Simkins, it was an impossible situation. There are just certain people who fit in that Joss mold, in that Joss world, and certain others did not, and never the twain shall meet. Edgar Allan Poe would've done really well there. But it was not his fault in any way, shape, or form; they should've given it to Jeff in the first place anyway. I don't know if they went for Simkins because he had more experience running a show or something.

JOSS WHEDON

(executive producer/cocreator, *Angel*)

David Simkins had a deal with the network. He's a smart guy, and I thought I'd give him a shot.

DAVID SIMKINS

I honestly think it would have been tough for *anyone* to come in there and try to figure out how the show worked. I didn't think it's about the show mechanics itself; it was about the personalities involved. Those guys were working together for so long [that] they all understood each other, and I just don't think there was any time. Especially for them. They had a lot going on. It was just easier for them to go on. And once they brought me in out of deference to the studio, then it was OK if they let me go. They tried, right? They were going to do it the way they wanted to. I get that, but I wish I'd listened to my inner warning system at the very beginning. I wished Joss well, hoped the season would be fantastic, and went off and did something else.

ELIZABETH CRAFT
(staff writer, *Angel*)

Part of the problem, in David Simkins's defense, is Joss was *so* busy at the time. It's not like he had a lot of time to spend with David, you know? You needed someone who could literally know what Joss would like and what he wouldn't. And coming from the outside, that's very difficult. Jeff Bell had been there, so it just was so much easier for Jeff to know what kind of things Joss responds to. And from our staff-writer perspective, it was terrifying. We were like, "Oh my God, we're going to be swept out." But in the midst of all this, Joss came in hours after the David Simkins situation went down. He was like, "Just so you know, everything is fine." [*laughs*]

SARA FAIN
(staff writer, *Angel*)

"You're not going to be out of here, so you can just relax." It was actually really thoughtful of him.

JOSS WHEDON

Honestly, who's going to walk into David Greenwalt's job and just be able to do it? It's a nearly impossible task. We'd hoped there would be a fit somewhere, but there wasn't and we sort of took care of it sooner rather than later, just because we needed to get the process working with the people who do it. It seemed abrupt and I felt bad that I put him in that position. It's a one-in-fifty chance that there was going to be a match there, like a marrow donor, and it didn't work.

CHARISMA CARPENTER
(actress, Cordelia Chase)

With season four, I felt that the Three Stooges—the main men who ran our shows and made it great—all left. David Greenwalt left to do *Miracles,* and I missed him terribly. My character missed him. Tim Minear wrote great stuff for Cordelia, but then he left to work on *Firefly.* And Joss had already been busy with other things for a while, although I knew he always had his hand in things, overseeing story lines and deciding what happens when, and the others would make it happen. Those decisions were obviously his and very important and key and brilliant, but without those three, how could the show possibly be the same? How could it *not* suffer?

TIM MINEAR

(consulting producer, *Angel*)

I had a hand in breaking stories pretty consistently through episode seven or eight. Then after I finished working on *Firefly*, I came back from episode fifteen, which was the last episode with Faith. I wrote that story with Mere Smith, and then did the season finale. When David Greenwalt left, there was much involvement on my part, and then *Firefly* eventually completely took over and I sort of abandoned them. That was actually a word that was bandied about.

Embracing the show for the first time was actor turned director Sean Astin (*The Goonies*, the *Lord of the Rings* trilogy), who helmed season four's "Soulless," an Angelus-centric episode.

SEAN ASTIN

(director, "Soulless")

I played in a friendly card game with a couple of writers—doesn't that sound like the start of an action movie? I was the actor in the writer card game, so they were really happy to take my money all the time. I was back from New Zealand and shooting *Lord of the Rings* and was reacclimating to American life with things like this card game. I really wanted to roll my sleeves up and get in the hour-drama directing chair. Basically, I draped myself over David Greenwalt, who would act nice even though he'd taken most of my money, and refused to let him leave our friend's house until he had promised me something. Anything. And he said, "Well, you can come and shadow Tim Minear, because we don't just hand out episodes like Chiclets. You have to be part of the show." So I followed Tim around learning what I needed to.

Angel was in its sweet spot. It was season four. The characters were well established; the way it was photographed had a very distinct look; the actors knew their thing. Basically the show was a well-oiled machine. Or a train going down the tracks and basically for a guest director to step in, it's like, "Oh, hey, can you be a conductor for a little bit," and your job is to not crash the train. Just let the train keep going in the direction it's going. There are little ways in which you can put your own stamp on it, but you know, you're not going to come in and reenvision. What I like about television compared to features is the pace. It moves a little faster.

My episode was a bottle show. There was one day out on location, to a house in downtown L.A. where there is a big mass murder. We also did a couple of vamp fights, which I loved. I love shooting the vampire fight sequences and I pretty quickly grasped how the visual effects guys were doing the dusting, when they "poof" a vampire. They hit them with the thing and they just dissolve or whatever. So just working with the stunt guys and working with the visual effects guys, I found that really fun. The rest of the time we were down in the basement of the hotel, with Angelus in a cell. David Boreanaz was great for the first two days, and then at the end of the third day of being in a four-by-four cell, he had this look in his eyes like, "OK, we need to *not* be doing this anymore."

Even with personnel in place, season four was a challenge in more ways than just an occasionally bored vampire. Season three had ended on a cliffhanger, with Angel sunk to the bottom of the ocean and Cordelia having ascended to a higher plane, though the rest of Team Angel—with the exception of the lying and duplicitous Connor—have no idea where either of them are. Angel's disappearance is resolved when Wesley, with a coerced Justine, puts clues together, locates the container, and rescues Angel and returns him to the hotel.

Eventually Cordelia, who had been helplessly watching matters unfold, also finds herself returned to the hotel, but with no memory of anyone. And *that* is just the start in a season that goes pretty far out there: an apocalypse is rising because of the birth of Connor—who never should have been brought into existence in the first place; the "Beast" for a time blots out the sun (thus giving full rein to vampires and demons); when the world seems to be ending, Cordelia, trying to give Connor something real to believe in, decides to sleep with him, which Angel witnesses; Angel's soul is taken through mystical means, and he becomes Angelus, in the belief the team can get some clues about the Beast; Angelus escapes; Faith is recruited by Wesley to break out of prison to help capture Angelus (which she does after what can best be described as an acid trip); Cordelia is pregnant, apparently with Connor's child, and the child's gestation is happening extremely quickly; Cordelia is manipulating Connor against his father; Willow uses magic to restore Angel's soul; the Beast is beaten, the sun begins to shine again, and Cordelia gives birth to a goddess named Jasmine (Gina Torres) before slipping into a coma; Jasmine seemingly brings peace and tranquility to everyone, though she hides her true nature (and the fact that she has to eat people to survive). All told, a simply insane year of storytelling, much of it triggered by the fact that in real life actress Charisma Carpenter had become pregnant, and the writers—who had intended on making Cordelia the Big Bad—were put into a corner so that, in essence, both Cordelia *and* Charisma gave birth to Jasmine.

Probably the most grounded relationship came from the romance between Fred and Gunn that heats up until the episode "Supersymmetry," where Fred wants revenge against her former professor, who purposely sent her to Pylea. Ultimately, she changes her mind, but Gunn steps in for her. That murder creates an unmovable wedge between them. Gradually, a relationship starts between Fred and Wesley.

J. AUGUST RICHARDS
(actor, Charles Gunn)

That change, I thought, was fantastic. I thought it was heartbreaking and fun. The killing of the professor character was probably the hardest scene I shot my entire time on *Angel*, because it was nearly impossible. There was so much that was not there that was happening. There was so much that had to be created. We had to talk loud even though it was quiet. That's just something I remember being very difficult.

Every season on *Angel* I remember specifically there being one day a year that I was afraid to go to work, because I was being asked to do something I didn't know if I knew how to do. One season I had to juggle in a scene. They offered to get me a stuntman, but up until that point I had done most of my own stunts, and I didn't want to stop there. I had a week to learn how to juggle and I did and it went great. In season five I had to do a scene with myself, and that was in the White Room with Joss directing.

Again, talking about great notes, he was giving me notes that I don't know if anybody else would understand, but he and I had a shorthand, I guess, or at least were on the same planet, because I know what he means. We do the scene a couple of times where I was with myself in the White Room, and the last take he said, "Now this time give me a little Laurence Fishburne and a little Southern preacher." I knew what he meant and we did it, and it was great. A lot of the work I'm most proud of is stuff that he's directed me in.

JOSS WHEDON

What was exciting about season three was that for once we weren't going to wrap everything up with a bow, which led to something very exciting to me, because I'd never really done cliffhanger endings. And the beginning of every season is always the hardest part of the season, because you really have to gear up and get people involved. Having solved the problems the season before, you have to introduce new ones. On *Buffy,* every year something is happening in school, but, still, we're always trying to find our footing. On *Angel,* season four we came in swinging, because we had already had all of this unresolved, exciting stuff.

STEVEN S. DEKNIGHT

I enjoyed the hell out of season four, and I even have some fond memories that aren't up on screen. Like the first episode where they dredge Angel out of the box at the bottom of the ocean. Originally he was supposed to have a beard he had grown, because he was down there for so long. We did makeup tests of David in the beard and raggedy clothes . . . I really wish I had a copy of this. My first reaction was he looked like the guy from *Monty Python's Flying Circus* who's on screen right before the music starts. And something I'd written in that episode was a whole bit we couldn't afford where Angel breaks out of the box at the bottom of the sea, and, after struggling through most of the episode, he swims to the top and breaks the water, but it's daylight and he gets incinerated. *Then* he realizes he's still in the box. I always regretted not being to shoot that bit.

JOSS WHEDON

What I came to at the start of season four was, "So *that's* why people always do cliffhangers. It makes everything much easier." As a result, with season four we just went to the mattresses. It was as twisted as you could imagine, and everything about it just excited me.

CHARISMA CARPENTER

It's weird, my stomach totally turns when I think about the relationship between Connor and Cordelia. I liked him as a person and everything, and I liked working with Vincent, but I didn't like my character being with him. It's icky to kiss someone else when you're pregnant. It's got to be icky for him, too. But if Angel and Cordelia had gotten together, that would have been a big snore fest, so what else were the writers going to do? . . . But Jesus, Mary, and Joseph, that whole season was rough. Like I said, I was pregnant, and we were doing these continuous episodes and my belly is growing and I was in the same costume—and it was *wow*! That was tough.

DAVID BOREANAZ
(actor, Angel)

The relationship between Angel and Connor was pretty volatile. Surprisingly, Vince and I, we always kind of laughed and said we'd like to do more scenes together where we're kind of more together, a father-son relationship, and build on that. But *then* he had to go off and screw my girlfriend. That was all wrong as far as Angel was concerned; that was just kind of weird.

KELLY A. MANNERS
(producer, *Angel*)

What's interesting is that in season four Charisma was going to become the evil character. Joss had broken the story arc, but about a month before we started, Charisma walked in and goes, "Oh, by the way, I'm pregnant." Joss almost tripped over. That's how Gina Torres came to be on the show as Jasmine. *That* threw a big wrench into Joss's plans. I thought he was going to cry, because it had to change his whole vision for that season. I know Joss loved having Gina; I think she brought quite a bit to the show. Like I said, she was a life vest because Joss's vision got fucked up. I think in a way she saved that season.

DAVID FURY

Charisma felt that everyone got angry at her over her pregnancy, and she's not wrong. I'm not going to say that I had a particular problem with her pregnancy, but the thing with Charisma is she led her life as she wanted to without considering ramifications on her role on the shows. For instance, she wound up getting a bunch of tattoos and one of them was a cross that was on her wrist. And I'm going, "You got a tattoo of a cross on your wrist when you're on a vampire show, and crosses have an effect on them? We have to hide that now." It's little things like that. These seem like little things. By all means she has the right to have a child, and I have no idea what the circumstances were, but it wasn't timed well. It *wasn't* timed to help us with production and allow us to write around it.

CHARISMA CARPENTER

My pregnancy in season four, that was a fucking mess. That whole season I wish I could undo or redo; that was kind of when the wheels went off. They didn't know I was pregnant; for whatever reason, over the summer I wasn't able to reach Joss to tell him. Then finally my agent told Kelly Manners and I got a call from Joss. The plan for the character was to go a different way, and then with the pregnancy news it was such a wrench that it changed *everything.* He said, "I have to change the entire season!" Now I don't know how much of that was just him being pissed off, disappointment, or if it genuinely was, "Oh, fuck," because there are lots of times where you just work with someone being pregnant or around it—you stand behind a desk or whatever. Maybe for my character, who was kind of sexy and was never behind a counter, and wearing midriffs and tank tops, maybe that just didn't work.

AMY ACKER
(actress, Fred)

That wasn't my favorite story line, but there are a lot of pieces in that I really like, like when Gina was on. You know, that was when Charisma was not sure if she was coming back, so I think the story kind of came with them figuring out what she was going to do. She was pregnant, so that was kind of a surprise, trying to work in this whole thing. That probably wasn't the original master plan for the show. It was sort of determined by circumstances. They made it work.

CHARISMA CARPENTER

I honestly have compassion, because I can't imagine being a storyteller and having a vision and working so hard on that idea and then, you know, the actor is throwing you for a loop and you have to adjust accordingly. I didn't really show for the first six months, but I was definitely working a lot of hours and having some side effects, so it became a concern, but, like I said, I have compassion for them *and* compassion for myself as well. I was in my thirties and had been with my partner for a really long time, had gotten pregnant, so that is my life and a forever thing. Acting is what I did for a living, so for me I was really torn. Not on whether or not to keep the baby, of course, but the fact that it was not greeted as good news. That the people I'd spent seven years with were left feeling like they were in a bind. And I'm such a people pleaser and spent so much time trying to do my best, because I'm not the smartest on set and it's very difficult for me to memorize lines and I had to work twice as hard as everyone else. So with that need to please, and the fact that nobody wants to be the bearer of bad news, it was unfortunate that it was seen in that way. And for it to have ultimately felt like a choice or sacrifice for anyone, that the truth is you *can't* have it all, was disappointing and a really big life lesson. And also it was difficult to be in the moment of being pregnant and to enjoy that process, because for the first six months I worked. And in the last trimester we had to make concessions for the schedule. Well, it is what it is, and I really think it affected my relationships with those people in a way. Of course, my son is worth it, but there's a sadness there as well that I'll probably always carry about that time.

DAVID FURY

There was a lot of rejiggering of thoughts about where the characters should be at this point and arcs of relationships. It just threw everything out the window. And these things happen all the time. You know, when Seth Green left *Buffy*, he was a big part of the show and then suddenly he left and we had to write him off, but that helped us introduce Tara. So some of these things worked out well, but we weren't looking to write off Charisma. She was very much a big part of the show, and having to suddenly present her pregnancy on the show and explain it . . . well, these are things that make it tricky for us, that's all. It wasn't for me to decide. All I'm told is the parameters of what I'm writing. "You don't have Charisma." Or, "You've got to use Charisma minimally." Or so and so has hurt his leg; he has to be sitting through the whole episode. Weird stuff, and you go, "OK, I'm going to go write that." I don't really involve myself with the personal lives, but, hey, it keeps things interesting.

JOSS WHEDON

The evil Cordelia was something we had been planning for a while, but not the Cordelia-being-pregnant part of the story. Season four saw a cap—except for one episode of season five—of the Cordelia arc. The thing with Cordelia that was beautiful is that I got to tell the Buffy story from the movie, which I could never tell on the series. The idea of the movie was that this girl is a ditz, because nobody has ever asked her to be anything else. When you actually put it to her, when there's more required of her, she steps up, she becomes stronger, she becomes interesting, and she becomes a hero. That's sort of what we got to do with Cordelia, but once that's done and she's having a baby, it's coma time. Can you squeeze more milk from something usually? Yes, but we really resolved what we wanted to do with the character and because we knew we had to have her go for a period, because of circumstances, it just felt right to wrap it up and move on to new things—which we did with season five.

CHARISMA CARPENTER

They *had* to write Cordelia out? I don't know if I'll ever believe it, but I accept it, although there's a part of me that feels like we were dealing with some of the most creative people that have ever been in TV, and they couldn't figure it out? I don't know. I think I'm a complicated person, I think I'm lovable, I think I tried really hard, but I also think there were things at work, and pressures and insecurities that the job made me feel would rear its head.

By the time I got pregnant, it was seen as the last straw. That's kind of what I suspect was where they were at with that, and it makes me sad. I've had lots of years to reflect on that, and I've seen Joss and Alyson and Alexis, and I saw them at Arizona Comic-Con recently, and they always have the most beautiful things to say about my talent and how amazing I was, and it's sweet and it brought tears to my eyes, because I didn't know they felt that way.

Who knows, maybe they were just being kind, but I really felt nice. And when I saw Joss, it was complicated. Not to say we're not friendly and I wouldn't hug his neck if I saw him tomorrow, but there's this feeling when I walk around him of, Does he think I ruined his TV show? Does he really believe that? And that makes me sad.

DAVID FURY

I don't know what the story direction originally was, but I think in terms of relationships and in terms of development between, say, Angel and Cordelia, it might have gone in a different way had her pregnancy not been introduced into it. It just affects how everyone relates to each other. Sometimes you write yourself into a corner. Here we have a romantic relationship developing between Angel and Cordelia, a love relationship that can never be, because there's no drama in that. Cordelia's back, what's going to be the big problem in getting these kids together? What if she's not herself and she's the one actually plotting Angel's demise? It just creates emotional resonance from the perspective of the fact she's a mother figure to Connor, and the fact that she was a potential lover of Angel. There's just a lot more emotion.

TIM MINEAR

And the audience knows her. It's like when Angel became Angelus on *Buffy,* and suddenly he was the bad guy. One of the other things, too, when we had her ascend to heaven because she was a higher being. I think we ended up hating that and that this was kind of a way to take it back.

DAVID FURY

It was her body being used by this thing, but there's an emotional connection there because you don't know what's going on with her. With the direction Cordelia's character took, it became impossible to bring her back to where she was. To bring her back to just superficial wisecracking Cordy. A lot of people missed that, but we felt we moved her out of that arena. To try and bring her back would be false and fake.

JEFFREY BELL
(co-executive producer, *Angel*)

Cordelia went through an amazingly remarkable arc. She came in as this very sort of self-absorbed cheerleader and wannabe actress and grew in depth and character and became a love interest for Angel. And as people who watched a lot of television will tell you, it's always more interesting if they *don't* quite get together but have the feelings. She kept growing stronger and then there was this whole paranormal thing happening with her that ended with her going away at the end of season three, coming back in season four, and we were excited to think, "Cordelia's the bad guy, or the thing inside Cordelia is the bad guy." We were talking about Angelus and that Faith was going to show up, and we were holding up sparkly things to the fans when we knew that Cordelia was going to kill Wolfram & Hart's Lilah Morgan.

STEPHANIE ROMANOV
(actress, Lilah Morgan)

In the script, they had it that Angel was the one who killed Lilah as Angelus, because they didn't want anyone to know the shock surprise that it was Cordelia. Although *I* knew it was her, it wasn't until the day of shooting that the final page was handed out where it spelled it out. Before it said, "Lilah goes down a hallway and Angelus follows." On that day the rest of the crew got the right script page. I was shocked, *but,* being that I was a Wolfram & Hart gal and everybody else had already gotten killed, I was shocked it went as long as it did. My question was always, "Do I finally get killed in this script?" I figured it was a matter of time, because they were killing off everyone else. I had only auditioned for a guest part, and they just kept adding to it and bringing me back. I never had a deal or anything, so it turned into a much bigger thing than I ever thought it would be.

I actually had a great time doing it. I loved playing Lilah, and that year was probably the most fun for me, because they were writing more for her and season four was the only year that we got to see some colors. That was always frustrating to me. Being there as part of the law firm, it was basically playing the same scene over and over again. But they always gave me the really fun lines, which is the nice sarcasm that is a joy to play. So I was happy it went as long as it did. Why look a gift horse in the mouth? I enjoyed it, but it was over for me and freed me up to audition for other things, which was OK. To all endings there are beginnings.

CHARISMA CARPENTER

It's hard for me to separate the realities of what was going on and the story line. I liked when Cordelia and Lilah would go head-to-head, but when Cordelia was doing it, because it was the right thing to do. Because she was so evil. Lilah had it coming, but I think that the performance could have been better if I wasn't so caught up in other stuff that was going on at the time, to be honest.

JEFFREY BELL

Trying to make things work with Charisma's pregnancy was tricky. I think we managed to do it and brought Gina Torres in as Jasmine. But I think at the end of the season, when we were needing the Big Bad to battle, Charisma was having a baby, so Gina came in and that worked out really nicely. We couldn't get Charisma back at the end of the season in a meaningful way.

TIM MINEAR

From the beginning, *Angel* had a reputation for the big turn.

CHARISMA CARPENTER

I'm glad to have been part of something so special. Having worked with David, Tim, and Joss heading up the show was a lifetime of lessons and information about writing. I can identify a piece of shit from something else in the writing process. Their work ethic was so strong. I don't know how Joss did it all, and I didn't know how it all turned out for him personally, but I felt really lucky to have been a part of that. It was a very good situation for a very long time, so I feel very lucky to have had that to use as a watermark for the future.

By season four, *Angel* had largely done away with the idea of crossovers with characters from *Buffy the Vampire Slayer* (Faith notwithstanding), but to help conclude season four, Alyson Hannigan's Willow was brought in to work a little of her mojo in fighting off ultimate evil.

JEFFREY BELL

Willow coming over came about because we needed sort of a powerful witch, wizard, magical person. Rather than bring in some guest star to do it, the thought was, "How about Willow?" Alyson came over and really served a huge help for us.

The evil Cordelia story line concludes with her giving birth to the goddess Jasmine, played by *Firefly*'s Gina Torres. This was also where Ben Edlund made his first major contribution as the writers were trying to solve the Jasmine threat.

DAVID FURY

We knew Cordelia was coming back from her ascension and that it wouldn't be entirely her. What we *didn't* know was how we were going to climax the season in what would have been a fight between a nine-month-pregnant lady and Angel. We figured she would give birth around episode eighteen or so, so we debated for a long time on how to work the pregnancy in. We'd already done Cordelia demonically pregnant, we had Darla, so what we realized was that whatever she gave birth to would have to be the Big Bad. But it wasn't until we were breaking the specific stories later on that we realized that our first idea, that the Big Bad might be a powerful guy, would work better if it was a woman. And not some big evil woman, but, instead, someone *wonderful*. She was going to bring peace and tranquility to the world, which was a big twist after the Beast. And she had a genuine point to make in her logic of giving the world peace—admittedly, without free will. There was a Garden of Eden parable there in the idea of, "You get to live in the Garden of Eden, but *I* make the rules and you can't choose to eat this apple."

BEN EDLUND

When I came in, they were still working hard on figuring out the Jasmine story line and how the mechanics of that were going to work with the cults. They brought Zoe from *Firefly* over to be Jasmine, so it was fun. It was a family affair. I helped Jeff Bell, who was running *Angel* at that point, break an episode he was going to work on called "Magic Bullet," if I'm not mistaken. I was raring to go. We sat down, and I felt like I was very handy in that break coming in from an outside point of view. Everyone had been in the same loops they'd been in for a season, so I had just come out and suddenly sat down and it was my job to assess where they were, try to possibly offer another pair of eyes. I was able to see a few things that turned out to be useful solutions. Part of it was the question of how to make it so that someone who had fallen for Jasmine could be woken up again. And my solve was you needed the blood of Cordelia.

TIM MINEAR

There were a lot of changes made because of Charisma's pregnancy. One example is that we had wanted Cordelia to come out of her coma in "Peace Out" and for *her* to be the one to put her fist through Jasmine's skull rather than Connor, but she couldn't work the kind of hours that were necessary. She *could* come in and be in a coma.

The other part of putting an end to Jasmine required, in the episode "Sacrifice," for Angel to travel to another dimension for answers. Edlund, who wrote the episode, believes that it captured just how insane—in the best possible way—*Angel* was as a series. Its insanity is particularly evident when Angel, a vampire, stands before crab-humanoid hybrids to find the solution to remove a goddess.

BEN EDLUND

It was all very, very nuts [*laughs*]. At *Firefly* and also at *Angel*, I had a tendency to do a lot of drawings, predesigning, while I was writing. Not to diminish all of the amazing foundational work done by the people who really had to do that stuff, but I draw *a lot*. So it was really enjoyable to be able to collaborate on that and throw in on the process to design this creature. And that shit is so over the top—*Angel* is great that way. *Angel* would do things no other show would do. Like Ray Harryhausen crap with these creatures. You know what I mean? Most shows just shirk away from that and go, "We're not going to get involved in that, it's too ambitious, it's going to look like crap." I *like* how it looks, even if it looks a bit computery and dated. I remember watching Ray Harryhausen when I was younger. *Star Wars* had come out, and then you would watch *Sinbad* and it was *still* cool. *Star Wars* blew it away, stripped the doors off it, and I *still* liked *Sinbad*, because I liked that little homunculus, or the little Pegasus, or whatever the hell they had. All that stuff was great. I feel that you can still have a design that feels good even if the CG is wherever it's at for the time. You can still have a sequence that's developed with filmmaking in mind, even if it's jittery and jumpy. It still does something. It's even more lovable, like the way Wes Anderson uses animation in *The Life Aquatic*.

The show in general and that sequence—Angel in the other dimension—was so hard-core in its fantasy. I loved being able to do stuff like the guy going to the humans, "You can't go there, because your little mouse lungs won't even take the atmosphere. It takes a dead man to go there." Those are things that are just woven down deep into this shit. You could also make a whole movie where the whole point is, "It takes a dead man to go there." But we're doing eighteen thousand things at once. At the end of the episode, they're like, "You gotta go, man, it takes a dead man to go there." But that's also while there's a hive mind being formed and a massive battle between the full cast and all of these National Guard dudes that Jasmine is running, and then she's taking all the wounds from the battle of the others . . . and *laughing* about it. So there's, like, six different genre overnotes going at once. I thought it was a good demonstration of where *Angel* had gotten up to, and running from that in year five we went from a Nazi-submarine episode to Angel turning into a puppet. The show was, like, a feast of crazy.

With dessert still to come after Jasmine's defeat. Her followers, without her, feel lost and are filled with despair, having believed they were experiencing pure joy. Connor, who always recognized Jasmine for what she was, now has nothing. Flipping out, he takes hostages—including the still-comatose Cordelia—in a condemnation of *everything*. Angel sets out to stop him, and seemingly fulfills the season-three prophecy of the father killing the son. In "reality," an alternative timeline is created (through a deal struck between Angel and Wolfram & Hart—in which Angel takes over the Los Angeles office of the firm, explored fully in season five). According to this timeline, Connor is a perfectly normal teenager being raised as part of a family. As far as the rest of the world (sans Angel, in an echo of season one's "I Will Remember You") is concerned, the son of vampires Angel and Darla never existed.

JEFFREY BELL

We were trying to be true to his character. As such, we didn't give him a break and ultimately realized there was no way to bring him into normal society, thus Angel's sacrificial decision at the end of the year, which I found emotional. That was the perfect payoff for that character.

TIM MINEAR

Connor's fate was something we discussed before the character was cast. We knew we were going to go to that sort of epic, mythic place with father and son. It was in season three that I had the prophecy "the father will kill the son," and that was a place we were really considering going. What we *didn't* know was the way that it would ultimately shake out. We decided that we didn't want Angel to kill Connor in way that *he* would kill him, so this was a good alternative. The whole notion of taking away free will in exchange for happiness, and Angel fighting against that and, in the end, doing that for his kid . . . that had an irony that I loved.

VINCENT KARTHEISER

I knew people were reacting really strongly to Connor, but I didn't know why, because I didn't know the show's history. To me, the character lost its thrill about four episodes in. From there on out, I felt like I was doing the same scene over and over and over.

CHARISMA CARPENTER

I remember that! It made everyone absolutely nuts!

BEN EDLUND

Something didn't quite satisfy with that character. I do remember there being kind of a fan reaction where they were not behind him, really. I don't think the writers loved him necessarily in terms of the net results of what they had written and what ended up on the screen. They were looking to figure out how to make him work the best way he could for their purposes.

VINCENT KARTHEISER

Every week I'd show up and have a scene with Cordelia, then Angel would show up and I'd have some sort of conflict with him. There'd be a couple of fight scenes where I'd fight with them, even though I didn't want to, and then I would sulk and leave. That to me was every episode, and ultimately they wrote him into a corner. There was nowhere for him to go. I think the majority of the fans really hated Connor and hated me and getting me off the show was the highest priority. And I don't blame them.

DAVID FURY

In "Peace Out," I got to give Connor a monologue to Cordelia's comatose corpse or whatever it was. With it, I was trying to buy back some feeling for him. People became very annoyed with his character and he was whiny and repetitive. In that speech I tried to kind of remind people he's this lost kid. I was trying to give a lot of empathy back to him, to allow people to kind of at least not hate him. I tried to give him a little speech that I thought gave him some humanity and made the character a little more three-dimensional. I felt like it was partially successful. And then of course he leaves the next episode where Angel gives him a new life.

Connor's speech is almost like my way of apologizing to the audience and he was kind of a pawn in this. It was kind of like, "This is all the things that's happened. I was stuck in a hell dimension and I'm kind of the victim of my circumstances." But doing it in a way that I thought was giving him some dimension. Steve DeKnight and I wrote "Awakening," and we got to do the whole fantasy thing of Connor and Angel united in battle against the Beast. I was able to avoid a lot of those episodes that had to dive so heavily into that Connor and Cordelia dynamic that people hated so much, so I feel like I dodged a bullet a little bit.

BEN EDLUND

Maybe Connor kept doing shit that was almost too profane to the characters the fans loved. This is just an opinion, but maybe he became an expresser of something that happens on a show in later seasons. It's strange, but as much as you get into a show and you do it for a long time, and there's a substantial church of love for the characters that gets built, there's an inverse of resentment built toward them. You have to be their gods from that point forward. They won't do anything without your sweat. After five years, the idea of a little punk kid coming back and fucking up the universe can be disproportionately alluring, because of elements that are inside the people creating the universe that they don't even know they might be expressing. I felt like in *Supernatural* there was a season there, in the latter part I was involved with, where we tore away everything from the main characters. Almost because we wanted to tear down the show. You know, because you're, like, "*Fuck,* this keeps going. What Jenga blocks do you pull away?" It is now a massive continent in our consciousness of what genre is and yet strangely hidden from the American populous. It's a world cult with 61 million people watching. Though I guess that's not on point.

STEVEN S. DEKNIGHT

I thought the whole concept of Connor was a fascinating idea. To start with, going all the way back to where Connor was born, that great Tim Minear episode in the alley where Darla stakes herself to give birth to this impossible baby. Then having the baby stolen and coming back older, wanting to kill Angel. The whole dynamic with Angel was great. Vincent Kartheiser was just an absolute joy to work with. He was so talented. And I loved where the whole thing ended up with Angel giving him up so he can have a life. It was just *so* painful.

BEN EDLUND

With everything that happened to him, I remember feeling that the one thing we were not going to be able to do was have Angel become angelic again, really. They had run that course, so he had to be postjoy almost at that point. And then become, like, heavy is the head that wears the crown. What a weird show.

JEFFREY BELL

As we were talking about what to do in year four, we came up with the idea that when Cordy comes back, it's not Cordy. It's this other thing. We knew we wanted to deal with the apocalypse. We had been talking about one for three years, and it felt like it was time that we should have one. But when we started, I don't think we had any idea that the show was going to be as serialized as it became in season four. *Entertainment Weekly* decided to list what was good and what was bad about the show. What was bad was that if you haven't watched from the beginning, it's like coming in at page 262 of a Stephen King novel—and that was an accurate criticism.

Now if you were inside the *Angel* umbrella, season four was the most emotionally satisfying year we ever had. But if you were outside of it, it was kind of cool and interesting, but the response was, "I don't know what the hell is going on, so I'm going to go and watch *The Bachelor*." It became too serialized, even for us. What we found out is that when you're telling a story that way, and you tell a stand-alone episode that doesn't address the central story, people say, "How can you do that? There's an apocalypse going on."

Also, our gang got their ass kicked almost every week. They constantly lost. They just rarely had any kind of victory at all. It was this sort of very dark, very linear type of storytelling. It was really a result of that one decision of let's host an apocalypse.

More than at any other time in its history, the future of *Angel* was uncertain toward the end of season four, the staff having to work harder than ever before to convince executives at the WB that the show should be renewed.

TIM MINEAR

The first thing I did was to sit down with one of our editors and we put together a clip package that ran about four and a half minutes. The idea was to show the executives all of the cool stuff we'd done over the past four years. We didn't assume *for a moment* that the network actually watched the show, so we wanted to prove to them that it was cool.

DAVID FURY

The funny thing is that we sat there, the people who actually made the show, and as we watched the clip package, we were saying, "Dear God, we do a *really* cool show. To achieve this kind of production value for the amount of money we have, it's like a movie." At the same time, we knew that we had to shake things up a bit to convince them.

TIM MINEAR

Joss had the idea of them taking over Wolfram & Hart before that meeting, but we showed them this clip reel; we took in reviews; there was a lot of great press about *Angel* at that point. So Joss, David, Jeff Bell, and myself pitched to them where we wanted to take the show in the fifth season. We decided that the season finale would actually serve as a pilot of sorts for what would happen the following year. We had to do that at the end of each year, laying out where we wanted the characters and arcs to go. But this was more drastic. This approach answered any concerns on the network's part that the show was too arcy, too soapy. The idea with them taking over Wolfram & Hart was that viewers could just tune in and understand it.

BEN EDLUND

What Angel does with Wolfram & Hart is selfish in a way, but it's a chance to minimize the harm *he's* inflicted on the world. And there's a lot of Faustian shit going on at the end of season four, but it's OK. *Angel* ultimately functions on tragic lives. Tragedy: you always know what's coming.

L.A. LAW

"I kind of want to slay the dragon. . . ."

The seeds for the fifth season of *Angel* were planted at the end of the fourth when Angel, in an effort to give his son, Connor, a *true* life, made a deal with Wolfram & Hart to provide an alternative reality for him. The price was that, in the aftermath of Jasmine, Angel would take over the Los Angeles office of the firm. Presented by the late Lilah Morgan as a "reward," there was obviously some sort of catch, though each member of Team Angel came into it believing they could nonetheless use the firm to fight evil from within. Angel's in charge, with Fred heading up science, Lorne taking on the entertainment division, Gunn (thanks to mental enhancement) made an uberlawyer, and Wesley in charge of archives.

These changes in the show, on a surface level, provided an opportunity to explore the nature of evil in a different vein, but more practically they had a lot to do with the struggle to get a fifth season renewal and with the need to cope with budget cuts.

KELLY A. MANNERS
(producer, *Angel*)

Before season five, Joss called me up and said they want to cut the budget if we're to go another season. He said, "Can we do it for two million an episode," which is plenty when I think back. I said, "We can't make the show we've been making for two million an episode, but we can make *a* show," and I actually thought season five was one of the better seasons. The big challenge, of course, was in tearing down another permanent set and then, with a reduced budget, to have another million-dollar set go up on a budget that's been severely cut as it is. That was my biggest concern.

STUART BLATT
(production designer, *Angel*)

Wolfram & Hart became the Big Bad, but on the surface they appeared to be a big law firm or advertising agency. And Joss wanted a set where you could wander from room to room to room, because he opened the season in that set with a long Steadicam shot. The large part of the set was the two-story lobby, which had Harmony outside of Angel's office, and then a lot of miscellaneous offices and hallways that went into Fred's lab. We had Fred's lab on another stage, and then there was a basement where we had holding cells. *So* many opportunities there.

JOSS WHEDON
(executive producer/cocreator, *Angel*)

The thing is, the debate about whether or not the show would come back was a money thing. The fact is, the junior executives at the network really cared about the show. But when you get up to the world of president Jamie Kellner, it's all about numbers. I was told that they would fight for the show and fight for a lead-in that makes sense. For them to take their biggest honking hit at the time, which was *Smallville,* and put it in front of *Angel* was a vote of confidence. And it showed that where it counts among the creative execs, it wasn't about money: it was about programming. And I really appreciated that.

KELLY A. MANNERS

I'm the money guy, so everything for me was how the hell are we going to do this and how are we going to do it for the money and working hard with the writers to try to keep them in reality as to how much we could do for the money we had. Surprisingly enough, like I said, I really loved the season. They had to really think about it when they were writing as well.

JOSS WHEDON

During season four, of which I'm very proud, at one point we were like, "Are we making *24*?" The events of the episodes seemed to happen in a two-week period. It played as this one dramatic arc. We all came out saying we had to shake up the paradigm. We had the characters we needed, but there wasn't enough for them. Somewhere in the middle of the season, I said, "Say, what if they actually *ran* Wolfram and Hart?" The exciting thing about it is not only the question of moral compromise, but the actual relatable question of, "I worked for Greenpeace, but now I work for Shell." So we then had the chance to get into different stories and milieus, and B stories—there was just a new kind of energy that wasn't so completely internal.

DAVID FURY
(executive producer, *Angel*)

The logical thing is good trying to defeat evil, but Joss would always say, "No, there has to be a balance, and it's much easier to balance evil when you're running evil. When you're the guys who run it, you can keep the balance going. You know you won't ever destroy it. Good will never defeat evil, but there has to be a balance. Without the balance, evil wins, or there's chaos," which essentially happens at the end of the series.

JEFFREY BELL
(executive producer/show runner, *Angel*)

Previously, we had been in the hotel. We were a family with everybody kind of living there. Gunn had been dating Fred, Wesley was around all the time, Lorne was living in the hotel, Angel was living there. They were all sort of there. It was very much a family dynamic. But suddenly we were in a big, corporate office. We were all grown up. It was like the difference between Buffy in high school and Buffy going away to college.

STEVEN S. DEKNIGHT

(supervising producer, *Angel*)

When I heard that idea from Joss, I thought, "Holy shit, that's brilliant." To be co-opted by your enemy; to basically say, "OK, we've been fighting you all this time. You think you can do better? Here are the keys." They go into it knowing it's a trap, knowing that Wolfram & Hart is up to something, but exactly what, they don't know."

BEN EDLUND

(supervising producer, *Angel*)

It was a very interesting way to solve what was becoming diminishing returns on premise. Yet they had all this cool stuff and Wolfram & Hart was one of the most interesting elements, with the idea of the Senior Partners and the Powers That Be and all that stuff. That was a really interesting way of playing out that shit. By the time you got to the end of season four of this crazy-ass show, what I really liked was that Wolfram & Hart was immense in their thinking. They were playing such a bizarre game. I understood that; it was like Angel understood that they legitimately were playing a cosmic sort of gambit. Of maybe good left unmolested trying to do its best job to make things better would achieve more evil than us working 24-7 against them. Just give them the reins. I felt like the idea at the heart of it, Wolfram & Hart's philosophy, was that they really felt the road to hell might be paved with good intentions, so they should give this over to people with good intentions and get it done faster.

JOSS WHEDON

The question of why Wolfram & Hart had given them the opportunity is one we were not going to answer in the first episode. They had an entire corporation under their control dedicated toward evil. Ultimately, there were questions that would definitely run through the entire season; we definitely kept the arc–soap opera nature that, quite frankly, was what we did well and loved. At the same time, we did them around episodes that would resolve themselves.

BEN EDLUND

Wolfram & Hart were not into Jasmine; she was an interloper to their plans. And then Angel took her out, and they sort of realized, "All right, then." It changed their thinking about what Angel was for them. What I liked was, as big as you could make your thinking as the protagonist, this particular villain who was the uberlawyer had the long-arc view. The uberlawyer had a bigger philosophy and a deeper, more jaded, darker, more cynical relationship to good versus evil than anyone could imagine. No investment in it. No interest. No ideological approach: "We need the humans, we'll heal in the face of this." All they wanted was some kind of inscrutable, horrific thing. In my mind, they just wanted hell on earth. They wanted the worst thing for people, and they thought maybe the best way to get it there was to have people who were trying their best to make the best thing for other people to happen. That was *very* heady shit.

JEFFREY BELL

So our big arc was, "What the hell are we doing here? Why do they have us here? We don't feel corrupted, but have we been corrupted? Have we been compromised beyond what we think?" That was something that, thematically, was in a lot of the episodes. It allowed us to tell stories with a little more scale in terms of the kinds of clients we deal with. We thought that, ultimately, we'd service both sides.

BEN EDLUND

I may not be 100 percent on this, but I'm in the ballpark. It was certainly investigated in the debate between the characters and how they kind of ended up taking the deal. "Even if it's a trap, it might be worth it." That was on screen, watching the characters reason their way into why maybe it's *not* crazy. "It might've helped if they just put the emphasis on that it's not a trap." "I think they really think we're going to make it worse." "I think we'll make it better." "We're willing to take that bet."

STEVEN S. DEKNIGHT

What was fascinating was the insidiousness of the way it slowly starts to dismantle the team and turn them against each other, especially with Gunn, who goes a little bit *Flowers for Algernon*. He gets a taste of what it feels like to be God and then slowly gets it taken away from him. Wesley going dark and stabbing Gunn, obviously the death and resurrection of Fred. There's just so much rich stuff that year.

J. AUGUST RICHARDS
(actor, Charles Gunn)

The only thing nerve-wracking about the whole change for me was that on my very first day back for that season, I had to do my big reveal as a lawyer. I didn't have the rest of the episode to build up to it; I just had to jump right in. That was difficult and I'd never done it before, but it actually turned out well. And it ended up setting me up for a lot of other roles as lawyers. It made me feel confident that I could do it.

JOSS WHEDON

Wolfram & Hart connected everything and made for a really interesting year, but it was never meant to be more than a year. That is to say, even before we were canceled, we said, "OK, this is year five. Year five is about, Can we stay pure in the heart of an evil place? Can we work for an evil corporation and still maintain our integrity? The metaphor and the question of what do they really want, what are they going to do to us, plays for the genuine flat-out suspense and the sort of overarching question of the season. But ultimately that is *not* a two-season question. We had a plan to shake up the paradigm for the next year. Of course, it no longer led to an exciting season six, but it's still a good series capper.

Going along with the reduced budget and the standing sets that most of the episodes would be filmed in was a return to stand-alone storytelling and a bit of a retreat from serialization, which had been *so* pronounced in season four.

TIM MINEAR

(consulting producer, season four, *Angel*)

It's very easy, when you start getting arcy, for things to begin to blur together. The mythology starts to get very convoluted. If the characters start to make references to the actions in previous episodes, then it starts to have no meaning beyond that. The art is then not relating to real life in any way; it's only relating to itself. When a show gets *that* arcy, it's easy for that to happen. Also, unlike *Buffy,* where the metaphor was very clear—the stages of growing up—*Angel* did not have a metaphor, despite attempts to do so at the beginning. It's a melodrama about men and women with a supernatural element—it's *Dark Shadows* in wide screen and color.

JOSS WHEDON

Going more stand-alone was a bizarre kind of symmetry to where we had started. Amazingly enough, we started out doing that and still weren't very good at it. I give you the werewolf episode we did, "Unleashed." Good guest star, good idea, nothing particularly wrong there, except for a failure to make a genuine emotional connection between what was going on with the guest star and our characters themselves. That was a fault of story breaking. And then the incredible amount of money we no longer had, because of budget cuts, really showed up on screen. It got pretty tough. Again, we found our footing as the season progressed. We got better at figuring out how to do stand-alone episodes with characters that we care about that we don't have to explain every single thing about, where we have a "previously on *Angel*" that's forty-five minutes long, as it felt like in season four.

STEVEN S. DEKNIGHT

Season four was like one big episode where you end it at the beginning of the next episode, because we would end on a cliffhanger. So you'd end that at the beginning of the next episode, and spend the next part of act one recapping what happened on the last episode to catch everybody up. That created its own difficulties. Everything was *so* interconnected that it was very difficult to make a move without thinking about the last twelve episodes or something. It was also really impossible to do stand-alone episodes, because we were so arcy, and in year five we went into a more stand-alone feel, which created a new set of problems, more in our brains than anywhere else. It was a different way of breaking a story, which was very challenging at first.

DAVID BOREANAZ
(actor, Angel)

Season four *was* very heavy in exposition, and it was deep with a lot of plotlines and story. In season five we wanted to open it up to more specific character bases and to keep it fresh on that level, rather than keep it so second story. The show worked best when it was about that, when you see each character go about doing their thing. It was interesting to watch. So season four got too serialized, but it did set up that whole Connor-Angel thing and the Cordelia thing. That kind of came to the forefront. It was important to go to those places, because it set up where we were going. That was the exciting part of it.

TIM MINEAR

Even though there's a logic to your audience being your audience when you're telling a story on a TV series, ideally you want it to have enough internal exposition that somebody could start at that place and begin to understand it. By the end of that episode, they start to get it. But that's hard with a story like ours. That's why you want to have a stand-alone episode in most instances. Some things will be arc heavier than others. You can do the episode where Darla goes into labor, she's going to lose the baby, and stakes herself to save the baby—that's what the episode is about. People can understand that story without understanding the entire mythology. Plus, with signposts throughout the story, in terms of internal exposition, you can help guide them through it. But it's tricky. The best example of a TV show that was able to do that, even though it wasn't arcy and it was a sitcom, was *The Mary Tyler Moore Show.* It didn't matter what episode you tuned into, if it was a story that took place in her workplace or home, you very quickly understood who these people were, what their relationships were to one another, and what their attitudes were. To some degree, you have to do that on a show like that.

STEVEN S. DEKNIGHT

But we definitely had to kind of find our way at the start of the season, since it wasn't the kind of storytelling that we were used to. Jeff Bell on *The X-Files* was probably more used to it, although that had been a while earlier. We were definitely trying to find just the right story and tried to figure out how to tell these contained episodes. I know there were episodes we were happy with, but my feeling is that we really started hitting it toward episode eight with the big throw down between Angel and Spike. It felt like it was starting to work.

JEFFREY BELL

The WB wanted more stand-alone episodes, and I'm a guy who really likes stand-alones. So that was the biggest difference in year five, telling more stand-alone type of tales and trying to take the best of what we did in the past in terms of keeping emotional arcs alive, so we were able to tell a whole bunch of different stories: horror, comedy, romance, fable, thriller, romp.

STEVEN S. DEKNIGHT

Because of the change, we got to do what I claim is an underappreciated episode called "The Girl in Question," where Angel and Spike went to Italy and the Italian Wolfram & Hart. They're trying to find Buffy and prove which of the two of them she loved the most. Then they realize that she really shouldn't be with either of them. It was that kind of crazy, kooky buddy-caper comedy that we could slide in there. I don't remember whose idea it was or how we were going to afford it, because we had to shoot a lot on standing sets. Soooo, it's an Italian Wolfram & Hart and the building is exactly the same, except they have Italian people. There's an Italian Wesley, who's never around. I don't know what other show you could do that on. It was just so delightfully wacky.

JEFFREY BELL

It was actually better that we didn't have Sarah on the show. As cool as it would have been, to me what five years of *Angel* was about was *not* whether Buffy would pick Angel or Spike. To bring her in at the end kind of doesn't honor what the five years of the series had been about.

STEVEN S. DEKNIGHT

There was also "Why We Fight," which took place during World War II on a Nazi sub. It felt like the stand-alone approach gave us a renewed vigor. We really felt like we started operating on all cylinders.

JEFFREY BELL

And we were able to have the show stay true to the characters and itself. I mean, we turned Angel into a puppet, we had the Mexican wrestlers . . . we went all over the place, yet [were] always true to the show. I loved that. That was my favorite thing about year five, the diverse kind of stories we'd earned the right to tell.

AMY ACKER
(actress, Fred/Illyria)

For the actors, I don't think there was much of a difference between stand-alone and serialized episodes. Even if there was just a sentence or something that furthered your character in a serialized fashion, it didn't feel like you had just paused everything else to get that. It just felt like that was a snippet of their lives, but it was still moving forward.

JOSS WHEDON

There was another side to it as well. You need the internal dynamic—it's what people love—but at the same time you need a show where if nobody's ever seen it, they can turn it on and not be so caught up in mythos that they're lost. I wanted to keep the serialized arcs in terms of the emotions and the relationships, but turned it back into the kind of show where you could watch an episode, there's a problem, it's resolved, there are outstanding emotional issues, but you have watched an hour and they have finished a case. Not that every episode would be that.

TIM MINEAR

What was needed was mininovels for television. We had some continuing stories in season one, then started to edge toward serialization in season two. In season three we threw in a couple of stand-alone episodes and a few that were stand-alone, but blatantly serviced the arc. My feeling is we became more successful when we said, "Fuck it, it's a novel." People didn't want to read a short story in the middle of a novel. They want to get to the next chapter of the big story, and *Angel* was most successful when it was just balls-out operatic melodrama. But in season five we changed the show significantly. People wouldn't feel like they were coming into the middle of something.

DAVID FURY

It was daunting sending the show in a new direction. Angel always existed in a true private detective paradigm. Cases came to him in different ways, but there was always the detective mystery and a clear moral goal: fight evil. Plus, there was always a "family" dynamic. The hotel was home, and Angel was "father" to his misfit crew.

STEVEN S. DEKNIGHT

What was frustrating for us is that in the early part of the season, the new approach resulted in the numbers going up, but the hard-core fans were complaining a bit about wanting it to be more arc-like, as it had been in previous seasons. You know, where's the Big Bad and that sort of thing? So it was really hard to strike a balance, especially that late in a series where you don't want to alienate the fans but you're trying to pick up new fans.

JEFFREY BELL

What we found is the change allowed us to tell emotionally compelling stories that involved our characters, and we could do that in stand-alone stories. But Wesley still pined for Fred. That didn't go away, so that emotional line was still there. Our characters still had their relationships. The big question for us in year five is we were telling stories from within Wolfram & Hart, our evil law firm.

STEVEN S. DEKNIGHT

What I loved, and this was as true in season five as any other season, was how dark they could take Angel and then, in contrast, how light and fun we could take him. Season five had Ben Edlund's "Smile Time," where we take our dark, brooding hero and turned him into a puppet. No other show could possibly do that.

No other episode is remembered by fans as being the true epitome of the diversity of *Angel*'s storytelling in season five as "Smile Time." Written and directed by Ben Edlund from a Joss Whedon story, the episode has Angel going to the studio of a children's television show that is stealing the life force from children. During his investigation, Angel finds himself transformed into a puppet.

STEVEN S. DEKNIGHT

Ben Edlund is a mad genius, and, quite frankly, the sweetest, most even-tempered person I have ever met in my life. It's like you physically cannot get him upset. I wish I had that in me, because I *do* get upset. I remember we were sitting in a room. I think it was me, Ben, and Jeff Bell. We were talking about the episode that Jeff did with the Mexican wrestler, the Hermanos Numero. Ben, out of nowhere, just says, "How about this? The phone rings and one of the brothers picks up and goes, 'Sí. Sí. Ah, sí.' He hangs up, looks at the other brothers and says, 'The Devil has built a robot.'" We looked at each other and we thought, "How fucking brilliant?" *That* was Ben. He worked on an absolute different plane than anybody else.

BEN EDLUND

"Smile Time" was my directing debut, and it was such a bizarre way to begin; to start with a show and go, "OK, we're not going to do the show that we normally do. We're going to do a show that should be built five feet above the ground, like a puppet show. And we're going to do things that, engineering-wise, have never been done in the pattern of this show, never been done on any show that anyone remembers." So *that* was impressive to me in terms of the challenge. But you couldn't know whether or not it would all fall apart once you started filming a puppet. And then you go, "Holy crap, we were so wrong." Every time we shot, all the dailies looked great. I also got to write all the songs for that episode, which had to be written in, like, three days. I was writing the songs with a guitar, sleeping overnight at Mutant Enemy, working on the script simultaneously, behind deadline, and turned it in with these songs.

So the idea was to make a TV show, a legitimate TV show, with the show that had a writers' room that looked like an actual writers' room, and all of the branding of the show looked like it wasn't just generic throwaway branding. When you see the puppets do their little performances, you really are watching what feels like excerpts from a legitimate ongoing show for kids. For me, that worked and I was happy with it.

STUART BLATT

We had a puppet company design and build the puppets, but we built the whole *Smile Time* theater stage, where all the sets were elevated, just like in *Sesame Street*. The puppets are working above and the puppeteers are standing or at least not laying down, so you can build sets that are four or five feet tall so that the puppeteers can walk underneath them and put their arms up. It was just super fun and creative.

JAMES MARSTERS
(actor, Spike)

They could do something like "Smile Time" because they know they can keep the audience. When you're that good, you can do *anything*. And they just went into doing *everything*. That episode was written by Ben Edlund, who was responsible for *The Tick*, a half-hour animated about mediocre superheroes. One of my favorite cartoons in the world. I remember going to him, because I had been waiting, and I got through one and a half scenes when I was like, "Ben! I'm funny. Come on. Why am I on the sidelines?" I wanted to get right in there, and he was like, "Oh, James, your scene is gonna be just fine for you. Don't worry."

There were numerous changes to the cast in season five. For starters, Charisma Carpenter's Cordelia was still in a coma as a result of events from season four. She did return in "You're Welcome," but at episode's end it was revealed that she had actually died, her visit to advise Angel coming from another plane. Additionally, with the end of *Buffy the Vampire Slayer,* James Marsters's Spike was brought over, now fully souled and after having helped save the world. Initially he's noncorporeal, but several episodes in he's whole again, triggering amazing back-and-forths—both verbally and physically—between him and Angel. On the creative front, the writers were genuinely pissed that the WB spoiled the fact that Marsters was joining the show, taking away from the character's death on *Buffy* and ruining any sort of surprise on *Angel.*

On the Wolfram & Hart front, Christian Kane returned as Lindsey McDonald, at one point even working with Team Angel toward the finale, though he was ultimately (and unexpectedly) killed by Lorne since Angel simply doesn't trust him. Sarah Thompson appeared as Eve, Angel's conduit to the Senior Partners; Mercedes McNab returned as the vampire Harmony and worked as Angel's assistant; and Adam Baldwin became the firm's Marcus Hamilton.

In regard to Lorne, season five of *Angel* was actor Andy Hallett's last starring role outside a voice-over part. He passed away on March 29, 2009, from congestive heart failure. The disease's origin came from a 2005 dental infection that spread through his bloodstream and to his heart. The pain of that loss is something still felt deeply by his costars, who cannot think of the show's final season without sharing that sense of loss.

JOSS WHEDON

Cordelia's situation was a little bit her call, because Charisma had just had a baby and was living the family life. Plus, you don't need visions when you've got assistants saying, "B story on line one."

CHARISMA CARPENTER

I did *not* leave the show, despite many people's suspicions, to raise my child. I am the type of person that I need work, I need to work. My work is super fulfilling to me. Yes, I wanted to be a mother. Yes, I am so grateful I have a child, but I love what I do. I would not be happy just being a mom, and I would not be happy just being an actress. Those things are beautiful things, and I think ultimately bring depth to me as a person, [and] therefore [to] my work. Unfortunately, it just didn't work that way with *Angel*.

The coma was a devastating way to go, and the fans love her, especially when Doyle passes the visions on to her and she grows. Her character gets multidimensional and multifaceted and gets a heart and gains perspective and is really a part of the team. And *then* to find out, "Gosh, what do we do with the character?" It's just devastating. Of my career, *Angel* is probably the greatest reward and the most disappointing thing all at once, but I know how special the show was.

BEN EDLUND

The coma may have come about due to some difficulties in what to do with Cordelia after she had given birth to Jasmine and what role to give this person, because the psychological truth of that person is really hard to navigate [*laughs*]. She had sex with Angel's son, got pregnant, and gave birth to their child, a goddess. It's a lot to deal with. So it was a kind of breakdown. This happens sometimes when a character in a narrative suffers a metanarrative breakdown of some kind. That may have been the strategy underlying Cordelia, leading her up to a certain point, and there was no exit strategy past that. A lot of times when you have a character go into a sustained coma, something's not working for that character.

CHARISMA CARPENTER

Honestly, I thought I was coming back for season five. I found out when they had the upfronts that year and journalists called me at home and said, "Why aren't you on the cast lists?" It was just kind of shitty, but not really a mystery. Look, it was a very complicated relationship, [in] which I definitely played a part . . . and there's no easy way to go about it. Am I bummed that it went the way that it did? Totally. Could it have been done differently? Probably, but that's the way it is. That's the way it happened, and that's the way it went down.

DAVID FURY

Look, there was a lot of anger about Charisma. I think probably mainly from Joss. It felt a little bit like we were all working our assess off to keep these people employed and it's like, you have to take that into consideration before you make any life choices. You just do. And you have to be much more vocal about it. If something happens and you tell them early on or whatever the thing is, that's fine. But it's the idea of just kind of showing up and, boom, "I've got tattoos," or, boom, "I cut my hair in the middle of an episode," which I think Sarah did. It's like, "Wait a minute, now you're just fucking with us. You're making it so hard to finish this episode, because you're changing it." There's always that attitude of, "It's my life and I can do anything I want to." Well, that's not great. Again, I don't know the specifics to Charisma's circumstances—I have a lovely relationship with her—I just know there was a lot of residual anger about what happened.

So, yes, they decided to write her out of the show. But I couldn't be more thrilled to be the one to bring her back for "You're Welcome." It was largely Joss figuring out she needed a proper farewell, and I was very grateful to be the one to do it, because it was great fun and it was great fun working with her. I've got to say, she was an absolute doll to work with and she and David got along great. It was a nice little reunion. There was no bitterness between anybody. You've got to give it up for that. Wherever the anger was, obviously it was all [water] under the bridge. She definitely deserved a better good-bye than going into a coma, and I'm so glad we were able to do that.

CHARISMA CARPENTER

Coming back was . . . complicated. I didn't want to do it. My only request was, "I just don't want Cordy to die. I'm not going to come back for you to kill her." At the time I was actually working on a show called *Miss Match* with Alicia Silverstone and having a great time there. It was shot on the same soundstages that *Buffy* used to shoot in. David Fury, who wrote the episode, came to see me in my trailer at *Miss Match* to talk to me about it. I was pretty angry with the way things were, and I had really no desire to give that show any more than I had already given. Then, of course, my personal feelings got put aside and I thought of the fans. You know, there's always two sides to me, where you want to act like the petulant child and be like, "Fuck you, I'm not coming back!" Then there's the other part of you that goes, "This is a huge part of your life. It's an amazing show and it's the right thing to do for the fans." The higher-minded self gives you the kind of closure that you need to move on.

So when David Fury came to see me, I said I'd come back, but I wanted *this* amount of money—my feeling was if you're having me back, you're going to pay me what I deserve for the first time ever in the history of the show—and the second thing was I didn't want Cordy to die. So I signed the contract and *then* David says, "I have to tell you something. We're going to kill Cordy," and I'm like, "Of course you're doing this *after* I signed the contract." But he goes, "Hold on, just hear it out." He tells me *how* she dies, and I'm in tears now for a completely different reason, which is that it was really well told *and* beautiful. That changed everything.

I came to set, Joss sent me a really nice bouquet of flowers and a beautiful note, which I have framed in my room. It basically said, "I think it'll be one of the sweetest stories you've ever told, thanks for coming and 'You're Welcome,'" which was a play on words with the title of the episode. And it was a really beautiful episode.

JEFFREY BELL

We were all excited that James Marsters became a part of the show. He's a good actor and an interesting character. Throwing him into the mix only helped. He died a glorious death at the end of *Buffy,* a truly heroic death, and we didn't want to shortchange that. What we needed to do was deal with that in an honest way that didn't diminish what he did and allowed him to come back in a meaningful way.

JOSS WHEDON

What Spike brought to the show is what he brings, which is a little anarchy and a blond: two things that we needed. He's the guy to confront everybody all the time over what they're doing. You can't have your characters constantly going, "What are we doing in this evil law firm? Make mine black with no sugar." Eventually you would start to think that they're patsies or idiots. You needed that voice, and to me Spike was that voice to start with. There was a lot more to do than that, but when I thought of it initially, he was the guy who was really bridling against what was going on.

JAMES MARSTERS

One of the great things about going over to *Angel* was that I could just be the dick again, like I had been on *Buffy* in the early years. I could just be the jerk and try to give Angel a headache on a daily basis. And, again, David is great. He was always really nice to me, so was Sarah.

J. AUGUST RICHARDS

It was really great to have James come to the show, because he brought so much. He's so invested in his character, and I love that about him. He's very easy to work with as well. When he came over, there was no friction at all. He's just about the work and he's so good. A great addition to the show.

STEVEN S. DEKNIGHT

James Marsters—I could not love him more. He was brilliant as Spike. He was brilliant on *Buffy* with the darkness and the rage and the passion, along with the humor. Then he just brought that to *Angel* with a new spin on it. He and Boreanaz together were just absolutely gold—the way they hated each other, but also kind of really meshed in a way they couldn't with other people.

JAMES MARSTERS

I got to go back to a version of Spike that was vicious and not as tortured as the Spike that *Buffy* had on its last few seasons. They were like, "Yeah, he has a soul, but he still is in competition with Angel. He's still gonna try to outdo him at all times" [*laughs*]. It was him coming into balance, you know?

Like, the character had gone through his fire walk. That character had come out of that difficult period of getting his soul and now he's coming to balance and becoming a fun character again.

JEFFREY BELL

The addition of Spike works on a drama level and a comedy level. Both James and David were really good at that. That, and the changes in most of the characters, just opened up a lot of storytelling opportunities. Once again, . . . some decisions made very early in the year allowed us to tell a very different kind of season in year five [than in] year four.

JAMES MARSTERS

My intent joining the show was to make life as miserable as possible for Angel. I just absolutely wanted to be pitted against him, to have to work with him and hate him anyway was absolutely hilarious. As I discovered with Principal Wood on *Buffy,* Spike functions well with an enemy or someone he can be surly to. David plays that really well, too. I don't know if it's about good and evil. Even if Spike's good, he hates Angel anyway, because Buffy could obviously never get over him. And Angel would hate Spike, because he's been with her. The dynamic was set up for some delightful conflict between the characters.

DAVID FURY

The most significant element we were looking to add to Angel's character was that of the ever-put-on big brother Spike. Spike was a character Angel was powerless to get rid of, first because Spike was a ghost, then simply because he's a vampire of virtually equal strength. It provided us with a true comic foil for Angel, allowing for some funny and sometimes interestingly poignant scenes.

BEN EDLUND

I remember we were pitching ideas about Spike—I was so excited—and I pitched this moment where Spike as the vampire ghost had drawn some enemies into some part of Wolfram & Hart. Nina the werewolf was staying overnight, so there was a moment where there could be some guys trying to get in. They're the equivalent of burglars or whatever the fuck they were—assassins—and they run into a ghost of a vampire and then a werewolf jumps *out* of the ghost [*laughs*]. Spike is just there and he goes, "Yeah, I'm a ghost, but *this* is a werewolf," and then the werewolf jumps out of his chest. This show is fucking awesome, man. The only time I've ever heard that as a possible game to play—the ole werewolf jumps out of a vampire-ghost's chest. That, to me, is *Angel*. At one point I was pitching that the Big Bad at a certain point was a scarab that they kept in a box, almost like the typewriter from *Naked Lunch*. It didn't even matter if it got in or didn't get in, because other things almost as crazy *did*.

CHRISTIAN KANE
(actor, Lindsey McDonald)

I'd been wanting to come back to the show, and when they asked me to, I asked Joss for a favor. Joss said, "You have to trust me. I can't tell you what's going on, but you have to trust me." I said, "I trust you, anything you want, but if I could just not get beat up by everybody . . ." I come back for season five, first episode I'm getting thrown around a strip joint by Spike. He's beating me up. I'm doing it, and during filming I look at Joss and go, "Duuuuude. This is exactly what we talked about. The first thing I'm shooting is this." He just repeated, "Trust me," and, sure enough, Lindsey got to kick some ass that season.

J. AUGUST RICHARDS

When I think about fifth season, I think about the episode "The Life of the Party," because Andy Hallett *was* the life of the party. He was the life of the set. He was so funny and made everybody laugh constantly. Losing him was a great tragedy. He was a really good friend. He was a really good man and a really good person, and all of us miss him very much. It was just wonderful working with him. I also had the pleasure of traveling a lot with him by doing conventions. He made the conventions a party.

AMY ACKER

Andy was awesome. We had a great friendship, too. We lived really close by each other. He had such a hard job; he would be there in the wee hours of the morning, when it was still dark outside, to start getting that makeup on and stay after to get it off. He worked harder than any of us and managed to still make everyone laugh and be the kind of center of it all, because he was pretty fantastic.

MARK LUTZ
(actor, Groo)

There's a lot of stuff that I hold private about Andy, but there's a lot of things that people *should* know about him. The best thing was his spirit, that show business quality they call "it." He had it in spades. He was a Pied Piper—everyone that met him loved him, and he was always his best to all of his fans. He had this innate ability to meet you and instantly find some common thread you both shared, whether it be the esoteric or something right on the surface. He would bond with you instantly and you'd feel like you knew him all your life.

CHARISMA CARPENTER

Andy was probably one of my favorite people to be around. He was always witty, always funny, and he's kind of like Jerry Seinfeld in a way, because there are a lot of funny people, but there's not a lot of people who are clean funny. The things he would say were so beyond his years; he was this old man stuck in a young man's body. I remember he saw a pair of pumps, and he said, "You have to have these. They reminded me of you and I'm going to get them for you." He was out with his girlfriend at the time and he said, "Charisma needs to have these." It was the weirdest thing anyone ever did for me, and he was just so sweet and fun and charming. Always lit up the room.

MARK LUTZ

When they started with the character of Lorne, they weren't sure if he was going to be a one-off or maybe a little bit recurring here and there. To go to full cast member by the last season, that's a testament to what he brought to the show. And it was an element that only bolstered what was an all-star lineup.

DAVID BOREANAZ

Andy was always laughing and always spreading his joy and his humor and his energy, which in itself was fantastic to be around. We would always compare jackets and where his came from, because his were always *so* loud [*laughs*]. A great, beautiful soul that was taken way too early from us. Every day was hard for him, because he endured, I think, two hours of makeup just to get into that character. But he was a trooper, and behind that was a great person and someone who was a lot of fun to work with.

One of the most shocking developments was the death of Fred, when she becomes "infected" with the spirit of an ancient, extremely powerful demon named Illyria. Even *more* shocking was the manner in which Fred died, and a moment later Amy Acker came to her feet as the resurrected Illyria.

AMY ACKER

Joss asked me to meet him for coffee, which was weird, because he didn't usually do that. I went and met him and we're sitting there and he said, "I'm going to kill Fred," and then waited an extremely uncomfortable time before adding, "I'm making you into this demon goddess." A few weeks later, Aly [Hannigan] and Alexis were getting married, and, at their wedding, Joss showed up and handed me and Alexis some scenes that he had written for Illyria and Wesley. They weren't scenes that were actually ever in the show; they were designed to test it out. Then, after Alexis came back from his honeymoon and we were all back, Joss had Alexis and me over to his house one night to work on those scenes. He had all these lights in his house that were different colored. We were reading the scenes and he said, "I want her to kind of move almost like an insect." So we were experimenting with different moves, and then he started changing the colors of the lights in the room. He had a red light, then he tried a yellow light, then he got the blue light and he was like, "Oh, yeah, she's gonna be blue." So we got to develop the character in a way that you wouldn't normally get to do.

STEVEN S. DEKNIGHT

Joss wrote and directed "A Hole in the World," and then I did the next episode, "Shells," where you see Illyria for the first time. Because Joss was directing it and she dies at the end of his episode, he directed the first scene at the top of my episode. I had something to work off of. But I cannot tell you how stunned we all were with Amy Acker's performance. She would just give this spot-on chilling performance as Illyria. I call, "Cut," and then she would be Amy again, who was the sweetest woman in the world. She would ask, "Was that OK? You want me to do anything different?" I'm like, "Holy shit!"

KELLY A. MANNERS

Amy Acker was just amazing in that moment. I never forgot that transition that she made. Illyria was, in a lot of ways, a better character than Fred was. I loved Fred, but Illyria was fascinating. The way that Amy created this entirely different person for us, within seconds [of] seeing it on screen, I was like, "Holy shit, what happened there?"

BEN EDLUND

If you were going to cast someone whom we'd only seen play Fred, the last thing you would ask for is super ice queen, strong woman. Because a lot of women who can do the kind of wilting-violet thing, they don't have the Geena Davis thing of putting real iron in. There's people who can do the accountant and there's people who can do the action hero. It's like you're asking a person to just pull it like an action hero trope, which is a villain element, out of their tool kit without casting them for it. She did *amazing*.

JAMES MARSTERS

Holy God, what a great actor! I was fooled by Amy. Fred is very close to the Amy that she presents to the world; just absolutely sweet and loving, patient and kind, and I had no faith that she could do Illyria at all. *And* I had no idea how talented she was. I just remember being blown over when I first saw her as Illyria. She just rocked it. It was amazing. I should know better, because she's a *great* actor. You get fooled. They're so good, you're just like, "Oh, that's just them." Same thing happened to me with Charisma Carpenter. I assumed that Charisma was like Cordelia and so I never bothered to get to know her. I avoided her, because I thought she was like that head cheerleader that drove me insane as a young, awkward punk rocker in high school. I just thought, "I am not going to get by that person." I guess it was an episode of *Supernatural* we were both on where we got to talk and I discovered she's a sweetheart, absolutely wonderful.

DAVID FURY

The death of Fred and birth of Illyria was pretty remarkable. That's all Joss. He loves Amy, but he loves pain as well. You want to kill a character and Amy was such an amazing actress that he went, "I'm going to kill Fred, because that's going to be devastatingly painful *and* I'm keeping Amy, but she's going to become this new character." It's *brilliant*. Even as you see Illyria, you hold the pain of Fred's death and the knowledge that that's *not* Fred. It was an amazing group of actors.

STEVEN S. DEKNIGHT

I loved how she got to really stretch. One of the great tragedies about the show being canceled at the end of season five is Joss had really great plans of where to take Illyria. It was also so bittersweet with Wesley still being in love with her, but trying not to be because he hates her—she actually killed the woman he loves. But she's kind of sympathetic, and he starts to fall in love with her again. It was just all so juicy.

AMY ACKER

I would say playing Illyria was definitely harder than playing Fred, because I had the makeup and the different movements and the different voice. I had been so accustomed to being Fred that, you know, it's kind of scary when you've got everyone used to seeing you in one part and then you show up the next day and you're like, "I'm this different person," and it's *really* different. At the end of the first week of Illyria, one of the camera guys came over to me and he was like, "Amy, we just wanted to say we're sorry we haven't been talking to you and hugging you like usual this week. It's that that we're all a little scared of you." I was like, "Oh, that's nice."

JOSS WHEDON

In season five we had to dance around a lot of things and I figured it out as we went and still tried to keep the integrity of it. I loved the sort of free associativeness of being able to do stand-alone that at the same time started to weave in the stuff that the people actually show up for, which is the character material that progresses things. Killing Fred was one of the most painful experiences of my career, and certainly one of the most lovely. It was like writing a big poem. I wanted to show people what else Amy could do, so I wanted to kill her and create an entirely new character for her to play. It's an opportunity you can only have on a fantasy show, and she pulled it off magnificently.

DAVID FURY

Joss's idea for Illyria was in the mix a long time before *Angel* was canceled. In fact, if we knew we were going to be canceled, we may not have done it, if only because we barely had any time to do anything with the character. It was almost as if Fred died in vain.

While year five was flourishing creatively despite the numerous obstacles placed before it, the WB nonetheless chose to cancel the series at the end of the season. There were a couple of factors that precipitated that decision, one being that Joss Whedon insisted on an answer about renewal earlier than usual so that he could craft a proper ending if necessary. And that fed into the fact that the network was developing a primetime reboot of the gothic-horror soap opera from the 1960s, *Dark Shadows,* which they would have, unlike the situation with *Angel,* owned a piece of. Additionally, did they *really* want two vampire-centric shows on the network at the same time? They delivered their answer with an early cancellation, a decision that bit them in the corporate jugular when *Dark Shadows* turned out to be a disaster and failed to go to series.

DAVID FURY

My memory is that Joss didn't want to be played with the way he was in season five of *Buffy,* so he wanted an early answer about season five of *Angel.* He said, "Tell us we're picked up. We deserve it. The show is doing better than ever: the ratings are up; the critics are praising the show." And they went, "All right," and then quickly came back that it was canceled. Which I believe they regretted almost immediately. And certainly since then I've heard a lot of things that they realized it was a bad mistake, but it's kind of like you can't let a creator, actor, or star dictate when they decide to pick up a show. So I don't know if they were making an example or what, but they kind of shot themselves in the foot by not picking *Angel* up.

IAN WOOLF

(first assistant director, *Angel*)

I don't think anyone was anxious to get out of there. It was actually a surprise to us when they canceled the show, because on the one hand they have this hundredth-episode celebration, with all of these speeches from the executives at the WB and Fox, how great we were, blah, blah, blah. Then, like a month later, we were told the show was being canceled. I was like, "What? Wait a second. What happened between the hundredth episode last month and now?" At the point we were told that we weren't going to come back for a sixth season; it was in January. We typically wrapped in March, so the last three months it was kind of a little bit sad. People were starting to jump ship to get on other shows, because it's all about paying your mortgage.

JAMES MARSTERS

We were not expecting to get canceled. When I came on the show, a lot of *Buffy* watchers who may not have been watching *Angel* came over to the show. And so our numbers were really good on that final season. We were really sure that we were gonna have a long run, but the network had a pilot in the works from the creator of *ER* [*Dark Shadows*], which was the medical show that launched George Clooney. They decided to run with that and cancel us, and I don't think the pilot turned out as well as they had hoped. They were looking for another *Angel* for many years and ended up regretting the fact that they didn't run with it.

JEFFREY BELL

Most of our people dealt with pain through humor. So there were a lot of horrible jokes, there were some tears, and there was also the feeling of, "What are you going to do?" The writing had been on the wall, and we escaped it for a couple of years, but at that point it finally caught up with us. So the reaction was all over the place. There was loss. When I first heard the news from Joss, I thought, "Oh, that's too bad." Then, when we went over to tell the crew, I found myself profoundly sad. It really didn't hit until we were over there on the set. That day, a Friday, was a bust. We came in on Monday to work and there was a really strange sense of humor in the office, because we were all still reeling.

STEVEN S. DEKNIGHT

Thankfully we knew early enough from the network that we weren't being renewed that we could plan how to wrap it up, which was vital instead of it just ending and never coming back.

KELLY A. MANNERS

We knew it was the beginning of the end, so we tried to enjoy it. Deep down in our hearts we knew there would be no season six. We all just went in with the best attitude we could and had as much fun as possible producing it, and that came out with what we put on the screen.

CHRISTIAN KANE

We were filming a scene where I was down in the basement, in the dungeon, getting my heart cut out every day by a demon. It was me, David, James Marsters, and Kelly Manners. Joss came in with Kelly and broke the news that we had been canceled. David took it very well and went to his trailer. David knew he was always going to have a career, because he was a good actor. He took it very well, and I walked Joss out. Right when we got to the stage door, I said, "Are you all right?" And Joss said, "Yes." I said, "What are you going to do?" And he replied, "I'm going to fucking kill you." And I was all right with it. I was fine with it at that point, because I knew it was over. I had, arguably, the worst death in the world, because I felt like I should have been there for the final fight. I felt like after all these years, Lindsey deserved to be there. Angel had a trust in him and he even said, "You're good in a fight." Interesting story: we filmed my death scene—where Lorne shoots me—two and a half months before the finale, even though it was in that episode. We filmed it at 6 A.M. on a blocked stage with six people. Joss did not want people to know. We filmed it and it took an hour and a half to film. By noon the next day, people knew I died. Somebody had leaked it.

Back then, it was very upsetting to me that A, I had to die. B, I was killed by a flunky. I hated it. Now, after all these years, I understood what Joss was doing. I was never upset about the fact of what he was doing, because in the middle of the show, when you think I'm going to be there at the end, I died. It was a great, great moment and it was shock value. I was upset about it until about five years ago with the passing of my dear friend, Andy Hallett. I thought, "There's no better way that I could've gone out." I was killed by my best friend. Andy didn't want to do it—he was very scared of guns—and he didn't like the fact that he was the one.

AMY ACKER

I would say the positive feeling stayed until the end of the series. From being on *Buffy* and then going on to *Angel*, David might have been ready to play a different character. But not in any sense that we weren't all crushed when it was canceled. In the last episode where I transform from the Fred form to Illyria and punch the demon through his face, that was the last day of shooting. I was just, like, crying a river everywhere. Joss wrote that scene even though I don't think he wrote that whole episode. He didn't direct that whole episode, but he came in to watch that scene be filmed.

JEFFREY BELL

The great thing about David is he really has the attitude of one door opens as another one closes. Joss said he took the news the same way he took the news when they said, "Oh, we're going to create a show around you." He was like, "Oh, cool."

DAVID BOREANAZ

I always prescribe to the idea that when every season is over, I consider the series over until it gets reordered and then I move on from there. So when I learned about the show not being picked up from Joss, I didn't really have much of a reaction. For me, you take the show for as long as you can, you learn from it, you work on a character for X number of years and you build with it and you take it as part of your résumé. For me, it was almost like a relief of pressure, so to speak. To have those words come in, it really took a lot of weight off of my shoulders. It wasn't like I was rejoicing, but at the same time it felt right.

IAN WOOLF

As the seasons go by—and this is typical—the cast gets more restless. In the first couple of seasons they're all happy to be there, but as the seasons go by, none of the actors want to be there. They don't want to come to work. They want to get their big salaries and they don't want to show up. That's typically what happens; they just get tired of it. Then when it's all over and said and done, it's like they don't realize how good they had it. Because being on a long-running TV show is like winning a lottery, especially for the cast. For the crew, there's so many more jobs out there for them. But for the cast, it's a finite amount of jobs for those people, especially the series regulars.

I remember Kelly Manners telling me about a year after *Angel,* after he was done, he was walking through the halls of Fox to go to an interview for another show, and who does he see sitting on a folding chair with some sides, waiting to go onto an audition? Alexis Denisof. He looked up at Kelly and he said, "You know, you were right. I didn't realize how good we had it." Because Alexis was one of the ones that complained. He really wanted out. Now he's sitting there in a folding chair, waiting to audition for a job. He didn't work for a long time. It's like there's nothing you can say to these guys, because the actors typically surround themselves with their PR people, their agents, their managers. Their egos get built up and up so they think that this is never going to end. And it does.

DAVID BOREANAZ

I actually felt stronger about leaving toward the end of season four, but when they kind of revamped the show in year five, it was a good enough thing to have happened just for the story structure and the people and the fans. Season five ended up being a thoroughly enjoyable year for me. Probably the best year of all the years since the first one. It just turned out better than I expected in terms of the characters and the story lines.

STEVEN S. DEKNIGHT

At the same time, the *Angel* cast knew it was the golden time. That's not to say that on occasion people don't get pissy, because everybody's human. You have a bad day; you're there for fourteen hours—it's going to happen. But we had such a fantastic cast and crew. Kelly Manners, our physical producer, kept everything moving and figured out a way to pay for the crazy stuff we came up with. Ross Barryman, our DP—without him the show would not have been the same. I mean, it's not just that he designed the lighting; he helped the director design their shots and helped them come up with better ideas of how to shoot something. I would not have been able to direct the three episodes that I did without Ross by my side. It was such a huge load off to have these people where it was not about egos, it was not about what they want, but it was about what's best for the show. It makes all the difference in the world.

DAVID BOREANAZ

In this business, things happen so quickly and so fast that I've always focused on getting the first episode done, then the following episode and not be so concerned about story lines and where the character is heading. I really kind of keep that unpredictable for myself, because you never know what's going to happen. Walking around thinking it's never going to end or that you're invincible—that's one of the traps of Hollywood, [so] that you have to really be cautious and aware of who you are as a person. And you have to remain strong in that foundation, which is something that I got from my parents growing up. They gave me that and it's helped considerably to get through it all.

JOSS WHEDON

We had such a hard time getting the fifth season at all that I came into it figuring that it might be our last. What I came up with at the very beginning of the year was a season ender that would have closure for the entire show as well, but also opened up a lot of interesting avenues should we get a sixth season. I then became convinced that we would continue, because things were going so well. So while it was a horrible blow to find out that we were being canceled, I didn't have to change what we were doing and could proceed straight ahead. What we planned to go out on was very much a statement that applies to what the show has been about since day one.

STEVEN S. DEKNIGHT

When we knew it was ending, the story became serialized again and it became much more about destroying-the-Illuminati kind of deal and taking out the enemies. A *Godfather*-esque bit that we had to plan for and have be a little more extended. But that was the interesting thing: nothing really changed when we found out we had gotten canceled. It still ended the same way. Joss devised an ending that would work as a series ender or a season ender. One thing that was different was that we had squirreled away enough money to try and make it slightly bigger. Besides that, it ended exactly the same.

I looked at the Internet response when we were canceled, and by then episodes sixteen or seventeen aired and a lot of people were saying, "They obviously made that last-minute change, because they were canceled," which of course is not true. By the time we found out we were canceled, episode seventeen, where Illyria appears, was already being edited. It had already been shot. One thing the fans often don't realize is the lapse between when they see an episode and we actually do an episode is a month. We usually had three or four weeks of postproduction and there would be two weeks of filming and a couple of weeks to write the script. Another hard thing about TV is that you can't adjust to the fans on a turn of a dime. If they express dislike of a character, chances are they're going to see that character for four or five more episodes because they're already shot.

DAVID FURY

The finale is very much how we discussed it would be before we got word of our cancellation. The body count would probably have been different since we were going to explore the Illyria-Wesley relationship in season six, but, otherwise, launching into what looks like a no-win battle was exactly where Joss had wanted the season to end up.

BEN EDLUND

The apocalypse was exactly where Wolfram & Hart wanted things to end up. Had Angel and the other characters not taken on the firm, they would have kept doing their battles against evil and coming out on top, but they got manipulated into taking on this thing, which triggered the apocalypse they wanted in the first place. You would say basically that Wolfram & Hart did not want the status quo. Angel and our plucky champions were protecting the status quo, which was a nonapocalypse universe. Wolfram & Hart decided the best way to actually get it to work the way they wanted was to just lay down and let the good intentions people pave the road right over you, straight to hell.

KELLY A. MANNERS

When you know a show is ending, morale definitely gets affected. You don't have the excitement you had every other season, because normally you're working to make sure you get the next season. When you're on a sinking ship and the band's still playing but you know it's sinking, you're not dancing.

BEN EDLUND

It was sad, but not tragic, is what I remember. But I had only done a year and a half at Mutant Enemy where others had done seven. So I had sort of blown in and had a really amazing time there and worked on one of the best sci-fi shows ever in *Firefly*. Then flipped over to something that was like an extraordinary toy box. That's what *Angel* was, the toys were all out and no one said, "Put those toys away!" They said, "No, put them on screen, let's go!" That was beautiful, and it was really wonderful people. And the way of working, although it was very demanding in terms of one's time, it was really fulfilling. I was in the right place to move on. It also felt like once that lock on all those talent jobs that had been drawn together broke, there was a kind of feeding frenzy in the air. It made it feel not that bad, because you got this feeling that people were getting a crack at all these amazing writers and producers that had been locked away in this one area. It was time, in a way, to open up the door and let these remarkable television craftspeople and artists out in to the mainstream.

AMY ACKER

It just didn't feel like it was supposed to be ending. I mean, Joss had already said he had an idea for season six, and it seemed like we still had good ratings and a great fan base and all of that. So it just felt a little bit wrong. Like, "We'll be back next year, won't we?" [*laughs*]. There was a fan movement to keep it going; billboards going around saying, "Save *Angel*." You know, they were motivated to try and keep the show on the air. You kind of had a little bit of hope that that might have happened.

STEVEN S. DEKNIGHT

I know the fans really threw their backs into getting the show picked up for a sixth season, but at the time it was definitely over at the WB, and UPN definitely passed, which was not surprising. I mean, ultimately it's kind of a numbers game. The WB really didn't make any money off the show and UPN just simply couldn't afford it. They really took a bath on *Buffy,* and the reason they took a bath on *Buffy* is that they couldn't come up with any product to launch off of it. They had a great lead in, but they couldn't get the material to be their next hit, and *Enterprise* wasn't really helping them either. So the feeling on *Angel* was that it was over, and it was very bittersweet. On the one hand, we would have loved for it to come back and for us to do another season; on the other hand, we also felt like we were finishing strong. And it's always nice to finish a show on the upswing and not when it's limping off into the sunset.

JOSS WHEDON

While this is a good note for the end of this particular movement, I didn't feel this particular symphony was over. Originally, I wanted to go out after five seasons of *Buffy,* because I was tired. It wasn't that I didn't think there were more stories to tell. And I'm glad I got to do those last two seasons. With *Angel,* the burnout level was not as high. I didn't have to run it day to day. I had great partners on the show, and it wasn't a drain on me. And it redefined itself so much so many times that it remained very fresh. The show had done extraordinary stuff from the very first season.

STEVEN S. DEKNIGHT

In the final year, we were able to do so many cool things and so many things that you just don't see on TV. The puppet episode is a great example. You know, one week we get a puppet episode, [and] the previous week you were at the bottom of the sea in a World War II sub, because the show was constructed in such a way that you could do anything. And Joss really would go to those places—to dark, scary places. He'd go for the lighthearted puppet places as well.

BEN EDLUND

The Whedonverse lived in a place where there was darkness plus this ability to let the air out, something that was not dissimilar from the pattern developed by *Xena*. What I thought *Xena* did very well, and part of why it got around the way it did, was that it wasn't *Conan the Barbarian* asking everyone to take these people seriously. "They're wearing animal skins—don't take them seriously!" Take their emotional truth seriously, and have fun with the fact that you're almost in a spaghetti barbarian movie. And there's a sense in the Whedonverse that you want the breeze to be blowing through there.

JEFFREY BELL

To me, what five years of *Angel* were about is asking specific questions. Why are we in Wolfram & Hart? What are we fighting for, why are we fighting, and what are we fighting against? Will Angel get to be a real boy? Will Spike? And these guys who clearly hate each other but also love each other, and this gang who has been with them—what's going to happen with them? We turned Angel into a puppet, we had Nazi subs and Mexican wrestlers, but we've always remained true to the show.

BEN EDLUND

The hinge between a Nazi sub and a puppet show was *Angel* finding its optimal versatility and true kind of muscle group. I don't know how much of *Angel* is what it is because of that. It's a rich field of ideas that manages to land our feeling story, but one of the things I enjoyed most about working there was how wild the ideas could get. Those were always helped by stand-alones, or at least some element of stand-alone in it. I don't have a particular axe to grind as far as the ratio of it, because I went in and worked on far more serialized shit and enjoyed that, too.

TIM MINEAR

It was the end of an era. For a moment there, there were three Mutant Enemy shows on the air with *Buffy, Angel,* and *Firefly*. Then there was *Buffy* and *Angel*. Then there was *Angel,* and then there were none.

JOSS WHEDON

People were asking why *Angel* was canceled when it was, and I sort of asked the same thing. That was a bit of a blow out of the blue. The message we always tried to give with the show is that redemption is really hard and it takes your whole life, and it involves fighting all the time, sometimes against things that can't be beaten. The last episode of *Angel* reflects that strongly. And the fact that through all the years of trying to find the format and trying to find the regulars and trying to find the relationships, that we held true to that premise and, in fact, came full circle to it, means to me that we really had something there. The whole time, in all the various incarnations, we always had the thing that I wanted, which was an exciting, strange, tough, funny, melodramatic show about the idea of redemption and what it is to be a human being.

STEVEN S. DEKNIGHT

Creatively the show accomplished so much. On a technical level, it's a beautiful show. Just stunning. We were one of the cheapest hour dramas on TV and you couldn't tell, because of the way it was filmed, thanks to the incredible Ross Barryman and our production values, and the choreography of the fights. Deeper than that, creatively I go back to the feeling that it created a mythological character in a battle between good and evil, where it's not always black and white. We were more than willing to go to a very gray place. Angel, our hero, has done some horrible things *with* a soul. I mean, he locked up the lawyers with the vampires, and, in what is the best episode ever done, Tim Minear's "Are You Now or Have You Ever Been," he has a chance to save these people in the hotel but instead says to the demon, "Take them all," because they deserve it. It's moments like that that you will not see on another TV show: where your hero will do something like that, and you're surprised by it.

DAVID BOREANAZ

The writers allowed me to do certain things that had been fantastic for me and exciting, because there's a lot of history to that character. I had the ability to use his palette really well with each show, depending on what they're asking for. Angel was multidimensional and had a lot of colors that I enjoyed tapping into. We opened him up and used his sarcasm in a very vulnerable way. The writers were great at using him in all sorts of different ways. I'd say the overall experience of doing the show was remarkably up-and-down. I kind of look at it as a huge arc for myself, personally striving and challenging myself every day, making the character fresh, unique, and different. Our job as actors is to communicate what the writer is trying to achieve, take their stories, . . . look at it as a whole, and . . . do our best to facilitate that. I was really a part of the whole, rather than an individual.

Personally, I was able to play a character that's 240 years old, and I've had the experience of playing the action hero, the experience of playing a demon, being very vulnerable at certain times. The palette that I had at my fingertips was a very rare thing. I wasn't flapping around in a cape like Dracula. There was a lot to this character that I learned from starting at the beginning.

STEVEN S. DEKNIGHT

I kind of compare Angel to Jack Bauer on *24*. Here's a guy who knows right from wrong, and knows about the battle between good and evil and realizes that to fight evil sometimes you have to do horrible things for the greater good, and he has no qualms about it. He regrets it and perhaps it haunts him, but he will do it. Angel's the same way. He will go to a very dark place to help save humanity, even if it means damning himself, which is something you don't see a lot on TV. There's not a lot of the antihero left. I've always loved antiheroes. You know, Luke Skywalker is great, but Han Solo, now you're talking: the rogue, the guy who's never on the up and up, but usually on the side of good. Those are the characters to me, where that gray area makes them interesting. And not just Angel. You can go to all of our characters and there's a lot of gray there. I mean, Wesley went all dark and kept a slave girl in his closet. Gunn being hooked on brain juice, and Spike of course, who tries so hard to be good.

Take the character of Fred. Sweet, innocent Fred, who almost killed a guy, but you know he was asking for it, and, still, you know what happens to her. She gets her soul destroyed and her body inhabited by an ancient demon, which really shows you that in this universe anything can happen to anybody. Nobody's safe, and it's kind of like the real world. Nobody's safe, but there's hope.

DAVID BOREANAZ

Buffy was a pop culture phenomen[on] from the start. Our show remained just under the radar, and I found that refreshing instead of being this huge success. We felt successful in our storytelling and what we did show to show. I wasn't looking to be number one in certain areas, I just wanted to do good work—*wherever* that landed us on the radar. The bottom line is that we remained loyal to our fans, and they were loyal to us.

STUART BLATT

Buffy was the flagship and, not taking anything away from it, but *Angel,* as far as I'm concerned, elaborated on that. Unfortunately, it always got looked at as a spin-off, and because it wasn't a girl-power show, it didn't get the same kind of credibility. And we did some crazy stuff on that show.

DAVID GREENWALT

You do a lot of things that don't always land, but the success of *Buffy* and *Angel*—and by success I mean the way it reached people of all ages and emotionally—was so satisfying, because you work so hard. Yes it's much more fun if it's a hit than if it's not. You've got to work as hard whatever one you're doing. I was very sad to kind of leave Joss and Marti. We were very close and that kind of broke my heart a little bit, but I was very happy. Then I went on to do my own thing and the shows I worked on were really good, but with the exception of *Grimm* they just didn't take off for whatever reason. That was a good six years, and I'll never forget that.

CHARISMA CARPENTER

Both *Buffy* and *Angel* were so layered. They really hit on themes that are quite deep, and there's a loneliness that people tap into with Buffy and Angel. Living your destiny at the expense of everything that you want for yourself. How do you negotiate those things through life? Just thinking about Buffy as a Slayer and Angel as a vampire, and sacrificing their relationship to a greater cause. Loneliness, and what it's like to take on that burden. I think people can relate to that. The dialogue . . . to this day, I don't think you can match it. The quipping, and the wit, and the way the language was made its own by all the wonderful writers.

Personally, I never grew more in my life or learned more about myself than working on those shows. It brought up everything for me—every demon, every button for you and about your childhood. "Am I enough? Am I smart enough? Am I talented enough? Am I worthy?" I learned work ethic. I learned when to keep my mouth shut. I learned what battles to pick and who *not* to piss off. I actually learned *a lot* by pissing people off.

JOSS WHEDON

Buffy had a paradigm that was new. Angel was a guy who looks like a hero and is a hero. There were things about it that make it a very unique show, but on the surface of it you could have looked at it and said, "That's an action show on the WB," and not many people got "the more" unless you watched it. With *Buffy*, even if you don't watch it, you say, "That's the idea," and it has that grand mission statement: high school is hell, little girl kicks butt. *Angel* didn't have that. *Angel* was only as good as the show itself. I honestly believe if *Buffy* had not been as good as it was, people still would have watched it, because they liked the idea. I'm glad that people thought it was good and I worked hard to make it good. *Angel* will always be perceived by people as only a genre show and you really have to sort of watch it to understand what we had going on.

DAVID BOREANAZ

This show and this character will be remembered for its sense of risk, its sense of style: a uniqueness to deliver story in a different manner; a uniqueness in character to expand with the other characters around him, to evolve into different types of characters, to be ever changing; the angst of conflict within him. There's so much to be remembered and so much to be proud of about this show. And its use of mythology and verse and language and texture—just the way it was shot. It will be remembered for a lot of things.

Angel's evolution remained an ongoing thing. I don't think for this type of character that there will ever be an end to his evolution. As far as his personal journey—God, it was leaps and bounds. The guy just completely came out of the shadows, opening up, and became more vulnerable with a better sense of himself from the people around him. The evolution was amazing; emotionally he evolved tenfold. And then with the show's ability to shift from the darker places to humor and back again . . . what a fantastic journey to be able to do that. It was great for me, because it enabled me to tap into those places on different levels and expand on those for different roles. I was able to use those opportunities in other parts. I really enjoyed the flexibility of the character and how the writers allowed me to interchange with him and move places. I welcomed that; it's one of the reasons I enjoyed it so much.

JOSS WHEDON

We never made an episode where it was, "Let's just do something cool." It's very much about the grown-up emotions, the decisions we've made. Territory that *Buffy* began to explore in its later seasons. The terrible decisions we've made and the life we've spent trying to come back from that. The show has an intense, epic melodrama that very much set its own tone. What it was trying to say, like *Buffy,* is mutable, but basically it was about, "How do I live? What do my actions mean? If I've made mistakes, how do I find peace and answers?" You never do. You have to keep fighting. I would never make an episode of television that didn't have something to say, because that would be pointless and the work is too hard.

It's an approach that may separate these from other shows, but I think it's also hurt. Television is designed to be comforting. It is designed for you to always know what you're in for. And my television is always designed for you *not* to. The idea that if this is a funny scene, someone should keel over dead. If this is a scary scene, there should be a joke. If this is a wacky farce, there should be sudden, gut-wrenching melodrama. I always want to change it up. Angel had had a more consistent tone, with the exception of the Pylea adventure, which was basically, "Can we make *The Wizard of Oz*?" Basically, it had always been very serious with a wry edge to it, whereas *Buffy*—who knew? My shows will never be giant hits, because they're not that. Ultimately, they work on a different model, and for a genre show to do that, I think it scares people a little bit.

DAVID GREENWALT

These shows were so personal to Joss. We sat in together on a lot of dailies, a lot of pages, and stuff that he's always been so generous to me in public and in private. But in my mind I was there to serve Joss Whedon and to do my best to write like him. Into every generation one is born. *That's* Joss Whedon.

And nothing seemed to sum up Joss Whedon better than the last episode of the series, particularly the final shot when hordes of the forces from hell have been sent by the Senior Partners to destroy Los Angeles and Team Angel, but to their last breath the group is willing to continue the battle, Angel raising a sword, stating he wants to slay the approaching dragon, and leading them to what will likely be their deaths.

CHRISTIAN KANE

Interesting bit of trivia about that final episode: David Boreanaz and I are the only two actors who appeared in the first episode and the last one. Our good buddy Glenn Quinn checked out, and Charisma had left the show. Alexis and my dear friend J. August Richards weren't on the show in the beginning.

JAMES MARSTERS

The problem with the ending was that we had no money. We had the big buildup of the monsters—hell is opening up; all the monsters are coming: oh, no! We only had enough budget for, like, a two-and-a-half-second shot of computer-generated Hellmouth opening up and all the dragons and stuff.

And the only thing left to do was just dump ice water on the cast for the rest of the night and hope for the best. I think a lot of shows put into the position that Joss was put into wouldn't have even tried. They would have said it was impossible to wrap it up, it would've been just another episode and then—surprise, surprise—we're not coming back. That does happen, but Joss was not satisfied with that, and he moved heaven and earth to try to wrap it up. I'm impressed that he did as well as he did.

STEVEN S. DEKNIGHT

I wish the show had continued on; we had more stories to tell. But I'm thankful that we got a chance to wrap it up. Where it ended, I love the fact that it didn't end with, "Oh, OK, everything's great. We defeated evil. We won." It ended, if memory serves me correctly, with Gunn wounded, probably going to die. They're going into this impossible battle against the forces of evil, but they're never going to stop fighting. I thought it was a great, great note to end on. I thought Jeff Bell did a phenomenal job with that last episode, and I'm very proud of where we ended up. That season, to me, was just so delightful.

J. AUGUST RICHARDS

I know that ending is really controversial. People love it or they hate it, but what's funny is that the more years that go on, the more I understand what Joss was trying to say or what they were trying to say with the ending of *Angel*. The essential question is, if you knew you were going to lose, would you still fight for what you believe is right? Would you still fight for good or what you believe to be good? The answer that the characters came up with was yes. My character was the one who asked the question. That means more to me now, especially in these times politically. I was actually just thinking about it over the last few days, and the meaning of that has become even more relevant for me right now in our history and where we are as a nation. I think it's beautiful and was perfect.

KELLY A. MANNERS

That last big fight in the rain was the last thing we shot, and there were lots of tears. You become a family when something like that goes for five years. We didn't make a lot of changes in the crew, so it was very emotional. And what a way to end. Standing soaking wet and then saying cut, print, good-bye.

J. AUGUST RICHARDS

That last scene was us in an alley, facing the giant in front of us, facing forty thousand on the left and forty thousand on the right. In an odd way, that was my good-bye to the characters and that world. When the comic books came out and continued the story, I had no desire to read them, because it was finished for me.

JAMES MARSTERS

When I produced theater, we would do a lot of shows that were big risks. I always said, "You guys. We're jumping off the cliff with this one. You know, we're either going to fly or we're going to splat . . . . so we better start flapping." And the cast started flapping *hard*. I'm reminded of the final scene in *Angel*, which was meant to be the most heroic thing that Joss could think of for Angel to do, which was to sacrifice his life for the good of other people when he knew he would lose. "Let's go to work!" That's the point of that episode; we know we're going to die, but we can't help but try anyway. And I think that that's the ultimate heroic act.

DAVID BOREANAZ

We ended *Angel* like an open-ended book. You kind of see the characters going out with a fight, which has been prevalent for Angel since the inception of the show. He's always going to be fighting, which is true today with humanity and all of the things that are going on in the world. It ends with a battle for his own self, and a battle for humanity. Striving for excellence and continuing the good fight, whatever that good fight is.

JOSS WHEDON

We got to see how efficiently Wolfram & Hart could pick these people apart. We got to see how that affects Angel. His attitude about what he does and why he does it has always been so shifting and, to me, so interesting. He has to go to a very dark, weird, selfish place to start playing at a level that Wolfram & Hart had been playing off of from the start. We tied up some loose ends, but not all of them, because life doesn't work that way. But the situation at Wolfram & Hart deteriorates to the point where there is a reckoning and a bloody one—because ultimately they're not going to sit down and play canasta.

BEN EDLUND

Best. Ending. Ever! What I love is the last shot where you get these fucked-up people, and the story, especially in a season where things got more grim, has Angel being like a pencil driven into a pencil sharpener, and the point was that shot, right? They will never stop fighting. *He* will never stop. He swings at the camera and it's over. But it's *never* over.

PART THREE

ACROSS
THE BUFFYVERSE

"If there is no great, glorious end to all this,
if nothing we do matters,
then all that matters is what we do."

BEYOND BUFFY

"You brought a date? Buffy, when I said you could slay vampires and have a social life, I didn't mean at the same time!"

Throughout *Buffy*'s long seven-season run and even before *Angel* had left the airwaves, creator Joss Whedon was already contemplating the next chapter in the Buffyverse. Even as fans clamored for a *Buffy* movie to continue the adventures of their favorite Slayer, Whedon had turned his attention to other offshoots of the original mother ship, using the Star Trek franchise as a template to Buffily go.

MARTI NOXON
(executive producer, *UnReal*)

Some of it is that Joss's energy is limitless. As the show started to function a little more smoothly and he had a little bit more time, unlike the rest of us, who would go home and take a nap, Joss goes and creates another show. Joss would say to me, "What'd you do this weekend?" and I'm like, "Well, I went to the mall, saw my brother, worked in the morning on Saturday." And I'll say, "What did you do?" and he'll reply, "I wrote a couple of songs, I did a comic book, I created this new show, and I'm working on a novel."

So some of it is that he's got a little more time to look and focus on things, which freed him up to do these things that people encouraged him to do. The other thing is that as the characters in the universe developed, we started to see possibilities in all of them. I look at almost every character on *Buffy* and I think, "Wow, they could have their own show." As you start to see the richness of that world, you realize there's all this potential for spin-offs and stuff.

The *Buffy* spin-off that came closest to being realized was the *Buffy* animated series, which would have been produced under the aegis of show runner Jeph

Loeb, now the major domo of the Marvel Television universe. But, at the time, he had a successful career as a comic book writer and was just finishing a stint on the TV series *Smallville*.

JOSS WHEDON
(writer/director, *The Avengers: Age of Ultron*)

It was an opportunity to do the things or the jokes that we only did in the writers' room. To do things that are so silly and postmodern or free associative that we could never do it on the show. Kind of like when the fear demon turned out to be really tiny and Buffy stepped on it. That's about as far in the direction of that humor that we ever went.

But with the animated series, we had a chance, while being cool, scary, and empowered, to be really whimsical. Like, everyone imagines what it would be like to have their driver's license, and Xander's imagination is that he's got a jalopy, and Cordelia and Buffy look like Betty and Veronica because they're in the back. It's very simple. It would have been a return to adolescence and year one and very freeing. A completely different kind of fun than the live show or the comics.

JEPH LOEB
(executive producer, *Jessica Jones*)

We had put together a class A animation team. We had all thirteen stories for the first season and nine scripts that were written by all *Buffy* writers and myself. We were beginning production. I spent a year and a half over there running the show. It just sort of stopped; everything was put in a box, and we waited.

Buffy: The Animated Series took place in year one. She's met Angel, but at the moment he's just this mysterious guy. She knows he's a vamp, but other than that she doesn't really know anything. While there are darker aspects, the show was absolutely geared to go a little younger, not much, simply because of the nature of animation. What would be the point of doing an animated version of the live-action show that's exactly the same? Do we really want to see cartoons have sex?

JOSS WHEDON

When the characters graduated from high school, I got all choked up and said, "But, wait, there are more stories, I have not told them all." So that opportunity was a well to draw from forever, and the relationships can be fluid within the boundaries of the show—that is to say, Cordelia could be supernice in one episode and completely awful in the next. Willow could find somebody else—and I think it's safe to say that it would probably have been a boy. One of the points of the show was that even though things may look like they're set a certain way, some days your best friend is your worst enemy, so these things are always fluid.

JEPH LOEB

On the animation side, we had Eric Radomski. He put together this extraordinary crew and it's an embarrassment of riches. Everybody wanted to work on the show. We recorded Alyson as Willow, Nicholas as Xander, and Tony for Giles.

In the presentation reel for the proposed series, many of the familiar tropes from the show's first season are readily apparent, beginning with Buffy staking a vampire who underestimates her resourcefulness in an alley. Afterward, she reconnoiters in the library with Giles, Willow, and Xander, cockily extolling her kill, when a dragon suddenly swoops down and swallows her and lifts her high into the sky above Sunnydale, leading into the title card.

JEPH LOEB

The show was about the grounding principles of Buffy as a metaphor for high school anxieties, high school troubles, and how they manifest themselves. Joss feels that the metaphor is never stronger than when you're in the middle of high school and you're trying to figure things out. So Buffy has moved to Sunnydale, she's friends with Xander and Willow, and she has begun to accept her role as the Slayer.

That's the joy of telling the stories. We could do things that are ironic in the sense that she can say things like, "I'll never do that," and we know that later on she does. You can't do that when you're doing the live show, because Joss was building a mythology year by year. We had all of that history to be able to look at. There's that side of it, and the other side of it is that these were stories that for one reason or another Joss always wanted to tell, but time got away. For example, Willow and Buffy going babysitting.

By the time they got around to something like that in the live show, they were too old to do that. We never saw why Buffy doesn't have a driver's license, and by the time the live show could have done that story, she was too old. In other words, these were stories that fall in between the stories that you know and love. Then there are just certain things that the budget of the live show would not allow that we would have been able to do. That's the most fun. We could do "Attack of the Sixty-Foot Buffy," not that we were going to, because on live action that would look ridiculous, but in animation it could be quite fun.

JOSS WHEDON

"Teenie Buffy" is the first script Jane Espenson turned in. We could never do "The Incredible Shrinking Buffy" on the live-action show. We referred to it as "Simpsons Beyond." We wanted the toughness of a Batman show, really good action, strong hero, but at the same time the completely off-center humor of *The Simpsons*.

But we couldn't find a home for it. Nobody seemed to want it, and it blew my mind. I feel like I'm standing here with bags of money. It's *Buffy* animated, what more do I need to explain here? People are just like, "We're not doing that sort of thing; we have a different agenda," and I'm wondering, did I miss the memo where this wasn't a cash cow? I had the *Buffy* writers writing it and the Buffy actors wanting to be in it. What did I miss?

Showtime was the last one we lost. They were interested, but they wouldn't do it without Sarah, and Sarah wasn't involved. But it just blows my mind.

Another enticing series that had been discussed and previously developed was a spin-off featuring Faith the Vampire Slayer.

MARTI NOXON

That's certainly one of the things we talked about, but I don't think that's where her career goals were. It's too bad, because if she were interested, that's a show I can totally see. She's a reluctant TV star, which is a shame because she's so good. We tried, believe me—it's not something that hadn't been discussed. It's funny; she's the fan of many *Buffy* folk and not the biggest *Buffy* fan. It doesn't seem like she's enough of a geek for the show to go, like, "Yes, I want to do this no matter what the cost."

TIM MINEAR

(executive producer, *American Horror Story*)

I had come up with the pitch. Eliza was gracious, kind of wonderful, but just felt she wanted to try something new. There are no hard feelings there. But the show was basically going to be "Faith Meets *Kung Fu*." It would have been Faith, probably on a motorcycle, crossing the Earth, trying to find her place in the world. I'm sure it would get arc-like at some point, but the idea of her rooted someplace seemed wrong to me. The idea of her constantly on the move seemed right to me. Oh, and she broke out of prison [on *Angel*], so there would have been people after her.

Faith wasn't the only proposed spin-off. Another that came tantalizingly close to fruition was *Ripper,* which would have been a coproduction with the BBC and shot in England. It intended to fill in some of the enigmatic mythology hinted at in the relationship between Ethan Rayne and Giles and his dark past while living in Britain.

MARTI NOXON

It would have been more adult. In our discussions, we realized because of the style of the show and the fact that it was a BBC series, we wouldn't have felt as beholden to hit every act break with a big cliffhanger. The pace can be a little bit more adult. The situations wouldn't have necessarily have had a monster in every episode. There would always be a supernatural element, but it wouldn't have to be quite so genre. It would feel a little more like *Prime*

Suspect with monsters. One of the writers joked this is the show where Giles can make himself a cup of tea and think about it, and that could be a whole scene. Giles's past is pretty dark. We were going to get to grow him up and show him in situations with women and all kinds of good stuff that he didn't get to do on *Buffy*.

It's no secret that Whedon is a huge comic book geek, having contributed scripts to some of the biggest comic book series ever published, but when he created *Fray* for Dark Horse, the story of Melaka Fray, the intention was always to see it one day make the jump to film or television.

JOSS WHEDON

I wrote the comic *Fray*, and it took place two hundred years in the future, thinking there's no way this can ever affect the Buffy universe and so it'll be safe. And then we ended up using a little bit; Buffy's scythe in season seven is from the comic book. So I felt some obligation to work in that mythology, and it would be lovely to make it all tie in.

MARTI NOXON

Joss is such a huge comic book geek that the opportunity to actually be the author of *Fray* was too enticing. Joss's passion for all of this is genuine; I don't think he'd do something that he really didn't want to do. He's had ample opportunity to exploit *Buffy* in ways that he has not and ample opportunities to produce other shows he would get credit for and money for that he didn't feel passionate about. Anything he does do is because he wants to see it.

More recently, fans were teased with the prospect of a *Buffy* Broadway musical, and after the success of "Once More, with Feeling," few could not salivate at the prospect. Unfortunately, it was Joss Whedon himself who pulled the plug on the prospect of the Slayer slaying the Great White Way.

DAVID FURY
(executive producer, *24*)

He was getting lots of offers to do it. But the realization was that the story doesn't work by itself. The story is a continuation of the whole series and where it was at that point. It just doesn't make any sense, so if you do a *Buffy* musical, you have to rewrite a different score and story, and at that point, Why am I doing a *Buffy* musical? The Buffy character is owned by other people, and the studio owns it. He'd be making money for so many other people, and he just didn't see any point in doing it.

He had been recently working on a musical for Broadway and then he went to see *Hamilton*, and suddenly he couldn't write anymore. I said, "That's how we felt when you delivered the *Buffy* musical to us. We all went, 'We can't do this anymore.' We're just not worthy of being able to do this." So, Joss had that same experience seeing *Hamilton* going, "I cannot do this; it's just too brilliant." He stopped writing the musical. I don't know if he's gotten the will to go back to it.

So will there ever be another Buffy TV series, a reunion film, or a reinvention? Whedon was outspoken in criticizing an attempted reboot that was announced in 2009 by Fran Rubel Kuzui, who still controls the Buffy rights. But after Whedon disparaged her efforts, no such reboot has materialized. But is it impossible that Whedon would revisit his most popular creation? Only time will tell.

CHARISMA CARPENTER
(actress, Cordelia Chase)

At this age it would be hard. You'd have to reboot it with new characters, and I just don't think that the fans would want that. I know I wouldn't want a younger, better-looking version of me. It's me or nothing! I'd be the grandma—I still got it! You know the young kids would be looking at me like I was a grandma, because if you're thirty-five, you're a grandma. *So* old!

GIRL POWER FOREVER

"Every Slayer comes with an expiration mark on the package, but I want mine to be a long time from now. Like a Cheeto . . ."

After twenty years, *Buffy the Vampire Slayer* is as potent as ever and frequently found on most critics' lists of the greatest television series of all time. Ubiquitous in its availability on a variety of streaming platforms today (Netflix, Amazon, Hulu, etc.), it's hard to imagine a world in which Buffy will ever go away.

For a generation of young girls, Buffy Summers has been a role model, and the show's metaphors and allegories of growing up remain timeless. It's a series that has not only inspired many others and changed the face of television but also encouraged strong roles for women in various mediums.

In addition, a generation of top show runners were mentored through the unofficial graduate program that was Mutant Enemy, ranging from *24*'s David Fury to *American Horror Story*'s Tim Minear to *Spartacus*'s Steven S. DeKnight to *UnReal*'s Marti Noxon, among others—like Oscar winner Drew Goddard.

Buffy the Vampire Slayer also launched Joss Whedon himself as a creative force. And Whedon has only grown more successful in the intervening decades, having written and directed two of the highest-grossing movies of all time, *The Avengers* and *Avengers: Age of Ultron* while continuing to relentlessly follow his eclectic passions, whether elevating a Nielsen-challenged TV series like *Firefly* into a major motion picture or adapting Shakespeare's *Much Ado About Nothing* in his backyard as a movie on a shoestring budget with a variety of familiar faces from the Buffyverse.

However, no matter what Joss Whedon does in the future, it's unlikely he—or the audience—will ever forget their first love: *Buffy the Vampire Slayer.* And thankfully that moment of perfect happiness won't turn them evil in the process, either.

STEVEN S. DEKNIGHT

(director, *Pacific Rim: Maelstrom*)

Joss did something unique. You look at what he did when he started with *Buffy*. It was a different way of talking. It was a different way of the characters interacting and the way the story would turn, from emotional to funny to emotional. You see the effect it had. To start with, I think it really solidified the WB as its first legitimate hour-long hit and really propelled it into the public consciousness.

KRISTY SWANSON

(actress, *Buffy the Vampire Slayer [1992]*)

I was house hunting, and I went over to Brentwood to look a place over. I walk in, and I look on the refrigerator, and there's a photo of Joss Whedon and his then girlfriend. I'm going, "That's weird!" Then I'm looking around the house, and I see some mail sitting out, and it says Joss Whedon on it. And then I see a *Buffy the Vampire Slayer* script, one of the TV-show scripts, resting on a table. I go, "Oh my God, this is Joss's house!" Obviously, this was the house he was renting and moved from, or whatever, and here I was innocently house hunting in Joss's house. It was very strange, a real trip—I just couldn't believe it.

STEVEN S. DEKNIGHT

Buffy also had the effect, the ripple effect, through the years since it was on; you can see the effect it had on the other shows, especially across the pond in England. I think *Buffy* had a profound effect on *Doctor Who*. You really saw that kind of Joss Whedon effect and that show continued on, a very strong influence. *Torchwood*, the same way. It's that Joss Whedon touch. You also see it in the Marvel movies, that combination of wit and humor that's not set-up punch lines. It's coming from a very different place. I think it is just what he created and how he created it, from an idea that, when you first hear it, "Buffy the Vampire Slayer" sounds ridiculous. He almost uses that to subversively slip in the meat and the emotion.

It just really takes you by surprise. I remember even before I was on the show, episodes of *Buffy*, you'd be sitting there at the end of an episode crying your eyes out, which was very unexpected. When Buffy finally gets Angel back and gets his soul back in and has to kill him. It's like, "Oh shit, no!"

DAVID FURY

(executive producer, *The Tick*)

It's definitely a couple of the most imaginative shows that have ever been on television. It was easier to do *Buffy* than *Angel,* but we tried to do it on both, which was telling story through allegory and metaphor. A lot of people don't appreciate that or think it's very obvious to do that. But I have to tell you, when you don't do it, the stories don't hold up. They don't last in your brains. You can look at all the external stuff and remember, but people still come up to me today and say how much those shows meant to them and how much they inspired them to become writers or actors. Just the idea that the show tapped into something special. There [were] a lot of shows that tried to emulate it, but they couldn't quite capture that magic.

Angel was a more difficult show to grab, but we tried to grab meaning in the episodes about the human condition. How to be good in a world that's not so good. All those things we tried to work into [the show]. I think that's a huge part of what those shows were, and it's something that I don't see in other places. When we talk about them when I'm on other shows, and I talk about those things, people turn their nose up at it. They think it's like, "Oh, *that* again." But I point out that when it doesn't have that, you're just telling plots. You're not telling stories, and there is a big difference. A plot is stuff people do, and a story is what it means and the thing you carry with you and the thing you can relay to somebody. And even as you're telling me how it felt when you watched Fred die, it's hard to manage that kind of emotional connection to a show. I don't feel that emotional connection to other shows often, only the best ones.

SARAH LEMELMAN

(author, *"It's About Power":* Buffy the Vampire Slayer*'s Stab at Establishing the Strength of Girls on American Television)*

I was pretty young when I started watching *Buffy*. I have an older sister, six years older, to be exact, so when the show came out, she was probably around thirteen, which was the audience that the WB was shooting for. I really looked up to my sister then, and I still look up to her now, so I would always watch the show with her, despite my mom's urging for me to get to bed. Some of the jokes may have been lost on me as a kid, but I appreciated it on a surface level back then—it was a fun drama/fantasy/supernatural show. Plus, I think I was always a feminist. I liked action movies, but I liked them even more when they had a female protagonist. Lara Croft was one of my heroes as a kid. Buffy also became one of them. And now, twenty years later, she's still one of my heroes, but I appreciate the show on a much more sophisticated level.

The show is filled with all kinds of references to feminism that the casual viewer is likely to miss. I can't tell you how many times I've watched the show, and each time I find something new to appreciate. Even the most overplayed episodes, like "Once More, with Feeling" or "Hush," you can't help but smile while watching it; even if you've seen it dozens of times.

JOSE MOLINA

(co-executive producer, *Agent Carter*)

I am really curious to see what Joss comes back as, because for the longest time he hasn't really had the full freedom to do whatever the hell he wants. The closest thing he got to doing whatever the hell he wanted was *Firefly*. *Buffy* came out of a movie that he hated, because they ruined the script. And so *Buffy* the series came out of him rescuing that. It's still very much his, but it was an existing title. *Angel*, of course, is a spin-off. *Dollhouse* came as an idea that he pitched over lunch to Eliza Dushku after he went to the bathroom and came up with this idea.

Firefly was the last thing that really came out of him fully formed that he loved. You can tell how much he loved it and loves it still. He's still involved in the *Firefly* fandom. He still supports some of the Browncoat charities. And when he went to the feature side to do *Avengers* and *Age of Ultron*, again it wasn't 100 percent his thing. These weren't characters that he was creating. They were characters that he loved, that he grew up with, but he had a responsibility within the MCU, and, you know, he had a lot of mandates that he probably wouldn't have chosen to impose on himself.

STEVEN S. DEKNIGHT

I, like many, many other writers, was deeply influenced by Joss and honored to be a part of the *Buffy-Angel* base. I always consider them like my post-graduate work. It's where I really learned so much, and I'm so thankful to have been a part of that and to have been able to work with so many amazing people and tell stories that were, especially for the time, batshit crazy. Now you've got more of a chance to tell crazy stories, but back then it was very unusual. It was just the high point of my life.

FELICIA DAY

(creator/actress, *The Guild*)

I don't think there's anything like it on TV now. There's something about *Buffy* that appealed to people of all ages, and I think right now if you look at examples of characters' ages, they're very much narrowly focused on teens. There's something universal about the point of view and the way that the themes were in the show that just appealed to people from all walks of life. That's when you really affect people in a bigger way with your art. And I think that's what *Buffy* did very singularly.

ARMIN SHIMERMAN

(actor, Principal Snyder)

Usually, I go to Star Trek conventions, so it's primarily Star Trek people. But since *Buffy*, and that's been many, many years now, there's always a sizable number of people who come up to me at Star Trek conventions and say we loved you as Snyder. And my response always is, you weren't supposed to love me as Snyder.

JAMES MARSTERS

(actor, Spike)

I kept saying to the cast, you know, I'm a Star Trek fan, guys. If you can provide the audience with a world that is delightful enough to go back to, even when you know what's about to happen, after the plot stops surprising you and you still go back for it—if we can do that, we could be the new Star Trek. And some of that is performance, so we gotta bring it right now. And if we become the new Star Trek, I'm the new Spock. I claim Spock. Shotgun, right now. Spock-Spike, Spike-Spock, same—so close. Anyway, I get to be Spock.

MERCEDES MCNAB

(actress, Harmony Kendall)

Anything you do, you never expect as an artist that people are still talking about it twenty years later. It's pretty outstanding. You can never appreciate how popular the show is even to this day and grasp there are millions of people out there that watch and love it and live and die on it until you go to the conventions.

DAVID FURY

That fan base is really extraordinary. People still approach me with their children who are fans. Or some eighteen-year-old will approach me and say my mom and I used to watch the show. And it's great. Especially when it's young women, because the show is so important to them. That was something I took for granted. I didn't realize how empowering it was. As the father of a daughter, I'm grateful I got to be a part of something that moved so many young girls that they are special, that they are all Potential Slayers. The idea that they have the power within.

JOSS WHEDON

(creator/executive producer, *Buffy the Vampire Slayer*)

I would never take all the credit for everything. There are definitely precursors. I don't think *Xena* gets nearly enough props for being an extraordinarily daring show. They were crucified, for God's sake. And credit for [having] an extraordinarily textured, believable, strong character. But it got heaped in genre world and didn't break through the mainstream in quite the same way. Ultimately, they didn't have our writing staff. I did. When I started, *Buffy* was kind of a radical concept, and I was like, "Really? Why?" The idea of a female carrying an action show—well it's all across the boards *now.* It's not even a question now. Even when we were pitching the animated show, they said, "Boys won't accept it. You need a boy character who's just as strong as Buffy who's in it with her," and we were like, "We really don't think you're getting the point."

That is no longer an issue. Now there will be some backlash, and a lot of shows with empowered women in them suck, because most shows are bad. The cream rises and that's the thing. But it's in the mix now, and that's a good thing.

SARAH LEMELMAN

It's a shame that many people watch *Buffy* on a surface level nowadays and either view it as campy, especially since some of the special effects have not held up, and give up on it or they enjoy it but don't see some of the subtler references to feminism and female empowerment in it, such as Whedon's turning the girl-in-peril trope inside out.

ANTHONY C. FERRANTE
(director, *Boo*)

I think the interesting thing about TV vampire series and other creature series is how often they want to be *Buffy* but miss the point of what made *Buffy* work. *Vampire Diaries, Moonlight,* and *The Originals* are a bit too serious at times—more *Twilight* than *Buffy.* They're romance novels, in essence, instead of allegorical tales. And while *Vampire Diaries* has done some amazing things, it's really in a different space than *Buffy.* I think both *Buffy* and *X-Files* created templates. Show runners and networks want to recapture those shows; both of those were lightning-in-a-bottle-type things.

What you need to succeed is having someone like Joss Whedon or Chris Carter, with their own point of view, coming in to subvert the genre and make it their own. If you're trying to think about, how can I create a show that's the next *Buffy* or *X-Files*?, it's almost guaranteed to fail or come up short.

STEVEN S. DEKNIGHT

I had a meeting with an unnamed executive at Spelling years ago and they openly admitted *Charmed* was their stab at doing a *Buffy* show. I had to respect them, because what they did worked and outlived us all and their ratings were better than ours ever were. It's what I call the *Joan of Arcadia* syndrome, which was not a bad show, but it definitely does not work outside the box. You usually don't go to the superdark places on these shows.

JOSE MOLINA

I left *Angel* to go to *Dark Angel*. After *Dark Angel*, I came back to the Whedon camp for *Firefly*. It was funny because working on *Dark Angel*, me and a couple of the members of the staff were still watching *Buffy* and *Angel* religiously, and we would come into work and go, "Why can't our show be as good as that one?" And so we would try to Whedonize our own show, but *Dark Angel* wasn't really designed to be that. So our pleas fell on deaf ears until season two of *Dark Angel*. The studio and the network decided that they wanted us to become *Buffy* and they wanted us to have the monster of the week, so we had to retrofit or reverse engineer our franchise to be theirs. And that didn't work, either. But it shows how seminal *Buffy* was becoming that other networks were starting to notice enough that they were like, "Yeah, we agree we want your show to be as good as their show."

SARAH LEMELMAN

Buffy has helped the popularity of vampires erupt. I'm only vaguely familiar with *The Vampire Diaries*, but I remember when it first came out, because my sister was very excited about it and talked about it a lot. The next day in school, I walked into my first class, which was Spanish II, and literally all the girls were talking about *The Vampire Diaries*. I wished that I watched it the night before, but I had marching band practice, which precluded me from watching it, and I just never jumped on the bandwagon after that.

As far as I know, *The Vampire Diaries* heavily focuses on the relationship between the lead actress and the vampire, Stefan. Later, Stefan's brother Damon enters, and we begin the love triangle. This reminds me of what happened with Buffy/Angel/Spike, but the viewers couldn't see it as drawn out as in *The Vampire Diaries,* because David Boreanaz left *Buffy* for his spin-off, *Angel.* Though we did see Spike always comparing himself to Angel, like in the penultimate episode of *Buffy,* where Angel has a guest appearance. In the episode, Spike sees Buffy and Angel kiss and gets very jealous.

Also, in season five of *Angel,* the episode "The Girl in Question" centers on Spike and Angel traveling to Italy upon news that Buffy is in trouble (but turns out, she's now dating their archnemesis, The Immortal, another vampire). Before the two heard this news, they started competing with each other over who Buffy *really* loves. The point of me saying all this is that *Buffy* sort of paved the way, showing that vampire shows can be successful, and other shows have used that and have then turned it into more of a love story as the main feature.

If we look at *True Blood,* there was so much going on there, but the thing that everyone remembers is, Who should Sookie choose? Bill, the "nice" vampire? Or Eric, the dangerous but alluring vampire? Teenage girls eat up love stories, especially when it involves vampires, because it's fun to fantasize about the dark and mysterious figure swooping you off your feet. It's why *Twilight* blew up, despite its source material being quite weak.

HARRY GROENER
(actor, Mayor Richard Wilkins)

I still meet fans who say, "I just started watching *Buffy,* and oh my God I just love it—it's great!" And you get stopped every once in a while by a younger generation that is just beginning to discover it. And then some of the older people in my generation . . . kind of go, "Don't tell anyone, but I love *Buffy.*" I enjoy all the fans talking about it, because I like talking about it, too. It was such a good time. It doesn't always happen that way in television. If you're doing an episodic, once in a while you get a part that's really interesting and fun. Most of the time, they're all primary colors. You're going to be red today, you're green, you're purple—that's all you are, and you can't be anything else. Or you're just information. If you're in a cop show and you're on the street and you're working at the store and they come and they ask you, "You see this guy?" "Yeah, I saw him. He's around the corner. He was wearing a purple shirt." That's it.

MERCEDES MCNAB

No matter how old you are, no matter where you live, where you're from, there is something for everybody. People can still relate to it. There's action; there's comedy. I feel like anybody can relate to that show.

THOMAS P. VITALE

(executive vice president, programming and original movies, Syfy and Chiller)

I'm not saying anything new here when I say that *Buffy* is definitely a top-fifty show in the history of television . . . Not just "genre" television, but all television.

HOWARD GORDON

(executive producer, *Homeland*)

Buffy was a brief experience, but a formative one. I was extremely lucky, because I really do think that Joss and [*Breaking Bad*'s] Vince Gilligan are the people I've worked with who have a voice that is extraordinary and unlike anyone else's. I'm glad I got a front-row seat to it.

FELICIA DAY

It has a legacy that hasn't been equaled in female empowerment. There's a lot of male superheroes on TV right now, not a lot of female ones. Back then, there were other shows like *Birds of Prey*. There were a couple of others, *Charmed* even, but *Buffy* really was the one that stayed apart from the rest, because there was something underneath it that really carries the legacy through. It's kind of sad that we're not there yet. We've kind of taken a left turn, but everything eventually comes back onto itself, and I'd love to see more shows with that irreverent tone with females in the lead, because the torch is a little bit out right now. But I think always *Buffy* will be the touchstone to that kind of genre.

JOSE MOLINA

So now that Joss Whedon has two of the top-grossing movies in the universe under his belt and a handful of hit shows, I'm really curious to see what he chooses to do next. If he's going to stay on the feature side or if he is going to come back to TV. I am of two minds about what I think he will do. Part of me thinks that he's going to want to do TV, because you get to write it, you get to shoot it, you get to air it, and it's done and you get to do that thirteen to twenty-two times a season. A lot of us writers thrive in that environment, where you're constantly up and at it. You don't have the two-to-three-year turnaround, the slog of getting a movie from pitch to script to production to post to everything else. But I think he may get more freedom and less commitment if he stays in features, and he's got a couple of kids who are both high school age now, so it wouldn't surprise me if the feature world allows him a little bit more time to spend with people that he honestly hasn't had a ton of time to see.

JOSS WHEDON

The thing I miss most is sitting in the writers' room, because I've never been around a group like that and I don't think I will be again. Just so funny, so dedicated.

DAVID GREENWALT

(executive producer, *Grimm*)

I'm very proud of the work. Joss used to tease me, like, "Well, doesn't every pilot go to a show and stay on?" Until he got into *Firefly* and *Dollhouse* and stuff that didn't go that long, but he used to give me a lot of shit. The success of *Buffy*—and by "the success" I mean the way it reached people of all ages and emotionally—was so satisfying because you worked so hard.

DAVID FURY

I was really proud to start my career in dramas working for these guys and these shows. We all kind of recognized what we were doing was amazing.

What Joss was able to do and put together and the way he looked at things was just very different than what we get from other people. I know a lot of people and it's not there. They're talented in their own ways, but they don't know that special something that seems to make a difference in a story that makes you go, "Oh, I get why we're telling this story now." We were doing that when we were doing twenty-two episodes a year minimally. Now, shows that have ten or twelve episodes. So when you think about quality control, I'm not saying all the episodes are good or great, but a lot of them are. The average is pretty damn high. In other words, the worst episodes are still worth seeing, and I couldn't say that for a lot of shows.

ELIZABETH CRAFT

(co-executive producer, *Dollhouse*)

I was terrified of Joss. I could barely speak around him. I was just so intimidated. He's so smart and he's so charismatic. Thank God I had Sarah, because I could not speak for the first season, which seems funny now, but I was just in awe of him. You know he really is 24-7 the way he is on a panel you might see at Comic-Con. That is how he is all the time, basically. He's that smart, that *on*. But he's also very inclusive. He cares about everybody. One year Sarah [Fain] wasn't going home for Thanksgiving, and he was like, "You're coming to my house."

SARAH FAIN

(co-executive producer, *Dollhouse*)

Later, I told him how terrified I was, and he thought it was totally absurd, of course. But it was a lovely Thanksgiving.

STEVEN S. DEKNIGHT

Joss has always been incredibly good to me, incredibly kind and encouraging. The last time I saw Joss was at the premiere of *Avengers: Age of Ultron*. I remember telling him, "I don't know how you even started to figure out some of that movie, of how to shoot it." It was so complicated. I know there were a lot of people that didn't like it and a lot of blowback about Black

Widow. I saw the movie, and, in fact, I still watch the movie whenever it's on. I enjoyed it. Call me crazy. I've got to say, when Vision hands Thor's hammer, I got teared up. I admit it. It was everything I ever dreamed of.

ELIZABETH CRAFT

What was great about also working for Joss was [that] you really felt like you were a part of something that had quality and, I want to say, was a movement. The cult of Joss is a good cult to be in.

CAMDEN TOY

(actor, a Gentleman)

I'm still actually amazed and lucky I've been a part of this television history and that it endures. Most shows, once they're done, even if they were popular at the conventions, they usually disappear. Remember *Heroes*? It was incredibly hot and those actors were incredibly in demand at conventions for autographs, but as soon as that show was canceled, you weren't seeing any interest anymore. It was like the shows didn't even exist anymore. At conventions today, there'll be three generations of women standing in front of me, and they'll say, "We love your show. You scared us so much." And I'm like, "Oh, thank you."

STEVE BIODROWSKI

(editor in chief, *Cinefantastique* magazine)

I do see influence on horror and fantasy shows featuring young, somewhat disaffected women who would like to return to their normal lives but cannot do so, because they are stuck in a situation that requires them to act responsibly. I'm thinking of Georgia Lass in *Dead Like Me* and Liv Moore in *iZombie*.

SARAH LEMELMAN

Buffy is hugely important for television. In my research, I found that *Buffy* was really one of the first shows that surrounded itself around a female cast and showed girls can be kick-ass just like boys. Sure, we have the '70s burst of strong female characters, but *Buffy* is the modern version of the female heroine. In the shows that came out during the women's movement in the '60s and '70s, we still saw females as being sexualized to hold their ground. *Buffy* satirizes this, and I think it is the greatest "F you" to the patriarchy that we've seen in a long time.

DAVID GREENWALT

There's been books and there's been classes on *Buffy*. The power of that really impressed me, and, again, it's the power of genre and the power of myth. I meet people to this day that are, "*Buffy* was so important in my life." People really connected to it. They were never given a cheap trick or a cheap product or a cheap manipulation. Not a bad day's work.

SARAH LEMELMAN

Moreover, unlike *Xena* or *Charlie's Angels,* Buffy is about powerful teenage girls, which is something that television really had never explored before. Since *Buffy,* we've seen a good deal of shows and movies that have powerful female leads with a supporting cast of women—*Orphan Black, Orange is the New Black,* and even *Game of Thrones*. Younger girls now are used to seeing strong female characters, like Katniss from *The Hunger Games,* and it's normal to aspire to be more than just a "girl." I don't think this was the case back when *Buffy* first aired, since a powerful female was an anomaly. *Buffy* showed the world the true strength of girl power, and we've never looked back since then.

STEVEN S. DEKNIGHT

The last time I saw Joss was at a party for Drew Goddard, who had been nominated for the Oscar for *The Martian*. Every time I see Joss, I love talking to him. I love finding out what's going on. He is just such a talent, and I think he has not just inspired and encouraged the immediate people around him but millions of people all over the world with what he's done.

DAVID GREENWALT

Buffy certainly made a bigger splash, there's no question about it. It was the first of that kind of thing to be seen. Now I see all of these vampire shows, and I'm like, didn't we already do that?

ACKNOWLEDGMENTS

The authors would like to profusely thank everyone who graciously took the time over the years to be interviewed by us, in some cases multiple times for many, many long hours. Thank you for your indulgence, enthusiasm, and candor.

Regrettably, Joss Whedon chose not to participate in the writing of this book, but interviews are taken from myriad previous interviews with Whedon conducted exclusively (and extensively) by Edward Gross over many years.

In addition, we're particularly indebted to *Buffy* scholar Sarah Lemelman, who was willing to share her own original material and insights to help supplement this volume.

Also, thank you to the publishers of *Cinefantastique* magazine over the years for their gracious assistance, ranging from the legendary Frederick S. Clarke to our good friend Mark Gottwald, Joe Sena, and current publisher Steve Harris, and a very special thanks to Mitchell Persons, who graciously allowed us to excerpt several interviews from his indispensible coverage of *Buffy* in *Cinefantastique* as well, including Kristy Swanson and Fran Rubel Kuzui, who declined to participate in new interviews for this volume.

In almost all cases, material is taken from original interviews, conducted by the authors, with the exception of the aforementioned material as well as public comments excerpted from personal appearances at press conferences, Paleyfest, Television Critics Association presentations, and conventions.

In addition, a very special thanks to our research assistants, without whose help we would probably be publishing this book for the fiftieth anniversary of *Buffy:* our indispensable senior research assistant, Jordan Rubio, as well as our additional research associates, Josh Rubin, Hilary Paige Taylor, and Lucille E. Brillhart. We would also like to single out the help of New York University professor Andrew Goldman for his gracious assistance in helping round up a group of talented and hardworking millennials (for the most part) to assist us as well as Brandeis University professor of American studies Thomas Doherty for his always-welcome advice, counsel, and inspiration.

We would also be remiss not to thank our patron saint, editor Brendan Deneen; Tor jack-of-all-trades, the awesome Christopher Morgan; and our intrepid literary agent, Laurie Fox, at the Linda Chester Literary Agency, for her boundless enthusiasm, undying love, and affection for Buffy.

You can follow the authors on Twitter at @markaaltman, @edgross, and @Slayersandvamps, or contact them directly at 50yearmissionbook@gmail.com.

ABOUT THE AUTHORS

MARK A. ALTMAN is a television and motion picture writer/producer/director who most recently served as co–executive producer of TNT's hit series *The Librarians*. Previous TV credits include *Agent X, Castle, Necessary Roughness,* and as executive producer and cocreator of *Femme Fatales* for HBO, for which he also directed several episodes.

Altman has also produced the $30 million film adaptation of the best-selling video game *DOA: Dead or Alive,* which was released by The Weinstein Company's Dimension Films. His first film was the award-winning *Free Enterprise,* starring William Shatner and Eric McCormack, which he wrote and produced and for which he won the Writers Guild of America Award for Best New Writer at the AFI Los Angeles Film Festival prior to its theatrical release. He is also a producer of the House of the Dead series, based on the video game from Sega, released by Lionsgate. In addition, he produced James Gunn's cult classic, *The Specials,* starring Thomas Haden Church, Rob Lowe, and Judy Greer.

His bestselling two-volume book written with Edward Gross, *The Fifty-Year Mission,* was released by St. Martin's Press in summer 2016 in hardcover to nearly unanimous critical acclaim, including raves in *The Wall Street Journal, Booklist,* and *Publishers Weekly.*

Altman is a former entertainment journalist. He is the founding publisher of *Geek,* a hip lifestyle magazine devoted to movies, television, technology, and pop culture. In the past, Altman has contributed to such newspapers and magazines as *The Boston Globe, Written By, L'Cinefage, Film Threat, The Manchester Guardian, The Boston Edge, Cult TV, Computer Player,* and many others, including *Cinefantastique,* for which he launched their independent film division, CFQ Films, which produced numerous successful genre features for DVD and VOD release, including *The Thirst,* starring Buffyverse alums Clare Kramer, Adam Baldwin, and Tom Lenk.

Altman has spoken at numerous industry events and conventions, including ShowBiz Expo as well as the Variety/Final Draft Screenwriters Panel at the Cannes Film Festival. He was a juror at the prestigious Sitges Film Festival in Barcelona, Spain. He has been a frequent guest and panelist at Comic-Con held annually in San Diego, California, and a two-time juror for the Comic-Con Film Festival. In addition to being a graduate of the Writers Guild of America Showrunner Training Program, he is also a member of the Television Academy.

EDWARD GROSS is a veteran entertainment journalist who has served on the editorial staff of a wide variety of publications, among them *Starlog, Geek, Cinescape, Life Story, RetroVision, Cinefantastique, Femme Fatales, Movie Magic, SFX,* and *Sci Fi Now*. He is the author of a number of nonfiction books, including *The Unofficial Story of the Making of a Wiseguy, X-Files Confidential, The 25th Anniversary "Odd Couple" Companion, Alien Nation: The Unofficial Companion, All in This Together: The Unofficial Story of High School Musical, Spider-Man Confidential, Planet of the Apes Revisited* (with Joe Russo and Larry Landsman), *Rocky: The Ultimate Guide, The Making of the Potterverse, Above & Below: The Unofficial 25th Anniversary "Beauty and the Beast" Companion, Superhero Confidential,* and, with Mark A. Altman, the two-volume *The Fifty-Year Mission*. Currently he serves as executive editor Film/TV for the Bauer Xcel Media digital network, which includes *Empire US, Life & Style, Twist, J-14, M, Closer, In Touch,* and *FHM*.